POLICE MEDALS OF THE WORLD

POLICE MEDALS OF THE WORLD

A GUIDE TO THE MOST COLLECTED AWARDS FROM AROUND THE GLOBE

by Roger Campion

A Token TITLE

TOKEN PUBLISHING LTD.
HONITON, DEVON
2002

First published in Great Britain, April 2002
by
Token Publishing Ltd., Orchard House, Duchy Road, Heathpark, Honiton, Devon EX14 1YD
Telephone: 01404 46972   Fax: 01404 44788
e-mail: info@tokenpublishing.com   Website: http//www.tokenpublishing.com

© 2002 Token Publishing Ltd

British Library Cataloguing in Publication data:
A catalogue for this book is available from the British Library
ISBN 1 870 192 47 8

No part of this publication may be reproduced, stored in a retrieval system or transmitted in any form or by any means, electronic, mechanical, photocopying, recording or otherwise, without the prior permission of the publishers

Printed in Great Britain by
Polestar Scientifica, Exeter

CONTENTS

Foreword x
Introduction xx
Australia 1
Austria 17
Belgium 31
Belize 35
Botswana 37
Canada 38
Denmark 59
Fiji 61
Finland 65
France 67
Germany 84
Great Britain 108
    Colonial awards 169
   British Commonwealth
      Bahamas 173
      Barbados 173
      Guyana 174
      Jamaica 175
      Lesotho 176
      St Lucia 176
      Sierra Leone 177
      Solomon Islands 177
      Trinidad & Tobago 178
Hong Kong 179
India and Burma 186
Ireland 200
Italy 209
Malawi 218
Malta 221
Mauritius and Seychelles 224
Namibia 228
Netherlands 231
New Zealand 245
Papua New Guinea 253
Poland 260
Portugal 267
Rhodesia 1965–1980 271
Russia 277
Sarawak 284
Singapore 286
South Africa 296
Spain 319
Sri Lanka 324
Swaziland 326
Uganda 327
United Nations 329
United States 334
Vanuatu 381
Vatican 382
Zambia 386
Zimbabwe 388

ACKNOWLEDGEMENTS

I am indebted to a number of collectors who provided information on medals in their possession and to various police officers, recipients of many of the awards listed throughout the publication. They are too numerous to mention each by name but without them and the enthusiasm of the publishers, this book would not have been written. Thanks are also due to my wife and family for their untiring patience and understanding when I was buried under papers and correspondence and our house looked more like an office than a home.

Roger Campion

INTRODUCTION

THE award of medals to police officers has long been a neglected area of study and research. When I first took an interest in the subject five years ago I was struck by the lack of a single source of information and reference. The award of national decorations for gallantry particularly in the Second World War following the introduction of the George Cross and George Medal, was reasonably well covered with a little effort but the existence of other awards made by individual police forces dating back to the 19th century was a well-kept secret. These medals, given for acts of bravery in some cases, for long service in others and as commemorative pieces to celebrate a royal event in a few instances, are a link to the history of the Police Service before the amalgamations and mergers of the late-20th century saw the end of a large number of borough, city and county forces. Interest in medals is most usually concerned with the armed forces and wars fought but police medal enthusiasts exist, albeit few in number, most of whom suffer from the same frustrating lack of a central reference point.

A similar situation occurs in many other countries where policing styles and practices can be very different from those of the United Kingdom, including members of the British Commonwealth where the basic concepts of law enforcement were imported from Britain. In other parts of the world where British influence was less pronounced or absent, policing structures evolved in quite different directions—evidenced by the thousands of individual police departments in the US, some large, some very small, or the Gendarmerie Nationale in France and Carabinieri in Italy, both a part of the Armed forces, all poles apart from the United Kingdom in structure although the duties of individual officers are much the same. The dangers faced from time to time by officers from all police forces in all countries are similarly very alike and most of the countries have their own methods of recognising acts of courage, particularly meritorious or distinguished service or long service with good conduct. Some countries have national awards, some are primarily local, some use a mix of both and a few have nothing at all. This guide attempts to provide a reference point for anyone with an interest in police medals and fill a gap in the knowledge generally available.

Emphasis is given to medals which are (or were) exclusively available to police officers although the variety of methods used to reward police officers is so wide that it would be unwise to restrict the guide to this category of award. In many countries (the UK included), police officers are rewarded in the same way as any other citizen for acts of courage although it was not always so, in others they are entitled to military awards only, no two countries are alike. For this reason, medals are mentioned for a number of sources including local lifesaving societies, regional governments if appropriate, a few military awards to reflect the nature of police forces in the past when the differences between them and the armed forces were blurred and a few privately struck awards, all in addition to any national awards. There are obviously gaps and many important awards will have been omitted, this was unavoidable—in many cases the medal concerned was very well-known and did not need further mention, in others information was hard to come by and there are undoubtedly those that have simply been overlooked. In some cases it has been frustratingly difficult to source suitable illustrations—a fact which is occasionally reflected in the quality of the reproduction.

A simple listing of the medals with descriptions and short histories would have told only a part of the story and I have tried to expand on the basic information by including a little local colour, the history of policing development in the country concerned, references to the use of heraldry on the medals where appropriate, a few case histories where possible or a miscellany of facts, figures and titbits of information, sometimes with little apparent relevance to the main subject but which add to the overall picture of the country under discussion.

AUSTRALIA

The effects of British rule can still be seen in the policing systems of a number of countries which remain in the Commonwealth although the model which worked well in a small island off the northern coast of Europe did not adapt easily to large sparsely populated countries or those where the diversity of cultures created problems not found in the UK. The policing of the new territories was a military matter for many years but transferred in time to the civil authorities as the situation became more stable.

The development of policing in Australia offers a good example of how the new challenges were met and how the needs of the time and the area of responsibility dictated how the police forces should be organised. Australia was first used as a settlement for criminals sent from the UK to a large under-populated country well away from civilisation where they would do no harm to anyone other than to each other, something that concerned nobody in the UK. From the time of the establishment of the first penal colonies in 1786 until 1810 policing was combined with guarding convicts and the officers were essentially paramilitary. The first police force as we understand it today was formed in Sydney in 1810 and gradually extended to cover the whole of New South Wales by 1862. It is the largest Australian force with a strength of almost 10,000 officers of all ranks.

As the continent was explored and settled the need for some form of police increased in all the new territories. The pattern of this development was similar to New South Wales with the duty first falling to the military until civil forces were established during the 19th century. The Victoria Police did not come into being as a civil organisation until 1852 but has grown since then to become the second largest force with more than 8,000 personnel including the executive officers, constables, trainees and cadets.

The area covered by the state forces is huge by any standards not simply in comparison with those in the UK or western Europe. Australia has a geographical area of 7.6 million square kilometres and a population between 15 and 16 million, mostly concentrated on the eastern coast. To the west of the Great Dividing Range and in the north are huge expanses of desert, still sparsely populated but with a need for policing, albeit infrequent. Western Australia Police is responsible for an area greater than 2.5 million square kilometres with only one city of any real size—Perth (pop 1.2 million)—and a number of small towns, none with a population greater than 30,000. The Force has a staff of less than 3,000 officers, including cadets and trainees, to police this vast area. Although more than 80 per cent of the people of Western Australia live in Perth the Force is represented in towns which may be up to 1,000 miles away from its headquarters.

The state and territory forces are supported by the Australian Federal Police (AFP), formed in 1979 by a merger of the Australian Capital Territories (ACT) Police and Commonwealth Police, a force which existed across the country alongside the state forces. The AFP is responsible for the enforcement of federal law and has offices in each of the states and territories. The Australian Police Service today is a modern, sophisticated and efficient organisation facing challenges unimaginable to its founders in the early years of the 19th century.

The award of medals to police officers in Australia showed a strong British influence until 1975 when the first of three local medals was introduced to replace a British one, the first step towards the establishment of a wholly Australian series of awards to recognise the achievements of Australians. The UK Police Long Service and Good Conduct Medal was introduced in the United Kingdom in 1951 for award to officers from all forces on the completion of 22 years long service with good conduct. It was extended to include all Australian forces on 1 May 1956 but became obsolete in 1975 when a local Australian medal was introduced.

NATIONAL MEDAL

The National Medal is awarded to members of the Australian Defence Force, any Australian police force, the fire or ambulance services, other emergency services and the prison service to recognise 15 years diligent service—signified by the 15 stripes on the ribbon. Further periods of ten years service are indicated by the award of a clasp inscribed with ten hemispheres.

Instituted: 14 February 1975.

Ribbon: Fifteen alternating stripes of gold and blue.

Metal: Bronze.

Size: 38 mm.

Description: (Obverse) the Coat of Arms of the Commonwealth of Australia with a raised outer band bearing the inscription THE NATIONAL MEDAL (above) FOR SERVICE (below). The medal is topped by the St Edward crown to which is attached a straight, plain suspender bar; (reverse) left plain.

The shield at the centre of the arms has six elements to represent the six states of the Commonwealth of Australia:

New South Wales
The cross of St George to represent England with a lion at the centre and the four stars of the Southern Cross on the arms.

Victoria
The four stars of the Southern Cross and a royal crown.

Queensland
A Maltese cross with a royal crown at the entre to symbolise allegiance to the Queen.

South Australia
The piping shrike, the state bird.

Western Australia
The black swan, the state bird.

Tasmania
A lion representing England.

The Northern Territory is not a state and is represented only in the Commonwealth Star above the shield which has seven points—the six original colonies and the Territory. The supporters—a kangaroo and an emu—are indicative of Australia's unique wildlife and the whole is superimposed on branches of the golden wattle plant, the national flower of the country.

AUSTRALIAN POLICE MEDAL

The final breaking of ties with the UK Police Service came with the introduction of an Australian medal to replace the Queen's Police Medal for Distinguished Service. Along with the QPM for Gallantry this award had been available to officers in UK and Dominion police forces since its introduction in 1909 as the King's Police Medal and awarded to senior police officers in Australia in a similar fashion to their British counterparts.

Awards for gallantry had ceased in 1977 in all countries but the practice of rewarding senior police officers for their service continued. The last QPM for Gallantry ever awarded went to an officer from New South Wales in August 1978 for an act of courage performed in April 1977. The QPM for Distinguished Service remains current in the UK and a number of Commonwealth forces but it was replaced in Australia in 1986.

Instituted: 1986.

Ribbon: White with a dark blue central stripe, all of equal width.

Metal: Nickel-silver.

Size: 38 mm.

Description: (Obverse) the head of the Queen on the seven-point Commonwealth of Australia Star with both superimposed on a pattern of fluted rays; (reverse) a wreath of golden wattle enclosing the words AUSTRALIAN POLICE MEDAL around the upper circumference and FOR DISTINGUISHED SERVICE in the central field. The medal is topped by the St Edward Crown attached to a plain straight suspender bar.

Recipients are entitled to the use of the letters APM after their name and the medal is awarded to members of the state and territory police forces and the Australian Federal Police on an annual quota basis of no more than one for each 1,000 members in each force plus one other for the whole of the country. No more than 39 awards can be made annually. A similar quota system operates in relation to other Australian medals and there have been occasions when the full quota has not been allocated.

POLICE OVERSEAS SERVICE MEDAL

A third purely Australian medal was introduced in 1991 which has no equivalent in the UK although officers from British constabularies have carried out similar duties often alongside their Australian colleagues without specific recognition.

Instituted: 25 April 1991.

Ribbon: A chequerboard pattern of black and white squares.

Metal: Nickel-silver.

Size: 38 mm.

Description: (Obverse) a globe of the world surmounted by a branch of golden wattle all surrounded by an outer band in a chequerboard pattern; (reverse) the Commonwealth Star with a rectangular central panel all surrounded by the inscription POLICE OVERSEAS SERVICE MEDAL. The medal is topped by the St Edward crown attached to a plain straight suspender.

This medal is awarded to recognise service by members of any Australian police force overseas in an international peacekeeping operation. Clasps in the shape of a globe are awarded to indicate for which of the six currently approved campaigns the medal was awarded—Cambodia (17 October 1992), Cyprus (6 April 1992), Somalia (1 July 1994), Mozambique (1 July 1994), Haiti and Bouganville. The globe depicted on the medal's obverse is centred on Cyprus, the first approved operation. Further symbolism is apparent in the design with the golden wattle (representing Australia) lying protectively over the globe and the chequerboard pattern indicative of the involvement of police forces from many countries. As the operations are all sanctioned by the United Nations, officers also receive the appropriate UN medal.

As a result of the withdrawal of the QPM for Gallantry there is now no national award for bravery in Australia exclusively available to police officers, the situation mirrors that in the United Kingdom where police officers are rewarded in the same manner as other civilians according to the level of bravery displayed although the nature of their work and their rôle in society usually means that a greater degree of courage is expected before an award is considered. Independent of the national awards, however, local medals and commendations are available in some forces to reward courage or meritorious service.

NEW SOUTH WALES POLICE COMMISSIONER'S VALOUR AWARD

Ribbon: Pale blue with dark blue edges and a thin white stripe towards each edge.

Description: (Obverse) a central medallion superimposed on a cross pattée whose arms are marked with an arched pattern to give the appearance of the top of a pillar. The medallion has a light blue enamelled centre bearing an eagle flying and the red cross of St George above (taken from the state coat of arms). This is surrounded by a band of dark blue enamel bearing the words NEW SOUTH WALES POLICE and FOR VALOUR. A silver wreath of leaves forms a second outer band. The medal hangs from a plain straight suspender by means of two small rings.

The award is made to members of the New South Wales Police who have shown extreme courage with a risk to their lives. Where the officer displayed courage in a dangerous situation which warranted official recognition but there was no immediate risk to life the Commissioner can present a Commendation Award (Courage). This takes the form of a badge affixed to the lower part of a ribbon. The badge is taken from the design at the centre of the Valour Award of a bronze eagle flying with the red cross of St George on a white circle attached at the top to the wing tips. The four stars of the Southern Cross are on the arms of the cross. The ribbon is pale blue with white edges and a thin white central stripe. A third award—for meritorious service—is available which is identical to the commendation for courage but attached to a ribbon lacking the central white stripe.

Police Medals of the World

QUEENSLAND POLICE VALOUR AWARD

A civilian police force was established in Queensland in 1869 after a number of years under military control. Today it is responsible for a large area ranging from the sophistication of Brisbane in the south to the wild and still very dangerous tropical area further north and from the popular coastal resorts of the Great Barrier Reef in the east to the wilderness of the Australian Desert at the State's western border.

Instituted: 1991.

Ribbon: Three equal stripes of dark blue, light blue and maroon.

Metal: Nickel-silver.

Description: (Obverse) the Queensland Police Service badge in the shape of a Maltese cross with a central medallion enamelled dark blue bearing the St Edward crown in the centre in silver surrounded by a silver buckled belt and with the words QUEENSLAND POLICE (above) and VALOUR AWARD (below) around the outside. The shape of the arms of the cross is mirrored by a line in blue enamel in each one and the area between each arm has a pattern of laurel leaves. A small wreath of laurel in engraved on the plain suspender.

The Commissioner of the Queensland Police Service has also introduced an award to recognise acts of extreme bravery performed in hazardous circumstances.

QUEENSLAND POLICE SERVICE MEDAL

Instituted: 1 January 1999.

Ribbon: Royal blue with a central stripe of pale blue, all of equal width with a thin silver line at each edge.

Metal: Nickel-silver.

Description: (Obverse) the badge of the Queensland Police Service and the Force motto—WITH HONOUR WE SERVE—in a banner below the central medallion all surrounded by an outer band bearing the inscription DILIGENT AND ETHICAL (above) SERVICE (below). It is attached to a plain straight suspender by the St Edward Crown.

This medal is awarded in recognition of diligent and ethical service for a period of at least ten years with sworn officers and members of the support staff both being eligible. After the initial presentation of the medal, clasps are awarded for each additional period of five years qualifying service. The bars are plain, of nickel-silver and carry at the centre the total number of years service in a small circle. Only the most recent bar can be worn. A roundel bearing this number is worn on the ribbon in undress uniform.

QUEENSLAND POLICE MEDAL FOR MERIT

Instituted: 4 October 1906.

Ribbon: Three equal stripes of red, white and blue.

Metal: Silver.

Size: 36 mm.

Description: (Original obverse) the crowned head of Edward VII with the legend EDWARDUS VII DEI GRA REX FID DEF around the circumference; (reverse) the Coat of Arms of the State of Queensland with the words QUEENSLAND POLICE (above) and FOR MERIT (below) around the circumference. A plain suspender and claw fitting are used.

    In 1910 when King George V ascended to the throne the medal was continued but the legend on the obverse was simplified to read KING GEORGE V only. The medal was awarded sparingly with 33 only issued between its introduction and 1936 when it was discontinued. A bar was available for any second award and there is one recorded example in 1917 when Constable John Scanlon was awarded a bar to his Medal for Merit for an act of courage displayed at Bundaberg. He had won his first award for conspicuous bravery displayed at Toowoomba railway station on 25 May 1913 when he arrested an armed man. He was also awarded the King's Police Medal for Gallantry for the same incident.

    On 3 August 1915 Constable Thomas Casey was awarded the Medal for Merit for the arrest of an armed man in Brisbane following a shooting in a brothel on 19 July. With the building in darkness, alone and unarmed and in the full knowledge that an armed man was inside, PC Casey entered the building, searched it and found and arrested the suspect. In addition to the award of the medal he was promoted to acting sergeant by the Commissioner in September. Thomas Casey was Irish by birth (b. 30 Jan 1877) and served with the Dublin Metropolitan Police until his resignation and move to Australia in 1909. He joined the Queensland Police on 21 January 1910 and retired as a sergeant after 27 years service in 1937. He spent the greater part of his service at Spring Hill, Brisbane, an area with a reputation for toughness, and recalled when interviewed by the local paper in 1951 that he had one lucky escape. He was attacked by a youth with a knife as he put his notebook back into his pocket after making an entry. The knife struck the book and broke which gave PC Casey the opportunity to disarm and subdue his attacker. On his retirement he was awarded the Imperial Service Medal in recognition of his contribution to law enforcement in Queensland.

    The award of the Imperial Service Medal (ISM) to police officers in Australia at the end of their service was not an unusual occurrence, in reality it was quite common if of doubtful authority. Of the 368 officers of all ranks who were awarded a silver medal at the time of the diamond jubilee of Queen Victoria in 1897 no fewer than 159 were subsequently presented with the ISM. Of the 421 constables and sergeants granted the commemorative bronze issue, 125 received the ISM, the last being in 1937 when the recipient must have served for at least 40 years.

    The arms of the State of Queensland which lie at the centre of the Medal for Merit reverse were first granted in 1893 although the two supporters were not added until the Queen's Silver Jubilee in 1977 and are not therefore included on the medal. The heads of the bull and sheep in the upper half together with the sheaf of wheat in the lower left half symbolise the State's agriculture with the column of gold rising from the heap of quartz and miner's tools at the lower right representing the mining industry. Above the shield and helmet are the Maltese cross and St Edward's crown symbolising allegiance to the Queen—devices which form the present badge of the Queensland State Police Service. On either side of the cross are two sugar canes, further agricultural symbolism. The two supports added in 1977 are the red deer for the old world and the State's bird (the brolga, a species of crane) for the native population. The State motto—*Audax et fidelis* (bold, aye, and faithful too)—is reproduced in a banner at the base of the arms.

    The Queensland Police Force had issued one other medal to its officers before the introduction of the Medal for Merit, to commemorate the Diamond Jubilee of Queen Victoria in 1897.

QUEENSLAND POLICE
DIAMOND JUBILEE MEDAL 1897

Instituted: 1897.

Ribbon: Crimson.

Metal: Silver and bronze.

Size: 36 mm.

Description: (Obverse) the Old Head of Queen Victoria with the words VICTORIA REGINA (above) and DIAMOND—1897—JUBILEE (below) around the circumference; (reverse) a Maltese cross with St Edward's crown in the centre (both devices taken from the State Coat of Arms) with a star between the arms of the cross. All surrounded by a circumscription which reads QUEENSLAND POLICE FORCE. The medal hangs from a plain straight suspender attached by a claw fitting. There was a top bar to the ribbon inscribed POLICE FORCE. The rank and name of the recipient were engraved on the rim.

The medal was issued in silver (368) to officers of the rank of inspector and above irrespective of their length of service and to sergeants and constables who had joined before 21 June 1887 at the time of Queen Victoria's golden jubilee and who were still serving ten years later on 21 June 1897—it was in effect a long service award for the junior ranks. The bronze medal (421) was awarded as a commemorative piece only to constables and sergeants who were sworn-in after 21 June 1887 and who were still serving in 1897. Permission was given to wear the medal in the colony only.

WESTERN AUSTRALIAN POLICE
QUEEN VICTORIA DIAMOND JUBILEE MEDAL 1897

Instituted: 1897.

Ribbon: Blue.

Metal: Gold and silver.

Description: (Obverse) an oval medal with the Veiled Head of Queen Victoria surrounded by an outer band inscribed with the words HER MAJESTY QUEEN VICTORIA'S RECORD REIGN. The dates 1837 TO 1897 are contained in a banner at the bottom of the medal; (reverse) the words POLICE WESTERN AUSTRALIA in three lines placed centrally with a rose above and below and LONG SERVICE MEDAL around the upper circumference inside the plain outer band. A banner at the bottom bears the date JUNE 29TH 1897. A straight suspender bar with a motif of laurel leaves is attached to the disc by a ring and crown.

Vying with Queensland for the honour of being responsible for the first official medal issued is Western Australia where another medal was introduced to commemorate the Diamond Jubilee. It was awarded in far lesser numbers—ten in gold to senior officers and 14 in silver to constables, corporals and sergeants—and was a long service and good conduct medal rather than a simple commemorative piece. Authority to wear the medal was granted in the colony only.

VICTORIA POLICE VALOUR AWARD

Another Australian police force has the honour of awarding the most long-lived award for courage of any police force in the UK, the Commonwealth or parts of the former Empire. The history of the Victoria Police Valour Award which is still current today can be clearly traced back to the last year of the 19th century, possibly earlier, although the design and name have undergone many changes since, the last being in 1987 when the current medal was introduced. There is some uncertainty over the initial design and the award was variously called the Merit Stripe, Valour Stripe, Valour Badge and Merit Badge. The term Merit Badge appears to have been adopted in 1905 and was used until 1921 when it became known as the Valour Badge. The first true metal badge introduced in or around 1904 was circular, of skeletal design and minted in silver with an outer blue enamelled band bearing the words VICTORIAN POLICE. The central medallion had the entwined initials of the force—VP—and the words FOR MERIT contained within a scroll also entwined with the two letters.

The rank, name and number of the recipient together with the date of the award were engraved on the reverse. On its introduction it was not intended for wear with a ribbon but, some time during the 1930s, the watered pale blue ribbon appeared and was first mentioned in official records in 1933.

The design of the badge remained unchanged until 1955 when it was altered to the pattern current today apart from one minor alteration made in 1987 when the word—FORCE—was removed from the legend on the outer band of the central medallion.

Between 1916 and 1923 a gold medal was awarded apparently alongside the Merit Badge and was of a totally different design. It was in the shape of a cross pattée with a large central medallion containing a King's crown within an outer band bearing the words VICTORIAN POLICE above and FOR BRAVERY below all surrounded by a wreath of laurel. A total of 22 awards were made during the lifetime of this medal.

Instituted: 1987.

Ribbon: Watered pale blue.

Metal: Silver.

Size: 38 mm.

Description: (Obverse) a four armed cross enamelled pale blue with a five-pointed star on each arm and five silver rays between each pair of arms. There is a central medallion also enamelled light blue containing the words FOR BRAVERY in white surrounded by an outer circle, enamelled dark blue, inscribed VICTORIA POLICE; (reverse) plain apart from the inscribed name of the recipient and date of the act for which the medal was awarded. The upper arm of the cross is surmounted by a Queen's crown attached to a plain straight suspender bar by three small rings.

The award is made to any sworn officer for an act which displays exceptional bravery in extremely perilous circumstances with provision for the award of a bar for any subsequent act of courage deserving of the medal. The bar is silver with a central rose design. Recipients are entitled to use the letters VA after their name in any official document in the State of Victoria.

The Victoria Police Force was founded in 1852 in the Colony of Victoria as it was then known but had no way of rewarding bravery displayed by its officers for many years although efforts were made to introduce some method of formal recognition. In June 1899 a Sergeant Rogerson was badly assaulted whilst arresting two burglars and this proved to be the incident which finally led to the introduction of the original Merit Badge a few years later.

In recent years the introduction of medals by individual state police forces in Australia has become widespread with Victoria now issuing an award very similar to the Queensland Police Service Medal.

VICTORIA POLICE SERVICE MEDAL AND AWARD

Instituted: 1997.

Ribbon: Royal blue with a broad central white band and a thin white stripe towards each edge.

Metal: Nickel-silver.

Size: 36 mm.

Description: (Obverse) a circular medal with a central medallion depicting a cross and five stars, one on each arm and one placed centrally. Surrounding this is a band bearing the legend VICTORIA POLICE and an outer band with the words DILIGENT (above) AND ETHICAL SERVICE (below); (reverse) left plain apart from the full name of the recipient. The medal hangs from a plain straight suspender attached by a Queen's crown.

The medal and award are available to sworn and unsworn members of the Victoria Police to recognise ten years uninterrupted diligent and ethical service. It is not a long service reward and not granted automatically. Recipients must show a record of honest hard work, dedication to duty and professionalism. Sworn officers are awarded the medal and unsworn staff given the award in the form of a lapel badge. Further periods of five years qualifying service meeting the same criteria are acknowledged by the award of a bar to sworn staff showing the total length of applicable service in a small central roundel, only the most recent being worn. Unsworn staff are presented with a replacement lapel badge with the relevant number of years' service in the centre. The criteria for eligibility are strictly applied and the Chief Commissioner has the right to refuse to grant or withdraw any medal or award if any member fails to meet or maintain the required standards of behaviour.

The medal is very similar to one recently introduced in Tasmania with the same criteria for its award. The Tasmania Police Service Medal differs only in the substitution of the badge of the Tasmania Police in the centre and its name above and below it. The main feature of the badge is the lion (representing England) superimposed on a map of the island—the smallest state in the Commonwealth of Australia with a population of not quite half a million people policed by around 1,100 officers without the difficulties of a large area and inhospitable climate faced by many officers in the police forces on the mainland.

Australia

NORTHERN TERRITORY POLICE SERVICE MEDAL

The youngest police force in Australia is the Northern Territory Police which dates from as recently as 1978 in its present form although it has been policed in a manner recognisable today since 1869. The first force was established under the command of a corporal from South Australia in December of that year who policed the huge area with six constables until 1884 when it was enhanced by the addition of the Native Police Corps. In 1911 it came under the control of the Commonwealth Police (later the Australian Federal Police) who stayed in control until self-government was won in 1978 and the Northern Territory Police as it exists today was formed. The Force is responsible for an area of 1,346,200 square kilometres—1,610 from north to south and 934 from east to west—but a population of less than one per cent of the Australian total (191,800) and a higher proportion of Aboriginal people than anywhere else. It manages with 912 sworn officers, 112 auxiliaries and 42 Aboriginal Community Police Officers. Outside of the main city of Darwin where more than half the population lives an officer at a rural station could be responsible for 2,000 people spread over 30,000 square kilometres with any back-up being many hours away but still expected to be able to deal with anything thrown at him including duties not normally associated with police work particularly in the UK.

It was (and to a certain degree still is) a dangerous area to police with hazards unknown in the UK. The first police officer from the Northern Territory to die on duty did so in unusual circumstances. Mounted Constable Davis decided to take a swim in the sea whilst on duty, contrary to orders, and paid for his misdeed with his life when he was killed and eaten by a crocodile. Another officer who died in 1933 illustrated the hostile nature of the country when he was speared to death by suspects in Arnhem Land whilst investigating the killing of a group of fishermen. The Northern Territory may be less dangerous today but it still presents challenges to residents and visitors alike. On 1 April 1999 the Force instituted a medal to reward officers for meritorious service with the design being very akin to similar medals introduced in other states.

Instituted: 1 April 1999.

Ribbon: Black with a broad central ochre band flanked by white stripes

Metal: Bronze.

Size: 36 mm.

Description: (Obverse) the badge of the Northern Territory Police within a raised outer band bearing the words NORTHERN TERRITORY POLICE around the upper circumference and SERVICE MEDAL at the bottom. A plain straight suspender is used.

The medal is awarded in recognition of ten years continuous and meritorious service with bars available after each additional period of ten years. The first presentation was made in June 1999 to 60 officers. The regulations included officers who had retired, resigned or died provided that they met the criteria. The badge at the centre has a kangaroo with a crown above, a banner at the bottom bearing the motto "to protect and serve" and a wreath in the upper half. It has the Force name in three banners on either side of and below the kangaroo.

page 11

AUSTRALIAN CAPITAL TERRITORY COMMUNITY POLICING MEDAL

Policing arrangements in the Australian Capital Territory (ACT) differ from the rest of Australia with the Australian Federal Policing having responsibility for supplying officers under a special contract. When the vogue for awarding medals for diligent service started in the state forces the special position of the ACT Police was not forgotten and a special award recently introduced. The medal is intended to recognise ten years service in the Territory since 6 December 1988 although this service need not be continuous. Further periods of ten years satisfactory service will be indicated by a bar worn on the ribbon. The first presentation of medals was made to 37 officers on 7 December 2001 followed by a further 35 four days later. It is thought that approximately 150 officers will be eligible for the medal in the first few months.

Instituted: 2001.

Ribbon: White with a dark blue band at each edge and a further dark blue stripe in the centre flanked by a yellow stripe separated by white stripes.

Metal: Bronze.

Size: An oval medal 36 mm wide by 42.5 mm high.

Description: (Obverse) the Coat of Arms of the ACT within an outer band bearing the words A.C.T. COMMUNITY POLICING MEDAL; (reverse) a panel for the recipient's name to be inscribed under the words FOR DILIGENT SERVICE. A plain straight suspender is used attached to the top of the medal.

The arms at the centre of the obverse consist of a shield carrying three elements—a castle with three towers to symbolise dignity, importance and the grandeur of the city, a white rose below the castle in commemoration of the contribution made by the Duke of York when Canberra was established as the seat of government and a crossed sword and mace (superimposed by a crown at the centre) above the castle. The supporters are swans (one white, one black) to represent the Aboriginal and European people. The original arms, first granted in 1928 also had a motto below the shield and a crowned portcullis above representative of a link with the arms of Westminster in London but these were removed when the arms were recently modified.

The ACT (which lies wholly within New South Wales) and the capital—Canberra, taken from an aboriginal word meaning "meeting place"—were established in 1908 to form the federal capital in an effort to end the rivalry between Sydney and Brisbane. The city has a population of about half a million and is the centre of Australian political and administrative power. Outside the city the rest of the ACT (more than 70%) is mostly bushland with almost half being within the Namadgi National Park, an area of mountains, river valleys, aboriginal rock art and the unique Australian wildlife.

NEW SOUTH WALES MEDAL FOR RESISTING AND CAPTURING BUSHRANGERS

The oldest medal known to have been awarded to police officers in Australia was introduced to recognise acts of courage performed in the troubles with bushrangers in the 1860s in New South Wales. It was officially sanctioned by the Colonial Secretary in NSW in 1870 but not presented until 1875, almost ten years after the acts for which they were awarded. The very last award made was in 1901 for foiling a bank robbery. Two different designs were struck.

Instituted: 1870.

Ribbon: Blue.

Metal: Silver.

Description: (Obverse) the Young Head of Queen Victoria with the words GRANTED FOR FAITHFUL AND DISTINGUISHED SERVICE around the circumference; (reverse) the Coat of Arms of the Colony with COLONY OF NEW SOUTH WALES inscribed around the circumference. A small loop suspender was used.

Second type reverse.

The second design was very similar and used the same effigy of the Queen on the obverse but with the inscription COLONY OF NEW SOUTH WALES around the circumference and VR below. The arms on the reverse were reduced in size and were placed above a wreath of flowers and banksia. The space below the crest was engraved with a variety of inscriptions including the recipient's name, sometimes the date and place and sometimes a few words to describe the circumstances leading to the award. The inscription around the circumference of the second version was amended to read GRANTED FOR GALLANT AND DISTINGUISHED SERVICES. The method of suspension was changed to an ornate scrolled bar attached by a claw fitting and a pinned brooch at the top of the ribbon. The first issue was produced in silver only but the amended version was available in gold for civilians and in silver for members of the police force. The medals were issued in very small numbers although just how many of the first type were awarded isn't known. Of the later version, 12 gold medals were awarded and six of silver.

Bushrangers have an unusual place in Australian folklore for a group of men and women who were no more than murderers, thieves and outlaws. Their total lack of respect and contempt for any form of authority struck a chord with large sections of the poorer people of Australia who understood only too well the desperate conditions in the early penal colonies and the severity of the authorities on anyone who stepped out of line. They were mostly Australian born free men who roamed the country in search of fortune and adventure and drifted into a life of crime although most achieved only notoriety and an early death. They were mainly horse, cattle and sheep thieves until the start of the gold rush in the 1850s and 60s when they very quickly recognised the easy pickings available as the gold was moved to Sydney and Melbourne from the diggings in the gold fields—it promised to be a lucrative time.

The forces of law and order ranged against them were seriously undermanned, a situation made worse by the numbers of police officers who resigned to seek their own fortune in the gold fields. Although the bushrangers found a place in Australian folklore and did little or no harm to ordinary people they were a murderous bunch. Clashes between the bushrangers and police were violent and bloody with six officers being killed and fifteen badly wounded from 1862 to 1868.

Frederick Ward first fell foul of the law when he was convicted of horse stealing at the age of 20 and sentenced to ten years hard labour although he was released on a ticket of leave (a form of early release on parole) after four years. Within a year, however, he was caught again for the same crime and sent back to prison. This time he escaped and soon found himself a job working on a farm owned by a former police officer who was married to a respectable, well-educated and literate part-aboriginal woman (Mary Anne). This unlikely couple fell in love and eloped together into the outback. Little was heard of either until a new bushranger—Captain Thunderbolt—and his female accomplice began to terrorise the district, stealing the mail and robbing travellers at gunpoint. For six years they stayed free until he was finally caught and sentenced to another five years in prison. Again he managed to escape after three years, rejoined his family and resumed his career in crime.

Sometime afterwards Mary Anne was captured and sentenced to six months imprisonment for vagrancy but was released to find that Captain Thunderbolt had started an affair with another part-aboriginal lady, the wife of a settler, and had taken off again. Mary Anne was dying and returned to the cave she had shared with Thunderbolt as their home. When his new lady tired of him and turned her attentions to a younger man, Thunderbolt himself returned to the cave where he found out about Mary Anne's illness for the first time although there was nothing he could do. With the death of his first love and the rejection by his second, he became careless and was cornered and killed by the police near the small town of Uralla on 25 May 1870. The officer who shot him—Constable A B Walker, stationed in the town—was awarded the New South Wales Medal for Resisting and Capturing Bushrangers for his courage during Captain Thunderbolt's final tussle with the forces of the law.

Not all bushrangers were uneducated men and not all died an early death—some were treated with a surprising degree of leniency considering the early history of Australia, their exploits and the severity of sentence handed down to others. Frank Gardiner was born in Scotland but taken to Australia at the age of five in 1835. He was a wealthy, educated man who owned a butchers shop from which he made a good living although it was suspected that most of the meat he sold had been stolen. He had several brushes with the law and served two terms of imprisonment for horse stealing. He took to bushranging in 1861 when he learnt that a warrant for his arrest had been issued for more horse stealing and led a gang which contained some of the most feared, and dangerous, of all bushrangers. His greatest coup was the theft of gold and banknotes to the value of £14,000, a huge sum for the times, and effectively retired from his life of crime to a small town in Queensland where he ran a store under a false name.

The police, however, tracked him down and he was arrested after a struggle in which the senior police officer—Sergeant Jon Middleton—was wounded in the face and wrist but succeeded in overpowering Gardiner. He was tried and sentenced to 32 years in prison but released after serving only eight years on the condition that he left New South Wales. He emigrated to America and settled in San Francisco but is believed to have been killed there in 1895 in a bar brawl. Sergeant Middleton was awarded the NSW medal for his part in his capture.

PENFOLD-HYLAND GOLD MEDAL

The concept of awarding medals for acts of courage has never been confined to governments, charities, commercial organisations and official bodies such as police forces, there are many examples of private individuals being prompted to issue their own, personal medals. Often they were special issues awarded once only as a reward for a specific act of courage which the donor thought worthy of something more than the official recognition available. On other occasions they were intended to be more permanent and awarded annually.

In November 1931, Mr H L Penfold-Hyland, a prominent businessman from South Australia and the son of a former governor of Castlemaine Gaol, offered to award a gold medal annually to the police officer from South Australia who had performed the most conspicuous act of bravery in a twelve month period to start on 1 January 1932. He had been prompted to make the offer after visiting Melbourne at the time a policeman was shot and killed causing him to reflect on the low value placed on the officer's life in particular and the poor regard for the police in general amongst large sections of the community.

The offer was accepted by the Police Commissioner—Brigadier-General Leane—and a board appointed to examine suitable cases and select an officer to receive the award. The criteria were simple, the gold medal was to be presented for:

(a)　conspicuous gallantry in saving life and property or in preventing crime or arresting criminals; the risks incurred to be estimated with due regard to the duties and obligations of the officer concerned, or

(b)　saving persons from drowning, or

(c)　protecting the public from injury at great personal risk.

The first award was made on 8 June 1933 for the year of 1932 to Foot Constable James Shannon from Hindmarsh police station for his bravery at an incident on 11 May when he entered a sewer in an attempt to rescue two men who had been overcome by fumes whilst working in a manhole.

Constable Shannon, with a colleague, had been sent to a sewer main in Thebarton where it was thought that two officials from the Sewers Department had been overcome by fumes whilst inspecting the main which ran towards the River Torrens. Despite the strong smell of fumes coming from the manhole Constable Shannon went down into the sewer and started to look for the two men. He was obliged to descend almost 25 feet down a narrow hole into a pit that was barely 12 feet square half filled with raw sewage. After a short while he was forced to the surface by the fumes but returned equipped with rods to resume his search standing waist deep in sewage. For almost 90 minutes he dragged the pit to the best of his ability in the cramped conditions but failed to find either man and was forced to give up when he was himself overcome by the fumes. For his courage in the face of the extreme danger to himself he was awarded the first Penfold-Hyland Gold Medal.

The actions of Constable Shannon were considered by a board of five officers in January 1931 and he was unanimously chosen from the eight officers put forward for actions arising from five sets of circumstances. Four officers had been involved in stopping runaway horses and two others for their tact, firmness and courage in handling a dangerous situation during a race riot between Greeks and Australians in March 1932. The act of stopping a runaway horse attached to a carriage of some description was a common occurrence of the time in most countries including the UK and were usually rewarded by some form of official recognition although the level varied greatly. In some forces in the UK a commendation from the chief constable was thought appropriate but in others—the Cornwall Constabulary being one—the officer's courage was rewarded by the King's Police Medal for Gallantry. There seems to have been no consistency at all.

There were no further awards until 1936 when the second, and last, medal was presented to Mounted Constable James Brock. In the evening of 23 April 1936 the officer was on duty at Cowell to oversee the arrival of the SS *Quorna*.

One of the passengers—Mr S Moyle—disembarked from the ship but slipped and fell into the water between the jetty and ship. Constable Brock immediately dived into the water and succeeded in finding Mr Moyle and dragging him to the safety of some submerged timber where he stayed until he was hauled to the jetty. It was found that Mr Moyle had broken his leg and the chances of him surviving were slim without the constable's actions. He was in danger of drowning, being crushed between the ship and jetty of being attacked by sharks known to be in the area. For reasons which are not known, these were the only two occasions on which the medal was awarded.

The medals were cast in 18 carat gold and of very similar design although they were specially made on each occasion and there were differences particularly in the inscriptions. The obverse contained a shield at the centre surrounded by a buckled belt with the words FOR BRAVERY at the top. The belt was surrounded by a wreath of laurel leaves topped by an imperial crown attached to a ring suspender. The reverse was plain. The first medal awarded to Constable Shannon was engraved in the shield of the obverse with PRESENTED TO - CONST - J A SHANNON - 1932 in four lines with PRESENTED BY H L PENFOLD-HYLAND ESQ on the reverse.

The second medal showed slight differences in the design of the imperial crown and the positioning of the engraving. The shield on the obverse was engraved with the ornate initials of Constable Brock - JLB and the reverse with TO - MOUNTED CONSTABLE - J L BROCK - 1936 - PRESENTED - BY - H L PENFOLD-HYLAND ESQ in seven lines.

The courage displayed by both Constables Shannon and Brock was also acknowledged by the award of medals by the Royal Humane Society of Australasia, a similar organisation to the RHS in the UK with similar aims and objectives—to give public recognition to people who risk their own lives in saving or attempting to save the lives of others.

ROYAL HUMANE SOCIETY OF AUSTRALASIA MEDAL

The Society was founded in September 1874 as the Victorian Humane Society but its remit was extended in 1886 to cover the whole of Australia and its territories (except New South Wales).

Instituted: 1874.

Ribbon: Dark blue with silver edges and a thin gold central stripe. Posthumous awards use a plain dark blue ribbon.

Metal: Gold, silver and bronze—dependant upon the level of bravery displayed.

Description: (Obverse) a female figure representing Australasia (standing left) placing a wreath on the head of a kneeling figure (right) who represents a person whose courage and humanity have been judged worthy of recognition. The five stars of the Southern Cross are included in the background above the kneeling figure. The words VIRTUTE (left and PARATUM (right)—bravery rewarded—are at the circumference; (reverse) a wreath of laurel and eucalyptus leaves with the central field ontaining the words AWARDED TO and the rest left blank for the details of the recipient. The name of the society is inscribed around the upper circumference and the words INST AD 1874 lie at the base.

In addition to the standard medals a special award (introduced in July 1881) is made each year to the person whose actions are thought to be the most outstanding of all those awarded the gold, silver or bronze medal. It is not awarded if there is no case of sufficient merit or where there are several of equal merit and it is not possible to differentiate between them—only one per year is ever awarded and it is not given posthumously. The design is identical to the standard medal and presented in gold or silver according to the class of the standard award made to the rescuer. The only differences are in the suspender bar which is rectangular and carries the name of the medal—CLARKE MEDAL—and the ribbon which is maroon with silver bands at the edges. The Clarke Medal is a prestigious and highly regarded award in Australia, it has been presented on four occasions by Her Majesty the Queen (the patron of the society) when she was visiting the country.

ROYAL HUMANE SOCIETY OF NEW SOUTH WALES

The State of New South Wales has its own humane society which awards medals to recognise acts of courage in saving life independently from the national organisation. Two classes of medal are available with the criteria for the award of each being dependent upon the level of bravery displayed.

Ribbon: Light blue with a dark blue stripe at each edge. In undress uniform the class of the award is indicated by a silver or bronze star worn on the ribbon.

Metal: Silver and bronze.

Description: (Obverse) the shield of the Coat of Arms of New South Wales within an outer band bearing the name of the Society; (reverse) a wreath of laurel with the words AWARDED TO (engraved name of the recipient and date of the act for which the medal was awarded) FOR BRAVERY. Each medal is numbered on the rim.

The highest example of bravery displayed during any one year in New South Wales is recognised by the award of a special medal in similar fashion to the Clarke Medal awarded by the national society. The Galleghan Award was introduced in 1996 and named in honour of Brigadier Sir Frderick Galleghan DSO OBE ISO ED who was the secretary of the Society for 14 years until his death in 1971. He won his DSO in Malaya during the Second World War. The design of the medal is the same as the silver and bronze awards with the only difference being the addition of a bar to the ribbon which is inscribed with the words GALLEGHAN AWARD.

page 16

AUSTRIA

Although there are similarities in the structure of the police forces of many European countries, methods of rewarding police officers for acts of bravery, meritorious service or long service and good conduct vary greatly. With a single exception, there are no medals exclusively available to police officers in Austria for any reason although they are entitled to federal and provincial awards in the same way as any other Austrian citizen if their actions are thought worthy of official recognition.

Austrian policing has three arms—the Federal Police (*Bundespolizei*), a Federal Criminal Investigation Corps and the Federal Gendarmerie which has its own Criminal Investigation Bureau. Control of policing activity (conducted by the Bundespolizei) in the provinces and major cities lies at a local level although all are responsible ultimately to the Ministry of the Interior. The Gendarmerie have a responsibility for policing rural areas in much the same way as their counterparts in France operate. All officers, from all branches of the Austrian police forces, are eligible for the primary federal award made for a variety of reasons which fall under the general heading of outstanding public achievement and exceptional services to the Republic of Austria.

GOLDENES EHRENZEICHEN

The Decoration of Honour for Merit of the Republic of Austria (*Das Ehrenzeichen für Verdienste um die Republik Österreich*)—introduced after the Second World War—is divided into five groups, each with a number of classes, and is subject to strict rules according to the rank or position of the recipient. Police officers are entitled to decorations from the fifth group (with one exception for very senior officers) and also to two medals which are a part of the system but which fall outside the five groups. The Decoration of Honour is also available to foreign nationals.

Instituted: 2 April 1952.

Ribbon: White with a red stripe at the edges, worn in triangular fashion with the apex at the bottom where it is attached to the medal.

Metal: Gold.

Description: (Obverse) a Maltese cross in red enamel with an inlaid white enameled Greek cross topped by the federal coat of arms in gold apart from the shields of the nine constituent länder which are enameled in their true colours and the national shield which is placed centrally on the breast of the eagle.

The Decoration of Honour in Gold is the highest award available to police officers other than those of the very highest ranks and is issued to officers of the rank of colonel. The same decoration is used irrespective of the reason for the award and there is no way to distinguish between those given for a single act (of courage or otherwise), particularly meritorious service over a period or as a reward for long service. These principles remain for the six other classes of the decoration available to police officers, the differences being only in the rank of the recipient. Officers of the next lowest rank—lieutenant colonel—are rewarded with the Decoration of Honour in Silver which is identical in design and differs only in the metal used and the colouring of the ribbon. For all silver medals the national colours of red and white are reversed from that used for gold medals and are red with a white central stripe. All are triangular in shape.

The next two ranks—major and captain—are entitled to one of the two medals which are attached to the honours system but are not a part of the five groups—the Cross of Merit—in gold or silver respectively. The design is identical to the Decoration of Honour and follows the same rules for the ribbon used but the medals themselves are of the plain metal only with no use of enamel.

The second of the two associated medals (Medal of Merit) is awarded in three degrees—gold, silver and bronze—to officers below the rank of captain. The same ribbon is used for all three classes.

MEDAILLE FÜR VERDIENSTE

Ribbon: Red with a central white stripe.

Metal: Gold, silver and bronze with no enamels.

Size: 35 mm

Description: (Obverse) a circular medal with the federal coat of arms (without the shields of the nine länder) surrounded by a wreath of pairs of laurel leaves with the provincial shields between each pair; (reverse) the words FÜR VERDIENSTE UM DIE REPUBLIK ÖSTERREICH (for services to the Republic of Austria).

The present Austrian arms were originally adopted after the country became an independent republic following the First World War. The national colours—red, white, red—were introduced first in October 1918 and are based on the seal of Duke Frederick II dating from 1230 which consisted of a silver bar on a red shield. This now appears (with silver changed to white) at the centre of the present arms. The eagle was taken from the arms of the Hapsburg dynasty and the mural crown, hammer, sickle and broken chain added to signify the liberation of the people from imperial rule in 1918. When Austria was incorporated into the German Third Reich after the anschluss the arms were abolished but re-adopted when Austria regained its independence in 1945 and have remained unchanged since.

Austria

In addition to the national awards, medals are issued by each of the nine provincial governments to citizens (including police officers) for life-saving or duty performed during any emergency, disaster or catastrophe, natural or otherwise. Not all provinces issue medals for all these reasons although most have a method of one sort or another of affording local recognition for saving life or for duty in times of need. These medals form an interesting group with most carrying designs or emblems of local significance and ribbons in the local colours. There are also individual medals issued in a single province only in commemoration of a particularly important event in local history. Austrian police officers are eligible for all these provincial awards irrespective of the branch of the service to which they belong.

The image of the modern Republic of Austria (the second) at the turn of the 21st century is one of a small, very picturesque, peaceful central European country and a very popular tourist destination in summer and winter. Its history, however, is far removed from this image. Prior to the Great War, it was the centre of the vast Austro-Hungarian Empire exerting a huge influence across most of the region and a past which included dominance of a number of modern states almost inconceivable today. In its time, it ruled Belgium, parts of modern Poland, Germany, Italy, Russia and the former Yugoslavia which belonged to Turkey at the time of its conquest. Its very easy to forget (or ignore) the fact that the first attack of the Great War was by Austro-Hungary on Serbia in retaliation for the assassination of the Empire's crown prince in Sarajevo by Serbian dissidents protesting against rule by the Empire. This triggered declarations of war by Germany on Russia and France, Britain (and its Empire) on Germany and the intervention of the rest of Europe and the USA into the first of the two conflicts which disfigured the 20th century. After the Second World War, Austria was occupied by the four allied powers until 15 May 1955 when agreement was reached to restore full sovereignty to the country and the Second Republic was established.

The position of the nine provinces in the Republic has also been the subject of dispute and conflict.

The province of the Tirol is usually thought of as typical of Austria but it was not until the end of the Great War and the plebiscite held there in 1921 that the people voted in favour of union with Austria along with Salzburg and Burgenland. The country's most recent problem area involved the southern province of Kärnten (Carinthia) following the break-up of Yugoslavia in 1991 and the war between the Serbs and Slovenia which borders the Austrian province. In December 1990 Slovenia became the first of the Yugoslav republics to vote in favour of independence and left the federation six months later. In order to assert its independence the new Slovenian government provoked a conflict with the federal forces over control of the border crossings, including those with Austria. Fighting was brief but fierce until a settlement brokered by the EU was agreed and Yugoslav federal troops were withdrawn. On 15 January 1992 Slovenia became an independent sovereign state for the first time in its history.

Although the fighting presented no direct threat to Austria, its proximity and the presence of the ethnic Slovenians in the province of Kärnten where they formed a sizeable minority resulted in officers from the Federal Gendarmerie who guard the borders and the Bundespolizei facing new challenges, duties and dangers few ever thought they would experience. The provincial government of Kärnten issued a special medal (*Cross for the Border Crisis Operation 1991*) to recognise their service in these particularly troubled times.

EHRENKREUZ FÜR DEN GRENZSICHERUNGEINSATZ

Ribbon: Red with a white stripe at one edge and one of yellow at the other, both 5mm.

Metal: Bronze.

Size: 35 mm.

Description: (Obverse) a cross pattée with a central medallion bearing the Coat of Arms of the Province of Kärnten surrounded by the word GRENZSICHERUNGEINSATZ and the date 1991 at the bottom; (reverse) plain apart from the inscription DANK DES LANDES KÄRNTEN.

page 19

Kärnten is one of the very few provinces that does not award a medal for life-saving although it does issue a reward in the form of a commemorative medal for duty during any operation following a catastrophe or disaster.

ERINNERUNGSMEDAILLE FÜR KATASTROPHENEINSATZ

Instituted: 14 December 1965.

Ribbon: Three equal stripes of yellow, red and white.

Metal: Bronze.

Size: 32 mm.

Description: (Obverse) the Arms of Kärnten; (reverse) plain apart from the inscription DANK- DES LANDES - KÄRNTEN - FÜR - KATASTROPHEN - EINSATZ (with thanks from the Province of Kärnten for disaster duty) in six lines

The Province of Kärnten was first established as a separate duchy in 976 and became part of Tirol in 1286. It has been a part of Austria since 1335. The shield at the centre of the provincial coat of arms is halved vertically with the right part having three equal bands in the national colours and the left three black panthers thought to have been adopted from the first dukes of the Province in 1237. On the provincial medals the shield has a helmet as the crest and mantling with the whole topped by an old musical instrument, all taken from the ducal arms although the meanings are not clear.

Austria

Most provinces award more than one medal for life-saving, duty at disasters or, in two cases, for recognition of service during the serious floods which afflict the country from time to time. The provinces of Vorarlberg, Wien (Vienna) and Burgenland all issue only a single medal for life-saving (*Rettungsmedaille* or *Lebensrettungmedaille*) without a separate medal available for duty during a disaster or floods although the saving of a life in either eventuality is recognised.

RETTUNGSMEDAILLE DES LANDES VORARLBERG

Instituted: 3 December 1979.

Ribbon: Blue.

Metal: Silver.

Description: (Obverse) the Coat of Arms of Vorarlberg with the words FÜR LEBENSRETTUNG (for life-saving) around the upper circumference and LAND VORARLBERG around the lower; (reverse) the image of a life-saver and a rescued person at the edge of a body of water against a backdrop of mountains. A lightning bolt is superimposed on the mountains to the left.

The Vorarlberg is the second smallest Austrian province with an area of just over 1,000 square miles and a population of about 350,000 in the far west of the country bordering Switzerland (west) and Bavaria (north). Until 1918 and the changes made in Austria at the end of the Great War it was a part of the Province of Tirol but has been independent since. It is the most highly industrialised province of Austria after Vienna but has a substantial tourist industry in summer and winter. The provincial arms consist of a simple shield with a red banner (the arms of the Counts of Montfort) and were granted as recently as 1923 although they were but one part of a more complicated set of features granted in 1863 by Emperor Franz Joseph I.

RETTUNGSMEDAILLE DES LANDES WIEN

Instituted: 14 July 1967.

Ribbon: Half red, half white.

Metal: Silver.

Size: 40 mm.

Description: (Obverse) the figure of a life-saver carrying the person rescued; (reverse) the Coat of Arms of Vienna with the words DEM RETTER AUS LEBENSGEFAHR (to the saver of a life in danger) around the upper circumference and DAS BUNDESLAND WIEN (from the Province of Vienna) in three lines at the base below the shield.

The Province (and city) of Vienna is the seat of government and home to most federal agencies. It is the smallest province (415 square miles) and entirely surrounded by the Province of Lower Austria (Niederosterreich) with a population of more than 1.5 million, about 20% of the total Austrian population. The coat of arms is a simple shield in the national colours—a white cross on a red background—and appears at the centre of the only medal awarded in the Province to police officers.

RETTUNGSMEDAILLE DES LANDES BURGENLAND

Instituted: 11 June 1971.

Ribbon: Four equal stripes of red, yellow, red and yellow.

Metal: Silver.

Description: (Obverse) an image of the hand of a life-saver gripping the wrist of a person in distress; (reverse) a central tablet bearing the words DAS LAND BURGENLAND in four lines with DEM RETTER AUS LEBENSGEFAHR around the circumference.

Burgenland (Land of Castles) is the most easterly of the Austrian provinces and was formerly a region of Hungary but became a part of Austria after the Great War in 1921 following a referendum of the mainly German speaking people although a part of the former area with a substantial Hungarian speaking population voted to stay a part of that country. The present name was adopted in 1920. The coat of arms shows a crowned eagle with outstretched wings perched on a rock and a small star above each wing. The eagle has a shield at its breast which has four vertical lines in red and white with three stars on the white lines. The elements have been taken from the two most influential and powerful families of the region in medieval times—the Counts of Mattersdorf-Forchtenstein and Güssing-Bernstein.

Three provinces award medals for both life-saving and duty at the scene of a disaster (*Katastrophenmedaille*). Two of them—Salzburg and Niederösterreich (Lower Austria)—use the same ribbon for both awards but the third province—Tirol—has differences, albeit slight.

TIROLER LEBENSRETTUNGMEDAILLE

Ribbon: White with a red stripe and a thin black line offset towards one edge.

Metal: Silver.

Description: (Obverse) the Coat of Arms of Tirol; (reverse) plain apart from the words FÜR - RETTUNG - AUS - LEBENSGEFAHR - DAS LAND - TIROL in six lines.

The Tyrolean award for duty in time of a disaster is very similar to the life-saving award, differing only in the inscription on the medals reverse which reads ZUM - DANK - FÜR - KATASTROPHEN - EINSATZ - DAS LAND - TIROL in seven lines. The ribbon is silver with lines of white and red offset towards one edge.

The Province of Tirol takes its name from a town which is now in Italy (since 1919) but which was once the home of the Counts of Tirol who ruled a much larger area than the present province. The provincial coat of arms has a crowned eagle with outstretched wings and a laurel branch framing its head. It first appeared in 1205 as a seal of the Counts of Tirol and doesn't appear to have been changed since 1567. The meaning of the elements has been lost although the eagle was a commonly used and popular symbol of authority and strength amongst rulers. The outstretched wings carry a yellow line ending in trefoils which is thought to have been added by the Counts of Tirol to distinguish their arms from others using the same basic eagle design.

Austria

RETTUNGSMEDAILLE DES LANDES NIEDERÖSTERREICH

Instituted: 27 January 1955.

Ribbon: Royal blue with a band of yellow towards each edge.

Metal: Silver.

Size: 40 mm.

Description: (Obverse) the image of a the figure of a rescuer holding the limp body of a person saved; (reverse) the Coat of Arms of the Province above the words DEM RETTER AUS LEBENSGEFAHR DAS BUNDESLAND NIEDER-ÖSTERREICH in five lines. Any second or subsequent award of the medal is indicated by a silver bar worn on the ribbon with the word LEBENSRETTUNG preceded by the number of the award—2, 3 etc.

KATASTROPHENMEDAILLE DES LANDES NIEDERÖSTERREICH

Ribbon: Royal blue with a band of yellow towards each edge slightly wider than the life-saving award.

Metal: Silver.

Description: (Obverse) an image from the scene of a disaster with a figure in the centre holding up a beam from a collapsed building with a scene of destruction and a fleeing figure in the background; (reverse) the Coat of Arms of the Province placed centrally over a branch of laurel with the words DANK FÜR KATASTROPHENEINSATZ around the upper circumference and the province name LAND NIEDERÖSTERREICH around the lower.

Lower Austria can best be considered as the cradle of Austria and has been occupied since prehistoric times. With Vienna wholly within its borders the Province has been at the heart of the history and development of modern Austria. It became an autonomous province separated from Vienna only in 1920 but continued to be administered by the national capital for a number of years despite the fact that the town of St Pölten had been the provincial capital since 1986. The provincial arms consist of a shield with five eagles with outstretched wings topped by a mural crown and are believed to have been taken from those of Duke Rudolf IV who had adopted them in 1360.

LEBENSRETTUNGSMEDAILLE DES LANDES SALZBURG

Instituted: 20 July 1955.

Ribbon: Half white and half red.

Metal: Silver.

Size: 50 mm.

Description: (Obverse) the Coat of Arms of the Province of Salzburg; (reverse) a wreath of laurel around the circumference with the words DEM RETTER AUS LEBENSGEFAHR AUS LAND SALZBURG in seven lines in the central field.

MEDAILLE FÜR KATASTROPHENEINSATZ

Ribbon: Half white, half red.

Metal: Bronze.

Size: 32 mm.

Description: (Obverse) The Coat of Arms of the Province of Salzburg above three wavy lines to represent water; (reverse) the words FÜR KATASTROPHEN HILFE (for help at a disaster) in three lines in the centre above a sprig of three laurel leaves with DAS LAND (upper) SALZBURG (lower) around the circumference.

The Province of Salzburg is dominated by the city of the same name which gained its power and influence from its position as the seat of an archbishopric dating from the 7th century. The city and the church dominated the destiny of the region for hundreds of years. The arms are very similar to those of the Province of Kärnten, divided into two vertically with the left half, however, having a single black panther. The most significant feature is the use of a hat as a crest, thought to have been taken into use in the early 19th century.

The history of the arms is uncertain but they are thought to have originated in the 13th century and be based on those of Archbishop Ulrich of Kärnten.

Austria

The Province of Steiermark (Styria) awards two medals, one for life-saving and the other for duty in times of flooding only with no mention made of any other type of disaster. The first of these—*Medal for Duty in the Floods of 1958*—was introduced after severe flooding had occurred in the Province in August 1958 causing severe damage and some loss of life. It was awarded to recognise the work of the local and federal emergency services and volunteers during and after the disaster.

MEDAILLE FÜR VERDIENSTE BEIM HOCHWASSEREINSATZ 1958

Instituted: 5 November 1958.

Ribbon: Half white, half green.

Metal: Bronze.

Size: 35 mm.

Description: (Obverse) the Coat of Arms of the Province with a laurel branch around the shield and the legend HOCHWASSEREINSATZ 1958 around the upper circumference; (reverse) the figure of a rescuer with his arm draped protectively around a young girl. He holds a shovel in his right hand and there is a branch of laurel behind the two figures. At the upper left circumference is a representation of heavy rain and in the lower left a series of wavy lines to indicate the floods.

STEIRISCHE LEBENSRETTUNGMEDAILLE

In 1965 the provincial government introduced a series of three medals, in gold, silver and bronze, as a permanent local award for anyone involved in any floods which affect the Province. The design was based on the 1958 medal and used the same ribbon. The medal was effectively reversed on the new design with the image of the two figures on the reverse of the earlier medal becoming the obverse of the new series.

The new reverse carried the arms of the Province but the wording was amended to read HOCHWASSERMEDAILLE (Flood Medal) with the date omitted. The diameter was also increased to 40 mm.

The life-saving medal also available in the Province uses the same ribbon as the flood medals and is a recent addition to the series of local awards, introduced only in 1997.

Instituted: 13 October 1997.

Ribbon: Half white, half green.

Metal: Silver gilt.

Size: 40 mm.

Description: (Obverse) the Coat of Arms of the Province with the words FÜR LEBENSRETTUNG (above) and LAND STEIRMARK (below) around the circumference; (reverse) left blank.

Most Austrian provinces are distinct historical areas rather than artificial groupings although the destruction of the Austro-Hungarian Empire after the 1918 armistice led to some being a shadow of their former selves—the Tirol, in particular, once covered an area of more than twice its present size. The borders of Steiermark (Styria) today have not changed since they were finally established at the beginning of the 16th century. The rulers changed many times but the provincial area has remained constant for more than 400 years. The panther which appears on the shield of the provincial arms was first known from a seal dating from 1260 belonging to Duke Ottokar III. Today the shield is topped by a ducal hat although its origins are unknown. The arms were officially adopted in 1926.

The Province of Oberösterreich (Upper Austria) currently awards life-saving and commemorative disaster duty medals (Erinnerungsmedaille) although they were both prompted by a special award made in 1955 after the Province was hit by severe flooding in November 1954—*Commemorative Medal for the Floods of 1954*. The current group of medals was introduced in 1962. Although the elements of the provincial arms have been known since the late 14th century when Oberösterreich became a part of Austria they were not officially adopted in 1930. Their origin is not totally clear but they were, in all probability, derived from those used by the Lords of Machland, the most influential family of the area in medieval times.

OBERÖSTERREICHISCHE ERINNERUNGSMEDAILLE AN DEN HOCHWASSEREINSATZ 1954

Instituted: *7 February 1995.*

Ribbon: *Half white, half red with lines of red and white (1 mm) at the edges.*

Metal: *Bronze.*

Size: *32 mm.*

Description: *(Obverse) the Coat of Arms of the Province above three wavy lines to represent flood water; (reverse) two branches of laurel in the lower half and the words HOCHWASSEREINSATZ 1954 above.*

OBERÖSTERREICHISCHE ERINNERUNGSMEDAILLE FÜR KATASTROPHENEINSATZ

Instituted: 9 July 1962.

Ribbon: The same as the previous medal (half white, half red) but without the coloured lines at the edges.

Metal: Bronze.

Size: 32 mm.

Description: (Obverse) a stylised representation of the two main elements of the Coat of Arms of the Province; (reverse) the words DANK DES LANDES - OBERÖSTERREICH - FÜR - KATASTROPHENEINSATZ in four lines with a design of lines and semi-circles above and below.

The Life-saving Medal was introduced at the same time and uses the same design for its obverse but with the reverse carrying the words DANK DES LANDES OBERÖSTERREICH FÜR LEBENSRETTUNG in four lines and a different design of a number of crossed lines above and below. The ribbon is identical to the medal introduced in 1954 including the use of lines of red and white at the edges.

The basic medal is bronze but there is a silver version available for any second or subsequent award to the same person.

The sole exception to the absence of any medal exclusively available to police officers is awarded in the Province of Vorarlberg only to the uniformed branch of the federal forces in recognition of an act of special merit.

SICHERHEITSMEDAILLE DES LANDES VORARLBERG

Instituted: 11 November 1984.

Ribbon: Red and white.

Metal: Bronze and silver.

Size: 34 mm.

Description: (Obverse) the Coat of Arms of Vorarlberg with the inscription LAND VORARLBERG around the circumference; (reverse) plain apart from the legend FÜR - BESONDERE - VERDIENSTE - IN DIE ÖRTLICHE - SICHERHEITS - POLIZEI (for outstanding service in the local security police) in six lines

BELGIUM

In June 1998 a fundamental reform of the policing structure of Belgium was announced with a proposal to amalgamate the many different police forces into a single Federal Police (*Federale Politie—Police Federale*). Implementation of the process started in 2000 although the changes are likely to take place over several years. The Federal Police will replace the 583 separate forces which make up the Municipal Police (*Gemeentelijke—Police Communale*), the *Landelijke Politie (Veldwachter)—Police Rurale (Garde-Champêtre)*, a rural police service, the Judicial Police (*Gerechtelijke Politie - Police Judiciaire*), special airport, maritime, railways and transport forces and the national force, the *Rijkswacht—Gendarmerie*.

The Municipal Police has the greatest strength with almost 18,500 officers at its disposal followed by the State Police with almost 16,000. The other forces are much smaller with specific jurisdictions and limited powers in some cases. Although the Municipal Police comprises a large number of very distinct forces under the control of the local mayor they are responsible at federal level to the Ministry of the Interior and have similar powers across the country. The Municipal Police has always been an entirely civil body since the first forces appeared before Belgium gained its independence from the Netherlands in 1830. The State Police, however, was modelled on the style familiar in France and Italy with the Gendarmerie Nationale and Carabinieri and was a part of the Belgian armed forces until 1992 when it lost its military status and became a civil police force. It continues to maintain a provost rôle within the Belgian army during service outside the Kingdom.

The range of awards given to police officers from any of the different forces for acts of courage, meritorious or distinguished service and long service with good conduct has always been limited with no medals exclusively available to police officers. The distinction between the two main arms of the police service, one civil, one military, meant that there were separate awards also available to the members. As a part of the Belgian armed forces, officers from the State Police were entitled to military honours although, in most normal circumstances, this was restricted to a single award. The *Military Decoration* was available in two divisions each with two classes. The design of the medal was identical in all cases, the only difference being in the ribbon colours for the two divisions and the use of a gilt chevron clasp on the ribbon to indicate a first class award.

The first division was for long service and seniority, the second for courage, self-sacrifice or particularly meritorious or distinguished service. The former hung from a yellow ribbon with three red and four black stripes all of equal width and equally spaced, the latter from a red ribbon with stripes of black, yellow and red (the Belgian national colours) at the edges. The second class award for service was made after ten years with the first class chevron following five years later. At the time of its introduction there was a single division (for long service and seniority) but this was changed in 1952 to introduce the second division—awards for bravery. The medal was introduced during the reign of King Leopold II (1865–1909) and there have been four further kings since—Albert I (1909–34), Leopold III (1934–51), Baudouin I (1951–93) and the present monarch Albert II. Each used his own device on the reverse of the medal.

DE MILITAIRE DECORATIE
(LA DÉCORATION MILITAIRE)

Instituted: 22 December 1873.

Ribbon: See above.

Metal: Gilt.

Description: (Obverse) a cross pattée with ribbed rays between the arms of the cross and a central medallion bearing the Belgian lion within an outer band inscribed with the legend L'UNION FAIT LA FORCE (unity makes strength). The upper arm of the cross was surmounted by a crown attached to a ring suspender; (reverse) the same basic design but with central medallion carrying the monogram or device of the reigning monarch and the outer band bearing the words ARMÉE - MÉRITE - ANCIENETÉ (army, merit, long service).

Belgium is a bi-lingual country—French and Flemish—but it wasn't until 1951 that this was recognised on the Military Decoration and the inscriptions surrounding the central medallion changed to include Flemish. The inscription EENDRACHT MAAKT MACHT was added to the French text on the obverse and LEGER - VERDIENSTE - DIENSJAREN to the reverse. The following year, when the statute governing the award of the medal was renewed, the design was changed once more and the inscription on the reverse removed.

When the State Police lost its military status the entitlement to this award was also removed and officers became eligible for the same honours as their civil counterparts in the Municipal Police and the other smaller forces. The *Civil Decoration* also comes in two divisions, one for long service and seniority, the other for bravery, devotion to duty or self-sacrifice with each division having five classes in all—a cross in first and second classes and a medal awarded in bronze, silver and gold.

DE BURGERLIJKE DECORATIE
(LA DÉCORATION CIVIQUE)

Instituted: 21 July 1867.

Ribbon: See below.

Metal: Gold or silver with white enamel.

Description: (Obverse) a Maltese cross in white enamel with a Burgundy Cross between the arms. The central medallion, also in white enamel, carries the monogram or device of the reigning monarch; (reverse) identical to the obverse. The upper arm of the Maltese cross is surmounted by the symbol of the House of Burgundy - a tinder box - attached to a ring suspender.

The design of the cross is the same for both divisions although the principle of using differently coloured ribbons follows the pattern of the Military Decoration. An award for long service or seniority hangs from a ribbon of four red and three black bands all of equal width, the bravery awards are red with two broad black band flanked by narrow yellow lines. The ribbons are the same for all five classes of the award.

The three medals, awarded in gold, silver and bronze, have the same basic design as the crosses but without the use of enamels, no tinder box above the upper arm of the cross and with the spaces between the arms of the Maltese cross being filled in but still carrying the Burgundy cross.

The crosses and medals of the Civil Decoration for Long Service in the Administration are awarded according to the rank of the recipient but the award for bravery or devotion to duty takes into consideration the degree of courage involved.

The two crosses are reserved for the most exceptional examples of bravery with medals being awarded for lesser acts which are, nonetheless, thought worthy of national recognition. The award for bravery can be made to foreign nationals.

Commemorative medals have been awarded in Belgium, some to police officers. to celebrate a variety of notable national events but the one most likely to be found on any group worn by an officer from pre-war days was instituted to celebrate the 100th anniversary of Belgian independence. The *Commemorative Medal of the 100th Anniversary of National Independence* was authorised by King Albert I and awarded to anyone who had served the country loyally for at least 20 years on the anniversary date of 1 January 1931. In reality recipients were holders of the Civil Decoration for Long Service in the Administration.

DE HERINNERINGSMEDAILLE AAN DE 100STE VERJAARDAG VAN DE NATIONALE ONAFHANKELIJKHEID
(LA MÉDAILLE COMMÉMORATIVE DU CENTENAIRE DE L'INDEPENDENCE NATIONALE)

Instituted: 20 July 1930.

Ribbon: White with lines in the national colours at the edges (red, yellow and black).

Metal: Silver.

Description: (Obverse) an octagonal medal the conjoined heads of the three monarchs since 1830 facing left; (reverse) the two dates 1830 and 1930 on a background of laurel branches. A ring suspender was attached to a royal crown fitted to the top of the octagon.

The most senior officers in all Belgian police forces, including the State Police, can be eligible for two of the Belgian orders of knighthood—the Order of the Crown and the Order of Leopold II, the class depending on the recipient's rank and length of service.

BELIZE

Formerly British Honduras and situated on the Yucatán Peninsula of Central America, Belize is a small country with a population of only 200,000, many of whom (40%) can trace their ancestry back to African slaves brought over in the 17th century. About ten per cent of the population are the direct descendants of the Maya people whose civilisation in the Yucatán pre-dates Christianity, the Romans, Greeks and Egyptians by centuries although it is now only remembered from the ruins of their towns and cities.

In the early days of European colonisation the country was of little interest to the Spanish until the British established a base there in the 1700s to take advantage of the logging industry that had been developed. Although the Spanish wanted the British out they were not in a position to do anything about it and the country effectively became a British Colony. Conflict between the two powers did take place but the Spanish fleet was routed with some ease and British control firmly established.

Belize gained independence from Britain in 1981 after a period in which British troops were sent to protect the country from the threat of invasion by neighbouring Guatemala who had claimed the territory for many years. It was the last of the Central American countries to achieve independence from the colonial power although it would have happened earlier but for the threat from Guatemala.

In 1985 three medals were introduced and made available to police officers to reward long service and good conduct, and distinguished or meritorious service alongside certain British honours which remained current although the colonial police series of medals to which officers were formerly entitled had been withdrawn in 1957. The first medal was awarded on completion of 18 years continuous service to officers of all ranks completed on or after 21 December 1982 with bars issued after a further seven and twelve years.

BELIZE POLICE LONG SERVICE MEDAL

Ribbon: Green with yellow stripes (3 mm) at each edge.

Metal: White metal.

Size: 40 mm.

Description: (Obverse) a circular medal containing a wreath of laurel with three bands at the four cardinal points and a truncheon superimposed over it diagonally (right to left downhill). There is an outer band bearing the words BELIZE POLICE FORCE in the upper half and FOR LONG SERVICE AND GOOD CONDUCT in the lower.

The reverse of this medal and the two following depicted the full armorial bearings of Belize—a shield divided into three parts with a ship in full sail in the lower part and tools of the logging trade in the upper two. The supporters are woodcutters one holding an axe and the other a paddle. A mahogany tree, the basis of the logging industry is placed above the shield. The motto—*sub umbra florero* (under the shade I flourish)—is contained in a banner at the base. The whole is surrounded by a circle composed of pairs of leaves of the mahogany tree.

MERITORIOUS SERVICE MEDAL

Ribbon: Three equal bands of red, white and blue.

Metal: Yellow metal.

Size: 28 mm.

Description: (Obverse) a square shaped medal with rounded corners and a central circular medallion bearing a design of a truncheon and wreath (black enamel) similar to the Long Service Medal with an outer band bearing the words BELIZE POLICE FORCE (upper) and MERITORIOUS SERVICE MEDAL (below) on black enamel.

This award is available to members of the Force up to the rank of superintendent for valuable service displaying devotion to duty or for extended service which showed exceptional ability, merit and exemplary conduct. Officers with less than 20 years service would not be eligible except in the most exceptional circumstances.

DISTINGUISHED SERVICE MEDAL

Ribbon: Green with yellow stripes at the edges and two others equally spaced towards the centre, all 1.5 mm wide.

Metal: Yellow metal.

Size: 32 mm.

Description: (Obverse) a straight armed cross the a central medallion of the same design as the MSM apart from the colour of the enamel (green) and the words DISTINGUISHED SERVICE MEDAL on the lower circumference of the outer band.

This award serves a dual purpose with its primary function being to reward officers above the rank of superintendent for particularly distinguished service. It is also, however, available to any member of the Force of any rank in recognition of an act of bravery in the execution of their duty.

The Police Force is a small organisation policing a relatively peaceful country although, in recent years, it has became a staging post for the export and transhipment of marijuana and cocaine from Colombia to the US, particularly since the withdrawal of the British garrison in 1994, and as a consequence the levels of drug-related crime in the capital—Belize City—has risen.

BOTSWANA

The Republic of Botswana was formerly the British Protectorate of Bechuanaland and achieved independence and republican status in 1966. It had long been neglected by the British but was the scene of the discovery of the three of the worlds largest diamond-bearing formations very soon after independence was granted. This discovery transformed the economy and led to a stable government not plagued by the troubles experience in other African states when colonial influence ended. Within a year of the granting of independence an honours system was introduced to replace the British system and included awards for police officers no longer entitled to any of the colonial police series of medals previously available.

The arms of Botswana have an oval shield at the centre with three elements—three cog wheels (mining and industry), three wavy lines (water) and a bulls head (the importance of cattle to the economy). The supporters are two zebra, one holding an elephants tusk to symbolise the former ivory trade and the other an ear of the main local crop—sorghum. In a banner at the base is the word "pula" which means water but which is also the name of the national currency and a familiar greeting. There are few rivers in this land-locked country and water is a very valuable commodity

POLICE MEDAL FOR MERITORIOUS SERVICE

Instituted: 1967.

Ribbon: Old gold with two broad maroon stripes.

Metal: Silver.

Size: 36 mm.

Description: (Obverse) the Coat of Arms of Botswana; (reverse) plain apart from the inscription BOTSWANA POLICE MERITORIOUS SERVICE. The name, rank and number of the recipient are engraved on the rim with the date of the award.

The medal was awarded to more senior officers only and they were entitled to the use of the post-nominal letters BPM. A long service medal was also introduced for award to officers of all ranks with the design being very similar. The only differences were in the inscription on the reverse which was amended to read BOTSWANA POLICE LONG SERVICE AND GOOD CONDUCT and the ribbon—maroon with gold stripes at the edges. Service prior to the achievement of independence was counted towards the qualifying period for the new award provided that there had been no issue of the Colonial Police Long Service Medal.

CROSS OF GALLANTRY

Instituted: 1967.

Ribbon: Blue with a central line in black and white lines at the edges.

Metal: Silver.

Size: 36 mm.

Description: (Obverse) a cross with a central medallion bearing the Coat of Arms of Botswana in the centre surrounded by the legend REPUBLIC OF BOTSWANA; (reverse) the central medallion was inscribed with the words FOR GALLANTRY and engraved with the name of the recipient and date of the award.

Acts of bravery by police officers are recognised by the award of the Cross of Gallantry which is available to any citizen. Recipients are entitled to use the post-nominal letters CG after their name.

CANADA

Canada is a huge country, the second largest after Russia, with an area of almost 10 million square kilometres but a population of less than 26 million, fewer than California. Although there is evidence that Vikings sailing from Greenland were the first Europeans to set foot in Canada in AD 1000, settlement in the true sense started in the 15th and 16th centuries with visits from the French and the British. The French established the first settlements watched carefully by the British as they expanded and the value of the natural resources of new country became apparent. Inevitably war ensued between the two powers resulting in the victory of General Wolfe at Quebec and the slaughter of the French forces. The Treaty of Paris in 1763 left the country in British hands although the French influence is as strong today as ever particularly in the Province of Quebec where calls for separatism persist.

Today Canada is one of the wealthiest countries in the world made up of ten provinces and two territories although Newfoundland remained independent until after the Second World War.

In policing terms Canada is inevitably associated with the Mounties—the Royal Canadian Mounted Police (*Gendarmerie Royale de Canada*)—a force with a mystique and romanticism about it not equalled by any other policing agency and often thought to be the only Canadian police force although most towns and cities and two provinces (Quebec and Ontario) have their own. The RCMP was founded as the North West Mounted Police (NWMP) in 1873 to take law and order to the provinces of Alberta and Saskatchewan with a strength of 18 officers and 257 men who took up their duties at the end of 1874. In addition to its law enforcement rôle the Force was responsible for the forging of friendly relationships with the local indigenous Indian population and the supervision of treaties between them and the federal government in addition to helping settlers cope with the hardships of life in the new territory—disease, poverty and natural disasters. In 1904 the prefix Royal was conferred on the NWMP in recognition of its performance. In 1920 the Royal North West Mounted Police was merged with the Dominion Police to become the Royal Canadian Mounted Police and its jurisdiction extended over the following decades until 1950 when the final province—British Columbia—was added to its area of responsibility.

The first name used by the NWMP was the North West Mounted Infantry until a member of government heard that the Americans were likely to take exception to the introduction of a Canadian military force into an area where the borders between the two countries had still to be finalised—the name was promptly changed to drop the word infantry and substitute police which was far more acceptable.

In the early days of the settlement of the far west of Canada the rôle of the mounted police was akin to that of the military and police officers there were called upon to put down insurrections by the indigenous people on more than one occasion. The officers were also rewarded in similar fashion to the military by the issue of campaign medals. In 1885 a rebellion broke out in Manitoba and Saskatchewan involving local Indian tribes and the Mitis, a people of mixed race descended from the Europeans who first settled the land and the local people. The rebels were led by Louis Riel, a man of French origin, born in Winnipeg, who variously studied for the priesthood, took an active part in politics in the far west, was banished from Canada to the USA and spent two years in an asylum. He is remembered as either a hero or a madman. The first troops to confront the rebels were from a 56 strong detachment of the North West Mounted Police at the Battle of Duck Lake. Twelve officers from the detachment were killed and many others wounded before they were forced to withdraw. When the serious nature of the rebellion became known to the Canadian government a force of 5,000 troops was mobilised and sent to quell the troubles. At the Battle of Batoche, the insurrection was finally put down. Louis Riel was arrested, tried for treason and hanged. The troops who took part in the action, including members of the NWMP, were all awarded a special medal

NORTH WEST CANADA MEDAL

Instituted: 1885.

Ribbon: Blue grey with a red stripe towards the edges.

Metal: Silver.

Size: 36 mm.

Description: (Obverse) the veiled head bust of Queen Victoria; (reverse) a wreath in the form of a branch of maple leaves with the date 1885 placed in the middle of the central field and the words NORTH WEST (above) and CANADA (below). The medal hung from a plain straight suspender attached by a claw fitting. 6,500 were issued. A clasp inscribed SASKATCHEWAN (where the bulk of the action occurred) was issued to some, but not all, members of the NWMP.

Since 1934 the RCMP has issued a long service medal to its officers on completion of 20 years service if they are of irreproachable character and whose conduct has been good and services satisfactory. A bronze bar with a single star is awarded after 25 years service, silver with two stars after 30 years and a gold star with three stars on completion of 35 years approved service. Only the most recent bar is worn.

ROYAL CANADIAN MOUNTED POLICE LONG SERVICE MEDAL

Instituted: 6 March 1934.

Ribbon: Dark blue with two gold stripes towards the edges.

Metal: Silver.

Size: 36 mm.

Description; (Obverse) the effigy of the reigning monarch; (reverse) the insignia of the RCMP consisting of the head of a buffalo within a buckled belt inscribed with the words MAINTENEZ LE DROIT all topped by a crown. On either side of the belt are five maple leaves. The name of the Force is contained in a banner below the belt. The words FOR LONG SERVICE (above) and AND GOOD CONDUCT (below) are inscribed around the circumference. A plain straight suspender is attached by a claw fitting.

When Queen Elizabeth came to the throne and the medal was redesigned to display her effigy on the obverse, changes were also made to the reverse to substitute the Queen's crown for the King's that had been used from the medal's introduction. The opportunity was also taken to reduce the size of the insignia of the RCMP and move the inscription to read continuously around the circumference. In 1989 a French language version of this new design was introduced with the inscription on the reverse reading POUR ANCIENNETÉ ET BONNE CONDUITE. The recipients have the right to choose which version they would prefer.

There is one other official national medal available to Canadian police officers other than members of the RCMP for long service. It is awarded on completion of 20 years service to officers of any recognised Canadian police force who showed industry, efficiency and good conduct during their careers. Although members of the RCMP or Canadian Military Police are not eligible, any full-time service in either of those bodies can be counted towards the necessary number of years service. Bars (bearing a stylised maple leaf) are available for additional periods of ten years. The medal is not a purely long service award and will be withheld if an officer with the required number of years service does not meet the appropriate standards of behaviour necessary. It can be awarded posthumously.

POLICE EXEMPLARY SERVICE MEDAL

Instituted: 12 August 1982.

Ribbon: Five equal stripes of dark blue and yellow.

Metal: Silver.

Size: 36 mm.

Description: (Obverse) a round medal with a maple leaf in the centre bearing a representation of the scales of justice and an outer band with the words EXEMPLARY SERVICE in the upper half and SERVICES DISTINGUÉS in the lower. It is of a skeletal design with the outer band attached to the leaves and stem of the maple leaf; (reverse) plain apart from the royal cypher EIIR topped by the Queen's crown in the centre of the maple leaf.

Prior to the introduction of the official national medal an unofficial medal was awarded to recognise long, efficient and faithful service in recognised Canadian police forces other than the RCMP. It was instituted by the Canadian Association of Chiefs of Police to correct the anomaly that existed whereby RCMP officers and those from some provincial forces were rewarded for their service but the majority of Canadian police officers were not.

CANADIAN ASSOCIATION OF CHIEFS OF POLICE SERVICE MEDAL

French version, obverse.

Instituted: September 1961.

Ribbon: 32 mm wide of royal blue with two narrow yellow stripes.

Metal: Silver.

Size: 39 mm.

Description: (Obverse) a maple leaf on which is superimposed the scales of justice and the letters CACP in Gothic script surmounted by a Queen's crown. The words POLICE SERVICE MEDAL are inscribed around the circumference in a raised band; (reverse) a wreath of laurel tied at the base with a bow bearing the words AWARDED BY with the recipients police force and name and the year of the award in the central field. Around the circumference are the words CANADIAN ASSOCIATION OF CHIEFS OF POLICE. All medals are numbered in a small tablet at the base of the reverse. The medal hangs from a ring suspender and a straight five-stepped suspender bar.

It was awarded after 20 years service with bars available to recognise each additional period of five years. After 25 years a bronze bar with a single maple leaf was issued, after 30 years one of silver with two leaves and to reward 35 and 40 years qualifying service gold bars were given, the first with three maple leaves and the other with four. The medal was discontinued on the introduction of the official medal in 1982.

In deference to the importance of French culture in Canada and the position of French as an official language the medal was produced in that language for award to officers of French origin and those from Quebec where French is the only official language. On the French language medal the wording of the obverse is amended to read POLICE at the top and MÉDAILLE DE MÉRITE at the base and the name of the Association on the reverse to ASSOCIATION CANADIÉNNE DES CHEFS DE POLICE. The inscription in the central field of the reverse above the engraved details of the recipient reads DÉCERNÉE À (awarded to)—the name of the recipient—PAR (by) the name of the force—a reversal of the order seen on the English language version.

Current official Canadian medals are all bilingual and the principle extends to the post-nominals permitted where the two versions of the medals name do not have the same initials. The Star of Courage, a national honour given to recognise acts of gallantry, has the post-nominal SC in English but EC (Étoile de Courage) in French. The RCMP Long Service Medal is also available in French for appropriate officers.

In addition to the CACP Service Medal, a second national unofficial medal is awarded to Canadian police officers who perform feats of outstanding police action in combating crimes committed against banks. Although it can be given in recognition of an act of great courage, it is not solely a bravery award and is most usually given to acknowledge particularly noteworthy investigations which result in the arrest of offenders who target any bank in Canada, domestic and foreign. The award is made annually by the Canadian Bankers Association at the conference of the Canadian Association of Chiefs of Police held in late August at different venues across the country. From its introduction in 1972 to 1999, 176 awards have been made to officers from a great many different forces. There is no limit on the number of awards that can be made in any one year.

CANADIAN BANKERS ASSOCIATION LAW ENFORCEMENT AWARD

Instituted: 1972.

Ribbon: Burgundy with a broad grey central band.

Metal: Gold.

Size: 36 mm.

Description: (Obverse) a circular medal with the representation of an arched panelled doorway and surround in the centre and the words THE CANADIAN BANKS (above) LAW ENFORCEMENT AWARD (below) around the circumference; (reverse) a floral wreath around the whole circumference and the inscription AWARDED BY - THE CANADIAN BANKERS - ASSOCIATION - FOR DISTINGUISHED - LAW - ENFORCEMENT in six lines in the central field. The medal hangs from a plain straight suspender attached by an ornate claw fitting.

The inscription on the medal is also available in French with the choice being a matter for the recipient. The circumscription on the obverse is amended to read MÉDAILLE D'HONNEUR DES BANQUES CANADIENNES (upper) and POUR ACTION POLICIÈRE MÉRITOIRE (lower). On the reverse the inscription in the central field reads —DÉCERNÉE PAR L'ASSOCIATION DES BANQUERS CANADIENS EN RECONNAISSANCE DE SA VALEUREUSE CONDUITE. Although the medal is highly regarded in Canada it is not approved for wear on a police uniform.

In 1999 a single award was made to an officer from the RCMP for his work in an operation which resulted in the arrest of members of two groups responsible for counterfeiting thousands of credit cards, banknotes and identification documents with a potential loss to the banks of 55 million Canadian dollars. In the previous year, five officers were honoured from three different forces. Three of these officers, two from the Toronto Police Service and one from the RCMP were also involved in credit card counterfeiting but the remaining two, from the Halton Regional Police Service, identified, arrested and convicted an armed bank robber responsible for a series of robberies where violence was used against bank staff.

Police Medals of the World

The Province of Quebec sits uneasily in the Canadian Federation, the majority of its citizens are of French origin and the calls for separatism remain as strong today as they did when Charles de Gaulle made his inflammatory speech there many years ago. A recent referendum on the subject was defeated by a small margin and is likely to return. The Quebec Police Commission awards two medals to officers from any police force in the Province and they are only inscribed in French with no provision made for the opinion of the recipient who might be of British origin. The medals are awarded for gallantry and meritorious service.

LA CROIX DE BRAVOURE DES POLICIERS DU QUÉBEC

Instituted: *11 February 1972.*

Ribbon: *Five equal stripes of blue, white, blue, white and blue.*

Metal: *Silver.*

Size: *32 mm.*

Description: *(Obverse) a medallion in the form of a cross with each arm bearing a fleur-de-lys. In the centre there is a wreath of laurel containing the emblem of Quebec and the words POLICE (above) and BRAVOURE (below); (Reverse) the words GOUVERNEMENT DU QUÉBEC above a space for the details of the recipient. It hangs from a ring suspender.*

LA MÉDAILLE POUR ACTION MÉRITOIRE

Instituted: *11 February 1972.*

Ribbon: *Diagonal stripes of gold and royal blue of equal width running downhill from the left.*

Metal: *Silver gilt.*

Size: *38 mm.*

Description: *(Obverse) a circular medal with a partial wreath of olive leaves in the lower circumference and the words ACTION MÉRITOIRE in the upper. The word POLICE is inscribed at the base over the join of the olive branches. In the central field is a fleur-de-lys in blue enamel; (reverse) the same as La Croix de Bravoure des Policiers above. A ring suspender is used.*

The medal is very often awarded posthumously to officers who died or were killed in the line of duty. Two examples from the Montreal Urban Community Police Service illustrate the circumstances in which awards of the medal would be considered.

At about 1.25 am on the night of 8 July 1973 Constables 1105 André Désilets and 1056 Claude Sarrazin heard the shouts of a young lady who had fallen into the lac des Dauphin in Montreal and was in danger of drowning. Constable Désilets went onto the slipway from which water-skies left to try to help her but slipped and fell into the dark, cold water. Although he was injured in the fall he ignored his own predicament and succeeded in helping the lady to safety on the quayside but couldnt get out of the water himself. His partner, who couldnt swim, tried to help Constable Désilets who was in serious trouble but also slipped and fell into the water. The two officers tried to get out and wait for help but failed. Their bodies were found 55 minutes later.

André Désilets was 25 years old with 4H years service. He left a wife and little boy. Claude Sarrazin was 37 years old with 12 years police service, he left a wife and seven children. Both men were posthumously awarded la Médaille pour Action Méritoire.

Eighteen months later, Constable 451 Aimé Pelletier and his partner were called to the scene of an armed robbery in progress in Montreal. When they arrived they saw three suspects running off but managed to block their way with the patrol car. One of the officers chased after one suspect and Aimé Pelletier took off after the two others, chasing them into a nearby apartment block. Inside the building one of them turned and opened fire with a handgun, seriously wounding the officer. Although he was badly wounded he managed to make his way back to his patrol car and call for reinforcements. He was still there when his colleague returned with the other suspect and tried to help but Aimé Pelletier died. He was a man of 17 years police experience and left behind a wife and three children. He was awarded la Médaille pour Action Méritoire for his courage.

Canadian police officers are eligible for British coronation and jubilee medals and they have also been awarded two special commemorative issues—in 1967 on the centennial of the confederation of Canada and again in 1992 to celebrate the 125th anniversary. In 1967 29,500 medals were awarded to a wide cross-section of the Canadian people including police officers on the recommendation of the national and provincial governments and a number of associations.

CANADIAN CENTENNIAL MEDAL—1967

Instituted: 1 July 1967.

Ribbon: White with a red band (5 mm) at each edge and four equally spaced thin (1 mm) red lines between the red edges.

Metal: Silver.

Size: 36 mm.

Description: (Obverse) a circular medal with a central maple leaf containing the royal cypher EIIR topped by the Queen's crown with a circumscription reading CONFÉDÉRATION - CANADA - CONFEDERATION; (reverse) the full Achievement of Arms of Canada above the dates 1867–1967. The medal was attached to a straight suspender by a claw fitting.

The 125th anniversary of confederation in 1992 was marked by the award of a further medal to 44,000 citizens who had made a significant contribution to their community or to Canada (including a number of police officers) on the recommendation of the Governor-General, Prime Minister, MPs, provincial government and a host of national organisations.

COMMEMORATIVE MEDAL FOR THE 125th ANNIVERSARY OF CONFEDERATION—1992

Instituted: 1992.

Ribbon: White with a blue band (4.5 mm) at each edge and five equally spaced thin (1 mm) red lines between the blue edges.

Metal: Rhodium plated copper and zinc alloy.

Size: 36 mm.

Description: (Obverse) a circular medal with a single maple leaf in the centre with the royal cypher EIIR and the Queens crown superimposed on it. Below the leaf are the dates 1967 - 1992 and the words CONFEDERATION - CONFÉDÉRATION; (reverse) the Coat of Arms of Canada (the shield) surrounded by the motto ribbon of the Order of Canada inscribed DESIDERANTE MELIOREM PATRIAM (they desire a better country) topped by a lion holding a maple leaf in its right paw. The Canadian motto A MARI USQUE AD MARE forms a circumscription covered the lower half of the medal. A straight suspender decorated with a maple leaf is attached by a claw fitting.

The Canadian coat of arms reflects the origins of the country with devices from England, Scotland, Wales and France contained within the shield above three maple leaves for Canada. The French influence is repeated in the use of a flag showing three golden fleur-de-lys on a blue field - the banner of royalist France—opposite the Union flag of Great Britain. The Canadian motto is taken from a biblical text (Psalm 72:8)—he shall have dominion from sea to sea and from the river unto the ends of the earth

page 45

In 1967 the first steps towards a wholly Canadian system of honours were first taken with the introduction of the Order of Canada, similar in most respects to the Order of the British Empire with three classes of award available for Canadian citizens who had showed the highest levels of service which enriched the lives of their fellow citizens. In 1972, a second step was taken with the introduction of the Order of Military Merit with similar criteria but restricted to members of the Canadian Armed Forces. In 2000, a third order was created exclusively for police officers. Membership of the Order of Merit of the Police Forces is available at three levels—Commander, Officer and Member—and intended to reflect long-term, outstanding service with varying degrees of responsibility. Her Majesty Queen Elizabeth is the Sovereign of the Order and the Governor General is the Chancellor and a commander. The Commissioner of the RCMP is the Principal Commander of the Order. It is intended that approximately 50 officers, who must be serving at the time of their appointment, will be admitted each year.

ORDER OF MERIT OF THE POLICE FORCES

Instituted: October 2000.

Ribbon: Royal blue with a gold central band, all of equal width.

Metal: Enamelled gold or silver.

Size: 38 mm.

Description: (Obverse) a cross pattée in blue enamel edged with gold for the highest level and silver for the two others. A central medallion carries a maple leaf (in silver or gold) within an outer band bearing the words MERIT MÉRITÉ CANADA in the appropriate metal. Above the medallion superimposed on the upper arm of the cross in gold or silver and red enamel is the St Edward crown; (reverse) left plain apart from a serial number. The medal is suspender from a straight bar bearing a design of laurel leaves.

For acts of gallantry Canadian police officers are treated no differently from civilians and are eligible for one of the national decorations for bravery dependant upon the level of courage displayed in the circumstances and dangers involved. The highest honour—the Cross of Valour—is awarded for acts of conspicuous courage in circumstances of extreme peril. Two other awards—the Star of Courage and the Medal of Bravery—are available where the level of courage does not reach the high standard required for the award of the Cross of Valour. All Canadians are eligible for the awards as are citizens of other countries for acts of bravery performed in Canada or outside the country but in circumstances which merits recognition by Canada as an act in the interests of the country. All awards can be made posthumously.

In addition to the national awards there are two unofficial provincial medals available to recognise examples of police courage. The Government of Ontario issues the Ontario Medal for Police Bravery to officers from any police force in the province to reward any act of superlative courage and bravery performed in the line of duty and is also intended to encourage the virtue of bravery and focus attention and support of the public behind the efforts of the police forces. The medals are presented at a special ceremony held in mid-November each year.

ONTARIO MEDAL FOR POLICE BRAVERY

Instituted: 1975.

Ribbon: Royal blue with two gold stripes towards the edges.

Metal: Gold plated sterling silver with blue and white enamel.

Size: 57 mm wide by 68 mm high (with crown).

Description: (Obverse) a cross in blue enamel on gold with the provincial flower (white trillium) in white in a small central medallion and a maple leaf between the arms of the cross. A Queen's crown tops the upper arm; (reverse) left plain.

At the ceremony held on 17 November 1998 in Toronto eight officers from four different police forces were awarded the medal, all for acts of bravery in saving or attempting to save a life in the previous twelve months. Two officers from the Ontario Provincial Police were honoured for rescuing a motorist who got into difficulties when his vehicle broke through the frozen surface of a lake. He succeeded in breaking free from the vehicle but could not make the shore in the freezing waters. The two officers—Senior Constables Esposito and Goodwin—borrowed a canoe and managed to reach him and pull him from the water safely. Both officers needed treatment for hypothermia following the rescue.

The medal can be given posthumously and the ceremony in 1998 unfortunately included one such award to an officer from the Waterloo Regional Police Service who lost his life trying to save the life of a 12 year old boy who had fallen into water near a dam and who had become trapped in a sluice gate. Constables Nicholson and Sauvé were both members of the Underwater Recovery Unit who responded to the call for help shortly after the boy disappeared under the water. Constable Nicholson made the first dive with the arrangement being the he should tug on his safety line when he had found the boy. When the signal was sent Constable Sauvé went into the water to assist his colleague but found that he had become trapped against the sluice gate by the pressure of water and was in severe difficulties. Constable Sauvé himself was pulled towards the sluice gate and his face mask filled with water to the extent that he as unable to breathe and forced to leave the water temporarily. He made several more attempts to reach his colleague until he was finally ordered out of the water. The body of Constable Nicholson was found alongside the 12 year old boy in the sluice gate. Both officers were honoured for their courage by the award of the Medal for Police Bravery.

Police officers are also eligible for a second provincial award as citizens rather than as a result of their position. The *Ontario Medal for Good Citizenship* is available to anyone as a tribute for excellence and achievement for the common good of Ontario. Police officers can be awarded the medal for personal sacrifices made provided that they are made outside the officers regular duties. The medal is silver and carries the coat of arms of Ontario on the obverse with the words FOR GOOD CITIZENSHIP at the upper circumference. The ribbon is white with a narrow central stripe in yellow and a green band at each edge.

page 47

Police Medals of the World

The Ontario Provincial Police (OPP) is one of only two such forces remaining in Canada, policing responsibility in the other provinces having been passed to the RCMP for many years. The RCMP maintains a presence in Ontario and Quebec but deals, in the main, with federal crime although it assists the provincial forces whenever necessary. The OPP is also one of the few which issued its own medals to reward officers for long service.

ONTARIO PROVINCIAL POLICE LONG SERVICE AND GOOD CONDUCT MEDAL

Instituted: 15 December 1949.

Ribbon: Crimson with two green stripes each bordered by white lines on both sides.

Metal: Silver.

Size: 38 mm.

Description: (Obverse) the Coat of Arms of the Province of Ontario with the word ONTARIO written below; (reverse) the inscription ONTARIO PROVINCIAL POLICE in three lines in the central field and FOR LONG SERVICE AND GOOD CONDUCT around the circumference and two crossed maple leaves in the exergue. An ornate, non-swivelling, suspender was attached to the top of the medal.

The medal was awarded to members of the Force who had served for not less than 20 years, the last ten of which must have been with good conduct and satisfactory service. Bars were awarded for each additional period of five years qualifying service. For 25 and 30 years service a plain silver bar decorated with one or two white trilliums (the provincial flower) was awarded and for 35 or 40 years qualifying service gold bars were issued also bearing one or two trillium motifs. The trillium is a small white flower with three petals and a yellow centre found growing wild in the spring in Ontario and which is widely used as the primary provincial emblem.

The Coat of Arms depicted on the medal obverse was first granted in 1868 and amended in 1909 when the supporters and crest were added to the original shield. The shield has two elements—the flag of St George in the upper third above three maple leaves with the provincial motto—*ut incepit fidelis sic permanet* (loyal she began and loyal she remains)—in a banner below. The two supporters (a moose and a deer) and crest (a black bear) are representative of the province's wildlife.

The Ontario Provincial Police is the largest force in Canada responsible for a vast area although the major cities have their own forces and there are many regional police organisations—Waterloo and Peel for example. It is responsible for areas not required to maintain their own police and also has a highway patrol covering some 130,000 km of roads.

The largest city in Ontario by some margin is Toronto with a population in the metropolitan area which exceeds 3.5 million. Officers from the Metropolitan Toronto Police are eligible for the two provincial awards and there are two available from their own force for bravery or meritorious service.

METROPOLITAN TORONTO POLICE MEDAL OF HONOR

Ribbon: Dark blue with a central dark red stripe (13.5 mm).

Size: 36 mm

Description: Obverse) a circular silver medal with a shield as the centrepiece depicting the force badge—a winged wheel at the top, a chevron below containing a crown, two opened books on either side of the apex of the chevron and a staff entwined with two serpents at the base. Around the circumference are the words METROPOLITAN TORONTO POLICE; (reverse) the words FOR DISTINGUISHED POLICE SERVICE around the circumference with the central field left blank for the details of the recipient. The medal hangs from a scrolled suspender bar.

The medal is awarded by the Chairman of the Board of Commissioners of Police in recognition of exceptional police service or outstanding valour in the performance of police duty, involving great personal gallantry and extraordinary risk. It ranks immediately below the Ontario Medal for Police Bravery in the order of precedence.

The second award, the Medal of Merit, is available to recognise acts of personal bravery or highly meritorious or intelligent police service which do not attain the high standards necessary for the award of the Medal of Honour but are thought worthy of official acknowledgement. It is cast in bronze and has the same obverse as the Medal of Honour and FOR MERITORIOUS POLICE SERVICE around the circumference on the reverse. The ribbon is also dark blue but with two dark red central stripes.

The Metropolitan Toronto Police Service is the sixth largest municipal police force in North America and the second oldest in Canada. It was founded in 1834 with a staff of five full-time constables supported by 14 unpaid special constables. For three years they performed their duty without uniforms and were primarily concerned with bootlegging, the sale of liquor to children, speeding horses, riding them on pavements and enforcing the strict rule that the Sabbath should be observed as a day of worship and rest. By 1998 the strength of the Service had risen to almost 5,000 uniformed officers using 1.161 cars, 129 motorcycles and 25 horses with a total budget of $522,145,800 (about £232 million). It is not a particularly violent city by North American standards—in 1998 there were 53 murders, almost 34,000 other violent crimes and 5,297 with each category of crime showing a decrease over the previous year. Toronto is a very cosmopolitan city and received calls in 51 different languages in 1998 reflecting the changes in its ethnic make-up. Efforts are being made to attract recruits which reflect more accurately the changing face of the city.

Law enforcement was first established in Manitoba in 1870 with a detachment of soldiers who were re-named the Mounted Constabulary Force and subsequently the Manitoba Provincial Police before their duties were passed to the RCMP in 1932. In Winnipeg, the first city force was formed in 1874 under the command of a chief of police who was at loggerheads with the Mayor for most of his short period in office. He had been in command for 18 months when a purge of the brothels and saloons was ordered by the city council in an attempt to curb the city's reputation as a den of sin. In July 1875 during a routine visit to a brothel by two constables the Chief of Police was found sampling the delights on offer.

He was arrested, charged and taken before the Mayor (also the magistrate) who took delight in fining and suspending him. The Chief resigned before he could be dismissed.

Today, the force has a strength of 1,206 officers of all ranks supported by almost 300 civilians to police the city of approximately 700,000. In 1995 in common with a number of Canadian agencies it changed its name from a police force to a service in 1995 and has developed from its uneasy start 130 years ago into a modern, efficient and well-respected Canadian police service.

The award of medals by urban forces has never been a Canadian tradition and, apart from Toronto, only one has ever been issued (in Winnipeg) although it lasted barely two years and was awarded only eight times. In May 1947 the Board of Police Commissioners Medal was introduced in Winnipeg to reward members of the public for assistance given to police officers. It was a small rectangular medal with the city crest in the centre of the obverse surrounded by the inscription WINNIPEG POLICE COMMISSION AWARD and leaves of laurel at the outer edges. The reverse also had the laurel leaves and the words FOR MERITORIOUS SERVICE IN LAW ENFORCEMENT in the upper half of the central field and a space below for the recipients details to be engraved. The crest was the original one before it was replaced in 1972 and showed the three most important factors in the establishment of the city—wheat, the railroad and a buffalo.

The last provincial police force to lose its identity to the Royal Canadian Mounted Police was in British Columbia. The British Columbia Provincial Police was one of the oldest forces in Canada, founded in 1858, some 15 years before the North West Mounted Police, the forerunner of the RCMP.

It was unusual in that its officers did not wear a uniform until 1925 although the dark green tunic and brown boots and belt introduced then remained virtually unchanged until the Force ceased to exist in 1950, allegedly for financial reasons. The Force was another which issued its own medal for a short time.

BRITISH COLUMBIA PROVINCIAL POLICE LONG SERVICE AND GOOD CONDUCT MEDAL

Instituted: 1 November 1946.

Ribbon: Dark green with a sand coloured stripe towards each edge.

Metal: Silver.

Size: 36 mm.

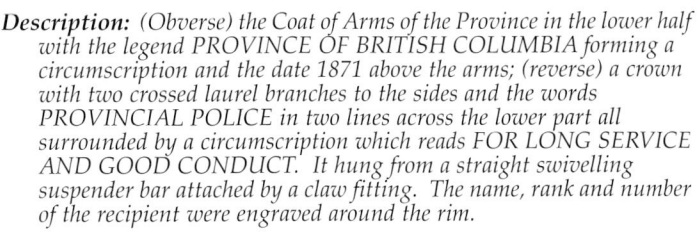

Description: (Obverse) the Coat of Arms of the Province in the lower half with the legend PROVINCE OF BRITISH COLUMBIA forming a circumscription and the date 1871 above the arms; (reverse) a crown with two crossed laurel branches to the sides and the words PROVINCIAL POLICE in two lines across the lower part all surrounded by a circumscription which reads FOR LONG SERVICE AND GOOD CONDUCT. It hung from a straight swivelling suspender bar attached by a claw fitting. The name, rank and number of the recipient were engraved around the rim.

It was awarded to recognise not less than 20 years satisfactory service although it had a short life and was discontinued when the Force was absorbed by the RCMP on 15 August 1950. The number of issues made is not known to any degree of certainty although the most commonly quoted figure is 63. For serving officers below the rank of inspector the medal was accompanied by a gratuity of $25 from the Police Reward Fund. When the RCMP took over the BCPP there was some resistance to the move, a situation not uncommon in many parts of Canada when the jurisdiction of the RCMP was expanded and the provincial forces disappeared. The move was not helped by the insistence that the local medal would no longer be authorised to be worn on the tunic. In an effort to placate the officers from British Columbia the RCMP Long Service Medal was issued to all holders of the local award, a situation which has resulted in both medals being worn together by more than a few officers.

The Coat of Arms depicted on the medal obverse is of a simple design with an uncomplicated symbolism. The upper part of the shield shows the Union Flag with a gold crown in the centre indicating the Provinces origins as a British colony. The lower half has a golden setting sun symbolising the position of British Columbia as the most westerly province of Canada superimposed on a ground of silver and blue wavy bars to represent the Pacific Ocean. The motto in a scroll below the shield reads splendor sine occasu (splendour without diminishment).

As recently as January 1999 the Government of British Columbia has introduced its own awards for police officers who have given some special service to the citizens of the Province. The awards are available to members of the municipal and regional police forces in addition to the RCMP. Two categories of award are available—for valour and for meritorious service—and are identical apart from the material used—gold for the valour award and silver for meritorious service. The award for valour is given where an act involves exceptional valour in the face of extreme hazard with the officer involved purposely taking action for the benefit of others whilst placing themselves at substantial risk of death or serious injury. It is the highest provincial award available in British Columbia. The award for meritorious service is given for any exemplary performance that enhances the image of police officers in the Province where the officer concerned acts in a manner significantly beyond the standard normally expected. Both awards take the form of metal bars, measuring approximately 36 mm by 13 mm and depicting the crest of British Columbia above a spray of dogwood, the provincial flower.

Lying next to British Columbia to the east is Alberta one of the three prairie provinces of Canada although the northern half is, in fact, characterised by large areas of coniferous forest. The province has an area of more than 250,000 square miles and a population of about 2.5 million, most living in the four main cities with the capital Edmonton the largest, supporting almost 800,000 people. Policing arrangements in the province follow the pattern of most of Canada with separate forces in most major towns and cities with the rural areas being the responsibility of regional forces and the RCMP. Only one of the individual forces issues its own medal to its officers but the provincial government issues a long service award to officers from any police force in the province whose service equals or exceeds 25 years in Alberta. Any service in any other province is not counted towards the medal even if it was police service, the 25 years must have been served within the province. There is provision for non-continuous service but the total must be at least 300 months in Alberta. The medal is available to police officers from any police force including the RCMP and also to members of provincial or federal correction services.

ALBERTA LAW ENFORCEMENT LONG SERVICE MEDAL

Instituted: 1 September 1980.

Ribbon: Dark blue with a green central stripe and a stripe of gold towards the edges.

Metal: Silver.

Size: 36 mm.

Description: (Obverse) the provincial crest with ALBERTA below and branches of wheat on either side; (reverse) the floral symbol of the province—the Alberta wild rose—placed centrally with the words TWENTY-FIVE YEARS above and LONG SERVICE below.

The shield of Alberta has the Cross of St George at the top above a rural scene of a field of wheat backed by a lake and mountains symbolic of the provinces geography. The first presentation of the medals actually took place on 19 March 1979 to twelve officers from five different police service and the Fort Saskatchewan Correctional Institute. The award of the medal is not automatic, recipients must be nominated by their chief officer, the chief of any force in which they served for more than five years or the person in charge of the pension fund if they have retired from the police service.

Recently, the provincial government has introduced a second medal for award to special constables. The system of using special constables in Canada is somewhat different than the UK, the officers are employed by authorised agencies and must serve for at least 20 years, all in the Province of Alberta, to be eligible for the medal. The medal can be awarded in addition to the RCMP Long Service Medal or the national Police Exemplary Service Medal.

ALBERTA LONG SERVICE RECOGNITION MEDAL FOR SPECIAL CONSTABLES

Instituted: 11 February 1998.

Ribbon: Five bands of red, blue, yellow, blue and red, all of equal width.

Metal: Silver.

Size: 36 mm.

Description: (Obverse) the full achievement of arms of Alberta including supports, crest and motto with an outer band bearing the words SPECIAL CONSTABLE (above) and LONG SERVICE MEDAL (below); (reverse) a sword pointing upwards with the scales of justice near the tip and a branch of wheat on either side. A plain straight suspender is used inscribed with ALBERTA of the front and the engraved name of the recipient on the back.

A system of bars is used to indicate the number of years service starting with a single bar inscribed 20 YEARS at the time the medal is first awarded. Each subsequent period of five years is indicated by the award of another bar bearing the total number of years served and placed higher up the ribbon with the first bar being replaced by a bar with no inscription. A special constable who served for 40 years, for example, would display four blank bars and an upper bar near the top of the ribbon inscribed 40 YEARS.

The only force in Alberta to award its own medals is the Edmonton Police Service and the introduction of the two awards to recognise acts of courage or the suffering of an injury in the course of duty occurred only in mid-2001.

EDMONTON POLICE SERVICE MEDAL OF VALOUR

Instituted: 2001.

Ribbon: Dark blue with a white central band bisected by narrow lines of yellow (left) and red (right).

Metal: Silver.

Size: 36 mm.

Description: (Obverse) a circular medal with the badge of the Force placed centrally superimposed upon a letter V; (reverse) a stylized wreath with the central field left blank for engraving. The medal is suspended from a straight bar inscribed with the words FOR VALOUR.

Awarded to recognise acts of heroism or the highest acts of courage in circumstances of great danger and a hazard to life. The award of the medal will be made retrospectively to 1961 when the Edmonton and Beverley Police Departments were amalgamated. It is the highest award available to any member of the Edmonton Police service.

EDMONTON POLICE SERVICE MEDAL OF HONOUR

Instituted: 2001.

Ribbon: Dark blue with a broad central band of white bearing three equally-spaced narrow lines of red, yellow and red.

Metal: Silver.

Size: 36 mm.

Description: (Obverse) an eight point star with the badge of the Force placed centrally surrounded by a circle of small rectangular blocks; (reverse) plain apart from a stylized wreath with the central field left blank for engraving. The medal is suspended from a straight bar inscribed with the words FOR HONOUR.

Awarded to officers who suffer a serious injury or permanent disfigurement in the course of their duty provided that they were acting in an appropriate and intelligent manner. It may also be awarded to the family of any member of the service who lost his or her life in the execution of their duty. The award of the medal can be made retrospective to 1982, the date the Edmonton Police Service was founded.

The badge of the Edmonton Police Service seen at the centre of both medals consists of a wreath of maple leaves surmounted by a crown with the coat of arms of the City of Edmonton in the centre. Around the coat of arms is an outer band bearing the words POLICE SERVICE (upper) and EDMONTON (lower). The coats at the centre of the badge were only granted in October 1994 and consist of a shield, supporters and scroll containing the motto, all superimposed on a mace intended to indicate that Edmonton is the capital of Alberta. The shield has four elements—a half sun at the top to represent the high level of sunshine in Edmonton, a winged wheel to symbolise the city's place as an aviation and industrial centre, a wavy line for the North Saskatchewan River on which the city stands and a sheaf of wheat to symbolise agriculture which is so important to the economy of city and province. The left supporter is an explorer, indicative of the city's past links to the former fur trade and the figure on the right (Athena, the Goddess of Wisdom) represents education and the University of Alberta in Edmonton.

The medals recently introduced in Edmonton are the most recent, in direct comparison to two much older awards once made in another force on the far side of the country. At the same time as the British Columbia Provincial Police ceased to exist as a separate body changes were made to another old force on the opposite side of the country in Newfoundland. This move gave the RCMP a presence across the whole country but, in Newfoundland, it did not result in the disappearance of the local force, the Royal Newfoundland Constabulary, which retained an area of responsibility which did not extend much further than the vicinity of St Johns, the provincial capital, although it recent years this has expanded to include a proportion of its former territory.

The Newfoundland Constabulary was founded in 1871 at the same time that the British military withdrew from the colonial garrison. The Constabulary was modelled on the Royal Irish Constabulary and headed by a former officer of that force—Thomas Foley—as the Inspector General. By 1879 the Force had a strength of 96 officers with stations across all of Newfoundland and a responsibility for policing large areas of the Labrador coast although there was no permanent presence there. In 1922 a dispute arose with the independent dominion over the boundary with Labrador which was resolved in 1927 resulting in the policing responsibility of Labrador staying with Newfoundland. In 1935 a new force—the Newfoundland Rangers—was established and assumed much of the former responsibility of the Constabulary although this all changed in 1949 when Newfoundland entered the Federation of Canada, the Rangers were disbanded and the RCMP moved into the new province. The prefix Royal was granted in 1979 to establish the Royal Newfoundland Constabulary and its authority expanded to include areas of Labrador once again. In the early years of its existence, the Constabulary flirted with the issue of medals to its officers and produced three which were awarded between 1892 when the idea was first mooted and 1921 when they were officially abolished.

NEWFOUNDLAND CONSTABULARY GOOD SERVICE MEDAL

Instituted: 1892.

Ribbon: Three equal stripes of green, red and green.

Metal: Silver and Bronze.

Size: Oval—40 mm by 31 mm.

Description: (Obverse) crossed tipstaves surmounted by a large state crown and with a scroll below bearing the Latin inscription words PAX NOBISCUM (peace be with us) all surrounded by an outer band with the words NEWFOUNDLAND (left) CONSTABULARY (right); (reverse) a wreath of laurel tied at the base with a bow and the words FOR GOOD SERVICE in three lines in the central field. A plain ring suspender is used with an open buckle top ribbon bar.

NEWFOUNDLAND SILVER STAR FOR BRAVERY AT SEA

Instituted: 1982.

Ribbon: Half dark blue and half crimson.

Metal: Silver.

Size: 38 mm.

Description: (Obverse) a six pointed star with a central medallion (22 mm) bearing a state crown in the centre and an outer band inscribed TERRA NOVA; (reverse) a depiction of a sailing schooner rescuing a man from the sea in the centre with the words FOR BRAVERY AT SEA in the surrounding band. A plain ring suspender is used.

The origin of both medals is shrouded in some mystery and there is a suggestion that the Star for Bravery at Sea was not intended as a medal for the Newfoundland Constabulary alone although it was commandeered as such shortly after its introduction was first muted. The first reference in official archives in 1892 mentions a letter to London regarding payment for medals and dies and a minute of the Legislative Council authorising the Governor to obtain a design for two medals - one for saving life and the other to the police force for meritorious service. In June 1893 authority to buy the medals was given followed a year later by an instruction to the Attorney General to draw up regulations for the grant of the medals to police officers. Somewhere between the first reference to the medals and the production of the regulations the original intention was obscured and they both became medals for award to police officers for gallantry.

The first presentations of the medals were made in 1897 to five members of the Constabulary for their actions in putting out a fire on a ship (SS *Aurora*) laden with gunpowder and dynamite docked in St Johns Harbour. Three officers were awarded the Star and two a silver medal for bravery. Later the same year, four officers were each awarded a bronze medal for saving life in two separate fires.

The original star differed from the piece later authorised and carried the name of the SS *Aurora* on the obverse in the band around the central medallion, the full inscription reading FOR BRAVERY AT SS AURORA. When the inscription was altered is far from clear.

Nothing was heard of either medal until 1914 when the dies were found in a safe in Government House and enquiries were set in hand to find out what they were and why they were issued. Nothing was done until 1918 when the Governor decided that the medals were all unofficial and that their issue should cease. A final presentation of five silver medals and nine bronze was made to long serving officers (38–40 years and 35–37 years respectively before it was withdrawn.

The Star for Bravery was also awarded at the same time, with official blessing, to a group of men who had assisted in one of the worst maritime disasters to occur off the coast of Newfoundland in 1918. A total of 23 were awarded in 1920 before a proclamation in the *Royal Gazette* on 5 March 1921 formally brought an end to the award of medals by the Dominion of Newfoundland. Thereafter officers from the Constabulary were eligible for the King's Police Medal for Gallantry or Distinguished Service or the Imperial Service Medal only.

The SS *Florizel* was the pride of the Red Cross Line used mainly on the run from St Johns to New York and doubled as one of the worlds first icebreakers.

On the night of Saturday 22 February 1918 she set sail for New York despite the fact that the conditions outside the haven of the harbour at St Johns were bad. The captain and crew were experienced in everything the North Atlantic could offer and were confident that it was all within the ship's capabilities. She sailed at 7.40 pm and weathered the storm as expected for several hours until conditions worsened and even experienced crew members began to become concerned. At 4.40 am, the captain ordered a change of course but was deceived by the weather and the ship ran aground at Horn Head Point, some 60 miles south of St Johns. The conditions were so severe that little could be done from the shore to help. Several ships tried but failed until the storm abated almost 24 hours later and attempts to reach the ship succeeded. It was all a little too late however and only 44 of the total of 138 people on board survived, the worst disaster in Newfoundland maritime history. During the rescue, small dories were used to take the survivors off the ship at great risk to the lives of the rescuers, including many members of the Newfoundland Constabulary.

The decision was made to award the Newfoundland Star for Bravery at Sea to those who took part in the rescue although it was discovered that there were insufficient medals remaining from the initial minting and more were ordered from the Royal Mint in London. After the presentations were made by the Prince of Wales in June 1920, the authority for the award of the medal was withdrawn.

Canadian police officers, primarily from the RCMP but also from 24 other forces, have participated in United Nations peacekeeping missions since the first involvement in Namibia in 1989-1990. Since 1947 a total of more than 125,000 Canadian military personnel, police officers and civilians have taken part in peacekeeping and observer missions with 113 having died in the service of their country.

In 1988 the work of peacekeeping forces from all countries was recognised by the award of the Nobel Peace Prize to all UN peacekeepers and this prompted the Canadians to introduce a special medal for award to all Canadians who had taken part in any mission, past or present. The introduction of the medal took many years and it wasn't formally approved until 1997 with the first presentation taking a further three years.

CANADIAN PEACEKEEPING SERVICE MEDAL

Instituted: 25 April 1997.

Ribbon: A light blue central band flanked by equal bands of white, red and green.

Metal: Silver.

Description: (Obverse) a depiction of three Canadian peacekeepers taken from the National Peacekeeping Monument in Ottawa. One figure is an unarmed UN military observer holding a pair of binoculars, another a kneeling female figure shouldering a radio and the third a guard with a rifle. The words PEACEKEEPING (upper) and SERVICE DE LA PAIX (lower) lie at the circumference; (reverse) a maple leaf with the royal cypher EIIR and crown in the centre with a branch of laurel on either side and the word CANADA below. The plain straight suspender bar is attached by a maple leaf.

The qualifying criteria call for a minimum of 30 day's service on a peacekeeping or observer mission and includes officers from the RCMP and other police forces (Royal Newfoundland Constabulary, Ontario Provincial Police, Metropolitan Toronto Police and Sûreté de Québec amongst them). Officers are also entitled to wear any UN medals issued but the Canadian government were keen to award national recognition of their services. The first presentation was made to a group of 89 recipients representative of the 125,000 eligible personnel at a special ceremony held in Ottawa on 6 September 2000. Further ceremonies will be held.

The colouring of the medals ribbon carries a great deal of symbolism. The white and blue bands are representative of the colours of the UN flag although the white also symbolises purity and the fact that peacekeeping is considered one of mankind's highest ideals. The red together with the white are the colours of the Canadian flag with the red further symbolising the blood shed by 113 Canadians who have died on the missions. The outer green bands are included to recognise the voluntary nature of much of the service performed.

Officers from the RCMP have been called upon to perform a number of unusual duties and a handful have been awarded one of the most attractive of all British medals—the Polar Medal—for a patrol they undertook during the Second World War through the North-West Passage from west to east, the first such voyage undertaken. A small ship, the *St Roch*, with a crew of eight under the command of a sergeant were detailed to patrol the Canadian Arctic waters from Vancouver to Nova Scotia, a voyage which took more than two years, from 23 June 1940 to 11 October 1942. The Polar Medal is awarded to members of the armed forces, civilians, explorers, researchers and scientists, including foreign nationals, who venture into the Arctic or Antarctic. It was introduced in 1857 as the Arctic Medal, redesigned once in 1876 and again in 1904 when it was renamed to take account of the expeditions to the Antarctic.

POLAR MEDAL

Instituted: 1904.

Ribbon: White.

Metal: Silver and Bronze.

Size: 33 mm—octagonal in shape.

Description: (Obverse) the effigy of the reigning monarch; (reverse) a depiction of the Royal Research Ship Discovery with a party of men in the foreground manhandling a sledge. An ornate swivelling suspender is employed.

The silver medals were initially awarded to officers with bronze going to all other ranks although this was changed in 1939 when the bronze issues were discontinued. All medals are awarded with a clasp bearing the dates of the service and the polar region concerned—Arctic or Antarctic. The Canadian police officers were all awarded silver medals with clasps which carried the inscription ARCTIC 1940-42. In July 1944 the *St Roch* returned to Vancouver by a more favourable route which only took 86 days and the crew members who had undertaken the original voyage were awarded a second clasp inscribed ARCTIC 1944. New members also received a medal bearing the same clasp. The number of medals awarded has increased greatly during the reign of the present monarch as exploration of the two polar regions expands. The officers from the Royal Canadian Mounted Police are likely to remain the only serving police officers ever to be awarded this coveted medal in the course of their duty.

DENMARK

The Kingdom of Denmark is one of the smallest countries in western Europe but has as one of its two overseas territories the world's largest island—Greenland. The other territory lies closer to Scotland and Iceland than it does to Denmark—the Faeroe Islands, a group of 18 islands with an area of 1,400 square kilometres and a population of 48,000. In policing terms both territories are independent districts of the national Danish Police Service. On the mainland there are a further 54 districts each under the control of a local chief constable who is also the public prosecutor and responsible for a team of lawyers to exercise this duty. The districts vary greatly in size, population and the number of officers in each. Aarhus police district, for example, on the eastern coast of the Jutland peninsula is responsible for more than 320,000 people but Kalundberg district in the north-west of the island of Sjælland serves a population of only 32,000. In terms of area the district of Herning is 200 times the size of Fredericksberg. Policing in Copenhagen stands apart from the other districts due to its population, the characteristics of a metropolitan area and the special responsibilities of being the country's capital city.

A police force has existed in Copenhagen since the late 16th century and many other large towns made their own policing arrangements in the 17th century. In 1919, however, the State Police (*Rigspolitiet*) was formed and absorbed every municipal force in 1938. There is now a single body with a total strength of approximately 10,000 officers and a responsibility for all aspects of policing on all Danish territory.

There is a single medal exclusively available to police officers, awarded in recognition of 25 years service with good conduct.

DANISH POLICE LONG SERVICE MEDAL

Instituted: 18 June 1959.

Ribbon: Green with a white central band, all of equal width.

Metal: Silver.

Description: (Obverse) the badge of the Danish police—a shield with the three lions facing left surmounted by the Danish royal crown; (reverse) a wreath of oak leaves with the word FORTJENT (for merit) in the central field.

Danish police officers can be rewarded for an act of courage or for saving a life from drowning with a disregard by the rescuer for their own safety by the award of one of two medals available to any Danish citizen who meets the strict criteria although, for police officers, the level of courage expected before an award would be considered is substantially higher due to the nature of their work. Both awards have been around for many years, the Medal for Heroic Deeds was introduced in 1793 and the Medal for Saving Life from Drowning since 1812. The design of both medals is similar—circular, cast in silver, hanging from a ribbon in red and white (the Danish national colours) with the head of the reigning sovereign on the obverse. The reverse of the Medal for Heroic Deeds has a wreath of oak leaves around the words FOR ÆDEL DAAD in the central field whilst the Medal for Saving Life from Drowning has the wreath made up of seaweeds surrounding the inscription AF FARENS SVÆLG FREMBLOMSTRER PRIIS OG LÖN (from the depths of danger honour and reward arise).

The most senior Danish police officers may be admitted to one of the two national orders of knighthood—Order of the Dannebrog, the Dannebrog being the name of the Danish national flag.

ORDER OF THE DANNEBROG

Instituted: 12 October 1671.

Ribbon: White with a red band at each edge.

Metal: Gold or silver with enamels.

Description: (Obverse) a Latin cross in white enamel on gold or silver with the crowned cypher of the founder (King Christian V) in the centre and the words GUD OG KONGEN (God and the King) on the arms of the cross. Royal crowns are positioned between the arms of the cross and it is surmounted by the cypher of the reigning monarch and a royal crown to which is attached a ring suspender; (reverse) the crowned monograms of Kings Valdemar II and Frederick VI with the dates 1219, 1671 and 1808. The earliest of these three significant dates is when the red and white Danish flag is said to have fallen from the heavens to commemorate victory in a battle by Catholic Danes over pagan forces.

The Order has four classes with the two lower ones each having two grades. It was originally restricted to a single class for 50 knights but membership was extended in 1808 to include any Danish subject irrespective of class or position and the current four classes established. Any senior police officer admitted to the Order would most usually become a simple knight.

FIJI

The Sovereign Democratic Republic of the Fiji Islands to give it its correct title, consists of a group of more than 300 islands (100 inhabited) in the South Pacific with an land area of 18,33 square kilometres scattered over a territorial area including the sea of 1.3 million square kilometres. The population of almost 800,000 people and standard of development gives the islands a certain influence in the area.

The first European interest came in 1643 when Abel Tasman, the Dutch explorer, sighted a part of the islands although it was left to the British with Captain James Cook and Captain Bligh of HMS Bounty fame to make the first real contact with the islanders after he had been cast adrift by his crew. In 1877 the formal annexation of the islands by Britain was announced and it subsequently became a British Crown Colony. The islands had attracted the attention of the Americans and French due to their strategic position and the decision to annex them was taken by the British before anyone else expressed too close an interest.

Fiji remained under British control until October 1970 when independence was granted although the early years of the new nation were very troubled. In the late 1970s the British had introduced a system of contract labour to harvest the sugar and copra and brought in workers from India. By the time independence arrived, these immigrants formed a substantial minority of the people on the islands to such a degree that the native Fijians felt threatened and rebelled after the Indian-based Federation Party won the election called in 1977. The racial tension continued over the following ten years and culminated in a coup dÈtat on 14 May 1987 which resulted in a military government, overtly racial policies and the expulsion of Fiji from the Commonwealth of Nations.

The achievement of independence, however, came before the racial tensions fully surfaced and was celebrated by the issue of a medal which was awarded to large number of local dignitaries, members of a variety of government agencies and ordinary Fijians, including police officers.

INDEPENDENCE MEDAL

Instituted: 1970.

Ribbon: Pale blue with stripes of white and red towards each edge.

Metal: Cupro-nickel.

Size: 36 mm.

Description: (Obverse) the crowned effigy of Queen Elizabeth II; (reverse) the Coat of Arms of Fiji with the words FIJI . INDEPENDENCE . 1970 around the circumference. A ring suspender was used.

The shield at the centre of the coat of arms of Fiji has four elements in the quadrants formed by the cross of St George in the main body below a lion, representing England, with its paws resting on a coconut, in the top third. The elements are sugarcane, a coconut palm and a bunch of bananas indicative of the countrys agriculture and a dove of peace with an olive branch in its beak in the bottom left quadrant, taken from the arms of Cakobau, a prominent local chief from the early days of colonisation.

The motto in the banner beneath the shield and two Fijian warrior supporters is *reveraka na kalou ka doka na tui* which means fear God and honour the Queen.

When independence was achieved, the need arose for an awards system to replace the colonial police series of medals which was previously made available to police officers for gallantry and meritorious service or long service and good conduct. In 1972, three new medals were introduced to fill this gap.

POLICE MEDAL FOR GALLANTRY

Instituted: 16 May 1972.

Ribbon: Pale blue with three stripes of green, white and dark blue at the edges and a red stripe placed centrally.

Metal: Silver.

Size: 36 mm.

Description: (Obverse) the crowned effigy of Queen Elizabeth II; (reverse) two crossed truncheons within a wreath of laurel and the words POLICE MEDAL FOR GALLANTRY around the circumference. A plain straight suspender bar was used.

The criteria necessary for the award of this medal mirrored those for the Colonial Police Medal and it was available for gallantry or meritorious service. Where an award was made for meritorious service the wording on the reverse was amended to read FOR MERITORIOUS POLICE SERVICE and the red stripe was omitted from the ribbon.

POLICE LONG SERVICE AND GOOD CONDUCT MEDAL

Instituted: 16 May 1972.

Ribbon: White with a broad pale blue central band and stripes of brown and black on the outer white bands.

Metal: Silver.

Size: 36 mm.

Description: (Obverse) the crowned effigy of Queen Elizabeth II; (reverse) the badge of the Royal Fiji Police with the Force name above and POLICE LONG SERVICE AND GOOD CONDUCT around the circumference. A ring suspender was used.

Long service and good conduct which was previously recognised by the award of the Colonial Police Long Service and Good Conduct Medal was recognised by the issue of a local medal although the requirement of 18 years unblemished service was retained.

FIJI POLICE MEDAL

When Fiji was expelled from the Commonwealth and declared itself a republic all entitlement to medals bearing the effigy of the Queen ceased and a new series was needed to ensure that the services of the country's police officers was appropriately rewarded. The Fiji Police Medal was effectively a replacement for the old medal awarded and was made available for bravery, valuable services or leadership although there was no difference in the design of the medal or colouring of the ribbon whatever the reason for the award.

Instituted: 8 March 1995.

Ribbon: Dark blue with orange stripes at each edge.

Metal: Cupro-nickel.

Size: 36 mm.

Description: An image of two Fijian police officers in uniform with the word FIJI (above) and POLICE (below) at the circumference. A plain straight suspender was used.

POLICE LONG SERVICE MEDAL

The medal introduced to acknowledge long service by Fijian officers replaced both the colonial medal and the local one available following independence but officers who had been awarded either were still entitled to wear them. Bars to the new medal, available after an additional seven years (22 years) and each five years thereafter could be worn on the new medal only.

Instituted: 8 March 1995.

Ribbon: Dark blue with a red central band, all of equal width.

Metal: Cupro-nickel.

Size: 36 mm.

Description: The badge of the Fiji Police with the words POLICE LONG SERVICE AND GOOD CONDUCT around the circumference. A ring suspender was used.

FIJI POLICE OVERSEAS SERVICE MEDAL

In common with police officers from many countries, officers from Fiji were called upon to serve as a part of United Nations peacekeeping forces outside of their normal area of jurisdiction. Following the example set in Australia a medal was introduced in Fiji to acknowledge this. It was, in effect, a general service medal for police officers and they were issued with a clasp showing the country in which they had served. Clasps available to date include *Sinai*, *Lebanon*, *Namibia*, *Cambodia* and *Iraq*.

Instituted: 8 March 1995.

Ribbon: A chequerboard pattern of dark blue and white squares of six squares width.

Metal: Cupro-nickel.

Size: 36 mm.

Description: Three four-point stars of different sizes, one superimposed on the other with the dove of peace and olive branch in the top right quadrant and the words POLICE OVERSEAS MEDAL around the lower circumference.

After several years of racial tension, the expulsion from the Commonwealth and international condemnation, the constitution of Fiji was amended to give equal rights to all citizens whether they were of native origin or of Indian background and the discrimination practised against the latter was removed. Having become rehabilitated in the eyes of the international community, Fiji was readmitted to the Commonwealth on 30 September 1997.

FINLAND

The Republic of Finland (*Suomen Tasavalta*) is a relatively recent European nation having earned its freedom from Imperial Russia following the war with its former masters precipitated by a declaration of independence made during the Russian Revolution. The decisive battle of the civil war between the Bolsheviks and the nationalist government fought at Tampere in 1918 ended in victory for the Finns and the establishment of the republic the following year. The new borders were recognised by the new Soviet Union in 1920 although the events of the Second World War resulted in Finland ceding one tenth of its territory to the Soviet Union.

Finland was a part of the Swedish Kingdom from the 12th century until it was handed to the Russians in 1809. It acquired a high degree of autonomy as a Grand Duchy although Tsar Nicholas II embarked on a programme of Russification in 1899 which only added to the resentment of the people and fuelled the calls for independence. Even after the republic had been declared, Finland's relationship with the Soviet Union was uneasy. In 1939, following the pact between Hitler and Stalin, it was invaded by the Red Army coming again under the control of its larger, stronger neighbour.

When Hitler invaded the Soviet Union in 1941, Finnish troops joined Germany to expel the Red Army but came once more under Soviet rule as the tide of the war changed and the Red Army invaded for a second time in 1944. In 1948 a friendship treaty was signed with the USSR although it was very one-sided and included an agreement to resist any attack on the USSR made through Finland by Germany or any of its allies. This uneasy relationship continued throughout the Cold War with Finland adopting a strictly neutral stance until the demise of the Soviet Union and the signing of a new treaty, with the Russian Federation, which contained no military references at all.

The Swedish heritage in Finland is strong and still reflected in the use of Swedish as one of the two official languages although there is no similarity between the two unlike other Scandinavian languages where the common roots are apparent. Finnish is like no other language in Europe with the exception of Hungarian, Estonian and several lesser-known tongues in Russia. Until the mid-19th century it had no official status although it is believed that speakers of a form of Finnish lived in the area 5,000 years ago. Swedish was a language of education, government and literature until 1863 after almost three decades of growing Finnish nationalism led to its adoption as a second official language. To English ears it is a strange language with features that can be difficult to understand. There are no articles of speech—*a* and *the* do not exist, there is no gender difference—*he* and *she* are the same word (*hän*) and there is no verb *to have* which would make the construction of many tenses of verbs impossible according to the rules of grammar of most European languages.

As a result of the country's history the honours system has developed since 1918 with the award available to police officers being of even more recent origin. *The Cross of Merit of the Police* can be awarded to police officers for meritorious service (including acts of bravery), civilians for aiding the development of the police service in a number of ways and also to foreign nationals for similar reasons. It can be awarded posthumously.

POLIISIN ANSIORISTI
(POLISENS FÖRTJÄNSTKORS)

Instituted: 19 June 1942.

Ribbon: Light blue with two narrow stripes of dark blue and white at the centre.

Metal: Silver (most awards) or gold (for special reasons) both with blue enamelling.

Description: (Obverse) a cross with the arms enamelled blue bearing a central medallion containing an heraldic rose. Between the arms of the cross are the emblem of the police—a lions crowned head.

Policing in Finland is organised nationally under the Police Department of the Ministry of the Interior although local responsibility and command is devolved first to the five provinces and then to local districts (including the capital—Helsinki—which has its own district police). There are 90 local districts each with their own police forces although only 24 of these offer a 24 hour service for emergencies. The day-to-day policing carried out in the districts is supported by three main national bodies—the National Bureau of Investigation (a detective force), the National Traffic Police and the Security Police. The total strength of all forces is approximately 8,000 officers of all ranks, supported by 2,500 other staff, who police a population of slightly more than five million albeit mainly concentrated in the south of the country.

The lion's head and white heraldic rose used on the Cross are both taken from the national arms but the honours system of Finland is notable for its use of the swastika, a symbol which will forever be associated with the Nazi regime in Germany although it is of ancient origin. It has occurred in early Christian and Byzantine art, on ancient coinage, amongst the Maya of Central America and the Navajo of North America. It also features in the Hindu and Buddhist religions although with different meanings. It is most usually seen with the arms bent in a clockwise direction to symbolise prosperity or good fortune although there is a left-hand version used to represent the night and magical or mystical forces.

The swastika was used on the first decorations introduced in Finland in 1918 after the declaration on independence and before it was adopted by the National Socialists in Germany in 1919–20 although is was first suggested as an anti-Semitic symbol in 1910. The Order of the Cross of Liberty, introduced on 4 March 1918 during the war to liberate Finland from Russian control, did not use a true swastika as it is commonly understood, the bent arms were much shorter and resembled the *fylfot*, a cross used in heraldry in many countries, including the UK, although descriptions of the Finnish decoration usually refer to it as a swastika. On 28 January 1919, a second decoration was introduced in Finland—the Order of the White Rose—which hung from a necklet for certain classes of award. The links of this necklet were in the shape of a true swastika. The design persisted even after the swastika was adopted by the Nazis and became a symbol of the atrocities committed by them but was finally replaced in 1963 by links in the form of branches of spruce.

FRANCE

The existence of national police forces in some European countries is the most fundamental difference between the policing structures on the two sides of the English Channel. In a few countries there is only the national force but in most local forces in cities, towns and regions are widespread and work alongside their nationally organised colleagues, sometimes with a different geographical area of responsibility, sometimes with a different policing priority but all contributing to law enforcement in the country concerned.

Although European police forces are invariably armed they are mostly civil organisations but with a few well-known exceptions. The Carabinieri in Italy and Gendarmerie Nationale in France are perhaps the two most familiar such bodies and both are units of the army answerable to their Minister of Defence but working alongside their civil counterparts with broadly similar remits in both countries.

The award of medals to police officers for either bravery or long service and good conduct varies between countries and can be as complex as the differences between the policing structures themselves. In Belgium there are no separate police medals at all—officers are awarded national decorations for courage in exactly the same way as any other citizen. The Carabinieri as a part of the Italian army are entitled to military medals for any act of bravery but in France the two arms of the police—the Police Nationale and Gendarmerie Nationale—each have their own distinct award.

MÉDAILLE DE LA GENDARMERIE NATIONALE

Instituted: 6 January 1950.

Ribbon: 37 mm wide. Dark blue with a narrow red stripe at each edge and a gold broad central band (10 mm) flanked by white lines (2 mm).

Metal: Bronze.

Description: (Obverse) a visored knight's helmet facing left superimposed on a sword pointing upwards with the inscription GENDARMERIE NATIONALE around the circumference; (reverse) a partial wreath of oak leaves with the legend COURAGE - DISCIPLINE above. The rank and name of the recipient are engraved in the central field. The suspender is incorporated into the medal and extends over the bottom of the ribbon. It takes the form of a flaming grenade (the emblem of the Gendarmerie) supported by two leaves.

The Gendarmerie Nationale has no counterpart in the UK and its position in the policing system of France dates from the Middle Ages. Although it performs a policing function it is a part of the French Army and holds a privileged position as the senior regiment with its members being the most highly paid. It is one of the oldest law enforcement agencies in the world although the exact date of its formation is difficult to determine.

A tentative line can be traced back to the 11th century and the corps of men used by an official of the King's household—the *sénéchal*—to administer military justice. This corps evolved over the next 400 years into the *maréchaussée* (the corps of marshals), the direct descendants of the Gendarmerie as it is known today. Up until 1536 they were responsible for the administration of military justice only but King Francis I expended their responsibility to all crime committed on the roads of France a direct connection to the present duties and responsibilities of the current force. The current name—Gendarmerie Nationale—was first used in 1791.

Responsible to the Minister of Defence, the Gendarmerie has a number of distinct units, the largest being the Departmental Gendarmerie responsible for policing rural France (including motorways) and towns and villages with a population of less than 10,000. It is officers from this unit that are the familiar sight outside the main towns and cities and on the roads. The Mobile Gendarmerie, the second largest unit with more than 17,000 officers, is primarily concerned with the maintenance of public order—they are effectively the riot police. Unlike the Departmental Gendarmerie it has no territorial jurisdiction and can be called upon to serve anywhere in mainland France or its overseas territories to maintain or restore order. The unit is equipped to deal with the most serious of situations and has access to a wide range of aids including light tanks and armoured cars for extreme emergencies. They are also trained to deal with the aftermath of natural disasters and can be used to supplement the Departmental Gendarmerie in times of great demand quite apart from the support rôle they offer when public order breaks down.

There are a number of smaller units performing specialised rôles—the Republican Guard (always based in Paris), the anti-terrorist group, maritime duties, mountain units, security at airports, bases of the French Air Force and armaments establishments and a presence in French overseas territories—altogether making a total regimental strength of more than 85,000.

The Médaille de la Gendarmerie Nationale is awarded sparingly to reflect the high standards expected of its officers and its position as the senior unit of the French Army. It is given to officers and NCOs who have been mentioned in despatches and to others (members of regiment or not) who have given important service of a permanent nature or particularly praiseworthy assistance on special missions deserving official recognition.

Any services given must have had a significant effect on the overall performance or efficiency of the Gendarmerie. Serving members mentioned in despatches must have shown special qualities of courage and a disregard for their own safety. These awards are symbolised by a small bronze (formerly silver) grenade worn on the ribbon and more than one emblem can be worn to indicate further awards for gallantry. The medal can be awarded posthumously.

As a part of the French armed forces, members of the Gendarmerie National are eligible for a range of medals for courage, devotion to duty and long or meritorious service in addition to campaign medals. Only one, however, bears the name of the regiment—the *Medal for National Defence*—which is awarded with a clasp inscribed with the geographic area of the operation concerned or the unit which includes specialisms within all branches of the armed forces. Any such medal awarded to a Gendarme carries a clasp attached to the ribbon which is inscribed "Gendarmerie Nationale".

It was instituted relatively recently to acknowledge service performed by regular members of the armed forces and those performing their period of compulsory national service. The medal comes in three grades denoted by awards in bronze, silver or gold with an unusual set of criteria for the award of each medal. It is a form of long service medal although there is a condition that there must have been some involvement in operation activities before its award would be considered. The progression from bronze to gold is based on the length of service of the recipient but complicated by a points system in addition to the number of years served. A bronze medal is awarded after six months service and the accumulation of 90 points. To qualify for a silver medal, five years service must be achieved with two of these in the bronze grade and for gold, ten years service is necessary with two in the silver grade. A silver medal also requires the accumulation of 600 points and gold 800. The points are awarded according to a formula defined by the Ministry of Defence and takes account of the nature of the actions and the duration of the recipient's service.

MÉDAILLE DE LA DÉFENSE NATIONALE

Instituted: 21 April 1982.

Ribbon: Dark red with a broad dark blue central band. The silver medal has a white stripe at each edge and the goldmedal one of yellow.

Metal: Bronze, silver and gold.

Description: (Obverse) the effigy of la Marseillaise by Rude with the words RÉPUBLIQUE FRANÇAISE inscribed on the upper circumference; (reverse) the Phrygien bonnet and the words ARMÉE-NATION and DÉFENSE NATIONALE. A simple ring suspender is used.

The Médaille de la Défense Nationale cannot be awarded to anyone who has been appointed to any grade of a national order or awarded the Médaille Militaire, France's second highest award for bravery.

In exceptional circumstances, the medal can be awarded to civilians and foreign nationals if they have rendered a particularly honourable service to France and its armed forces.

The motifs on the medal are reminders of the French Revolution of 1787–1799. The effigy of la Marseillaise on the obverse is indicative of the marching song of the revolutionaries which developed into the French national anthem and the Phrygien bonnet is the familiar pointed red hat associated with the revolutionary soldiers which became an official state emblem in 1792.

MÉDAILLE D'HONNEUR DE LA POLICE NATIONALE

Instituted: 3 April 1903.

Ribbon: A central blue stripe 8 mm wide separated from two 6 mm red stripes at the edges by white stripes each 5 mm wide.

Metal: Silver.

Size: 27 mm.

Description: (Obverse) a visored female figure holding a sword and shield protecting a kneeling woman and child with the words POLICE FRANÇAISE to the left around the edge; (reverse) there are two styles available, both inscribed with the words RÉPUBLIQUE FRANÇAISE around the edge and MINISTÈRE DE L'INTÉRIEUR in the centre. One has a rectangular tablet containing the name of the recipient and the date of the award in the lower half, the other has the inscription on a plain field but with a wreath around the right side. This round medal is suspended by an ornate wreath of olive and oak leaves open at the top left and covering the lower half of the ribbon. It is attached to the medal itself in three places.

The Police Nationale is the civil arm of the French police answerable to the Department of the Interior with its basic policing function being the same as the Gendarmerie Nationale, the major difference being in its area of responsibility. Where the Departmental Gendarmerie has a predominantly rural remit the Police Nationale can be found in any town or city with a population in excess of 10,000 inhabitants. The growth of urban areas in recent years has caused there to be some overlapping of responsibility but the basic rule exists throughout the country and includes the police in Paris who are a part of the Police Nationale.

The history of the Police Nationale can be traced back almost as far as the Gendarmerie but the basis of the structure found today was laid down by Napoleon Bonaparte in the early 19th century although major changes and reforms have taken place several times, usually as a result of the major civil disturbances that have affected France from time to time, most recently in 1968. It is the largest of the two French policing organisations with more than 108,000 personnel including the support staff necessary in a national body of such size and complexity providing administrative, technical, scientific and specialist functions.

There are two separate forces within the overall umbrella of the Police Nationale—the Air and Frontier Police and the Republican Security Companies known as the CRS, an organisation with a reputation, not wholly undeserved, for taking firm and decisive action at times of civil unrest although they are a highly trained, disciplined and professional body. They are the civil equivalent of the Mobile Gendarmerie with a total strength of almost 16,000 officers organised in groups across France ready to go anywhere in support of a local police chief who has requested their assistance. In theory, the French authorities can call on the services of almost 30,000 riot-trained officers from the Mobile Gendarmerie and CRS in extreme circumstances—a formidable force.

The Médaille d'Honneur de la Police Nationale is awarded to all members of the Force for at least 20 years exemplary service and includes those working in administrative, technical or scientific posts. It can also be awarded to people, including foreign nationals, who have given exceptional or particularly significant service to the Police Nationale. Recipients who have previously served in the Armed Forces, the Gendarmerie, a number of other specified agencies and in times of war are permitted to count up to a maximum of ten years service in those bodies in the qualifying period. From 22 October 1929 the award of the medal was extended to all French protectorates and overseas territories with the exception of Morocco, Algeria, Tunisia and Indo-China.

When it was originally introduced in 1903 the medal was known as the Médaille d'Honneur de la Police Municipale et Rurale but this was changed in November 1936 to the Médaille d'Honneur de la Police Française following the riots of February 1934 and the resulting changes to the structure and function of the Force. On the introduction of the medal in 1903 the legend on the obverse read POLICE MUNICIPALE ET RURALE but was changed to the present design in 1936. The current name was adopted on 22 April 1996 although the design of the medal was left unchanged.

There is provision for the award of the medal for bravery to serving officers where the life of the recipient was in danger and exceptional devotion to duty was displayed. In these cases a silver star is worn on the ribbon to signify the special circumstances of the award. This special award can be made posthumously.

Medals awarded to police officers by the French government were not confined to France itself. During the Age of Empire between 1830 and 1914 when European countries expanded their influence to all corners of the globe, the French controlled large areas of north-west Africa and the countries we now know as Vietnam, Laos and Cambodia, all called French Indo-China from their colonisation in 1887 until they gained their independence in the 1950s. In 1918 the French government introduced a medal to reward police officers for service in this far-flung outpost of the Empire.

MÉDAILLE DE LA POLICE DE L'INDOCHINE

Instituted: 9 March 1918.

Ribbon: Three horizontal bands of red, black and green, first broad but soon changed to narrower bands. In 1925 the ribbon was changed again to horizontal bands of red, bright yellow and pale green.

Metal: Silver.

Description: (Obverse) the right facing female head representing la République by Maurice Borrel with the words INDOCHINE FRANÇAISE at the circumference to the left and right of the head; (reverse) a branch of laurel in the lower half of the medal with the words HONNEUR ET MÉRITE in the central field above and POLICE DE L'INDOCHINE around the circumference. A plain ring suspender was employed.

After a bloody war with local insurgents in all three countries but especially Vietnam fighting for independence from European influence the French left Indo-China in 1954 and the medal became redundant.

In Africa the three primary French possessions were Algeria, Tunisia and Morocco although great swathes of the Sahara Desert were also under French control along with the island of Madagascar in the Indian Ocean. Different medals were awarded to police officers in each country on the mainland. In Algeria the medal and ribbon were the same as the Médaille d'Honneur de la Police Municipale et Rurale with the only difference being the addition of a clasp on the ribbon in the shape of a crescent and star. The award was introduced on 4 February 1905 but became redundant when Algeria achieved independence in 1962. In Tunisia and Morocco, separate medals were issued.

MÉDAILLE DE LA POLICE TUNISIENNE

Instituted: 10 August 1927.

Ribbon: Three yellow and two red stripes, all of equal width.

Metal: Silver.

Description: (Obverse) a trophy of arms surmounted by a crescent and star with the name of the medal inscribed around the circumference in French; (reverse) an inscription in Arabic script— MUHAMMAD AL-HABIB, BEY OF TUNIS. The medal hung from a ring suspender in the shape of a crescent and star attached to a half wreath.

Issued to reward 20 years service with irreproachable conduct, the medal stayed in existence until independence was granted to Tunisia in 1956.

The issue of the medal in Tunisia was preceded on 9 March 1918 by an award in Morocco available to native officers only.

MÉDAILLE DE LA POLICE CHERIFIENNE

Instituted: 1 March 1924.

Ribbon: Three orange and two green stripes, all of equal width.

Metal: Silver and enamel.

Description: (Obverse) the five-pointed star of Morocco in green enamel at the centre surrounded by Arabic script which read THE MOROCCAN STATE WITH GOD'S PROTECTION all within an outer band in red enamel bearing a motif in the shape of a zig-zag; (reverse) an elaborate Arabic motif surrounded by an inscription in Arabic script which broadly translates as THE MEDAL OF HONOUR FOR LOYAL POLICE SERVICE. A ring suspender was used.

The earlier issues were of silver only without the enamel and hung from a ribbon or red and green. The medal remained in existence throughout the French occupation but finally became redundant when independence was achieved in 1956. Chérif (sharif in English—meaning noble, high-born or illustrious) is of Arabic origin and a title of respect. Its use has been restricted since the advent of Islam to descendants of the prophet Muhammad through his daughter Fatima although it broadly means a person of noble ancestry or political importance.

A feature of the French honours system is the issue of a range of awards to people from a wide cross-section of the community for their service in their chosen profession (the Médailles d'Honneur) and a number of commemorative medals which are similar to the campaign medals awarded in the UK although civilians are eligible in addition to the Armed Forces. In the 1950s the break-up of the former French Empire took place but not without a struggle by the locals and resistance by the French which involved the police amongst others. After independence had been granted to a number of former possessions in Indo-China and North Africa a special medal was introduced for award to all those who had been involved, including police officers, in the French government action against the local insurgents.

MÉDAILLE COMMÉMORATIVE DES OPÉRATIONS DE SÉCURITÉ ET DE MAINTIEN DE L'ORDRE

Instituted: 11 January 1958.

Ribbon: A medium blue central band flanked by red and white stripes of equal width and thin red lines at the edges.

Metal: Bronze.

Description: (Obverse) the left facing helmeted head of la République with the words REPUBLIQUE (left) FRANCAISE (right) at the circumference; (reverse) the name of the medal within an open wreath of branches of laurel and oak. It hung from a small ring suspender and wreath of oak leaves.

The police officers eligible for the medal were those who had been placed at the disposal of the military authorities and who had played an active part in the security operation during the time of crisis. The award of the medal was authorised for five operations in Tunisia (1 January 1952 to 5 May 1958), Morocco (1 June 1953 to 5 May 1958), Algeria (31 October 1954 to I July 1964), The Sahara (31 October 1954 to 27 June 1961) and Mauritania (10 January 1957 to I January 1960). For each a clasp was awarded bearing the location of the operation—*Tunisie, Maroc, Algérie, Sahara* and *Mauritanie*—and any number could be awarded and worn with the medal.

Other commemorative medals for involvement in operations elsewhere could have been awarded to police officers but this is the most widespread and familiar.

During the Second World War the Vichy government in France produced what is possibly one of the rarest police medals ever issued. It is believed to have been awarded on 34 occasions only between December 1943 and summer 1944.

Following the surrender of France in June 1940, Marshal Pétain, a French hero from the Great War, established a government in the unoccupied area of France centred on the town of Vichy to the north-west of Lyons and some 250 miles south of Paris. In return for the promise of a level of co-operation, Hitler agreed to withhold his troops from southern France and to allow the establishment of what was effectively a puppet regime. The agreement lasted until November 1942 when Hitler ordered his troops to occupy the whole of France after the Anglo-American landings in North Africa. The Vichy government survived but with limited power and influence and very little credibility. After the Allied forces landed in Normandy in June 1944, its days were numbered although it held on for a further few months until Paris was liberated in August and the authority of the new government established under Charles de Gaulle was recognised by the British, American and Soviet governments in October. Pétain and most of his officials had moved eastwards with the Germans but the legacy of the Vichy government remained. In the following years, some 125,000 collaborators were tried in the special courts set up for the purpose and 40,000 received terms of imprisonment. Between 700 and 800 were executed with a further 10,000 thought to have been executed by the Resistance without any form of trial. During its time in power the Vichy government issued its own medal for police officers.

MÉDAILLE D'HONNEUR DE LA POLICE DE L'ÉTAT FRANÇAIS

Instituted: 15 December 1943.

Ribbon: Three equal stripes of red, white and blue — the French tricolour.

Metal: Silver.

Size: 27 mm.

Description: (Obverse) a standing figure of a lady holding a branch of palm and a wreath with two other figures in the right background and scenes of lifesaving; (reverse) a cartouche for the name of the recipient in the lower half of the medal with the words MINISTERE DE L'INTERIEUR above and ÉTAT FRANÇAIS in relief around the upper circumference. The medal hung from an ornate wreath of oak leaves attached to the disc in two places and which extended over the ribbon. The obverse and method of suspension are identical to the current Médaille d'Honneur pour Actes de Courage et de Dévouement awarded by the French government.

The medal was awarded in recognition of acts of service which displayed exceptional courage or a high level of devotion to duty or for 20 years distinguished service with no defaults on the recipients record in the previous ten years. It could be awarded posthumously and very often was—three awards notified in August 1944 went to police officers from the area of Dijon who were killed by terrorists—as members of the resistance movement were known by the collaboratist regime. A total of 34 awards only are known and the medal is the rarest of all French police medals. It fell into disuse with the demise of the Vichy government in August 1944.

One further medal which was made available to French police officers and could be found in groups commemorates the resistance mounted against attacks by the Japanese during the Sino-Japanese War of 1937–45 by citizens of the French concession in Shanghai between August and November 1937.

The position of the foreign concessions in Shanghai was unique and resulted from the Treaty of Nanking after the Chinese were defeated by the British and surrendered the city in 1842. It was opened up to unrestricted foreign trade and the British, Americans and French took control of areas within the city where they were granted special rights and privileges. They were effectively sovereign foreign enclaves in the Chinese city unaccountable to Chinese law. The Japanese were granted a concession in 1895 and extended their influence over the Chinese in the first half of the 20th century as Japanese imperialism increased, culminating in the war of 1937-45 when they occupied the city. In 1937 as fighting between the Chinese and Japanese forces threatened to involve the city many French people, including regular police officers, volunteer special police officers and civilian volunteers took part in the resistance and were rewarded by the issue of a special medal in their honour.

MEDAILLE DE CHANGHAÏ CONCESSION FRANÇAISE

Instituted: 1937.

Ribbon: Blue with an arrow white and red stripe at each edge.

Metal: Silver and bronze.

Description: (Obverse) a dagger pointing downwards with the top of the handle forming the mounting point for the ring suspender and the words SERVIR (to serve) across the centre; (reverse) the name of the medal inscribed in five lines in the centre with lines of laurel leaves above and below.

The same medal was awarded to a number of groups of people who played a part in the resistance but ribbons with alternative designs and colouring were used to differentiate between them. In addition, clasps were attached to the ribbon, each inscribed (in relief) with a description of the group. Medals awarded to regular police officers bore a clasp with the words MÉDAILLE COMMEMORATIVE - CHANGHAÏ - POLICE FRANÇAISE in three lines. Members of the voluntary special police received a medal with a ribbon very similar to that awarded to regular officers but with the white and red lines at the edges being narrower and a clasp bearing the words POLICE SPECIALE - VOLONTAIRE - AOÛT-NOV-1937 in three lines. The medal awarded to other volunteers hung from a mauve ribbon with narrow stripes of red, white and blue at each edge. The clasp was inscribed VOLONTAIRE - FRANÇAIS - AOÛT-NOV-1937 in three lines.

An additional medal to commemorate the emergency was issued by the municipal authorities to a wide range of people including police officers from the foreign concessions and members of the local force who were responsible for the policing of the rest of the city.

SHANGHAI MUNICIPAL COUNCIL EMERGENCY MEDAL

Instituted: 1937.

Ribbon: Red with a white central band and yellow edges. All the colours were separated by a thin black line.

Metal: Bronze.

Size: 40 mm.

Description: (Obverse) an eight point rayed star with a central medallion bearing the seal of the city within an outer band inscribed SHANGHAI MUNICIPAL COUNCIL; (reverse) a wreath of laurel with the words FOR SERVICES RENDERED - AUGUST 12 TO NOVEMBER 12 1937 in the central field. A ring suspender was used.

SHANGHAI MUNICIPAL POLICE LONG SERVICE MEDAL

The Shanghai Municipal Police was an international body staffed with officers from China, India, White Russia and many European countries, typical of the cosmopolitan nature of the city.

Good service of at least 12 years was rewarded with a silver medal and bars for each additional period of five years. It was abolished in 1942 after the Japanese occupation of Shanghai the previous year.

Instituted: 1925.

Ribbon: Brown with a yellow central band edged with white.

Metal: Silver.

Size: 36 mm.

Description: (Obverse) a circular medal with the seal of the Municipality in the centre surrounded by an outer band bearing the words SHANGHAI MUNICIPAL POLICE; (reverse) plain apart from the words FOR LONG SERVICE in two lines. An ornate swivelling suspender was used. The recipients name and rank were engraved around the lower rim.

The design on the obverse was repeated on a second award given to regular officers to acknowledge particularly distinguished conduct although it was awarded very sparingly with only six ever being issued from its introduction in 1924 to its demise during the Second World War. The only difference in the design was the substitution of the words FOR DISTINGUISHED CONDUCT on the reverse. It was produced in two classes—silver and bronze—with each using different ribbons. The silver first class award hung from a red ribbon with a blue central stripe and the bronze from a red ribbon with two blue stripes at the edges.

A similar medal to the long service medal with the same qualifying criteria was available to members of the special constabulary with the major differences being the omission of the outer band containing the force name from the obverse and the six-line inscription on the reverse which read SHANGHAI MUNICIPAL POLICE (SPECIALS) FOR LONG SERVICE. The ribbon was dark brown with three white bars each with a thin yellow stripe. Shanghai finally fell to the Japanese in 1941 who remained until the end of the Second World War although the changes signalled the end of the foreign concessions and the start of a new era for the city.

The municipality seal was unusual and made up of the flags of most of the countries which had treaties with China and who maintained a presence there. It takes the form of three shields joined by their points in the centre. Each shield has a representation of four flags, Britain, the USA, France and Prussia in one, Russia, Denmark, Italy and Portugal in another and Austria, Spain, the Netherlands and Norway and Sweden (joint) in the last with the motto *Omnia juncta in uno* (all joined in one) around the circumference between the tops of the shield and repeated in Chinese characters below each word. The design was introduced in April 1869 although there was a considerable amount of resistance from the local people who objected to the total lack of any Chinese motif apart from the motto. Alternative designs were proposed but it remained in use until after the Second World War.

Acts of courage or lifesaving in France are recognised by the award of two medals and any person is eligible irrespective of their occupation or nationality although the level of courage expected of a police officer is greater than that of a civilian in common with the accepted practice in many countries, including the UK. Although differences occur where lifesaving from water is involved with different ministries becoming the appropriate authority. Any person who helps another who is in danger at the risk of his or her own life can be rewarded in one of a number of ways dependent on the level of courage displayed.

Medals to reward acts of courage and devotion to duty and humanity were introduced by Napoléon 1, probably in 1808 and certainly existed in 1810. Whether or not they were available to police officers or the Gendarmerie isn't known. It isn't until the reign of Louis-Philippe (1830 to 1848) that awards to the Gendarmerie can definitely be verified although they are scarce as most acts of courage by gendarmes were rewarded with the Médaille Militaire. The design of the medal has undergone a number of changes since its introduction although the current award has remained constant since 1931.

MÉDAILLE D'HONNEUR POUR ACTES DE COURAGE ET DE DÉVOUEMENT

Instituted: 31 January 1931.

Ribbon: Equal vertical bands of blue, white and red.

Metal: Bronze, silver, silver-gilt and gold.

Description: (Obverse) a representation of a female figure holding a branch of palm and a wreath placed centrally with scenes of lifesaving and two smaller figures in the background after a work by the sculptor Coudray; (reverse) a cartouche for the name of the recipient and the words RÉPUBLIQUE FRANÇAISE around the upper circumference and MINISTÈRE DE L'INTÉRIEUR in the central field. The medal is attached to the ribbon by means of a wreath of oak leaves.

The earliest awards came in two forms—a large (50 mm) silver medal—with another, smaller (27 mm) award being presented with a ribbon in the national colours for wear on a uniform. The very first award is believed to have been made in 1782 during the reign of King Louis XVI to a youth of 17 years who rescued two children from drowning after they had fallen through the surface of a frozen pond at Versailles. The King was so impressed by the act of selfless courage that he authorised the award of a medal to the youth. Further individual medals followed until the matter was placed on a formal footing. The practice of awarding two medals, one large and one small for wear, was retained for a number of years. They were available to any citizen, including police officers and Gendarmes, although the earliest date officers from either body received an award is the subject of speculation. It is known that one was awarded in 1844 (during the reign of Louis-Philippe I) to Sergeant Jean-Louis Suzanne for his courage and humanity on a number of occasions at Blois. The medal carries the King's head on the obverse with the words LOUIS PHILIPPE I (left) and ROI DES FRANÇAIS (right) around the circumference. The reverse has an ornate depiction of the figures of a male with a lion representing courage and a female and child representing humanity holding a wreath of laurel above a specially struck oval central medallion giving the details of the award.

The design of the obverse changed in these particularly troubled times for France and exist with the effigies of Napoleon, Louis XVIII, Napoleon III and Charles X before a representation of la République was chosen. The reverse stayed similar irrespective of the head on the obverse although a more simple design existed during the period of the Second Republic—a wreath of oak leaves with the words RÉPUBLIQUE FRANÇAISE in the central field.

There are seven classes of the award currently available with the simplest being a letter of congratulations from the Minister for the Interior, followed by an Honourable Mention which takes the form of a diploma.

At the next level of courage a bronze medal is awarded, followed by silver in two classes, gilt and finally gold to honour courage of the highest degree. The class of the medal is indicated by the use of certain devices on the ribbon apart from the bronze medal. The device is usually in the form of a five-pointed star. The award of a silver medal, second class, is indicated by a single silver star but the first class award carries two stars. The award in gilt carries a gilt star but the gold medal uses a device that is common in France, Belgium, the Netherlands and other European countries but which plays no part in the honours system of the UK—the use of a rosette on the ribbon, in this case in the colours of the ribbon.

Award of the more prestigious medals is restricted by a series of conditions which must be satisfied before they will be considered, conditions which often insist upon the recipient already being the holder of a lower award. The silver medal, for example, is only awarded to holders of the bronze medal who perform a second act of courage which displays great courage. The gilt medal is reserved for the most extreme examples of courage or to holders of two silver medals. This protocol is not repeated for a second medal available to French civilians.

MÉDAILLE D'HONNEUR DE LA MARINE MARCHANDE

Instituted: *31 January 1931.*

Ribbon: *Equal vertical bands of blue, white and red with an anchor on the central white band.*

Metal: *Bronze, silver, gilt and gold.*

Description: *(Obverse) the effigy of la République by Marey consisting of the head facing right with the words REPUBLIQUE (left) FRANCAISE (right); (reverse) a cartouche for the details of the recipient and the date of the award with a marine trophy of arms and the words MARINE MARCHANDE—COURAGE ET DEVOUEMENT. A plain ring suspender is used.*

The anchor on the ribbon is in red for the bronze, silver and gilt medals and in gold for the highest award—the gold medal, which also carries a rosette. Devices in the form of stars of silver, gilt or gold are worn on the ribbon to indicate the class of the medal. The medals are available to anyone who saves a life from drowning in the sea, a river or any water not the responsibility of the Admiralty where a further medal is awarded. The award is available to police officers and gendarmes and includes those serving overseas in present and former French territories.

In addition to the national medals, there are awards made to police officers by local lifesaving societies although there are only three remaining today compared with the situation in the early years of the 20th century when there were no fewer than 183 regional and departmental societies who all issued medals of some description to recognise acts of courage in saving life by citizens of the area including police officers and members of the Gendarmerie. The three societies which remain were all founded in the mid to late 19th century but have survived the effects of time. By the very nature of their work, police officers in the three areas have been regular recipients of the medals awarded by the three societies including one officer who saved the lives of two people on two separate occasions in the space of a few weeks in the town of Châtellerault in Vienne.

André Quelen was serving as a *"Gardien de la Paix de la Brigade Aniticriminalité de Châtellerault"* at Christmas 1998 when he was sent to help a woman who had attempted suicide by throwing herself into the River Vienne. Although the water was close to freezing point he jumped into the river and succeeded in bringing the woman to safety. Her injuries were so severe than she was in hospital for a month but survived thanks to the courage of André Quelen.

Barely two weeks later, on 12 January, he rescued a young lady of only 21 from a fire in the town and his courage was subsequently recognised by the award of the gold medal (the highest honour) from the *Société des Sauveteurs de la Vienne*. The medal was presented on 25 September 1999 together with the Diamond Jubilee Medal of the Alberta and Northwest Territories Branch of the Royal Life Saving Society Canada by the Honorary Life Governor who is also Honorary President for the French society in Canada. It was the first occasion that the Canadian award had been made to a Frenchman.

MÉDAILLE DE LA SOCIÉTÉ DES SAUVETEURS DE LA VIENNE

Instituted: 1892.

Ribbon: Five equal bands of red, yellow, blue, white and red.

Metal: Bronze, silver and gold (silver-gilt).

Description: (Obverse) a female figure with a tablet to her right bearing the words in three lines SOCIETE - DES - SAU - VETEURS and another to her left inscribed DE LA - VIENNE - LXXXVI; (reverse) left blank apart from a plaque for the recipient's name to be engraved above the words POUR QUE VIVENT LES HOMMES.

The two other societies which remain in France both award medals to anyone who saves the life of another from danger whatever the source and police officers are regular recipients.

MÉDAILLE DE LA SOCIÉTÉ DES SAUVETEURS DE LA GIRONDE

Instituted: 1855.

Ribbon: Red with a green central band, all of equal width sometimes seen with a rosette placed centrally.

Metal: Silver-gilt.

Description: (Obverse) the Coat of Arms of Gironde superimposed on an anchor and topped with a mural crown with a banner bearing the words SAUVIR OU PERIR; (reverse) the words SAUVETEURS DE LA GIRONDE around the upper circumference and the date 1855 at the base with the central area marked by a circle and with the words DÉCERNÉE A above a space for the name of the recipient to be engraved.

France

MÉDAILLE DE LA SOCIÉTÉ DES SAUVETEURS DE LA CHARENTE

Instituted: 1865.

Ribbon: Half blue and half white separated by a narrower band of red sometimes seen with a rosette placed centrally.

Metal: Silver-gilt.

Description: (Obverse) the Coat of Arms of Charente within an outer band bearing the name of the Society and the date 1865; (reverse) a partial wreath of laurel leaves around a central field for the recipients details with the words SAUVER OU PERIR at the top.

Medals previously awarded by the local societies still crop up from time to time, often attractive pieces, they usually have the coat of arms of the city, town region or district on the obverse and a variety of desisns on the reverse. The political changes that have taken place in France since the local lifesaving societies first appeared in the mid 19th century have seen many historical place names disappear and many of those that remain have become secondary to the country's 22 regions.

Each region is made up of a number of departments (95 in all) many of which retain their historical names.

The Department of Loiret lies south of Paris in the Region of Centre with Orleans as its major city and it is generally thought of in the UK as a lesser-known part of the Loire Valley. Loiret once had is own lifesaving society (founded on 10 May 1868) that awarded a medal to any citizen whose actions were thought worthy of official recognition although they have long since been discontinued.

MÉDAILLE DE LA SOCIÉTÉ DES SAUVETEURS DU LOIRET

Instituted: 1868.

Ribbon: Half yellow, half red.

Metal: Silver.

Size: 25 mm.

Description: (Obverse) the Coat of Arms of Loiret within an outer band inscribed at the circumference with SAUVETEURS DU LOIRET (upper) and the date 10 MAI 1868 (lower); (reverse) a depiction of the head of a wild boar. A simple ring suspender was used.

Medals awarded by local lifesaving societies are not invariably circular although this is true of the majority. The Société des Sauveteurs des Alpes-Maritime, situated in the south-east corner of France and including the Côte d'Azur the city of Nice, once awarded a medal in the form of a cross.

MÉDAILLE DE LA SOCIÉTÉ DES SAUVETEURS DES ALPES-MARITIME

Instituted: 1871.

Ribbon: Half red, half yellow.

Description: (Obverse) a cross with trefoils at the end of each arms superimposed by an anchor and a pair of crossed axes. The date of the founding of the society (1871) is inscribed on the upper arm of the cross. The medal has a large ring suspender attached to a mural crown and the upper part of an anchor joined to the upper arm of the cross; (reverse) usually engraved with the name of the recipient and date of award.

The use of devices such as bars, clasps and rosettes on full-size medal ribbons seen on many French medals is more widespread and varied in other European countries than the UK. Clasps or bars on British medals have existed since 1847 when the Naval General Service Medal was introduced with a large number of bars being made available in subsequent years to identify the action for which the medal was awarded, the earliest being the fleet action clasp of 1 June 1794. The concept has continued to the present day and the combination of medals and clasps that have been awarded is extensive. Bars are also used to signify a subsequent award for gallantry to someone previously awarded the same decoration. They are naturally uncommon although more than 5,700 first bars to the Military Medal were awarded during the Great War. Second awards of the Military Cross during the same conflict were made on 3,000 occasions. During the Second World War the importance of air power and the number of missions undertaken led to the award of 1,550 first bars to the 20,000 Distinguished Flying Crosses granted to air crew.

The most widespread device likely to be seen on the ribbon of a British medal, however, is the oak leaf emblem denoting a Mention in Despatches. Many thousands were awarded during the two major conflicts of the 20th century and they can be seen on many Victory Medals from the Great War or War Medals 1939–45 from the Second World War. The design is different but the reason why it was awarded remains the same.

Arguably the most familiar examples of the variety of devices found on foreign medals can be seen on the French Croix de Guerre which is itself the equivalent of the oak leaf awarded in the UK. There are four devices available of the French award according to the author of the "despatch" leading to the award of the medal. An Army despatch would entitle the recipient to wear a bronze laurel branch on the ribbon, an Army Corps despatch carries with it the right to wear a silver gilt star, a Divisional despatch—silver star and one from a brigade or regiment—a bronze star. Any subsequent awards are denoted by the device on the ribbon of the original and, in theory, there is no limit to the number of stars or branches which can be worn on one ribbon.

The recipient of five bronze palm branches, however, wears instead a single silver palm branch.

The criteria for the award of the Belgian Croix de Guerre followed similar lines with the most obvious difference being the replacement of stars for regimental or divisional despatches by bronze, silver or gilt lions.

A second Belgian medal—the Commemorative Medal of the War 1940–45—made use of a variety of emblems to denote the branch of service of the recipient or their contribution to Belgiums war effort. The medal was introduced on 16 February 1946 and awarded to all members of the Belgian Armed Forces who served between 10 May 1940 and 7 May 1945 including members of the resistance movement. The most common emblem is two crossed sabres used to recognise someone who took part in the campaign against the invading Nazis in 1940 or members of the resistance. Crossed anchors denoted maritime service, crossed bolts of lightning—service as an intelligence agent, a bronze crown for volunteers, red crosses to indicate the number of times wounded and thin bars to indicate that the recipient had been a prisoner-of-war (one bar for each year in captivity). There was also a device to indicate an act of courage which was not sufficient to merit the award of the Croix de Guerre but which deserved official recognition—a bronze lion. A recipient could be awarded a number of emblems and was entitled to wear them all on the same ribbon. Bars similar to those seen on British medals to recognise a particular battle or campaign were also awarded—*Liege 1940, Flandres 1940, Ardennes Belges, Canal Albert* and many others. Four separate elliptical devices were available to recognise the major theatres of war in which the recipient fought—*France 1944, Pays-Bas 1944-45, Allemagne 1944-45* and *Tchécoslovaquie 1945*.

The method of signifying the second award of a decoration for gallantry is a common feature in a number of countries but the method varies considerably. In the Netherlands any subsequent awards of the *Bronzen Leeuw* (Bronze Lion)—the country's second highest award for bravery—is denoted by a large figure 2 worn on the ribbon. Similar conditions apply to the *Bronzen Kruis* (Bronze Cross)—the next level of gallantry award available. The use of Arabic figures for second or subsequent awards in the Netherlands is varied for the *Vliegerkruis* (Flying Cross)—here a winged bar with a Roman numeral in gold in the centre is used.

GERMANY

The impact that Germany has had on the history of Europe in the 20th century cannot possibly be understated although it was once a hotchpotch of many hundreds of small states and principalities often in constant rivalry with each other. The first steps towards the unification of these states into something resembling the Germany we know today came in 1815 at the Treaty of Vienna following the Battle of Waterloo and the end of the Napoleonic Wars. The dominant German state was Prussia which had fought alongside the British and Hanover to defeat the French although the decades which followed were marked by civil unrest and demands for changes to the old political order. In 1862 the Prussian King Wilhelm I appointed Otto von Bismarck as his Chancellor and he embarked on a programme to establish a united country - also under Prussian domination. He partially succeeded in 1866 with the northern states forming a confederation although it took a war with France provoked by Bismarck in 1871 to bring the southern states of Bavaria, Baden and Württemberg together to form the Second Reich.

Resentment over the war, the loss of territory and the humiliating defeat smouldered in France until the outbreak of the Great War in August 1914 when the opportunity to exact revenge presented itself and she sided with Britain and Russia to confront Germany and Austria. This desire for revenge had its effect on the tough conditions laid down by the allied powers in the treaty which saw an end to the slaughter.

The Treaty of Versailles signed at the end of the Great War laid the foundations for the discontent and upheaval in Germany which led, ultimately, to the rise of Adolf Hitler, the establishment of the Third Reich and the Second World War. The Treaty called for huge war reparations, a shift in the European balance of power and the confiscation of large areas of territory which had been controlled by Germany for centuries. When Germany suffered from the economic disaster of hyper-inflation and very high levels of unemployment in the 1920s and 1930s, the weaknesses of the Weimar Republic resulted, almost inevitably, in the rise of extremists political parties, in particular the National Socialist German Workers Party (the Nazis), led by Hitler.

He was made Chancellor in January 1933 and President shortly afterwards after the Reichstag was burnt down and a state of emergency declared by the former president—Paul von Hindenburg. All other political parties were banned—Hitler was a dictator with a huge level of public support. The Third Reich, which was to last a thousand years, was established and the first steps along the road to the Second World War were taken.

Germany

THE THIRD REICH 1933–1945

A strong, ruthless and amoral police force is a cornerstone of any dictatorship, Germany in the 1930s being no exception. Some five years after Hitler's rise to power but before the start of the war he had authorised three awards to police officers to recognise 8, 18 and 25 years faithful service to him and the Third Reich.

MEDAL FOR EIGHT YEARS FAITHFUL SERVICE IN THE POLICE

Instituted: 30 January 1938.

Ribbon: Cornflower blue.

Metal: Silvered white metal.

Description: (Obverse) a circular medal showing the Nazi police emblem of a stylised eagle with outstretched wings holding a wreath of oak leaves containing a swastika all superimposed on a wreath of oak leaves; (reverse) the figure 8 placed centrally with the words FÜR TREUE DIENSTE IN DER POLIZEI (for faithful service in the police) around the circumference. A ring suspender was used.

CROSS FOR EIGHTEEN YEARS FAITHFUL SERVICE IN THE POLICE

Instituted: 30 January 1938.

Ribbon: The same cornflower blue as the medal but with the police emblem embroidered on the ribbon in silver.

Metal: Silvered white metal.

Size: 42 mm.

Description: (Obverse) a cross pattée with the Nazi police emblem as described for the 8 year medal in the centre; (reverse) the words FÜR TREUE DIENSTE IN DER POLIZEI in five lines in a central medallion. A ring suspender was used.

The cross awarded for 25 years service differs in two respects—it was finished in gilt and the emblem embroidered on the ribbon is in yellow. When the ribbon was worn alone, a metal police emblem was worn with it, in silver or gilt. On 12 August 1944 provision was made to recognise 40 years service—an ambitious and fanciful thought given the progress of the war at the time and the inevitable outcome. A metal motif with the number 40 for wear on the ribbon was authorised but it is not thought that it was ever produced or issued. Nine months later the surrender of Germany rendered all Third Reich medals redundant.

page 85

The loss of one particular area of German territory after the First World War was used as an excuse by Hitler to launch his invasion of Poland in 1939. The city of Gdansk (Danzig) is situated on the Baltic coast of present-day Poland but ownership has changed hands frequently since it was founded in 997 as a Polish city. As the fortunes of Poland changed over the centuries the city was ruled in turn by the Teutonic knights (1308), Poland again (1466), Prussia (1772), France (1807 to 1814), Prussia again (1814) and Germany (1866) until it was granted the status of a free city in 1919 although it was administered by Poland. In 1938, Hitler demanded its return to Germany and used the refusal of the Poles to comply to attack on 1 September 1939. During the period in which it was occupied by Germany a series of police long service awards was introduced by the Nazis along with a range of other decorations. Several of the awards were actually introduced in 1938 as Hitler's intentions became obvious. The Danzig Police Long Service awards followed the pattern of those issued in the Fatherland with a medal available after eight years service, a cross in silver after 18 years and one in gold after 25 years.

POLIZEI-DIENSTAUSZEICHNUNG (MEDAILLE FÜR 8 JAHRE)

Instituted: 1938.

Ribbon: Blue.

Metal: Silver.

Description: (Obverse) circular with the Coat of Arms of Danzig above a small circle bearing a swastika all within a wreath of single oak leaves around the circumference; (reverse) the figure 8 at the bottom with a sprig of laurel on either side and the words FÜR TREUE DIENSTE IN DER POLIZEI in script in three lines above. A simple ring suspender was used.

The shield at the centre of the arms contains two crosses, one above the other, which first appeared in the early 15th century when the city was under the rule of the Teutonic knights, topped by a crown which was added in 1457. At the same time the two lion supporters were added. The swastika was added during the period of the Third Reich.

KREUZ FÜR 18 UND 25 JAHRE

Instituted: 1938.

Ribbon: Blue.

Metal: Gilt and silver.

Description: (Obverse) a cross pattée with a central medallion bearing the Coat of Arms of Danzig above a small circle containing a swastika. A second smaller cross with rayed arms was positioned between the arms of the larger cross; (reverse) left blank.

GERMAN DEMOCRATIC REPUBLIC (EAST GERMANY)

The *Deutschen Demokratischen Republik* (German Democratic Republic or GDR) was born out of the partition of Germany at the end of the Second World War by the four major allied powers—Britain, France, the USA and the Soviet Union. From 1945 it was the Soviet Occupation Zone but established as a separate country in its own right on 7 October 1949 five months after the three other occupation zones in the west were united to form the Federal Republic of Germany (West Germany). The GDR had a short, troubled existence, always under Soviet domination and the scene of the most likely flashpoint between east and west—Berlin. The end of the GDR as a separate state started at the most potent symbol of the divide between the two halves of Germany when the Berlin Wall was opened on 9 November 1989. After the Wall was opened, the end of the GDR was inevitable and it passed into history four days before its 41st birthday, on 3 October 1990, when the two Germanys were reunited.

The basic policing structure of the GDR was based on the *Volkspolizei* (People's Police) which grew from a force founded in East Berlin in 1945 to support the Soviet troops in maintaining order and which was expanded to cover the whole of the new country in 1949. The Volkspolizei were very different from the two bodies most usually associated with policing in East Germany, the State Security Service (Stasi) and those guarding the borders. Although they were commonly known as border police, the *Grenzschutztruppen* (Border Security Troops) were a part of the Armed Forces and trained and equipped as such. Their official remit was to guard the borders of the GDR against subversive elements from the west but, in reality, they were there to prevent any East German from leaving without the authority of the government, an authority very rarely given. They were authorised to use whatever force was necessary to secure the borders and had no hesitation in opening fire on anyone brave (or foolish) enough to try to cross the Berlin Wall or death strips which ran from the North Sea to the border with Czechoslovakia.

The lengths to which the authorities were prepared to go to prevent anyone from leaving had to be seen to be believed. The secured area running the length of the border, between the entry control points in the east and west, extended for five kilometres with the actual "death strip" being anything from 100 to 2000 metres wide. A potential escapee from the east was first faced with a wire fence several metres high fitted with electrical and acoustic alarms. The open area beyond the fence was patrolled regularly by guards with dogs overlooked by watchtowers fitted with searchlights, listening equipment and eager, dedicated guards armed with machine guns that they were very ready to use. Beyond the towers was a concrete patrol road and reinforced concrete vehicle barrier with openings only at the 14 authorised crossing points. The last barrier was a second wire fence, three metres high, also equipped with electrical and acoustic alarms. The actual border with West Germany was a hundred yards away across an area specially cleared of all trees, shrubs and bushes to allow the guards a clear sight of (and shot at) any hopeful escapee who got that far. If a village, hamlet or even a single house stood at the border on the eastern side, it was shielded by a high concrete wall. Despite these precautions many tried, and some succeeded, in escaping to the west although most failed and many died in the "death strip".

In April 1990, five months after the Wall was opened, but before reunification of the two Germanys, I was fortunate enough to visit the border area and Berlin to study the border controls (*above*). The watchtowers remained but were not staffed and the wire fence was still there. In places where it had crossed a road, however, it had simply been cut and rolled back, opening another crossing point which the authorities did their best to control. Some were staffed by border guards or customs officials from east and west, some by the west alone and some by a handful of East German guards who were a little uncertain of their new duties. In a few short months more than 150 new crossing points were opened in the fence. At one new crossing, a few miles from an official border crossing point at Helmstedt-Marienborn, the office was an old caravan and the actual checkpoint marked by three orange traffic cones placed in the road (*right*). Three East Germans carried out rudimentary checks on a few villagers cycling from east to west enjoying their new found freedom. My guide, a member of the West German Border Police, took me to meet them. We shook hands, exchanged a few words, asked a few questions and posed for photographs but, on the way back to the west, my guide reminded me that "a few months ago the bastard would happily have shot us".

Part of the agreement between east and west over the position of Berlin included a proviso that there should be free access between West Germany and West Berlin through GDR territory. The routes were strictly defined and we were told that we should, under no circumstances, stray from the transit route or exceed the 100 kilometre an hour speed limit. As drivers of a car registered in West Germany we would have been stopped and relieved of a sum of West German marks very quickly and more than once. The Volkspolizei in their green and white Lada patrol cars were everywhere paying no attention to anyone not driving a car registered in the west—we heeded the advice. Close to Berlin the evidence of security increased with watchtowers at every junction before the fence and death strip that surrounded the city appeared. In the enlightened times, however, controls were lax and amounted to no more than a brief stop to hand back the transit visa we had bought for five marks (West German) a few hours before.

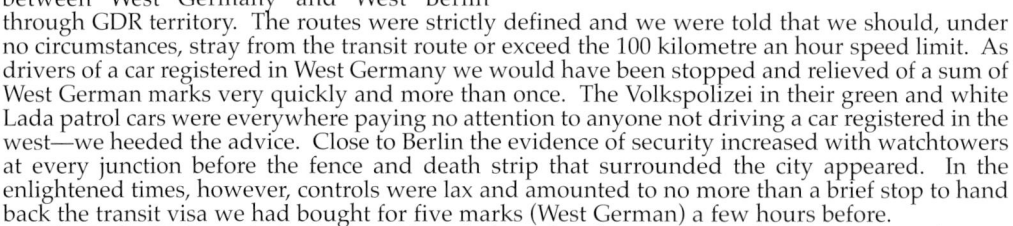

The Berlin Wall was intimidating although the sight of a major from the US Army standing on a wheelchair chipping away at it with a hammer and handing the pieces to tourists within sight of Checkpoint Charlie somewhat reduced its threat. Crossing over to East Berlin at Checkpoint Charlie for a short visit was atmospheric, aided by the fact that my occupation—police officer—was clearly printed in my passport and interested the guard sitting in his little booth handing out day visas—for another five Deutschmarks. He examined it for an eternity and photocopied every page before handing it back with what was meant to be a smile. For the next three hours as we wandered along Unter den Linden and in and out of the back streets we were aware of our "friend" not far behind following our every move. He gave up shortly after I was approached by another man wearing a long leather coat, looking every inch the caricature of German security man, who asked in perfect English if I wanted to change some money. Once I had refused, not wishing to spend the rest of the day sampling the hospitality of an East Berlin police station, both men wandered off to annoy someone else and left us to enjoy the delights of the city.

The most obvious example of the differences between the two halves of the city, apart from the fact that no-one in the east ever smiled, was the lack of almost anything worth buying in the shops, the more noticeable the further we strayed from the city centre. In a toy shop, the range of toy cars available was comparable with those we give away in garages for buying a few gallons of petrol and in a corner shop the choice of anything was limited to one brand—tins of peas, toilet rolls, jam, butter, toothpaste, virtually everything—all plainly packaged and very dull. The only thing available in abundance was alcohol (spirits) with a range comparable with anything in the west.

Crossing back to West Berlin should have been easy if we had known that we were obliged to leave by the same route that we had entered. I wanted to cross at the Brandenburg Gate but, as we had entered through Checkpoint Charlie, that was the way we had to leave and no amount of pleading with the guard was going to change his mind. Back at our proper crossing point I managed to get back to safety easily enough but not without a few anxious moments as my passport was examined in detail again and I wondered if they would find the handful of East German currency I had in my back pocket and was determined to take out with me—in direct breach of their law. As I stopped halfway across no-mans land to take a few photographs of the control point (*left*) and border guards I gained the impression that some of them longed for the good old days when they could have shot me.

The East German authorities awarded a range of medals to their police officers for long service and meritorious conduct. Most medals were available in three classes—gold, silver and bronze—with the same design and the same basic colour and design of ribbon but with the class indicated by the addition of stripes, sometimes using different colours, sometimes different numbers of stripes of the same colour. The emblem of the GDR was a common feature of most medals—a motif of a hammer and pair of compasses within a wreath of wheat entwined at the base by a banner in the national colours—red, black and yellow. This use of modern industrial and agricultural symbolism was a recurring feature of the coats of arms of most communist states. The medals were available to several groups under the control of the Ministry of Internal Affairs including the Fire Brigade and Prison Service.

To reward faithful service, there were two sets of three medals (six in all) available for service ranging from five to 30 years. Each set of the *Faithful Service Medal* was awarded in bronze, silver and gold with the class of the award also being indicated by the ribbon.

MEDAILLE FÜR TREUE DIENSTE IN DER DEUTSCHEN VOLKSPOLIZEI—5 TO 15 YEARS

Instituted: 1954.

Ribbon: Light green with three central stripes of red (bronze), white (silver) or yellow (gold)—worn in the Russian style.

Metal: Gold, silver and bronze.

Description: (Obverse) two six-point stars, one superimposed on the other with a central disc containing a shield with three horizontal bars to represent the national flag and the Coat of Arms of the GDR at the centre and the words FÜR TREUE DIENSTE (for faithful service) around the edge; (reverse) The Coat of Arms in a central disc surrounded by a wreath of laurel. A ring suspender was used.

The bronze medal was awarded after five years service, the silver after ten and the gold after fifteen years faithful service. To reward further periods of service a second group of three medals was available.

MEDAILLE FÜR TREUE DIENSTE IN DER DEUTSCHEN VOLKSPOLIZEI—20 TO 30 YEARS

Instituted: 1954.

Ribbon: Red with one (20 years), two (25 years) or three (30 years) stripes of yellow at each edge—worn in the Russian style.

Metal: Gold.

Description: (Obverse) a twelve-point star and central disc bearing the Coat of Arms slightly offset towards the top with the words FÜR 20 JAHRE TREUE DIENSTE below. Above and below the star were branches of laurel; (reverse) the same as the previous award.

The figure in the inscription was amended to indicate the appropriate number of years served. In undress uniform a device in the shape of the twelve point star which forms the centrepiece of the medal was worn on the ribbon.

Meritorious service by officers from any organisation under the control of the Ministry of Internal Affairs rather than the achievement of a certain number of years served was rewarded by one of a further set of three bronze, silver and gold medals available. The criteria for the award of the *Meritorious Service Medal of the Ministry of the Interior* demanded more than the completion of a certain number of years service and the class was decided by the level of the service performed. The group of medals were all of the same design with the class being differentiated only by the metal used and the colouring of the ribbon.

VERDIENSTMEDAILLE DER ORGANE DER MINISTERIUM DES INNERN

Instituted: 1966.

Ribbon: Green with a thin red stripe at each edge and stripes in the national colours—black, red and yellow, in the centre. This was for the basic bronze medal, the silver medal had an additional stripe of white towards each edge and the gold medal one of yellow.

Metal: Gold, silver and bronze.

Description: (Obverse) a circular medal with a twelve-point star containing a central disc bearing the national emblem with four oak leaves below and the words FÜR HERVORRAGENDE VERDIENSTE (for excellent meritorious service) around the upper circumference half; (reverse) the same as for the previous two sets of medals. A plain ring suspender was used.

Apart from the service medals, three others were available for particularly meritorious service which went beyond the criteria for the previous award. The medals were not different classes of the same group but individual awards in their own right. The first of the three—the *Medal for Excellent Performance in the Armed Services of the Ministry of the Interior*—was not solely available to police officers and came in a single class.

MEDAILLE FÜR AUSGEZEICHNETE LEISTUNGEN IN DEN BEWAFFNETEN ORGANEN DES MINISTERIUM DES INNERN

Instituted: 1959.

Ribbon: Green with a thin white stripe towards each edge.

Metal: Gold.

Description: (Obverse) a circular medal with a twelve point star surrounding the state emblem in the upper two-thirds flanked by oak leaves above a banner bearing the words FÜR AUSGEZEICHNETE LEISTUNGEN in two lines; (reverse) the state emblem.

Germany

The two remaining medals were both more colourful and made use of enamels to identify them as the highest awards available. They were both solely police awards. The first, the *Medal of Honour of the German People's Police*, was particularly colourful and the design was typical of many medals produced in the former Eastern European communist states and the Soviet Union.

MEDAILLE EHRENZEICHEN DER DEUTSCHEN VOLKSPOLIZEI

Instituted: 1949.

Ribbon: Green with a thin red stripe at each edge.

Metal: Silver with multi-coloured enamels.

Description: (Obverse) a circular medal in a dark green enamel with a twelve point star in silver in the centre superimposed by the figures of two members of the Volkspolizei in gold carrying a banner in the colours of the national flag (horizontal stripes of black, red and yellow) with the state emblem in the centre. The flag was in the shape of an arc overlapping the upper medal circumference. Below the star, in gold lettering, were the words FÜR DIENST AM VOLKE (for service to the people); (reverse) left blank.

EHRENTITEL VERDIENTER VOLKSPOLIZIST DER DDR

Ribbon: Red with thin gold and black stripes towards the edges and two golden oak leaves at the base of the two parts of the ribbon which followed the Russian style.

Metal: Gold with red enamel.

Description: (Obverse) in the shape of a twelve point star with rayed arms with the state emblem (including the sheaves of wheat) in gold on a red enamel background in the centre surrounded by a circle of oak leaves.

The *Outstanding Police Officer of the GDR Award* was the highest honour available to any police officer and was awarded sparingly for acts of courage or outstanding police work above and beyond the call of duty. In October 1990 when the GDR ceased to exist the medals all passed into history. Medals for outstanding achievement were awarded in almost every field of work including metalworkers, bank workers, vets, teachers, those involved in the building and construction industry and farm workers. Very few occupations did not have some form of award available.

FEDERAL REPUBLIC OF GERMANY

In May 1949 the three occupying powers of the western part of Germany—Britain, France and the USA—recognised that political development of the country's two halves were diverging and unlikely to change, the chances of the Red Army leaving the Soviet zone were slim. In a move guaranteed to antagonise Stalin the *Bundesrepublik Deutschland* (BRD)—(the Federal Republic of Germany, more familiar before 1990 as West Germany) was established to enable the rebuilding of the country to progress without the delay, hindrance and political interference sure to come from Moscow.

The new German constitution forbade the wearing or display of any symbol of the Nazi Party or the swastika and this included many medals won by members of the German armed forces during the War although they may have been awarded for acts of bravery performed by ordinary men and women in extraordinary circumstances not of their making. On 26 July 1957 when the new Federal Republic had become established the government agreed to a proposal that veterans of the conflict should be allowed to wear their medals provided that all Nazi symbols had been removed. The three long service medals awarded to police officers during the Nazi regime were amongst those approved for wear, suitably altered. The Nazi eagle and swastika were removed from the obverse of all three awards and replaced by a wreath of oak leaves bearing the words FÜR TREUE DIENSTE IN DER POLIZEI (formerly inscribed on the reverse) in the centre of the medal and as a central medallion for the two crosses. The reverse carried the number of years service— 8, 18 or 25. The cornflower blue ribbon was retained but without the embroidered emblem previously seen on the two highest awards. The fourth medal in the series, introduced in 1944 to reward 40 years service but never produced during the Third Reich, was re-instated in 1957 and awarded to a few suitably qualified officers.

The provisions of the law included the medal most associated with the Third Reich—the Iron Cross (*Das Eiserne Kreuz*)—although it was a much older award dating from 1813 but renewed by Hitler in 1939 and altered in design to show the swastika in the centre of the obverse in place of the traditional oak twig. The German Cross (*Das Deutsche Kreuz*) and War Cross of Merit (*Das Kriegsverdienstkreuz*) were purely Nazi awards introduced by Hitler and both carried the swastika as a prominent feature. Their wear was outlawed immediately after the defeat of Germany in 1945 but holders were permitted to wear both medals in 1957 provided that the Nazi emblems were removed.

In the years following the end of the War policing activity was very much under the control of the occupying powers, it wasn't until the establishment of the BRD that the allied authorities considered handing responsibility back to the Germans. It was directed that each state could begin to organise its own police force in September 1949 but they were not finally authorised for more than a year after, in November 1950. Strict conditions were applied; they were not to be paramilitary although they could be armed on occasions and they were to have no involvement whatsoever in politics, a situation which would cause the ordinary police officer no problems at all. Each of the eleven German *länder* had its own separate force responsible to the state government in all matters, general duties (*Schutzpolizei*), criminal matters (*Kriminalpolizei*) and emergency duties such as riot control, civil unrest and training (*Bereitschaft Polizei*). Federal bodies existed to investigate federal or international crimes (*Bundeskriminalamt*), border duties (*Bundesgrenzschutz*) and to police the railways (*Bundesbahnpolizei*).

It was only a year from the appearance of the first cracks in the Berlin Wall on 9 November 1989 to the unification of the two Germanys into the present federal republic with the capital returned to Berlin as a symbolic gesture although the seat of government remained in Bonn for a further decade. The 15 districts of the former GDR were absorbed into the western political structure as five new *länder* bringing the number to sixteen, each with the same degree of autonomy enjoyed by the original eleven in the west. The policing structure also adapted to the western pattern although the absorption of officers from the *Volkspolizei* and their retraining and indoctrination into the ways of the west took some time.

The award of medals to German police officers is limited with no provision for national recognition of long service other than a certificate and modest increase in salary after 25 years and a further certificate at retirement which comes on reaching the age of 60. Any act of courage, lifesaving or particularly meritorious service by an officer from any one of the sixteen forces is recognised by the individual state authorities with the award of a medal which is available to any citizen, not solely police officers or members of the emergency services. Two types of award are generally available—the *Verdienstmedaille* (medal for merit) and *Rettungsmedaille* (lifesaving medal)—although some states have none, others have one but not the other and some states have both with the criteria for the award of either varying from state to state. There are also awards for more specific reasons available in one state only.

The award of the *Rettungsmedaille* to police officers is only made where the level of courage displayed far exceeds that of other citizens; the saving of human life or protection of the public from danger are expected as a normal part of an officers professional duty and awards are made only in exceptional circumstances. In Schleswig-Holstein, for example, only one officer has received the medal in the past several years such is the expectation placed on the police.

Covering an area of more than 35,751 square kilometres and with a population of 10 million the State of Baden-Württemberg (capital—Stuttgart) lies in the south-west corner of Germany bordered by France, Switzerland and Austria. It includes in its territory the industrial area around the capital and the Black Forest. The police force has a total strength of more than 24,000 officers in all branches. The Medal for Merit awarded by the Minister of the Interior is available to any citizen to mark an individual particularly meritorious or distinguished act or as a reward for service to the *Land* over a period of years.

VERDIENSTMEDAILLE (BADEN-WÜRTTEMBURG)

Instituted: 15 January 1975.

Ribbon: Half black, half yellow with bronze edges.

Metal: Silver.

Size: 26 mm.

Description: (Obverse) the Coat of Arms of the Land with its name below; (reverse) the words FÜR VERDIENSTE (for merit) in two lines with a stylised branch of laurel.

The coat of arms on the obverse (authorised in 1956) takes the form of a shield with three lions surmounted by six smaller shields carrying the arms of the six original states which make up the current *land*. The two supporters are a deer and a griffin taken from the arms of Baden and Württemberg. There is also a Lifesaving Medal awarded, introduced not long after the BRD was established.

RETTUNGSMEDAILLE (BADEN-WÜRTTEMBURG)

Instituted: 1953.

Ribbon: Gold with a white band towards the edges.

Metal: Silver.

Description: (Obverse) an outer circle with two rows of laurel leaves around a central medallion bearing the words FÜR - RETTUNG - AUS - GEFAHR in four lines; (reverse) the same design but with the name of the Land in the central medallion in three lines (BADEN - WÜRTTEM - BERG).

This original design was short-lived and changed in 1956 to one using the State Coat of Arms on the reverse with the State name inscribed above and two laurel leaves below. The double row of laurel leaves on the outer band of the reverse was changed to a single row more in the form of a wreath but the wording was unaltered. The ribbon design and colouring were unchanged.

The largest German state by some margin is Bavaria (*Bayern*) although it is not the most populous with approximately 11 million citizens compared with Rhineland-Westphalia (*Nordrhein-Westfalen*)—17 million—which includes the heavily industrialised area of the Ruhr and the cities of Cologne (*Köln*), Düsseldorf, Dortmund and Essen. Bavaria covers the whole of south-east Germany and is bordered by Austria to the south and the Czech Republic to the east. The State is today thought of as an integral part of Germany with the impression that it always has been although it was an independent territory (and a kingdom from 1805) until the end of the Great War and ruled by the same dynasty for more than 750 years. The present boundaries (with a few minor changes) were established in 1805 after ten years of occupation by the French, the Austrians and the French again.

Organised policing in Bavaria began in 1812 shortly after the kingdom was established with the forming of a gendarmerie along the lines of the French equivalent. Many towns and cities, including the capital—Munich (*München*)—had their own independent bodies although these were absorbed by the Gendarmerie over the years. The Gendarmerie survived the changes made to the structure of Germany after the Great War and the early years of the Nazis regime with their stronghold in the State. In 1936, three years after Hitler came to power, the Gendarmerie was abolished as the policing structure of the whole of Germany took on a more sinister rôle. In 1948, Bavaria became a *Land* of the new Federal Republic of Germany and the foundations for the present body were laid.

The first medal to be made exclusively available to police officers in Bavaria was introduced during the period between 1886 and 1912 when the Kingdom was ruled by a prince regent—Luitpold—the uncle of the two previous monarchs—Ludwig II and Otto—who were both certified as insane and unfit to rule. The *Security Service Decoration* was awarded to members of the Gendarmerie and the police force in Munich, in two classes, in recognition of 20 and 35 years service.

SICHERHEITSDIENST-AUSZEICHNUNG (ERSTE KLASSE)

Instituted: 22 February 1906.

Ribbon: Light blue with a white stripe towards each edge.

Metal: Gilded bronze.

Size: 40 mm.

Description: (Obverse) a cross with a small round knob at the end of each arm and a central medallion bearing a pattern of a crown superimposed on a rayed background. Between the arms of the cross were three laurel leaves finished in green enamel; (reverse) the central medallion showed a lion facing left and the four arms of the cross carried the inscription FÜR XXXV - JAHRE - DIENST - ZEIT.

The enamelled laurel leaves were omitted from the second class cross awarded for 20 years service and the number on the upper arm of the reverse was amended to XX. The medal became redundant when the rule of the Wittelsbach dynasty came to an end after the Great War and Bavaria was declared a socialist republic.

One legacy of the ruling family can still be seen in the Bavarian coat of arms—the striking pattern of light blue and white diamond shapes on the central shield of the full arms and the more commonly used small arms which consists of this shield surmounted by a crown. The pattern also appears on the badge of the Bavarian Police—a shield with the pattern on a background of a rayed twelve-point star.

In common with a number of other states, Bavaria introduced the first of a range of awards for its citizens—the Lifesaving Medal—within a few years of the establishment of the BRD.

Germany

RETTUNGSMEDAILLE—1952 TO 1974 (BAYERN)

Instituted: 22 December 1952.

Ribbon: Three light blue and two white stripes, all of equal width.

Metal: Silver.

Description: (Obverse) the full Coat of Arms of Bavaria with the words FREISTAT (above) and BAYERN (below) around the circumference; (original reverse) a wreath of oak leaves with the words FÜR - RETTUNG - AUS - GEFAHR in the central field.

In 1974 the design of the reverse was changed although the obverse and ribbon used were unaltered. The wreath of oak leaves was removed and replaced by a spring of three laurel leaves in the lower right of the medal and the inscription changed to read FÜR - OPFERBEREITEN - EINSATZ DES - EIGENEN - LEBENS (for a willingness to put at risk and sacrifice one's own life)

Ten years later a further medal was introduced, awarded in the name of the State President. *The Commendation Medal for Saving Life from Danger* was radically different from the two versions of the *Rettungsmedaille*. It is also known as the St Christopher Medal from the design on the obverse.

BELOBIGUNGSMEDAILLE FÜR RETTUNG AUS LEBENSGEFAHR

Instituted: 25 September 1984.

Ribbon: White with a broad central band in light blue bisected by a thin white lines and a thin light blue line at each edge.

Metal: Silver.

Description: (Obverse) the figure of St Christopher holding the child on his shoulders with the words OFFENTLICHE BELOBIGUNG (public commendation) around the upper circumference and FÜR RETTUNG AUS LEBENSGEFAHR (for saving a life in danger) around the lower; (reverse) the small Coat of Arms of Bavaria with the legend DER BAYERISCHE MINISTERPRÄSIDENT around the circumference.

page 95

Three of the German States are cities—Berlin, Bremen and Hamburg, the first being the largest and most populous by some margin. Berlin grew from a small fishing village in the 13th century to the capital city of one of the most powerful nations in Europe, arguably the world. From the end of the Second World War in 1945 November 1989 it was a potent symbol of the Cold War, divided by the Berlin Wall for a significant period of that time. The West Berlin Police faced problems unknown elsewhere, entirely surrounded by a hostile neighbour, the most likely flashpoint for the Third World War and with their freedom and ability to do their job frustrated by the presence of troops from the three western occupying powers. Working alongside the regular officers were a band of reserve volunteers, *die Freiwillige Polizei-Reserve*, whose service was recognised in 1984 by the introduction of a special medal, unique in the German policing system.

The decoration was awarded in three classes, two of which (first and second) were hung from a ribbon and a third special class which was worn as a breast badge. The design of the special class award differed slightly from the others in the shape of the cross but was broadly similar.

EHRENZEICHEN FÜR DIE FREIWILLIGE POLIZEI-RESERVE

Instituted: 1984.

Ribbon: Red with a white central stripe, all of equal width, and a line of white or yellow at the edges according to the class of the award.

Metal: Gold and silver with enamels.

Description: (Obverse) an enamelled cross patonce with concave arms and a motif of laurel branches between the arms. A central medallion in white enamel carries the badge of the Berlin Police—a twelve-point star with the city crest at the centre; (reverse) plain apart from a rectangular plaque with the words FÜR VERDIENSTE UM DIE FREIWILLIGE POLIZEI-RESERVE DES LANDES BERLIN (for service to the Volunteer Police Reserve of the State of Berlin) in two lines.

Germany

The badges of all German police forces follow the same pattern—the star with the State Crest at the centre, in the case of Berlin, a shield with a standing bear surmounted by a mural crown. The crest forms the centrepiece of all medals issued in Berlin including the Lifesaving Medal which follows a pattern of design seen in several of the German *länder*. Since its introduction the design has been altered once—in 1983.

RETTUNGSMEDAILLE (BERLIN)

Instituted: 28 May 1953.

Ribbon: Orange with a white band towards each edge.

Description: (Obverse) circular with the Berlin Crest superimposed on two branches of oak leaves with the words LAND BERLIN below; (reverse) a wreath of oak leaves around the circumference and the words FÜR - OPFERBEREITEN - EINSATZ - DES EIGENEN - LEBENS (for a willingness to put at risk and sacrifice ones own life) in five lines. A triple ring suspender is used.

The use of an orange, yellow or gold ribbon with white bands towards each edge is a feature of lifesaving awards made in several länder although it originated in 1833 as a Prussian medal and was subsequently adopted as a national award in the early days of the Third Reich. They were awarded to anyone who saved a life in circumstances of extreme peril or at great risk to their own life. With the establishment of the Federal Republic many states introduced their own award using the same, or similar, criteria.

Brandenburg, the new *Land* in the former GDR which surrounds Berlin, is one of the very few which does not award either a *Verdienstmedaille* or *Rettungsmedaille* although it is likely that this will change. Decorations are available to members of the Fire Service (regulars and volunteers) but not police officers. There is one commemorative medal, however, which was awarded to members of the police force, amongst others, following a flood in the summer of 1997 on the River Oder at the border between Germany and Poland. Two versions were produced, one for civilians and one for members of the emergency services, including police officers and border guards.

ODERFLUT-MEDAILLE (BRANDENBURG)

Instituted: 15 August 1997.

Ribbon: Half red, half white.

Metal: Bronze.

Description: (Obverse) the Coat of Arms of the State (an eagle in a shield) with the word LAND above and BRANDENBURG below, all within an outer band at the circumference inscribed with ODERFLUT 1997 at the top and IN DANKBARKEIT UND ANERKENNUNG (in gratitude and appreciation) in the lower half; (reverse) a map of the area flooded.

page 97

Police Medals of the World

The smallest *Land* in size and population is the old Hanseatic town of Bremen situated on the River Wesser surrounded by Lower Saxony. It covers an area of only 404 square kilometres and has a population of approximately 700,000, less than half that of the next smallest—Hamburg. The State awards a *Rettungsmedaille* although it is unusual in Germany in that it is not intended for wear and comes without a ribbon. The medal first appeared in November 1908 but the current regulations covering its award were re-instated in 1973. The choice of a silver or bronze award is made on the basis of the degree of courage displayed by the rescuer.

LEBENSRETTUNGSMEDAILLE (BREMEN)

Instituted: 8 May 1973.

Ribbon: None.

Metal: Silver and bronze.

Description: *(Obverse) The full Coat of Arms of Bremen with the words DER SENAT D FREIEN HANSESTADT BREMEN below; (reverse) a narrow wreath around the circumference with the words FÜR RETTUNG AUS GEFAHR in four lines in the central field.*

As an Imperial free city and member of the Hanseatic League, Bremen's position near the mouth of an important river has always assured it prominence in German history and led to the granting of special rights from the 10th century. This prominence and history led to the granting of *Land* status in 1948 when all other criteria seemed to point away from the decision. The Coat of Arms is based on a simple shield bearing the key of St Peter (the city's patron saint) with a crown above the shield and two lions as supporters. The key has appeared on city seals, coins and a number of documents from the early 13th century.

In addition to a *Rettungsmedaille*, the remaining city state of Hamburg was alone in once awarding a series of cloth merit badges (*Polizei-Verdienstabzeichen*) to its police officers between 1947 and 1981. A number of different grades of badge were awarded using different coloured cloth although they all followed the same basic design of a circular badge with a partial wreath of oak leaves and the letter "V" in the centre. The *Rettungsmedaille* awarded in Hamburg differed substantially from the design adopted by most other states.

RETTUNGSMEDAILLE (HAMBURG)

Instituted: 2 October 1951.

Ribbon: Red with a white band towards each edge.

Metal: Silver.

Size: 37 mm.

Description: (Obverse) the full Coat of Arms of Hamburg within a band around the upper two-thirds of the circumference inscribed with the words FREIE UND HANSESTADT HAMBURG. The lower quater of the medal bears the words FÜR RETTUNG AUS GEFAHR in Gothic script; (reverse) within an outer band an image of a man entwined in the tentacles of an octopus.

Hamburg achieved its prominence and status as a result of its position on the River Elbe in much the same way as Bremen grew on the Wesser. It was also an Imperial free city and member of the Hanseatic League although it spent many years under the control of the Kings of Denmark. It joined Germany in 1815 and was recognised as a state in 1919.

The State of Hessen is less well-known than many of the other German *länder* and is mainly rural in nature with only one city of any real size—Frankfurt-am-Main. The State has awarded a medal for saving life since 1953 although three versions have been produced one of which was used for one year only (1988) before being replaced by the current design. The original design was in use from 1953 to 1988 and was very similar to those awarded in other states. The ribbon design and colouring remained constant through the changes in medal design.

RETTUNGSMEDAILLE (HESSEN)

Instituted: 1953.

Ribbon: Orange with a white band towards each edge.

Metal: Silver.

Size: 25 mm.

Description: (Obverse) the Coat of Arms of the Land of Hessen with its name below; (reverse) a wreath of ten single oak leaves and the words FÜR RETTUNG AUS GEFAHR in the central field.

The present Arms of Hessen—a shield with a striped lion rampant all surmounted by a crown—are very simple compared with earlier versions which reflected the nature of Germany before 1871 and the number of principalities, counties and city states which had existed. The old royal arms of Hessen-Darmstadt had no fewer than nine separate shields although the present arms were at the centre. When the Federal Republic was established the simplified arms were adopted although they are very similar to those of the first Count of Hessen who died in 1234.

With the demise of the former GDR five new *länder* were created from the fifteen districts of East Germany and absorbed in the Federal Republic. Although civic heraldry in the east was as old as that in the west, the new states all needed new coats of arms. Mecklenburg-Western Pomerania (*Mecklenburg-Vorpommern*) is situated in the far north-east of modern Germany bordering Poland, covers an area of 22,500 square kilometres and has a population of over two million. The new arms of the *Land* were officially adopted in January 1991 and contain elements from the old territories of the area and which reflect its early history including periods when large areas were under Swedish domination. The shield of the arms is quartered with a bulls head (upper left and lower right), the Brandenburg eagle (lower left) and a griffin (upper right).

This new state was the first from the east to introduce a lifesaving medal following the pattern set in the west and adopted similar design features, ribbon colours and criteria. In the old GDR there was no room for any locally awarded orders, decorations or medals, everything was controlled from the centre with the national coat of arms being very prominent on many awards.

RETTUNGSMEDAILLE (MECKLENBURG-VORPOMMERN)

Instituted: 23 October 1992.

Ribbon: Orange with a white stripe at each edge.

Metal: Silver.

Size: 25 mm.

Description: (Obverse) the Coat of Arms of the Land with its name at the circumference on either side; (reverse) plain apart from the words FÜR RETTUNG AUS GEFAHR. A ring suspender was used.

The difficulties involved in the creation of new states experienced in 1990 was not new; in 1949 the western occupying powers in Germany came across the same problems as they established the new Federal Republic. Several of the existing states are a modern creation with little historical basis other than the fact that they lie in the same area of Germany. Lower Saxony (Niedersachsen) is a combination of several old territories, principalities and kingdoms situated in the north-west of Germany and has the *Land* of Bremen within its borders. The artificial nature of the State caused additional difficulties in finding a suitable coat of arms. The final design is very simple—a prancing horse in a shield with no further embellishments. A horse appeared on the arms of a number of prominent old families and was accepted as a reasonable compromise for the new state. The horse appears without the shield on the obverse of the Lifesaving Medal introduced in the State in 1953.

RETTUNGSMEDAILLE (NIEDERSACHSEN)

Instituted: 1953.

Ribbon: Gold with a white band towards each edge.

Description: (Obverse) the prancing horse taken from Coat of Arms of the Land; (reverse) a wreath of single oak leaves with the words FÜR RETTUNG AUS GEFAHR in the central field.

Lower Saxony is one of a few German states which issue medals to remember the work performed by the emergency services and others during and in the aftermath of natural disasters. Such medals have been awarded in Brandenburg (floods), Sachsen-Anhalt (flood) and Schleswig-Holstein (floods). The first medal awarded in Lower Saxony came after the devastation caused by storm damage and floods in the winter of 1962. The work of all involved was acknowledged by the issue of a special *Commemorative Medal on the Occasion of the Storm and Flood Catastrophe of 1962*. In 1975 the State was struck by a forest fire which caused a large amount of damage and some loss of life. Although the lions share of the work involved in containing and subsequently overcoming the fires fell to the Fire Service, a number of police officers were awarded the *Commemorative Medal on the Occasion of the Forest Fire Catastrophe of August 1975*.

GEDENKMEDAILLE AUS ANLAß DER STURMFLUTKATASTROPHE 1962

Instituted: 1962.

Ribbon: Red with a white band towards each edge.

Description: (Obverse) a stylised image of a large wave breaking against the shore; (reverse) the Coat of Arms of Lower Saxony and the words STURMFLUTKATASTROPHE 1962 around the lower three-quarters of the circumference.

GEDENKMEDAILLE AUS ANLAß DER WALDBRAND-KATASTROPHE IM AUGUST 1975

Instituted: 1976.

Ribbon: Red with a white central band, all of equal width.

Description: (Obverse) a stylised image of flames against a background of a forest represented by three trees; (reverse) plain apart from the words WALDBRAND - KATÁSTROPHE - IN - NIEDERSACHSEN - AUGUST - 1975. A simple ring suspender was used.

The industrial heartland of Germany lies in the State of Rhineland-Westphalia (*Nordrhein-Westfalen*), the most populous state although it is not the largest in area. The police force is the largest in Germany. The State awards few medals but has issued a lifesaving medal since 1951 with police officers being frequent recipients.

RETTUNGSMEDAILLE—1951 TO 1970 (NORDRHEIN-WESTFALEN)

Instituted: 16 October 1951.

Ribbon: Orange with a white band towards each edge.

Metal: Silver.

Size: 33 mm.

Description: (Obverse) the Coat of Arms of the State with the words LAND (above), NORDRHEIN (left) and WESTFALEN (right) at the circumference; (original reverse) a wreath of oak leaves with the inscription FÜR RETTUNG AUS GEFAHR in the central field.

In 1970 the design of the medal was subjected to minor changes although the use of the State Arms on the obverse, the inscription on the reverse and the ribbon colouring and pattern were retained. The shield on the obverse was reduced in size and the name of the State moved to the lower circumference, the word LAND was omitted. On the reverse the wreath was removed leaving only the inscription.

The Arms of the State have three elements, a rose taken from the former Principality of Lippe, a prancing stallion and a white fess to symbolise the River Rhine flowing through fertile green fields.

Police Medals of the World

The design of the *Rettungsmedaille* is very similar in most states that award them, the Coat of Arms usually appearing on the obverse and an inscription on the reverse which is usually the same. The criteria for the award of the medals differ slightly but they are most usually given where a life is saved and the recipient displays great courage and a disregard for his or her own life although the standards expected of police officers are substantial greater. The State of Rhineland-Palatinate (*Rheinland-Pfalz*) has awarded a Lifesaving Medal continuously since 1951 although the design was amended in 1971.

RETTUNGSMEDAILLE—1951 TO 1971 (RHEINLAND-PFALZ)

Instituted: 1951.

Ribbon: Gold with a white band towards each edge.

Metal: Silver.

Size: 33 mm.

Description: (Obverse) the Coat of Arms of the Land *with its name below at the lower circumference;* (reverse) the inscription FÜR RETTUNG AUS GEFAHR *within a wreath of oak leaves.*

The design changes made in 1971 were minor with all the elements of the earlier medal being retained in the same position. The Coat of Arms of the *Land* on the medals obverse consists of a shield divided into three parts with a lion in the lower third, a red cross on a white background at the upper left and a wheel in the upper right. The shield is surmounted by a crown. The *Land* is situated in the west of Germany north of Baden-Württemberg and bordering France, Luxembourg and Belgium. Its capital is the city of Mainz (represented by the wheel of the arms) and it has within its territory the renowned wine producing regions of the Rhine and Mosel. The oldest city in Germany—Trier—also lies within its borders close to the border with Luxembourg at the entrance to the Mosel Valley. The importance of the city is recognised by the inclusion of the cross on the State Coat of Arms. The third element—the lion—and originated in the 11th century as the arms of the ruling family of the Pfalz (Palatinate). It is a medium sized state with an area of 19,849 square kilometres and a population of approximately four million.

page 104

The smallest *Land*, apart from the three cities, is not an historical state and was created only in 1919 by the League of Nations. Saarland lies on the border with France and Luxembourg and covers an area of only 2,570 square kilometres with a population of just over one million. Almost from its creation it has been the subject of dispute between France and Germany in much the same way as Alsace and Lorraine have been argued and fought over. After the Second World War it was ruled by France and not returned to Germany until 1957, many years after the establishment of the Federal Republic. There is an independence movement in the State and the coat of arms adopted between 1945 and 1957 can still be seen although new official arms were granted when it was returned to Germany. These arms are those used on the obverse of the *Rettungsmedaille* awarded in the State.

RETTUNGSMEDAILLE (SAARLAND)

Instituted: 24 November 1958.

Ribbon: Red with a white band at each edge.

Metal: Silver.

Size: 25 mm.

Description: (Obverse) the Coat of Arms of the State (a quartered shield containing elements indicative of its past) with the name below; (reverse) a wreath of laurel with the inscription FÜR RETTUNG AUS GEFAHR in the central field.

The use of a wreath with an inscription in the central field on the obverse of a medal is common in many countries. In the UK and the Commonwealth it is most usually a wreath of laurel leaves, occasionally oak and sometimes a combination of the two. On the medals awarded in the German states any wreath is usually of oak leaves, Saarland being one of the few exceptions. The State of Schleswig-Holstein, situated in the far north of the country bordering Denmark, followed the more traditional pattern when it introduced a *Rettungsmedaille* shortly after the Federal Republic was established whose design was almost identical to those issued in Rheinland-Pfalz, Hessen and Bayern with the inscription on the reverse contained within a wreath of single oak leaves. The design, however, was used for only three years (1951 to 1954) when a more distinctive pattern was adopted which gave the oak leaf symbol more prominence than its use as a wreath. The ribbon colour of orange and white and design which was identical to ribbons used in Hessen and Nordrhein-Westfalen was retained.

RETTUNGSMEDAILLE—SINCE 1954 (SCHLESWIG-HOLSTEIN)

Instituted: 1954.

Ribbon: Orange with a white band towards each edge.

Metal: Bronze.

Size: 33 mm.

Description: (Obverse) the Coat of Arms of the State with its name around the upper circumference in ornate script; (reverse) a motif of three oak leaves with an acorn at the centre placed centrally on the medal and the words FÜR RETTUNG AUS GEFAHR around the circumference, also in ornate script. A simple ring suspender was used.

   The Coat of Arms of the State are a simple halved shield with two lions (taken originally from the Danish National Arms) on the left to represent Schleswig and a stylised nettle leaf on the right to represent Holstein which has its origins in the 13th century and comes from the Counts of Schaumburg who also ruled Holstein. The meaning is unknown.
   The position of the State on Germany's North Sea coast brings with it the risk of flooding in severe weather. One of the most severe storms and subsequent floods in February 1962 led to the issue of a special commemorative medal for those involved in rescue work during the storm and clearing up operations afterwards.

STURMFLUTMEDAILLE 1962

Instituted: 1962.

Ribbon: Blue with a red central stripe flanked by white stripes.

Metal: Bronze.

Description: (Obverse) a stylised scene of a large wave crashing over a house; (reverse) the two elements of the State Coat of Arms without the shield placed centrally with the word STURMFLUT at the upper circumference and the date 16/17 FEBRUAR 1962 around the lower circumference half. A simple ring suspender was used.

   The German people are proud of their federal system of government and individual *länder* are keen to emphasise their autonomy. This desire can be seen in the use of the term *"Freistaat"* in official documents. When the new State of Saxony (*Sachsen*) was created in 1990 and subsequently introduced its Lifesaving Decoration nine years later it used the term on the medal to reinforce its status, particularly important after the years behind the Iron Curtain.

page 106

LEBENSRETTUNGSEHRENZEICHEN (SACHSEN)

Instituted: 14 June 1999.

Ribbon: Dark green with a white central band, all of width and narrow yellow edges.

Metal: Silver.

Description: (Obverse) the Coat of Arms of the State (a shield striped horizontal and crossed top left to bottom right by a crown-ring) with the words FREISTAAT (upper) and SACHSEN (lower) at the circumference; (reverse) a partial wreath of oak leaves at the lower circumference and the words FÜR RETTUNG AUS GEFAHR at the top with the central field left blank for the name of the recipient and date to be engraved.

The new State of Thüringen lies at what was formerly the border between the two Germanies and suffered from the worst aspects of the neglect of the communist rulers particularly in the areas close to the dividing line. The disappearance of the border in 1990 and subsequent new found freedoms led to massive regeneration of the area which has some of the finest old German towns—Weimar, Erfurt and Eisenach—as well as a reminder of the darkest days of German history—the concentration camp at Buchenwald a few miles from the State capital at Weimar. The *Land* is predominantly rural and covers an area of 15,209 square kilometres and a population of more than 2.5 million.

Four years after the State had become a part of the Federal Republic the authorities introduced a *Rettungsmedaille* to bring the local honours system into line with the western states. The design of the medal followed the pattern familiar elsewhere on its obverse and reverse although the authorities resisted the temptation to adopt the usual orange and white ribbon and chose one very similar to Decoration for Service in the Volunteer Police Reserve awarded in Berlin.

RETTUNGSMEDAILLE (THÜRINGEN)

Instituted: 18 August 1994.

Ribbon: Red with a white central band, all of equal width, and a gold stripe at each edge.

Metal: Silver.

Description: (Obverse) the Coat of Arms of the State (a shield containing a striped lion rampant and eight stars) with its name below; (reverse) a wreath of oak leaves around the inscription FÜR RETTUNG AUS GEFAHR in the central field.

Although the issue of medals by the individual states in Germany is not unique—Austria has a similar system—it is a natural consequence of the federal system of government and contrasts with the procedure elsewhere in western Europe where there is more centralisation.

Officers proudly display their medals at an inspection parade.

Mobile unit on parade circa 1935.

GREAT BRITAIN

Police officers serving in Great Britain today can expect to be awarded a medal after 22 years service with good conduct unless they rise to the very highest ranks or perform an act of great courage which is thought worthy of national recognition—no mean feat given the seeming reluctance of the authorities to do so—when they could become eligible for others. Acts of gallantry are rewarded according to the level of courage displayed. The highest award is the George Cross which is only given where there is a risk of death of 90 to 100 %, followed by the George Medal (50 to 90%), Queen's Gallantry Medal (20 to 50%) and the Queen's Commendation for Brave Conduct where a risk of up to 20% is necessary before an award is considered. Where courage is displayed but is not thought to merit national recognition or where this is refused by the Home Office, chief constables can award their own commendations.

The Long Service and Good Conduct Medal, the standard issue which all police officers receive, commonly referred to as awarded for "22 years undetected crime", was introduced in 1951 after a long tussle with those who thought it unnecessary to reward police officers for simply doing their job and keeping out of serious trouble for 22 years.

Most medals issued by watch committees and local city or borough police forces were awarded for long service and good conduct with a few having provision in their conditions for recognition of acts of gallantry by officers (Plymouth City for example). Others introduced them solely to reward bravery. In March 1904 the Chief Constable of Reading Borough Police—Captain John Henderson—suggested to his Watch Committee that it should introduce such a medal to reward officers for saving life or for acts of special bravery, a suggestion that was accepted at the next meeting held a month later on 26 April.

At the time there was no national recognition available for any acts of bravery performed by police officers. Rewards were sometimes given locally in the form of a gratuity or the presentation of a watch, clock or similar article although this varied greatly from place to place. *The Police Review and Parade Gossip* once carried reports from forces across the country of "honourable mentions and presentations" which included details of rewards and gratuities for gallantry or meritorious service. In Canterbury in May 1896 Sergeant Hollands was *"awarded a gratuity of £1 in recognition of his conduct in connection with the cases of theft from Messrs. Court Bros"*. and in Lancashire a month later it was reported that *"rewards have been granted to the following for meritorious acts performed in the execution of their duty:- PCs Bowen, Rushton and Radcliffe, £1 each, and PC Haines, £2"*. Similar reports were found in almost every edition. Members of the public were also allowed to reward officers personally with the authority of the chief constable but no national form of recognition existed.

This was changed in 1909 with the introduction of the King's Police Medal (KPM) which was awarded for distinguished service or gallantry although the design of the medal was the same. The first recognition of the difference came in 1933 with the additional of thin red lines to the blue and white ribbon to signify that the award was for gallantry. The following year saw the reverse of the medals changed with the legend *for distinguished service* or *for gallantry* appearing in the exergue. In 1947 the Chief Constable's Associations of the UK put forward a recommendation that the award for gallantry should be re-designed as a cross and re-named the King's Police and Fire Service Cross to distinguish it clearly from those awarded for distinguished service—the suggestion did not find favour in government circles and was never pursued. In all probability the reasons lay in the class distinctions then applicable in the Armed Forces and society in general—"crosses" for gallantry (DFC, MC and DSC) were available to commissioned officers and medals (DFM, MM etc) were for "other ranks". Most recipients of the KPM for gallantry were constables or sergeants and awards for distinguished service were almost invariably given to high ranking officers—the thought of "other ranks" receiving crosses and officers being awarded "medals" was never likely to be received with much enthusiasm.

When Queen Elizabeth II ascended to the throne the medal became known as the Queen's Police Medal (QPM) and the reverse was re-designed but the difference between the two retained. From 1951 the gallantry award was only ever made posthumously and became effectively redundant in 1977 with changes to the Royal Warrant covering the grant of the George Medal.

The George Medal (GM) was introduced by King George VI in September 1940 as a direct result of the need to reward members of the public, including police officers, fire-fighters and the other emergency services, for acts of courage performed during the blitz on British towns and cities. It could not, however, be awarded posthumously. The KPM for Gallantry was the equivalent of the GM for police officers who lost their lives in the course of their duty in circumstances where the GM would have been awarded had they lived. When the criteria for the award of the GM were changed in 1977 to allow it to be given posthumously the need for a separate medal for police officers ceased and the QPM for Gallantry fell into disuse.

Police officers are rewarded in the same fashion as other members of the public for acts of bravery. Today they are eligible for the George Cross, the George Medal, the Queen's Gallantry

page 109

Medal or the Queen's Commendation for Brave Conduct, dependent upon the level of courage displayed, in exactly the same way as other civilians. There is some suggestion that the degree of courage expected from police officers in the face of danger is higher than members of the public due to the nature of their work and that the level of any award given in similar circumstances would reflect this. Certainly the level of awards made today appears to be less than that of the past.

The British Empire Medal for Gallantry was frequently awarded to police officers most noticeably during the Second World War until its abolition in 1974 with the introduction of the Queen's Gallantry Medal. A number of societies concerned with particular aspects of protecting and saving life awarded medals to police officers and other civilians—the RSPCA, the Royal Humane Society, the Society for the Protection of Life from Fire and many others have long recognised the need to reward those who performed acts of bravery within their particular area of interest and continue to do so today.

Those forces which issued their own awards for bravery retained them long after the introduction of the national awards. Still others introduced local forms of recognition notwithstanding the existence of a suitable national decoration for most circumstances.

In common with official medals in the UK the majority of those produced by police forces and watch committees used ribbons which were of a conventional design—a base colour with stripes of varying colours and widths running vertically, or a single colour. A great number employed the traditional police colour of dark blue with the stripes usually being of red, sometimes green and occasionally white. Awards for gallantry only most commonly hung from a ribbon of a single colour—crimson in Manchester, royal blue in Brighton and Aberdeen and red in Rochdale—a simple, almost classical design, as if to signify the special reason for the award—an act of courage.

Of all locally issued medals, two in particular stand out for their unusual use of colour or unique design. The Exeter City Police Long Service and Efficiency Medal awarded between 1928 and 1939 hung from an attractive grass green and white ribbon—the city colours—and the Cardiff City Police and Fire Brigade Conspicuous Bravery Medal used yellow as the basic colour with three red chevrons to produce a ribbon whose design was probably unique amongst all medals issued in the UK.

The symbolism of medal ribbon colours is not well recorded and a somewhat neglected aspect of medal research. One of the earliest campaign medals issued where the colours of the ribbon are significant and recorded is the Central Africa Medal of 1895 awarded mainly to local forces for services in Central Africa between 1891 and 1898. The ribbon consists of three vertical stripes of equal width in black, white and terracotta to represent the Africans, Europeans and Indians who were involved. The campaign to re-conquer the Sudan, fought in 1896–97, led to the issue of the Queen's Sudan Medal in 1899 with a ribbon where the symbolism has been recorded. It is half-yellow and half-black to represent the desert and Sudanese nation separated by a narrow crimson stripe to symbolise the British forces. Ribbons of other medals issued during the reign of Queen Victoria undoubtedly have a meaning although few are widely known.

Probably the most well-known examples of the symbolic colouring of ribbons are the eight campaign stars issued for the Second World War, the design in each case representing those who took part, the theatre of war or the conditions of the combat. The 1939–45 Star, the most widely issued of the eight, has a simple ribbon of three colours in vertical stripes all of equal width—dark blue, red and light blue—to represent the three Armed Services in order of seniority. The three colours with the same meaning but of differing widths also appear on the ribbon of the Africa Star on a buff background to symbolise the desert. Where stars were awarded to one particular arm of the services, the Atlantic Star, for example, which went, in the main, to the Royal and Commonwealth Navies, the colours were chosen to represent the theatre of operations—in this instance being of watered silk in blue, white and green to signify the ocean. The most coveted of all stars—the Air Crew Europe Star—awarded to aircrew only, had a pale blue background to signify the sky with black edges (for night-flying) separated from the blue by narrow yellow stripes to represent searchlights.

Most medals awarded in the UK had ribbons of conventional design and colouring but recently authorised issues in Australia and New Zealand include some striking designs and vivid colouring. The Queen's Service Order and Medal of New Zealand employs a red, white and black ribbon based on a traditional Maori stepped pattern used to signify the stairway to Heaven. In Australia, the Fire Service Medal uses the national colours of green and yellow but with a central red stripe in the shape of a flame. The Police Overseas Service Medal bases its ribbon on the chequered police hat band in black and white and is very striking.

LONG SERVICE AND GOOD CONDUCT MEDAL

Instituted: 14 June 1951.

Ribbon: Dark blue with twin white stripes towards each edge.

Metal: Cupro-nickel.

Size: 36 mm.

Description: (Obverse) the head of the reigning monarch; (reverse) a standing female figure representing justice holding a wreath in her right hand and set of scales in her left with a circumscription reading FOR EXEMPLARY POLICE SERVICE. A truncheon is seen in the exergue. The medals are engraved around the rim with the rank and name of the recipient. A straight bar suspender is employed.

The medal is awarded to officers of all ranks in any police force in the United Kingdom. In May 1956 it was extended to include police forces in Australia, Papua New Guinea and Nauru but replaced in Australia in 1975 by the National Medal.

Officers who achieve the rank of superintendent or above could find themselves being awarded the Queen's Police Medal for Distinguished Service (QPM) although the higher the rank the more likely the award with chief officers being the most usual recipients. Officers of lower rank than superintendent have been awarded the medal although this is an unusual event.

QUEEN'S POLICE MEDAL FOR DISTINGUISHED SERVICE

Instituted: 19 May 1954.

Ribbon: Silver with two broad dark blue stripes.

Metal: Silver.

Size: 36 mm.

Description: (Obverse) the head of H M Queen Elizabeth; (reverse) a robed standing figure with his right arm resting on a sword and the left on a shield on which is inscribed TO GUARD MY PEOPLE. A laurel wreath is in the exergue and the words FOR DISTINGUISHED POLICE SERVICE are inscribed around the circumference in an outer band. A ring suspender is employed and the recipients name, rank and force are engraved around the rim.

The QPM was introduced as the Kings Police Medal (KPM) on 7 July 1909 during the reign of Edward VII and carried his effigy on the obverse. It was instituted to reward courage and devotion to duty by police officers and originally hung from a silver ribbon with a single blue stripe, the central silver stripe was added in 1916. The obverse of the first medal made no distinction between medals awarded for distinguished service or gallantry and differed from later medals by having the robed figure on the obverse with a spray of laurel in the exergue. The first recognition of the special nature of awards for gallantry was made in 1933 when thin crimson lines were added to the blue stripes to signify to differentiate the two types of award. Later the same year inscriptions were added to the reverse to indicate if the medal was awarded "for gallantry" or "distinguished service" with these words written in the exergue. This design remained until Queen Elizabeth ascended to the throne and the reverse was altered to the existing design.

In 1940 when the blitz of British towns and cities had started the name was changed to recognise the courage of the Fire Service to the King's Police and Fire Services Medal. The design and criteria for its award remained the same until it was discontinued in 1954 and a separate medal was established for the Fire Service when the QPM was introduced. From 1950 onward the KPM for Gallantry was only ever awarded posthumously, it was in effect the police equivalent of the George Medal where recipients lost their lives and the GM could not be awarded. When the Royal Warrant of November 1977 made it possible for the George Medal to be given posthumously the QPM for Gallantry effectively became redundant and its award ceased.

The KPM was available to police officers in the UK and all parts of the British Empire and large numbers were awarded in India, Burma, Australia, South Africa and the smaller nations until the 1930s when a range of separate medals was introduced although the entitlement to the KPM remained. In 1932 the Indian Police Medal was introduced followed in 1937 by the Burma Police Medal and a special bi-lingual version of the KPM for South Africa.

The South African medal was very similar to the basic medal but with the reverse re-designed to incorporate the reason for the award and the inscription on the shield in English and Afrikaans. The shield was inscribed TO GUARD MY PEOPLE and OM MY VOLK TE BESKERM and the reasons for the award moved from the exergue to the circumference. Awards for gallantry were inscribed FOR BRAVERY (left) and VIR DAPPERHEID (right) and awards for distinguished service FOR DISTINGUISHED SERVICE (left) and VIR VOORTRFLIKE DIENS (right). Minor changes were made to the obverse. It was continued as the Queen's Police Medal (South Africa) after 1952 but withdrawn when South Africa left the Commonwealth. About 50 were awarded of both types.

With the advent of these more local medals the numbers of KPMs being awarded decreased and fell further after 1938 when the Colonial Police Medal was authorised by King George VI.

Apart from the national medals available to police officers in the UK a number of forces have awarded their own rewards for long service or gallantry or to commemorate a royal event. These were unofficial medals but some continued after the introduction of the KPM for Gallantry in 1909 and the Long Service and Good Conduct Medal in 1951 although they were all were discontinued many years ago.

ABERDEEN CITY CONSTABULARY MEDAL FOR SPECIAL SERVICE

Instituted: 5 July 1909.

Ribbon: Royal blue.

Metal: Silver.

Size: 39 mm.

Description: (Obverse) the Coat of Arms of the City of Aberdeen with the legend AWARDED BY THE TOWN COUNCIL OF ABERDEEN around the circumference; (reverse) a laurel wreath with the inscriptions FOR SPECIAL SERVICE in two lines at the top and CITY CONSTABULARY in larger letters placed centrally with a space between the two for the rank and name of the recipient and the date of the award. The exergue has a motif of a constables helmet superimposed on a pair of crossed truncheons. The ribbon was attached by a ring suspender with a claw fitting of unusual design.

Aberdeen City was the only Scottish police force to award medals to regular officers apart from one commemorative issue in Dumbartonshire. Many forces—Edinburgh, Govan and Dundee for example—recognised the services of members of the Special Constabulary during the Great War by issuing medals but regular officers weren't rewarded by any force in Scotland before or after the War other than Aberdeen until very recently with the introduction of the Tayside Police Medal.

The Aberdeen medal was first awarded on 5 July 1909 to the widow of Constable Say, an officer who had lost his life attempting to effect an arrest. It was cast in gold although later issues were of silver. The Chief Constable of the Constabulary had thought for some time that acts of courage or specially distinguished conduct by his officers should be recognised and rewarded. The death of Constable Say in the course of his duty prompted the Town Council to agree with him and authorise the medal.

The coat of arms on the obverse depicted three castle turrets within a shield surmounted by a King's crown below a banner containing the town motto—*bon accord*. The motto is thought to be a reminder of a battle with the English during the reign of King Robert the Bruce between 1274 and 1329. The town was loyal to him and had supported him during his struggle and was consequently attacked by the English. Legend has it that the Castle of Aberdeen was stormed by English troops who *"were killed all in one night"* with the watchword for the campaign being *"bon accord"*—retained as the town motto thereafter in memory of the victory. The three castle turrets on the shield are accepted as a representation of the fortifications which once stood on the three hills on which the town was founded—Castle Hill, Windmill Hill and St Catherine's Hill.

An example of the medal exists with the obverse showing the arms of Aberdeen as described but with the addition of the supporters (leopards) on either side and no crown. It also lacks the circumscription and has a plain reverse. It is possible that this version was a pattern for the authorised piece and never issued. Similarly it may have been struck for a totally different reason and have little or nothing to do with the later medal or the police.

One month after the first award a silver medal was presented to Constable William Ritchie *"who had specially distinguished himself in effecting an arrest of a burglar in Torry the previous February"*. Constable Ritchie was working night duty, passing the University Bar in Sinclair Road at about 4 am, when he heard the sound of breaking glass coming from the bar and went to investigate the cause. He came across two men searching the bar and moved towards them. When he was seen one of the men dived through a window managing to escape leaving Constable Ritchie to tackle the remaining felon. A heavy object was thrown at him followed by a fifteen minute fierce struggle between the two men as each tried to overpower the other, Constable Ritchie to effect an arrest and the burglar to make good his escape.

William Ritchie prevailed, eventually succeeding in binding the feet of his assailant with a clothes line and subduing him. Constable Ritchie took a hard kick to his left temple during the struggle which left him with a prominent swelling for the rest of his life. His assailant served a lengthy term of imprisonment with hard labour for his pains.

In all probability Constable Ritchie was fighting for his life. His assailant was prepared to use any means at his disposal to escape and, as the example of Constable Say showed, the threat of death was very real for officers in the early years of policing with no effective means of summoning help if such help was readily available. Constable Ritchie fully deserved the recognition he received.

Professional police forces as we know them today were established in Scotland many years before they were first seen in either England or Wales. The first properly established force in England is believed to be the Preston County Borough Police, formed in 1815. It existed as a separate body until 1969 when it was amalgamated with the Lancashire County Constabulary along with a number of other borough forces. The Force was relatively short-lived in this form, lasting only until 1974 when large parts were lost to help form the Cumbria, Greater Manchester, Cheshire and Merseyside forces which exist today—overnight it went from the largest provincial force in the country with 6,674 officers to one of medium size with its authorised establishment more than halved to 2,743. Its headquarters lies close to Preston, the oldest of its constituent forces.

In Wales, the Brecon Borough Police was established in 1829—the first in the Principality—and survived for 60 years until it merged with the Brecon County Constabulary. Changes in the title to the Mid-Wales Police (1948) and Dyfed-Powys (1968) were followed in 1974 by the loss of some territory as the Gwent and South Wales forces were formed. Brecon remains a divisional headquarters of the Dyfed-Powys Police.

The two oldest forces in the United Kingdom were in Scotland—the Blairgowrie Burgh Police was first formed as far back as 1757, almost 60 years before anything similar was seen in England and 72 years ahead of Brecon Borough. It ceased to exist as a separate body on its amalgamation with the Perthshire Constabulary in 1875. It now forms a part of the Tayside Police. The Kelso Burgh Police, also formed in 1757, lasted a few years longer than Blairgowrie (until 1881) before it too became a part of a much larger shire constabulary. Kelso is now within the area of the Lothian and Borders Police. The oldest large police force in the UK is Glasgow City, established in 1800.

The amalgamations of the 1960s and 1970s saw the demise of a large number of long established county, city and borough forces with magnificent names. The Lothian and Borders Police doesn't have quite the same ring as the Berwick, Roxborough and Selkirk Constabulary and the Cumbria Constabulary in England is far less attractive a name than the Cumberland, Westmorland and Carlisle Constabulary which it replaced in 1967 together with parts of Lancashire and West Yorkshire

The Aberdeen City Constabulary was founded in 1818 and ceased to exist as a separate force after 157 years in 1975 when it was amalgamated with the Scottish North-Eastern Counties Police to form the Grampian Police. The evolution of the Grampian Police provides a good example of the development of policing in the United Kingdom and how mergers and amalgamations over many years have resulted in the loss of some wonderful place names and a certain amount of local identity. Following on from the establishment of the Aberdeen City Constabulary came two shire forces in 1840—Banffshire and Aberdeenshire—with Kincardineshire joining them a year later and Elginshire in 1844. The final shire force—Nairnshire—was formed in 1850 along with the first of the small burgh forces at Elgin.

During 1859 four further burgh forces at Nairn, Macduff, Banff and Fraserburgh were established leading to full professional policing arrangements across the whole of the region. These four forces were to last for a short time only with Nairn and Banff being merged with their respective shire forces, Fraserburgh joining with Aberdeenshire in 1866 and Macduff Burgh also merging with Nairnshire four years later in 1870. The oldest of the burgh forces—Elgin—was the last to be absorbed by its shire force in 1893 leaving the region policed by the four shire forces and Aberdeen City. A period of stability followed, the only change occurring in 1919 with the re-naming of Elginshire to Morayshire.

In 1930 the Nairnshire and Morayshire Constabularies were amalgamated to form the Moray and Nairn force, a situation which was to remain until 1949 when the four shire forces were brought together in one large force with an awful name—the Scottish North-East Counties Constabulary. The final act occurred on 16 April 1975, the Aberdeen City Police joining the amalgamated constabularies to form the Grampian Police which exists today.

BIRKENHEAD BOROUGH POLICE DIAMOND JUBILEE GOOD SERVICE MEDAL

Instituted: 13 September 1897.

Ribbon: Red with two stripes of dark blue all of equal width.

Metal: Silver and bronze.

Size: 39 mm.

Description: (Obverse) left-facing conjoined Young Head and Old Head of Queen Victoria surrounded with the inscription VICTORIA DIAMOND JUBILEE above and the dates 1837 - 1897 below; (reverse) the Coat of Arms of Birkenhead and town motto in a scroll all contained within an oak and laurel wreath tied at its base and surrounded by the legend FOR GOOD SERVICE (above) and BIRKENHEAD CONSTABULARY (below). The recipient's name, rank and number were engraved on the rim. A plain straight swivelling suspender was employed. It was attached to the tunic by a plain flat buckle.

Long service medals awarded by police forces and watch committees were issued to officers irrespective of rank provided that they met a number of criteria, usually a certain length of service with good conduct and no defaults recorded on their personal records. The length of qualifying service varied and any defaults could be expunged on the authority of the Chief Constable and Watch Committee to allow the award of a medal to an officer with a good career other than a minor lapse or two. The one common feature was that they were only ever issued to serving police officers—with one known exception and a suspicion that there were others although something of a mystery exists.

In September 1897 the Birkenhead Watch Committee authorised the issue of a medal to celebrate the Diamond Jubilee of Queen Victoria to officers with 20 or more years service. The medal was struck in bronze for constables and sergeants and in silver for officers of inspector and above. A very unusual award, however, was made to the Prosecuting Solicitor for the Birkenhead Police—a Mr James Fearnley.

James Fearnley was a local man, born at Moreton close to Birkenhead on 25 May 1865, the son of the local rector. He chose a career in the legal profession, studying in Liverpool until he

page 115

qualified in 1887. Eight years later he was appointed as the Corporation Assistant Solicitor in his home town and was to spend the rest of his career in public service with the Corporation. He became the Deputy Town Clerk and Prosecuting Solicitor in 1899, the Town Clerk in September 1907 and, finally Clerk of the Peace of the Borough in 1916. He married a Liverpool girl in 1899 and had two children, a boy born in 1900 and a girl in 1902. He died at the comparatively young age of 59 on 20 April 1924.

In Victorian times and for many years after the Magistrates Courts were known and accepted as police courts and there was no perceived need for there to be any appearance of independence between the two unlike the latter half of the 20th century when it was seen to be of great importance and ultimately led to the formation of a totally independent prosecuting body—the Crown Prosecution Service. Prosecutions in court were very often conducted by police officers, usually the local superintendent or head constable, but he was advised by the Borough Solicitor where necessary and represented in court in particularly complex matters. The Office of Chief Constable in most police forces was a more political appointment than nowadays with the responsibility for running an effective police force being a matter for all Officers of the Corporation through the Watch Committee. When the commemorative medal was awarded in Birkenhead, it would have been quite understandable for certain members of the Corporation such as James Fearnley to be included.

The *Police Review and Parade Gossip* published on 17 September 1897 carried a report of the presentation of the medals at Police Buildings, Birkenhead a week earlier and reported that they were awarded to the Chief Constable, Superintendent and ten inspectors. The twelve bronze medals struck were all awarded to serving constables and sergeants. All medals (silver and bronze) were engraved on the lower rim with the rank, number and name of the recipient (for police officers) and the name and position held for James Fearnley and any other civilian recipients. The medals were presented in a black box of issue which carried the recipients rank and number in gold lettering. This was the only occasion when medals were awarded by the Birkenhead Borough Police. There is no mention of an award being made to James Fearnley, any member of the Watch Committee or other Corporation Officers. The medal named to James Fearnley could have been struck privately or there could have been a separate issue to the borough worthies not reported in *Police Review*—a little mystery. The silver medal named to James Fearnley hung from a plain blue ribbon.

The shield of the town coat of arms depicted on the medal reverse is quartered with each part being representative of an area of the town and its history. The upper right quarter shows an oak tree representing Tranmere, the lower right depicting two lions to indicate Oxton and the bottom left with a star to represent Bebbington. The meaning of the single lion shown in the upper left quarter must be considered in conjunction with the crozier (abbot's staff) which runs down the centre of the shield and forms a cross. These two features were taken from the great seal of Birkenhead Priory—a Benedictine Abbey founded in 1150—and are included to recognise the importance of the priory in the towns history. The parts of the shield also illustrate the meaning of the motto—*ubi fides ibi lux et robur* (where there is faith there is light and strength). The cross and crozier indicate faith (*fides*), the star and two crescent moons at the top of the shield represent light (*lux*) and the lions and the oak tree mean strength (*robur*)—the three elements of the motto. The arms were granted on 28 August 1878.

The Birkenhead Town Police was founded in June 1833, three years before the majority of borough police forces, by a special Act of Parliament with five officers only. By 1856 this had risen to 27. In 1889 the name was changed to the Birkenhead County Borough Police. The Force existed separately until 1967 when it was merged into the Cheshire Constabulary together with Stockport Borough and Wallasey County Borough. On 1 April 1974 parts of the Wirral in Cheshire, including Birkenhead, were amalgamated with the Liverpool and Bootle Police to form the Merseyside Police.

Great Britain

BOLTON BOROUGH POLICE GOOD SERVICE MEDAL

Instituted: 30 July 1913.

Ribbon: Medium blue with a 5 mm red stripe at each edge.

Metal: Silver.

Size: 36 mm.

Description: Obverse) the Coat of Arms of the Borough of Bolton surrounded by a raised outer band which bore the legend FOR GOOD SERVICE in the upper half and BOLTON BOROUGH POLICE in the lower; (reverse) a wreath of laurel tied at the base with a bow around a central field in which was inscribed PRESENTED - BY - THE - WATCH COMMITTEE - date of the award) in four lines. The recipient's rank, number, name and date of joining were engraved around the lower rim. An ornate scrolled suspender was used attached to the medal by a claw fitting.

The medal was awarded until the outbreak of the Second World War when it fell into disuse and was finally superseded by the national long service and good conduct medal in 1951. The medals were cast in silver for issue irrespective of rank although there is evidence that bronze versions were struck. One such medal was dated 1888 and named to a sergeant. It is possible that early awards followed the pattern seen in some forces of a distinction between senior officers and constable and sergeants with the former receiving silver medals and the latter bronze. The date on the medal seen could have been the date of the sergeants appointment which would have qualified him for the award in 1913, shortly after its introduction, possibly one of the very first made. Later issues in silver were made irrespective of the rank. When the change was made isn't known.

Initially the medal was awarded for 25 years service with good conduct and no adverse record on the officer's personal file. In 1931 the qualifying period was reduced to 20 years and provision was made for the issue of clasps to denote each additional period of five years service. The clasps were plain and of the slip-on type inscribed with OVER 25 YEARS and OVER 30 YEARS and the recipient's details engraved on the reverse.

The shield of the arms on the obverse is divided top left to bottom right by two bands with a second shield at the bottom left and an arrow, mule spinning spindle and weaving shuttle together in the top right corner. The small shield contains the Lancaster red rose to indicate that it is the Bolton in Lancashire and not Yorkshire or Northumberland. The three devices on the right remember the archer soldiers of Bolton, the inventor of the mule—Thomas Crompton—who was born at Tonge in Bolton Parish in 1753 and Philippa, daughter of King William III, who is said to have introduced weaving to Bolton and other English towns from her native Holland in 1337. Standing atop the shield is an elephant with a castle on its back which was taken from the central feature of the coat of arms of Coventry and is meant as a reminder that the founder of the County of Coventry in the 14th century was King Henry VI—a Lancastrian. Below the shield, in a scroll, is the Borough motto—*supera moras*—which means overcome thou delays in classical Latin but a more appropriate "on the moors" in dog Latin, a reminder of the old name for the town—Bolton-le-Moors.

Prior to April 1974 and the establishment of the current large metropolitan police forces in many parts of the UK most towns and cities of any size boasted their own force with the rural area and small towns being the responsibility of county constabularies. The north-west of England was particularly well served by these local forces who exhibited a pride in the fact that they were local and an efficiency that came from the relatively small area and close-knit camaraderie of officers in comparison with their county colleagues. In the area now covered by the Greater Manchester Police these local forces could be found in Wigan, Rochdale and Bolton in addition to the two forces in Manchester itself—Manchester and Salford Cities which had merged some six years earlier.

The Bolton Borough Police was founded November 1839 after a false start with a temporary police force which was established in the face of a great deal of local opposition. Although the first constables were under local control they had been sworn in by a Government Commissioner and faced substantial resentment in the Borough. The first 40 years of the Force's life coincided with a particularly violent period in Bolton's history with the Chief Constable being obliged to issue his

page 117

officers with cutlasses for their protection. In 1867 the Force had grown to 70 officers but the demands of policing an area troubled by the "Fenian Brotherhood" led to the swearing in of more than 2,000 special constables to assist the regular officers. The Force assumed control of several neighbouring towns and had seen its strength rise to 166 by the end of the 19th century. It ceased to exist as a separate entity in 1969 when it was merged into the Lancashire Constabulary together with the other borough forces.

The years immediately following the Great War saw large numbers of former servicemen choose their local police force as a career, some undoubtedly influenced by their experiences in a different uniform. Albert Bentley (*pictured left*) was a collier by trade when he enlisted in the Loyal North Lancashire Regiment (2nd Battalion) in December 1915. He served for the duration and applied to join the Bolton Borough Police after his demobilisation in December 1918, being sworn in on 30 January 1919 (Constable 140). Apart from the first two years service he spent his time at the village of Darcy Lever, near Bolton until he retired on pension at the age limit of 55 in 1946 after 27 years with the Force. He worked until he was 70 as a security guard and lived until he was 94. He was born close to Bolton, served his community for 27 years and was rewarded by the Watch Committee in 1939 with the award of the silver good service medal. At the time of his death in 1985 he was the oldest surviving pensioner of the Bolton Borough Police and last known living holder of the medal.

BOOTLE BOROUGH POLICE DIAMOND JUBILEE ISSUE GOOD CONDUCT MEDAL 1897

Instituted: August 1897.

Ribbon: Five equal stripes of blue, white, blue, white, blue.

Metal: Silver and bronze.

Size: 32 mm.

Description: (Obverse) the Old Head of Queen Victoria with the inscription VICTORIA DIAMOND JUBILEE (above) and 1837 - 1897 (below); (reverse) the Coat of Arms of the Borough with the words BOROUGH OF BOOTLE above. This is surrounded by an outer ring bearing the words AWARDED FOR GOOD CONDUCT 1837 - 1897. The rank and name of the recipient were engraved on the lower rim. The medal hung from a plain straight suspender attached by a claw fitting.

The medal was primarily a commemorative issue although there was a long service element in the conditions for its award and was only made available to officers with 10 or more years service without any default being recorded against them although there is evidence that this was relaxed for certain senior officers. Plain bars were awarded for unblemished service in excess of the 10 year qualifying period.

In the late 19th century and the first half of the 20th century the class system which operated for the issue of official medals by the Crown was also apparent in the Police Service. Very often medals were issued in silver and bronze with the former going to officers of the rank of inspector and above and the bronze issue to sergeants and constables. This changed in the Police Service many years before changes were made to awards available in the three Armed Forces in 1993 as a result of the review of the gallantry awards system. In 1897 when the Bootle Borough Watch Committee authorised the issue of the medal to commemorate the Diamond Jubilee it came as no surprise that this practice was continued and the distinction between the ranks was made. A single presentation of medals was made by Alderman Mack, Mayor and Chairman of the Watch Committee, on 8 November 1897 in a ceremony held at the Police Buildings, Bootle. A total of four officers were awarded the silver medal including the Chief Constable (James Cumming) and 11 bronze medals went to constables and sergeants from a total force strength of 66.

The ceremony served a dual purpose—it also presented an opportunity for the award of St John Ambulance Association medallions and certificates to a number of people including several police officers. The instruction of police officers in first aid and ambulance work was begun in Bootle 15 years earlier when it was a part of the Lancashire Constabulary and so impressed the Chief Constable that he soon extended it to the rest of Lancashire and, finally, the idea was copied across the whole of the UK. It was considered of such importance in Bootle that 62 of the Forces 66 officers were qualified in 1897, the highest percentage by far in the country.

One distinguished recipient of the silver medal was Detective Inspector John Stewart who was later to became the Chief Constable. He initially joined the County Constabulary and was stationed at Bootle until 1887 when the Borough Force was created. He was immediately promoted to the rank of sergeant in the much smaller Force, followed shortly after by a second promotion to inspector and chief clerk. At the time of the Jubilee he was in charge of the Detective Department and held the rank of detective inspector. He succeeded Mr Cumming as the Chief Constable on 1 January 1906 and led the Force for 12 years until ill-health forced him to resign in December 1918. His services to the Force were recognised by the Magistrates at the Borough Police Court in March 1919 when he was presented with a gold watch and chain and a purse of treasury notes.

Earlier in his service he was awarded the Liverpool and Shipwreck Humane Society General Medal for Bravery in silver for *"stopping a runaway horse attached to a cab in Pembroke Road, Bootle on 4th May 1899"*. This medal was one of several awarded by private bodies and charities to police officers and other members of the community for acts of bravery. Many are national societies—the RSPCA and Royal Humane Society, for example—but a few are local to a city, the Liverpool Society being one of the largest and most familiar. The Society was founded in 1839 following a hurricane in the Irish Sea when a number of people distinguished themselves by saving lives. The first medal—the Marine Medal—was issued in 1844. In 1883 a second type of medal was issued for saving life from fire. The General Medal was introduced in 1894 to reward anyone who saved a life irrespective of the cause with the first award being made on 9 June to two officers from the Liverpool City Police (Constables Twizell and Dean) who were both injured whilst stopping a runaway horse.

The obverse of the general medal won by Inspector Stewart carries a cross patée with a crown surrounded by a wreath of laurel in the centre. The cross has a circumscription which reads FOR BRAVERY IN SAVING LIFE with the date of the introduction of the medal—1894—at the foot. The reverse has the Liver Bird surrounded by a wreath and the name of the Society around the circumference. It was issued in gold, silver and bronze and hung from a red ribbon with two white stripes, all of equal width.

The coat of arms of the Borough depicted on the reverse of the Bootle Borough medal was in the shape of a shield and consisted of a chevron with three stags' heads all taken from the arms of the Earls of Derby, and three fleur-de-lys. The upper third of the shield depicted three mural crowns which originated from the arms of the Bootle family. A mural crown has the appearance of being built with bricks and has battlements to represent a castle wall and appears in the arms of distinguished soldiers and civic crests associated with such men. The crest showed a lighthouse which is a rare device in heraldry and is presumed to indicate the towns position at the mouth of the River Mersey. The motto—*respice, aspice, prospice*—means reflect on the past, consider the present, provide for the future.

Policing in Bootle was initially the responsibility of the Lancashire County Constabulary—it was not until 1 July 1887 that the Borough formed its own force which survived until May 1967 when it was amalgamated with the neighbouring Liverpool City Police to form the Liverpool and Bootle Constabulary. It is now a part of Merseyside Police. As the Force was only ten years old at the time of the Diamond Jubilee an officers total service in both the county and borough forces was counted when his eligibility for the medal was calculated.

Liverpool Shipwreck and Humane Society's Marine Medal.

RSPCA Life-Saving Medal.

Royal Humane Society Medal.

BRIGHTON BOROUGH POLICE MEDAL FOR MERITORIOUS CONDUCT

Instituted: 7 February 1902

Ribbon: Royal blue.

Metal: 22 ct gold.

Size: 34 mm.

Description: (Obverse) the Coat of Arms of Brighton Borough within a wreath of laurel; (reverse) engraved with the rank and name of the recipient, the date of the award and brief details of the circumstances. The medal was hung from a gold suspender ring with a plain brooch bar inscribed BOROUGH OF BRIGHTON POLICE MEDAL for fixing to the tunic. Examples exist with this brooch bar having no inscription.

The majority of medals awarded by individual police forces to their officers for either bravery or good service were cast in silver or bronze, very few in gold. Occasionally a specially struck medal was presented to reward an act of bravery but they were very often unique and never became regular issues. Gold was sometimes used on these occasions. One such award was made by the Birmingham Borough Police in 1885 to Detective Inspector Edwin Bennett for bravery displayed effecting the arrest of two men for burglary.

Edwin Bennett joined the Force on 15 September 1876 and was quickly identified an a promising officer with good potential. He served in a number of branches in the Force and was rapidly promoted to the rank of detective inspector in the early 1880s. He received his first commendation by the Magistrates when he became involved with the investigation of the campaign of violence and terrorism conducted by the Fenians in a number of English towns and cities. He was badly assaulted on duty and incapacitated for three months. The Magistrates commended him for his courage at the subsequent trial of his assailants. He suffered a further assault in 1885 which resulted in two more months absence from duty and was again commended by the Justices and presented with a gold medal by the Watch Committee as a mark of their appreciation for his bravery. On 25 April 1887 he left Birmingham to take up the post of Chief Constable of the Kidderminster Borough Police, a force of some 24 officers. He died in office in 1918 at the age of 67 after 45 years police service.

The only police force in the United Kingdom believed to have regularly awarded a medal in gold to its officers as a reward for bravery was the Brighton Borough Police. The medal was introduced at the suggestion of the Chief Constable, Sir William Gentle, who submitted a design to the meeting of the Watch Committee. The design was approved and one dozen were subsequently ordered at a cost of 10/6d (52.5 p) each.

The suggestion of a medal had been prompted by the courage shown by Borough Constable George Edward Larner in the previous December at the scene of a fire in Dorset Gardens, Brighton which resulted in a life being saved. At the same meeting of the Watch Committee on 7 February it was also resolved that Constable Larner should be the first recipient of the medal. The medal was awarded sparingly and fell into disuse with the introduction of national awards to recognise acts of bravery performed by police officers. It is thought that it was presented on five further occasions only, the last occasion being in 1921 although a second award bar was issued two years later. The examples with the brooch bar for pinning the medal to the tunic having no inscription are most likely the un-issued examples from the initial batch of a dozen pieces.

The second award was made on 11 November 1903 in somewhat unusual circumstances to Superintendent William Hale for *"his plucky and praiseworthy conduct in fearlessly attacking and destroying a ferocious dog by which he was bitten"*. Three years later on 11 July 1906 Constable Frank Ware was presented with the medal in recognition of the conduct, courage and ability he had shown arresting an armed ex-convict. His medal is inscribed on the reverse with the detail of his actions—*"Presented by The Watch Committee to PC Ware 24A for courageous conduct in arresting an armed burglar in the Western Road on the night of 30th May 1906"*. The inscription on the reverse of the other medals followed this same pattern.

Fourteen years were to pass before the next award was made to two officers for rescuing two men from drowning in rough seas. Sergeant David Morgan and Constable Robert Samuel Minton were jointly involved in the rescue and each was presented with his medal on 22 September 1920. The final award of a medal was made just over one year later, on 19 October 1921, to Constable William Rowland Calder for the rescue of a boy from the sea.

When approval for the medal was given initially by the Watch Committee there was no provision made for the issue of a bar to acknowledge a second award to the same officer. Sergeant David Morgan was to cause the matter to be addressed on 21 December 1922 when he attempted to swim to a grounded vessel with a lifeline in an attempt to save the lives of the boats occupants. His courage was thought worthy of the medal but, as an existing holder, the award of a bar was the recognised course of action. The Watch Committee approved the award on 17 January 1923 and a bar was specially commissioned for Sergeant Morgan. It was very ornate in design—a gold rectangle with laurel leaves along the top and sides and inscribed SERGT D MORGAN - BAR AWARDED 17 JANUARY 1923 in two lines.

The coat of arms of the Borough of Brighton shown on the obverse consists of a central shield depicting two dolphins facing left within a border with eight martlets (in heraldry—swallows without feet) representing the County of Sussex surrounding the town of Brighton. The origin of the dolphins cannot be traced clearly and it is uncertain if they represent the town's association with the sea or were adopted from the arms of one of Brighton's two leading families. The number of martlets on the medal also highlights a discrepancy—the official heraldic description refers to six martlets but the medal shows eight, the reason for the difference is not known. The two dolphins appear again above the shield, facing downwards with their tails entwined and flanked by two branches of coral. This is thought to represent the sea and climate of the south coast.

The Brighton Borough Police was founded in 1838 but was amalgamated with the West and East Sussex county forces and borough forces of Eastbourne and Hastings to form the Sussex Combined Police on 1 April 1943 for the duration of the Second World War. This happened to a number of forces under the Defence Regulations with many never regaining their identity. In Devon, the Tiverton Borough Police had the distinction of being the smallest remaining independent police force in the UK with 14 officers and had resisted all suggestions that it should amalgamate with the Devon County Constabulary. In common with Brighton and many others this came to an end in 1943 for wartime purposes but, unlike Brighton, Hastings and Eastbourne in Sussex, Tiverton Borough was gone forever and never re-formed. On 31 March 1947 the five Sussex forces resumed their separate identities for a further 21 years until 1 January 1968 when they were again amalgamated, this time permanently, to form the Sussex Constabulary—renamed the Sussex Police from 1 April 1974.

BRISTOL CITY POLICE GOOD SERVICE MEDAL

Instituted: 8 December 1926.

Ribbon: Dark red with a central green stripe 6.5 mm wide.

Metal: Silver.

Size: 36 mm.

Description: (Obverse) the Coat of Arms of the City of Bristol surrounded by a band with the legend FOR GOOD SERVICE above and BRISTOL CITY POLICE below; (reverse) a laurel wreath tied at the base by a ribbon with the recipient's name, rank and number in the centre. It was suspended from a plain straight bar attached by a claw fitting.

Awarded to officers of all ranks who had completed 17 years service without default with bars available for each additional five years good service. The bars were also of silver and attached to the suspender by lugs at each end with the length of service written in raised letters within a thin raised border—TWENTY TWO YEARS or TWENTY SEVEN YEARS, whichever was appropriate. The central field on the reverse usually carried an inscription with the recipients details although some were engraved on the lower rim. The medal was discontinued in 1951 after 498 medals and 477 bars had been issued.

The city coat of arms shown on the obverse was most likely granted when it was made a county in 1373 although this is by no means certain. The original arms consisted only of the shield which shows a castle standing on a mound from which comes a ship on its way out to sea. This is symbolic of the citys reputation as a seafaring port and major trading centre, dating from the Middle Ages. Above the shield is a visored helmet below two arms crosse— one holding a pair of scales (representing justice) and the other a serpent (for wisdom)—which are rising from clouds to signify that all good gifts come from above. The supporters on either side are unicorns sitting on a mound and the motto contained in the banner below the shield—*virtute et industria*—means by virtue and industry. The crest and supporters were formally added to the shield and granted to the city on 24 August 1569.

Researching the police careers of recipients of locally issued good service medals such as the Bristol City award can often unearth evidence of a police tradition in families. Delving into the history of most forces will usually uncover at least three generations from the same family making their careers in the Police Service, in some cases spanning almost 100 years. The effect became less pronounced as the county, city and borough forces were swallowed up by the rationalisations and amalgamations of recent years and the working population became more mobile. The first noticeable change came after the Great War when some looked further afield than their local force for a police career—the Metropolitan Police attracting large numbers of young men away from the provinces. Brothers too have often followed their father into the local constabulary.

In 1874 James Perry joined the Bristol City Police and had risen to the rank of detective sergeant when he retired in 1900—he was the first of three generations to serve, although one of his grandsons yielded to the lure of London and built an illustrious career in the Metropolitan Police. James's son—Samuel John—followed his father into the Bristol City Police at the age of 21 on 8 November 1911 after serving in the Royal Navy for a few years. He began his career as a constable with the Fire Police in the days before the establishment of a Fire Service totally separate from the police but moved to the River Police after a few years.

During the Great War he enlisted in the Royal Artillery as a gunner and served for the duration. He returned to the Bristol City Police, River Section, on demobilisation and was promoted to sergeant on 31 July 1924. He retired on pension on 24 November 1937 emigrating to South Africa shortly afterwards to become a farmer. He died in Pretoria in 1958. In 1928 he was awarded the Bristol City Police Good Service Medal in recognition of his 17 years service with a 22 year bar being added five years later. His time spent away from the Force on military service during the Great War was counted for the purposes of his entitlement to the medal.

Samuel Perry had two sons who followed him into the Police Service although the youngest— Jack Lenton Perry—served only as a cadet for a very short period before the Second World War intervened and he enlisted in the RAF—83 Squadron, Sgt 581034—volunteering for flying duties as an observer. He was killed in action on 4 June 1940 on a sortie over Germany at the age of 20.

Jacks elder brother—Howard James Perry KPM BEM—chose not to join his local force in Bristol, instead he opted for a career in the Metropolitan Police after eight years military service as a bandsman with the Gloucestershire Regiment. He joined in 1936 and was awarded the Kings Police Medal for Gallantry two years later for *"effecting the rescue of several persons from premises infected by poisonous gas at St Pancras, London"*. He was promoted to sergeant in 1946. He became a very active member of the Police Federation, several social bodies within the Police Service and was the Secretary of the Police Seaside Home Supporters Group for a number of years. One year before he retired in 1967 his work was acknowledged by the award of the British Empire Medal for Meritorious Service (Civil Division) in the New Years Honours List.

Originally known as the Bristol Constabulary, the Force was established on 20 May 1936 with a strength of 228 officers. In common with a number of similar forces the name changed on more than one occasion, first to Bristol County Borough Constabulary (1892) followed by the Bristol City and County Borough Police (1894) until the more commonly accepted Bristol City Police was formally adopted. It survived as a separate body until April 1974 when it was amalgamated with the Somerset and Bath Constabulary and a part of Gloucestershire to form the present Avon and Somerset Police.

Police Medals of the World

CAMBRIDGE CITY POLICE LONG SERVICE MEDAL

Instituted: 1913.

Ribbon: Red with a blue central stripe.

Metal: Silver.

Size: 36 mm.

Description: (Obverse) the Coat of Arms of the City of Cambridge with the legend CAMBRIDGE BOROUGH POLICE FOR LONG SERVICE around the circumference; (reverse) a wreath of laurel tied at the base by a ribbon with the rank and name of the recipient and date of the award inscribed in the centre. The medal was attached by a claw fitting to a plain straight swivelling suspender.

The medal was authorised for award to members of the Force after 25 years service without a blemish on their personal records. It appears to have been a short-lived medal with no record of any award after 1914, possibly due to the outbreak of the Great War in August.

The Cambridge City coat of arms was granted in 1575 and consists of a bridge across the centre over a river with three ships. A fleur-de-lys and two white roses are shown in the upper third of the shield. The elements emphasise the importance of river trade to the borough and the patronage of the Royal Family for many centuries. In addition to its use on medals issued by police forces, the coat of arms of a county, city or borough was a recurring feature on their helmet plates and cap badges. There were exceptions, however. A number of forces, the Devon Constabulary for example, employed a royal cypher appropriate to the reigning Monarch—VR, GvR etc with a few having only the initial letters of its title— MC for the Monmouthshire Constabulary, G for Gloucestershire or W for Wiltshire in the centre. Individual helmet plates were equally widespread which displayed the officer's number and often the division (Bristol, Leicestershire, Dorset and others). The basic design of the plates usually followed one of two patterns—the Brunswick Star (a seven point star) topped with a crown or a wreath of laurel also usually with a crown. The central field showed the coat of arms with the force's name inscribed on a surrounding band inside the star or wreath. The crown was very occasionally absent (Brecon Borough) on plates with a wreath design but almost invariably appeared with the star.

In Victorian times and during the first half of the 20th century with the large number of small forces then existing the helmet plates were subject to a great deal more variation than in the years that followed as the numbers reduced. When the Cambridge Borough Police was founded in 1836 the first helmet badge consisted of the full achievement of arms including the crest and supporters with no other identifying feature, something not considered necessary until much later. The Brunswick Star style plate with the Tudor (King's) crown was adopted early in the 20th century with the central field retaining the full coat of arms and the Force name—Cambridge Borough Police—in the surrounding band. This was changed to Cambridge City Police when city status was granted in 1951 and the Tudor crown was replaced by the Edward (Queen's) crown in 1954 on the accession to the throne of the present Monarch. The Force ceased to exist as a separate body in 1965 when it was amalgamated with the Cambridgeshire Constabulary to form the Mid-Anglia Police—renamed the Cambridgeshire Constabulary on 1 April 1974.

Helmet plates were often issued in two forms by some forces (Cambridge included)—one of white metal for daytime use and one painted black for night duty. The coat of arms or royal cypher in the central field was often also painted black although many were of white metal, again including the Cambridge Borough Police.

The use of the coat of arms alone as the badge led to a number of very attractive plates being produced. One in particular stands out from the forces which also issued medals to their officers— Leamington Spa. The Borough's connection with the Royal Family was recognised by the use of the royal coat of arms as the police badge with the only addition being a scroll beneath the arms which carried the name of the Force—Royal Leamington Borough Police. Authority to use the royal coat of arms or any part of it was granted rarely and its use in the Borough by the police reflects its standing with Queen Victoria. By the mid-20th century the Force had, however, adopted the Brunswick Star design.

In recent years the use of the Brunswick Star and Edward (Queen's) crown has become standard although the central field retains a local symbol in many cases—but not all. The royal cypher (EIIR) has become increasingly evident as the present forces encompass several counties with no one local device being appropriate—Devon and Cornwall for example with the two very different counties, the cities of Exeter, Plymouth and Truro and twenty former borough forces. The City of London Police and Hampshire Constabulary are the only two forces in England and Wales which have not adopted the star design.

CARDIFF CITY POLICE AND FIRE BRIGADE CONSPICUOUS BRAVERY MEDAL

Instituted: 11 May 1908.

Ribbon: Yellow with three red chevrons. The riband for wear in undress uniform had only one chevron.

Metal: Silver.

Size: 39 mm.

Description: (Obverse) the Coat of Arms of the City of Cardiff with the legend FOR CONSPICUOUS BRAVERY below; (reverse) a seven line inscription PRESENTED BY THE - CARDIFF - WATCH COMMITTEE - TO - (rank, number and name of the recipient) - FOR - CONSPICUOUS BRAVERY in seven lines with two intertwined laurel branches below. A claw fitting and ornate swivelling scroll suspender were used.

The coat of arms of Cardiff depicted on the obverse of the medal was initially granted in 1907 and amended in 1956. The full armorial bearings of the present City and County of Cardiff were adopted as recently as 1996. Central to the shield is the Red Dragon, the emblem of Wales, standing on a grass mound and holding a flag pole topped by a banner with three chevrons pointing upwards. The floral symbol of Wales—a leek—grows from the mound. The three chevrons are attributed to Iestin ap Gwrgant, the last Prince of Glamorgan, who lived in Cardiff Castle from 1030 to 1080. Whether or not the chevrons on the medal ribbon derived from this ancient source is unknown.

This medal was the only one issued by any Welsh police force to regular officers and was authorised by the Watch Committee on 11 May 1908 to all ranks of both services to reward acts of conspicuous bravery. Examples of such acts include rescues from drowning in rivers and canals or, as in one recorded instance, entering a basement filled with coal gas to rescue a man who had been overcome by the fumes and was unconscious and close to death. Bars were available for further acts of courage which merited the award of the medal. The clasp was generally plain with a raised border and the name of the recipient engraved on the reverse. Medals were struck in silver and the award carried with it a non-pensionable weekly allowance of 2 shillings (10 pence) for life. The last award of the medal is believed to have been made in 1929.

The Cardiff Borough Police was founded in 1836 with an establishment of five officers although this very soon rose to a number more in keeping with the size of the area policed. The name was changed to the Cardiff City Police in 1906 with the granting of city status and it existed as a separate force until it became a part of the South Wales Police in June 1969.

DEWSBURY BOROUGH POLICE MEDAL

Instituted: 1906.

Ribbon: Not intended to be worn with a ribbon although an example exists suspended from a dark blue ribbon believed to be unofficial.

Metal: Silver.

Size: 38 mm.

Description: (Obverse) the Coat of Arms of the Borough of Dewsbury; (reverse) a wreath of laurel tied at the base by an ornate bow with an engraved inscription in the central field. A small ring suspender was attached to the top of the disc.

The first suggestion that a long service medal should be awarded in Dewsbury was made to the Watch Committee by the Chief Constable on 16 October 1906 at the request of members of the Force. It was proposed that officers should receive the medal on completion of 21 years service and that they should be of silver for those of the rank of inspector and above and that sergeants and constables should receive one that was electro-plated. The first award appears to have been made at about the same time to former Deputy Superintendent Palmer of the Corporation Fire Brigade (then a part of the police service) with two others going to sergeant Joseph Dransfield and Constable Walter Hargreaves in September 1912. The Watch Committee minutes refer to other awards being made in June 1913 (Fireman White) and June 1915 (Deputy Superintendent Healey of the Corporation Fire Brigade). The records are known to be incomplete; two medals have been seen with no corresponding record in the minutes. The total number of awards made is not known.

The inscription on the reverse of the two medals seen differs and the period of service necessary before an officer became eligible for the medal differs. On one the inscription reads PRESENTED TO DETECTIVE INSPECTOR J SHAW FOR 25 YEARS FAITHFUL SERVICE and on the other TO INSPECTOR A BROWN FROM THE DEWSBURY CORPORATION FOR 21 YEARS SERVICE 11 NOV 1913.

The crest of Dewsbury depicted on the obverse consists of a shield with a chequerboard pattern in the lower half taken from the arms of William de Warenne, the Earl of Surrey, and a kinsman of William the Conqueror who held areas of land including the Manor of Dewsbury. Above this is a cross flanked by a pair of owls drawn from the arms of two other powerful land-owning families in the area for more than 600 years.

Dewsbury Borough Police was a small force although typical of the time with a strength of 57 officers of all ranks in 1911 serving a population of 53,358. Other forces of similar size awarded long service medals to their officers (Bolton, Bootle and Grimsby amongst them) although they were very few out of the large number of borough forces that existed. The Force was founded in 1863 and survived as a separate body for just over 100 years until 1968 when it was absorbed by the West Yorkshire Police which later amalgamated with the Leeds and Bradford City forces in 1974 to form the current organisation.

DUMBARTONSHIRE COUNTY COUNCIL CORONATION MEDAL 1902

Instituted: 1902.

Ribbon: Royal blue.

Metal: Silver and bronze.

Size: 34 mm.

Description: (Obverse) the crowned and robed bust of King Edward VII facing right with the words EDWARD VII and the date 1902 on the left and KING - OF - GREAT - BRITAIN - & IRE - LAND - EMPER - OR OF INDIA in nine lines in the right third of the medal; (reverse) the Coat of Arms of the County of Dumbartonshire consisting of the Scottish saltire and four roses with the date JUNE 26 (left) 1902 (right) in a scroll to each side. The legend DUMBARTONSHIRE COUNTY COUNCIL lies around the upper circumference. In a scrolled panel in the lower half of the medal is the inscription PRESENTED TO THE MEMBERS OF THE - DUMBARTONSHIRE CONSTABULARY - TO COMMEMORATE THE CORONATION OF - HIS MAJESTY - KING EDWARD VII in five lines. The medal hangs from a plain ring suspender. It was issued unnamed.

This medal was the only one believed to have been issued by a county constabulary to regular officers for any reason although there are examples where medals were awarded to members of the Special Constabulary to reward service in the Great War in some counties. The number of medals issued in Dumbarton is believed to have been fewer than 100 of both types (silver and bronze together). The authorised establishment of the Force in 1902 is known to have been 93 officers although there is a possibility that issues, probably in silver, were made to local dignitaries as occurred elsewhere in the UK. Very little is known about the medal and it is the subject of speculation that it was awarded in silver to officers of the rank of inspector and above and in bronze to sergeants and constables. This would follow the pattern of awards made in other forces in the UK to celebrate the coronation and Queen Victoria's jubilees of 1887 and 1897.

The Dumbartonshire County Constabulary was founded in 1840 and expanded over the years as it absorbed three neighbouring burgh forces—Kirkintilloch in 1872, Helensburgh in 1876 and Dumbarton Burgh in 1949. It ceased to exist as a separate body in 1975 when the Strathclyde Police was formed by the amalgamation of a number of similar smaller forces.

EXETER CITY POLICE
LONG SERVICE AND EFFICIENCY MEDAL

Instituted: 24 May 1928.

Ribbon: White with two broad (8 mm) grass green stripes.

Metal: Silver.

Size: 36 mm.

Description: (Obverse) the arms of the City of Exeter with the legend FOR LONG SERVICE AND EFFICIENCY around the circumference; (reverse) the hat of maintenance superimposed on two crossed swords with the legend CITY OF EXETER POLICE FORCE around the circumference. It was suspended from a plain straight swivelling suspender bar attached by a claw fitting.

The ninth Chief Constable—Arthur F Nicholson OBE KPM—who served from 1 May 1913 to late 1930—was responsible for the introduction of the medal. It was awarded to officers who had completed 17 years service provided that they satisfied three conditions which were very similar to those in many other forces who issued such medals;-

(a) that they were zealous and efficient in the discharge of their duties,

(b) that no default had been recorded against them in the preceding 17 years, and

(c) if a constable, that they were in receipt of the special increment in pay in accordance with paragraph 58 of the Police Regulations 1920.

Bars were awarded for further periods of five years service again with conditions that no default had been recorded during that period and that the officer was in receipt of the second special increment in pay available under the Police Regulations of 1920. The bars were also of silver, of the slip-on type and carried the legend TWENTY TWO YEARS, TWENTY SEVEN YEARS or THIRTY TWO YEARS. Only two of the latter are thought to have been awarded.

The medals were supplied by a local jeweller and hallmarked in Birmingham in 1928. A second striking was made in 1936 but there is no record in the Watch Committee minutes of any issue being made from this batch. The cost of the dies, striking and engraving of the initial batch amounted to £37 14s 9d. There was no provision for the award of the medal for gallantry, it was solely a long service and good conduct reward.

The coat of arms on the obverse has a shield showing Exeter Castle supported by a winged horse (Pegasus) on both sides and surmounted by a visored helmet facing left on which stood a crowned lion holding an orb. The city motto—*semper fidelis* (always faithful)—is written in a scroll beneath the shield and horses. The hat and swords of maintenance on the reverse are part of the city regalia and the design is believed to have been the idea of the town clerk—Mr Lloyd Parry.

The recipient's initials and surname or full name were engraved on the lower rim. The medal was never officially issued unnamed although examples are known to exist.

In all probability these came from the second striking which was thought to have been lost when the jewellers shop was destroyed when Exeter was bombed in the Second World War or, alternatively, from a number which disappeared when the Force was amalgamated with the Devon Constabulary in 1966.

Two miniatures of the medal (without bars) exist although it is not known if they were official issues. One medal hung from a full size ribbon that had been folded inwards to the appropriate size leaving it as three stripes of equal width—green-white-green—and was pinned to the tunic by means of a plain silver bar at the top. The other bore a correct ribbon and had no such silver bar. The holder of the latter medal is known although it is unnamed but the recipient of the first is a mystery.

The first presentation of medals in Exeter was made on 25 October 1928 when 24 were awarded to officers of all ranks from constable to the Chief Constable himself who received three bars in recognition of his 33 years service. Four officers received two bars, ten received one and nine medals only were awarded. Further issues were made until the medal was discontinued in 1939 at the outbreak of the Second World War. The last two awards were made on 11 October 1934. A total of 36 medals and 26 bars were presented.

There is no record of any medal or bar being awarded after 1934 which calls into question quite why the second striking of medals in 1936 was ever authorised. A number of officers qualified for a medal or bar after this date but Watch Committee minutes and personal records do not record any presentations of either. Several officers became due for the medal or bars after 1936 and before it was discontinued in 1939 but their personal records make no mention of either ever being issued.

The medal and any bars could be withdrawn if the officer failed to continue to conduct his duties with zeal and efficiency or if any default were to be recorded against him. It wasnt difficult to record a default. Discipline was harsh with officers regularly appearing before the Chief Constable charged with any one of a number of offences against the disciplinary code which seem trivial today. An officer caught *"gossiping"* on his beat could expect a fine ranging from 5 shillings (25p) to 20 shillings (£1)—a week's wages—and be forever barred from receiving his good service medal irrespective of how well he conducted himself for the rest of his service. There was a procedure for expunging a default from an officer's record but this only on the personal authority of the Chief Constable who often showed a degree of inconsistency with some quite serious offences being removed from one officer's record and minor matters remaining on another. There is one recorded instance in 1920 of an officer in Exeter being summoned and convicted of assaulting a boy whilst on duty. He was fined 20 shillings (£1) but continued to serve and the record was expunged by the Chief Constable ten years later on October 1930 coincidentally a mere 17 days after he would have become entitled to his medal. Less than six months later it was awarded. A number of officers benefited from a benevolent decision by the Watch Committee in Exeter taken in October 1928 at the time that the first issue of medals was made to expunge from their records any defaults which should have disqualified them from receiving the medal.

It should be remembered that the educational standard of many recruits was low—the candidate's application form for the Cornwall Constabulary in the 19th century asked if the applicant could read *or* write and there is one recorded instance in the same force of an officer with three years service being dismissed for *"illiteracy"*. The caricature of a rotund constable with mutton-chop sideburns licking the end of his pencil before laboriously recording details of a trivial incident in his notebook is not too far from the truth—failure to make a note of anything and everything reported to him would result in an appearance before his Chief Constable on a charge of neglect of duty and the recording of a default on his personal record.

Once an officer had been accepted into his chosen force it was relatively easy to find himself dismissed sometimes through no fault of his own and often under circumstances which called into question the recruiting procedures of the force. On 1 December 1879 Third Class Constable 26 John Britton of the Devon Constabulary was dismissed for *"having an impediment in his speech"*. Quite why this was not picked up when he joined three months earlier was not explained in the register of dismissals. A second constable from Chulmleigh in the same force in March 1880 suffered a similar fate *"in consequence of being unable to get a cottage to live in"*.

The majority of dismissals were, however, well deserved. When Third Class Constable 297 John Horrill, stationed at Ideford, was found to have been *"convicted of manslaughter in 1856"* it should have come as no surprise to him to find his services were no longer required and he was dismissed (4 May 1865). Similarly David Leonard was sent packing from headquarters on 12 March 1857 when it was revealed that he had been *"released from gaol 7 days before enlisting after 10 months imprisonment"*.

The scant information recorded of the reasons why officers were dismissed are easily understandable but intriguing and hide stories which were, in all probability, very interesting, but we can only speculate on the detail. Why a constable who joined in March 1857, rose to first class in two years but was demoted to third class three years later should be dismissed in August 1864 for *"stupidity"* was not explained. Nor is it made clear why a superintendent in Exeter should be listed as a *"deserter"* two days before Christmas 1862.

Drink and sex were recurrent reasons for the early dismissal of officers. Drinking on duty, frequenting public houses in uniform and drunkenness off duty were problems affecting most forces from their foundation to the beginning of the Great War when the incidence of such offences diminished rapidly. Trouble with ladies was punished severely as chief constables imposed their moral code on the constables although many fully deserved their punishment. *"Gross misconduct as a married man"* without further explanation was recorded several times as the reason why officers from the Devon Constabulary were dismissed. On occasions the reason was more specific. A constable in 1858 who *"passed off an improper female as his wife"* and another who *"contracted venereal disease as a married man"* in 1865 must surely have suspected that their careers might be curtailed once the matter had come to the attention of their superiors.

Chief Constables were not noted for their tolerance although they sometimes showed compassion. In February 1863 a constable at Teignmouth was called upon to resign for *"misconduct"* but re-instated a few months later. He failed, however, to take advantage of this change of heart by the Chief Constable and appeared before him again in September the same year and was dismissed for good for *"gross indecency and immorality in having connexion with a prostitute on a highway"*.

Such was the life of a constable in the early years of the existence of the Devon Constabulary with similar tales being recorded in the borough and city forces which issued good conduct medals. By the turn of the century discipline had improved and the incidence of an early end to a career for such reasons diminished. It was still a simple matter to record a default but large numbers managed to avoid them and collect their medals.

The Exeter City Police was founded in 1836 and existed as a separate body for 130 years until 1 April 1966 when it was amalgamated with the Devon County Constabulary to form the Devon and Exeter Constabulary. The new Force lasted in this form for barely a year before it was joined with Plymouth City Police and the Cornwall Constabulary to form the present Devon and Cornwall Constabulary on 1 June 1967.

At its birth the Force boasted a strength of 27 officers of all ranks including the first of the 12 chief constables who would serve during its 130 year life. The constables were rewarded at rates of pay varying from 18 to 21 shillings a week (90p to 105p) with the Chief Constable receiving £120 per annum. By early 1913 the strength had more than doubled to 64 officers and was again increased to 78 in November of that year when the Parish of Heavitree, a part of the Devon County Constabulary, was annexed as the City of Exeter expanded. When the Force ceased to exist in 1966 the authorised establishment of officers had risen to 136.

The two officers who are believed to have been the last surviving recipients of the medal both lived into their 90s. William Wood was born in Winkleigh on 4 November 1886 and joined the Force at the age of 20 as constable 65 on 11 February 1907. Following his retirement from the Force he lived in Exeter and had reached the grand old age of 96 when he died in 1983. When the medal was introduced in 1928 he had completed 21 years service and was one of the first to receive it. One year later he was presented with his bar denoting the completion of 22 years service. He had a chequered career and fell foul of the disciplinary code on three occasions for trivial offences in the early years of his service but was also later commended by the Chief Constable.

In October 1910 he appeared before the Chief Constable for *"failing to properly patrol his beat and visiting the Hippodrome when on the sick list"*. He was fined one day's pay for the first offence and cautioned for the second. The two other infractions were of a similar nature but on 25 October 1928 all three matters were expunged from his record by a resolution of the Watch Committee. He was awarded his medal ten days later on 5 November. His commendation by the Chief Constable came on 17 April 1916 for *"stopping a runaway pony and milk cart in Fore Street, Heavitree"*.

Tom Farrant was a few years older than William Wood (born 11 July 1883) and joined the Force in February 1905 after working as a farm labourer for eight years from the age of 14. He had a good career and never recorded a default. On three occasions he was commended by the Chief Constable for stopping a runaway horse and wagon and once received the praise of the Watch Committee and the Chairman of the Justices (Lady Owen) for *"his conduct in connection with the arrest of two men for possessing housebreaking implements by night"*. He was also awarded £2 by the Watch Committee for this *"highly praiseworthy conduct"*—11 February 1932. The practice of rewarding officers with money for particularly good work was an accepted and relatively common practice in some forces in the years before the Second World War. The sum involved (£2) was substantial for the time with the average weekly wage of an experienced constable being 95 shillings (£4.75p).

Constable 68 Farrant retired on full pension with 30 years service in February 1935. He died in Exeter in 1978. The deaths of Constables Wood and Farrant severed the last links with the Exeter City Police Long Service and Efficiency Medal although an officer who joined the City Force shortly before it ceased to exist in 1966 was still serving in the Devon and Cornwall Constabulary in the first year of the 21st century—164 years after it was founded.

CORPORATION OF GLASGOW MEDAL FOR BRAVERY

Instituted: 1924.

Ribbon: Green with a 3 mm red stripe at each edge.

Metal: Silver.

Size: 32 mm.

Description: (Obverse) a standing figure of a robed angel facing left blowing a long trumpet and holding a wreath of laurel in her left hand. In front of the angel was an ornate round shield bearing the inscription FOR - BRAVERY in two lines; (reverse) the Coat of Arms of Glasgow surrounded by a wreath of thistle inscribed with the words PRESENTED BY THE - CORPORATION OF GLASGOW TO (details of recipient) in three lines. It hung from a ring suspender and was fixed to the tunic with a top clasp of ornate design bearing a thistle overlain by a panel containing the word GALLANTRY.

Although not exclusively a police medal and available to anyone to recognise an act of courage performed in the city, the Corporation of Glasgow Medal for Bravery was nonetheless awarded to police officers on many occasions. Before it was introduced in 1924 there had been one award of a medal for bravery to a officer from the City Force—in 1871—although it is thought to have been a unique event and the medal specially commissioned. It is also believed to be the first such award made in the UK by any police force.

The medal was oval and very unusual in design with the obverse showing the armorial bearings of Glasgow within a surrounding garter belt bearing the words CITY OF GLASGOW POLICE. The suspender consisted of a constable's helmet sitting on top of the medal with a pair of crossed truncheons on either side and joined at the handles above the helmet to a ring. An oval garter brooch buckle was used to attach the medal to the tunic. On the reverse was an inscription giving details of the circumstances leading to the award and the name of the recipient—*"Presented by the Lord Provost, Magistrates and Board of Police to John Kerr, Constable, A Division of the Police Force of the City in recognition of meritorious services rendered by him in saving by his intrepid conduct, the lives of the inhabitants of a tenement, 4 stories in height, at Old Wynd, Glasgow, immediately preceding the fall of that tenement on the 23rd November 1871".*

From its introduction in 1924 until it was discontinued on 1 May 1975 the Glasgow Corporation Medal for Bravery was awarded to police officers on no less than 226 occasions. In addition nine first bars, two second bars and one third bar were granted. The first award to a police officer occurred in 1925 with Constable James Sparks receiving the medal for *"pursuing and attempting to arrest an armed man".* The reasons for the awards in the years following reflected changes in society, the demands placed on police officers and an increased expectation of the level of bravery displayed by a police officer before he or she would be considered for an award—mirroring the situation nationally. In the early years the majority of medals and bars were awarded for saving or attempting to save lives from rivers, canals and fires in tenement buildings (105 occasions) or for stopping runaway horses (89 occasions). There were instances of awards being made in connection with the arrest of violent, dangerous or armed criminals but they were rare until after the Second World War when they became far more prevalent. Between 1950 and 1972 there were 38 such awards out of a total of 42 made since 1924.

The city's armorial bearings which appear on the unique medal and the three versions of the Corporation award date back to the 13th century although they were not officially granted for more than 600 years in 1866. They were, however, in common use for some time before. The shield which forms the central feature of the bearings has four distinct elements—a tree which forms the centrepiece with a bird at the top, a fish at the base and a bell to the right of its trunk.

The earliest known element is the fish (a salmon) holding a golden ring in its mouth. Its inclusion is built around a story involving the Patron Saint of Glasgow—Saint Mungo—and the present of the ring made to Queen Languoreth by Hydderch Hael, King of Cadzow. The Queen subsequently gave the ring to a knight which caused the King to suspect there might be an intrigue between the two. Some time later, whilst on a hunting party he took the ring from the knight as he slept and threw it into the River Clyde. When he returned home to the Queen he demanded to see the ring and threatened her with death if she could not produce it. Neither she nor the knight could produce it and she was forced to approach Saint Mungo and confess. He in turn sent a monk to the river with orders to bring back the first fish he caught. When the fish was returned to Saint

Mungo he retrieved the ring from its mouth which was later presented to the King, saving the Queen's life. The fish first appeared on the seal of the Bishop of Glasgow (William Wyschard) in 1270. Two also appear as supporters for the shield in the full armorial bearings.

The bird first appeared a year later, in 1271, on the seal of Bishop Robert Wyschard and commemorates a wild robin which was tamed by Saint Mungo's old master—Saint Serf. The bird was accidentally killed by disciples and blamed on Saint Mungo. He picked it up, however, and prayed over it, bringing it back to life and sending it flying back chirping to its master.

The most dominant feature on the shield is the tree although it is pre-dated by both the fish and bird. It first appeared as a hazel branch but is now an oak and illustrates another event in the life of Saint Mungo, this time when he was a boy in the monastery. He had been left in charge of the holy fire in the refectory but fell asleep. Other boys there who were jealous of him put out the fire hoping to cause disfavour with the monks. When he found out what had happened, Mungo broke branches from a hazel tree and prayed over them causing them to burst into flames and re-light the holy fire.

This history of the bell is something of a mystery although there is a suggestion that it was given to Mungo by the Pope. It had, however, become a city institution by the 15th century and was used to call the people of the city to prayer from 1450 for many years. The fate of the original bell is unknown but a replacement was bought in 1641 and still exists today. The city motto which appears beneath the shield—*Let Glasgow Flourish*—is a shortened form of a text which appears on the bell of the Tron Church cast in 1631—*Lord let Glasgow flourish through the preaching of thy word and praising thy name*.

In 1935 the medal was re-designed although the ribbon was retained and the metal used and size were unchanged.

Description: *(Obverse) a wreath of laurel tied at the base by a bow with the words FOR BRAVERY in the central field; (reverse) the Coat of Arms of Glasgow with an inscription below which read PRESENTED BY THE - CORPORATION OF GLASGOW - TO - (details of the recipient and date) in four lines. The upper brooch bar was of a plain design.*

There was provision for the medal to be awarded posthumously although this was, thankfully, a rare event. On 4 September 1952 Detective Constable John MacLeod was shot and killed in the city when he was about to question a local bank clerk in connection with an allegation of theft made against him. As he was about to approach the person—a youth of 18 named Edwin Finlay—with Detective Constable Thomas MacDonald, the youth fired at them, killing DC MacLeod and seriously wounding DC MacDonald. Finlay held off three other officers who had arrived and attempted to arrest him but eventually shot himself. He was found to be in possession of three revolvers and £100 in cash, part of the £900 he was thought to have stolen. John MacLeod (aged 31) who was married with a four year old daughter, died soon after his admission to hospital. Thomas MacDonald made a full recovery. The two detectives and three constables who had come to their aid and attempted to arrest Finlay—Charles Hill, Arthur Scott and Thomas Crawford—were all awarded the medal for bravery later the same year.

One officer was awarded the medal on four occasions—Sergeant James Robertson. As a constable he was rewarded for stopping a runaway horse, with a bar being awarded in 1938 and a second three years later for similar acts of courage. In 1954, as a sergeant, he received an unprecedented third bar for rescuing a woman from a tenement building in imminent danger of collapsing.

In 1965 a further re-design of the medal was authorised and it was issued in 22 carat gold rather than silver. The ribbon was again retained.

Description: *(Obverse) the Coat of Arms within an oval shield with a surrounding narrow band in which was inscribed FOR BRAVERY at the top and which had two palm leaves in the lower half (reverse) left plain apart from the engraved details of the recipient. The suspender was ornate with two thistle leaves joined in the centre by a thistle flower attached to the top of the medal's main disc—the ribbon hung from a ring attached to the thistle flower.*

From its inception in 1924 the medal was intended to reward acts of courage performed in the city by anyone but it has been awarded twice to city police officers for their actions away from their home force area. One unusual award was made to Detective Sergeant Hugh Wilson for his conduct whilst on holiday in Blackpool in 1972 when a local police officer there (Superintendent Richardson) was shot and killed by armed bank robbers.

In 1975 the reorganisation of regional government led to the demise of the medal although it was replaced by the Strathclyde Regional Council Medal for Bravery with changes to the medals design and the ribbon colour.

Great Britain

Ribbon: Medium blue with a gold stripe (5 mm) at each edge.

Description: (Obverse) the words FOR BRAVERY placed centrally above two crossed laurel leaves with the circumscription STRATHCLYDE REGIONAL COUNCIL; (reverse) left plain apart from the engraved details of the recpient.

Glasgow City Police is the oldest large police force in the whole UK, established in 1800. Over the years it grew as the city boundaries were pushed ever outwards absorbing a number of smaller burgh forces including the Gorbals (1846), Clyde (1867) and Govan (1912) until the major restructure on 16 May 1975 when the current Strathclyde Police was formed with the loss of the Lanarkshire, Dumbartonshire, Renfrew and Bute, Ayrshire, Argyllshire and Stirlingshire Constabularies. The Strathclyde Police is now the largest force in Scotland by some margin with 7,000 officers, only slightly less than the whole of the rest of the country. In mainland Britain it is exceeded only by the Metropolitan and Greater Manchester forces.

COUNTY BOROUGH OF GRIMSBY POLICE GOOD SERVICE MEDAL

Instituted: November 1914.

Ribbon: Dark blue with crimson edges and a crimson central line.

Metal: Silver and bronze.

Size: 35 mm.

Description: (Obverse) the Coat of Arms of the County Borough of Grimsby within an oak wreath. Around the circumference is the inscription FOR GOOD SERVICE above and COUNTY BOROUGH OF GRIMSBY POLICE below; (reverse) a laurel wreath tied with a ribbon around a central field containing the legend PRESENTED - BY THE - WATCH - COMMITTEE and the date in five lines. The recipient's name and rank are engraved on the lower rim. The medal employed a claw fitting and plain straight swivelling suspender.

The Grimsby Watch Committee introduced the medal to reward officers who had achieved 25 or more years service with no misconduct recorded on their personal file. It was struck in silver for issue to officers of the rank of inspector and above and in bronze for constables and sergeants—a practice quite common before the Great War. The rank and name of the recipient were engraved on the lower rim although there are differences with the date of the award also appearing on the rim. The medal was formally abolished in 1941 but officers were permitted to continue wearing the ribbon on their tunics until their retirement from the Force.

The Grimsby coat of arms consists only of a shield, there are no supporters, no crest and no motto. The cockle shell seen on the medal above the shield has no official authority although its significance to the local fishing industry is obvious. The arms comprise a shield with a chevron between three boars' heads. The meaning of the devices is far from clear but they are believed to have derived from the arms of important families with some connection to the Borough. A popular alternative explanation for the appearance of the boars' heads derives from the right of the Mayor and Aldermen to hunt boar in Bradley Woods, although there is little supporting evidence. The chevron could have come from a number of sources including the family of de Grymesby although the arms of the Member of Parliament for Grimsby in 1762 and later the Mayor and Recorder of the town—William Broxholme of Barrow—comprised a chevron between three badgers' heads. The earliest use of the Town Seal with the arms dates from the mid-17th century although they were not officially granted until 1974. The origin, however, will remain subject to some discussion.

One recipient of the medal was the Chief Constable—John Stewart OBE KPM—who was to

page 133

become one of the longest serving police officers in the UK at the time of his retirement on 8 July 1930 when he had accumulated more than 48 years police service in eight different forces from Glasgow to Eastbourne. Born in New Deer, Aberdeenshire, he first applied to become a constable in the Aberdeen City Police at the age of 18 after four years of farming work near his home. He was turned down at Aberdeen because of his age but succeeded in obtaining a post across the border in Sunderland on 18 March 1882. For the first four years of his police career he served with five forces, some appointments being for very short periods. His longest stay was at Glasgow City where he served for 14 months before moving back south to Bootle and finally Accrington where he put down roots for six years until his ambition took him to Eastbourne.

The founding of the Eastbourne Borough Police in 1891 saw John Stewart take up one of the six patrol sergeant posts although his obvious talent resulted in a mere six weeks in this position before he was appointed the station sergeant and later the Chief Constable's clerk in 1892. He was promoted from 4th class to 1st class sergeant and the Warrant and Coroners Officer during the following twelve months but his now rapid move through the rank structure did not end there—by April 1894 he had been promoted to inspector and then chief inspector until he left Eastbourne on 1 June 1898 to become the Chief Constable of the Newcastle-under Lyme Police, being selected from 72 candidates.

He applied twice for the post of Chief Constable at Grimsby but was passed over on the first occasion in 1900 by John Fisher, an inspector from the Liverpool City Police. The procedure for the selection of chief constables was very much a local affair, the decision being one for the local watch committee alone without any interference or guidance from central government. It was not unusual for the rank of the applicant to be ignored or play a relatively minor part in the decision, the fact that John Stewart held higher rank than John Fisher meant little. It wasn't unknown for a sergeant to be appointed as a chief constable in some smaller forces particularly if he had come from a large city force, especially the Metropolitan Police in London. John Fisher, however, served for a very short period until he died suddenly in 1901. The Watch Committee offered the post to John Stewart without further interviews or selection procedures—he accepted and took up his new post on 28 August 1901. He was to stay at Grimsby until his retirement in July 1930.

He joined the Force at a time of an industrial dispute in the Grimsby fishing industry and subsequent civil unrest with extensive damage being caused in the docks. The situation deteriorated to the extent that the Riot Act was read in Rigby Square and 400 police officers from Manchester and Sheffield together with a detachment from the Lincolnshire Regiment were drafted into the town to help restore and maintain order. A further period of unrest during the rail strike in 1911 tested his abilities but was handled with a high standard of efficiency and no injury or damage. During his time in command of the Force he was to mould it into an efficient and effective unit and his abilities were recognised nationally in the New Years Honours List of 1915 when he was awarded the King's Police Medal for Distinguished Service with the citation published in the *London Gazette* reading *"he has shown exceptional administrative ability and has brought the Grimsby Force to a state of great efficiency"*.

Later the same year he received his Grimsby Police Good Service Medal although he had only 14 years service with Grimsby but had served as a police officer for 33 years since he first went to Sunderland as no more than a youth in 1882. John Stewart was further honoured nationally in 1920 when he was awarded the OBE for *"exemplary conduct during the Great War"*. He was one of four brothers who chose a police career, one serving at Glasgow, one in Edinburgh and another who rose to the rank of chief inspector at his previous force in Accrington. John Stewart died in his native Scotland in May 1938.

The Great Grimsby Borough Police was founded in April 1846 with a strength of four officers although this was increased to seven over the next ten years and later to more realistic levels as the idea of professional policing became accepted. The Force survived until April 1974 when the idea of small independent forces fell from fashion and it was amalgamated with the Lincolnshire Constabulary. It now forms a part of Humberside Police.

LEAMINGTON BOROUGH POLICE AND FIRE BRIGADE CORONATION MEDAL 1902

Instituted: 1902.

Ribbon: Royal blue.

Metal: Silver.

Size: 32 mm.

Description: (Obverse) the conjoined heads of the King and Queen facing left with the words H.M. EDWARD VII KING and H.M. ALEXANDRA QUEEN around the circumference and PROCLAIMED 1901 below; (reverse) plain apart from the inscription PRESENTED BY - ALDERMAN WACKRILL J.P. - TO THE - LEAMINGTON BOROUGH POLICE FORCE & FIRE - BRIGADE - ON THE OCCASION OF THE - CORONATION OF - HIS MAJESTY - EDWARD VII - JUNE 26th 1902 in eleven lines. A straight suspender and ring fitting were employed. They were issued unnamed.

In addition to the officially produced medal awarded to officers from the two London forces and the unofficial award made in Windsor with its obvious royal connections, Leamington Spa was the only other force in the UK to issue a medal to commemorate this coronation. It was the first medal issued by the Force and was never repeated at any subsequent royal event.

One recipient was the Chief Constable—Alexander Thomson—who took up his appointment with the Force two years earlier. He started his police career with the Nottingham Police and was awarded the Royal Humane Society Bronze Medal in June 1893 for attempting to save a life. He stayed at Leamington until 1904 when he left to become the Chief Constable of Walsall Borough Police where he stayed until his retirement at the age of 58 in 1921. He was also awarded the County and Borough Police version of the Coronation (Police) Medal 1911 whilst at Walsall.

The Leamington Spa Borough Police was founded in 1835 with an establishment of 21 officers although this was reduced to 14 when the Warwickshire County Constabulary was formed in 1857. In 1947 the Leamington Spa Borough Police amalgamated with the County Force.

In May 1903 the King and Queen embarked on a post-coronation tour of Scotland with a commemorative medal being issued to 2,950 police officers, troops, the Fire Brigade and members of other ancillary services who were involved in parades and escort duties during the tour. The Visit to Scotland Medal 1903 was very similar to the previous year's official Coronation Medal apart from the change of the year on the reverse to 1903 and the inscription SCOTTISH POLICE around the upper circumference to replace the name of the English service. The ribbon was plain red and an ornate clasp decorated with a thistle was worn above the plain straight suspender bar.

The coronation of 1902 was the last occasion at which the issue of official medals was restricted to police officers from the two forces in the Metropolis. In 1911 when the next issue was made the practice was extended to the whole country.

LINCOLN CITY POLICE GOOD SERVICE MEDAL

Instituted: 17 June 1926.

Ribbon: Dark red with a green central stripe 6.5 mm wide.

Metal: Silver.

Size: 32 mm.

Description: (Obverse) the Coat of Arms of the City of Lincoln surrounded by a laurel wreath and surmounted by a scroll bearing the city motto with the legend FOR GOOD SERVICE above and LINCOLN CITY POLICE below; (reverse) a wreath of laurel tied at the base with a ribbon usually with the recipients name, rank and number inscribed centrally. Examples exist with the central field left blank and the recipient's name inscribed on the lower rim. It was suspended from a swivelling straight bar attached by a claw fitting.

Although there were a great many unique designs amongst medals issued by borough watch committees and police forces several were almost identical in appearance with the only differences being on the obverse where the name of the force and the coat of arms used were changed. Most were presented to reward officers for "good service" with a qualifying period ranging from ten years to 25 years without a blemish on their record. Bars for further periods of five years service without black marks were awarded by some forces and one—Rochdale Borough—issued two separate medals—one bronze, one silver, with different ribbons—on the achievement of 20 and 25 years service respectively.

The medal issued in Lincoln followed the pattern of using the city coat of arms in the centre of the obverse surrounded by an outer band with the words FOR GOOD SERVICE in the upper half and the name of the Force—LINCOLN CITY POLICE—in the lower half. The coat of arms is surmounted by a scroll inscribed with the city motto—*floreat lindum* (Lincoln Flourishes)—all contained in a wreath of laurel. Lincolns coat of arms is very simple in design—a red cross with a golden fleur-de-lis (representing the Virgin Mary, the Patron Saint of the City and the Cathedral) on a silver shield. It is thought to be at least 500 years old.

The reverse was also very similar, almost identical, in design to many others with a wreath of laurel tied at the base by a flowing bow surrounding a central field for the recipients rank, name and date of the award to be engraved although, in the case of the Lincoln City medal, it was sometimes left blank with the details engraved on the lower rim.

Although the basic design on the reverse of many medals was similar, the inscription with the recipients details varied greatly. Most carried the name of the recipient, usually with the rank held and the officer's number. In some cases the date of the award was engraved, in others the date the officer joined the Force and occasionally with neither date recorded. Many also carried a few words noting that the medal had been awarded by the Watch Committee although the wording often differed from force to force.

In Lincoln the medal was awarded to officers of all ranks on completion of 20 years service without a default being recorded against their name. It was formally abolished in October 1941 although holders were permitted to wear the ribbon until they retired from the Force. The city force was founded in 1836 but ceased to exist on 1 April 1967 on amalgamation with the Lincolnshire Police.

The use of the Latin name for Lincoln (*Lindum*) in the motto is indicative of the Roman influence in the development of a number of place names in the UK although it is far less widespread than might be expected from the length of time the country was under Roman rule— 400 years. The first mention of "*Lindon*" referred to the pool at the foot of the hill where it is believed a 2,000 year old ancient Briton settlement was founded. With the arrival of the Romans this was latinized to "*Lindum*" and changed again as it achieved the status of a colony to "*Lindum Colonia*" (the Colony of Lindum for retired legionaries). As the Roman influence declined the name was altered twice in keeping with the evolution and development of the English language, first under the Saxons to "*Lindcylene*" —(Saxon Chronicle of 942 AD)—and later to Lincolia in the Domesday Book of 1086. Lincoln still means the *Colony of Lindum* despite these changes.

Modern English place names all derive from one of three basic sources—the name of a person or family, a significant geographical feature of the area or an early form of habitation or a combination of two of these sources, occasionally all three. The first written record of place names usually occurred long after the Romans had left with many first appearing in something close to their present form in the Domesday Book of 1086. The origin of many names is relatively easy to understand—Plymouth, for example, was first referred to in 1230 as *"Plymmue"*—the Mouth of the River Plym—taken from the Old English *"mutha"* and the name of the local river although it is doubtful if *"Plym"* was ever its true original name. Some names have a less apparent origin—Bristol appeared in the Domesday Book as *"Bristou"* although it was known earlier in the 11th century as *"Brycg stowe"* taken from the Old English for the assembly place by the bridge.

The use of personal or family names appears less frequently than the two other sources but is an important feature of a number of well-known places. In 1086, Brighton was recorded as *"Bristelmestune"*—the farmstead of a man called Beorhthelm using his personal name and the Old English word—*"tun"*—meaning enclosure, farmstead, village, manor or estate. At the same time Grimsby appeared as *"Grimesbi"*—the farmstead of a man called Grimr—although, in this instance, the derivation came from Old Scandinavian (the language of the Vikings) with the use of the personal name and the word—*"b"*—meaning homestead or village in Old Norse or Old Danish. The influence of the Viking invasion and settlement is very evident in the north and east of England and occurs in a large number of place names. Old English is, however, the predominent source and has given rise to some very descriptive names with some also being quite attractive in their original form, others less so. Birkenhead in the Wirral was first recorded around the beginning of the 12th century as *"Bircheveth"*, taken from the Old English—*"birce"* and *"heafod"*, and meaning "the headland where birch trees grow". Liverpool, on the other hand, although also first appearing at the same time, was known as *"liuerpol"*—"a creek with thick or muddy water".

One corner of England is unique in the origin of a large number of its place names. Cornwall was one of the few areas of England not reached during the Anglo-Saxon conquest and settlement between the 5th and 9th centuries AD. The Old Cornish language survived the influence of the invaders and is preserved in many place names, a feature which becomes quickly apparent to any visitor to the county. The language has suffered less corruption over the years than Old English with many words which appear in names being the same as they were when they first appeared in written form almost 1,000 years ago. The word *"tre"*, meaning farm, which appeared in written form before the Domesday Book in 1086 has the same meaning and is spelt the same in the current Cornish language as it was then. Similarly, *"porth"*—harbour or port—with an equally old origin and spelling remains the same and can be seen in place names around the Cornish coast.

Medals issued by watch committees and the small local police forces which once existed in the UK can reveal a great deal about many aspects of our history beyond a few bare details of an officers service and his reward for a number of years good service. They can tell us much about many aspects of local history going back long before the concept of policing as we know it today was first established.

LIVERPOOL CITY POLICE ORDER OF MERIT

Instituted: 24 October 1851.

Ribbon: Blue with red edges and a red central stripe.

Metal: Silver.

Size: 32 mm.

Description: *(Obverse) the Coat of Arms of the City of Liverpool surrounded with a laurel wreath and with the city motto DEUS NOBIS HAEC OTIA FECIT in a banner above and the date 9th OCT 1851 along the bottom; (reverse) the inscription PRESENTED - BY - THE WATCH - COMMITTEE - TO - (engraved name of recipient in italics) - AS A REWARD - FOR GOOD - CONDUCT in nine lines in the central field with ORDER OF MERIT (above) and LIVERPOOL POLICE FORCE (below) around the circumference on a raised circle. The medal hung from a plain swivelling suspender bar.*

This Force is thought to be the first to issue a medal of any description to its officers in 1851 and followed this with two more until 1951 when they were discontinued. Two issues were cast in both silver and bronze with the colouring of the ribbon of the last issue also being different for each and changed once, leading to a combination of medals and ribbons which can be confusing and which has led to the publication and spread of misleading information over the years.

The first medal authorised resulted from a visit made to the city by Queen Victoria in October 1851. The initial suggestion was put to the Watch Committee by the Head Constable—M M G Dowling—in a report submitted by him at the committee meeting held on 24 October. The Force was very young, barely 15 years old, with no experience of dealing with such a prestigious event—a step into the unknown for all officers with many potential pitfalls. At the conclusion of the successful visit Mr Dowling was prompted to suggest that a medal be struck to reward his officers for their conduct and to commemorate the visit - a suggestion quickly approved by the Watch Committee a few weeks later. Six months after the approval was given an order was placed for 112 medals and 176 bars. Fourteen officers were to receive a first class medal with three bars, 26 a second class award with two and the majority—72—with a single bar (third class).

The estimate of cost initially put forward proved to be wildly inaccurate. It was suggested in October 1851 that the dies would cost "around £3" and each medal "about three shillings" with the total cost for an anticipated 150 medals being £22 10s (£22.50p). The true cost for 112 medals and bars in July 1852 when they were delivered had risen to £71 12s (£71.60p).

The banner above the shield on the obverse with the depiction of the Liver Bird carried the motto of Liverpool—*Deus Nobis Haec Otia Fecit*. There is more than one translation for the motto, one reads "God has given us this leisure" which is a literal interpretation of the Latin but the one which is believed to convey the intended meaning more accurately reads "God has bestowed these blessings on us" a quotation from Virgil (The Eclogues) and was suggested by James, the 10th Earl of Derby.

One condition only was attached to the award of the medal, that the officer should show a good conduct record for at least five years prior to the visit. Each five-year period of good conduct back to the founding of the Force in 1836 was recognised by the award of a bar—a maximum of three available. Any future misconduct by an officer would have resulted in the temporary withdrawal of the medal as a punishment and a dismissal in its forfeiture altogether. There was a single presentation by the Chairman of the Watch Committee to all 112 eligible officers at a grand parade of the whole Force held in Hatton Garden on 5 August 1852.

The Liver Bird is arguably one of the most familiar and well-known parts of any city or town coat of arms in the country but very few people know its origin. Some think it is a mythical creature and, if they should ever fly away, Liverpool will be doomed. The truth is even less likely. Liverpool was founded on 28 August 1207 by King John who wanted to rule Ireland and needed a port under his control for his troops and the new town adopted his seal as its own. The seal showed the eagle of St John holding a sprig of broom (the symbol of the Royal House of Plantagenet) in its beak. During the English Civil War 437 years later in 1644 the seal was lost. A new one was made but looked more like a cormorant with the sprig of broom becoming a piece of seaweed—both familiar sights to the local artist who had probably never seen an eagle. The official coat of arms granted in 1797 accepted that it was a cormorant holding a piece of seaweed.

The name of the bird is also subject to a certain amount of controversy with the simplest explanation being that it is taken from the first half of the cities name although the origin of "Liver" is far from clear with a number of spellings (more than 14) appearing over the years. One possible explanation for the bird's name arises from a gift made to the city in 1668 by the Earl of Derby—a silver mace *"engraved with the arms of the town, viz a leaver"*. A leaver or liver was thought to be the Dutch name for a water pelican of shoveller (a species of duck) and could be the origin although there is a school of thought that it refers to the Welsh name for seaweed—laver—less convincing but interesting. Whatever the origin, the Liver Bird admirably serves its purpose as the symbol of the city recognised world-wide.

LIVERPOOL CITY POLICE DIAMOND JUBILEE GOOD SERVICE MEDAL

Instituted: 1897.

Ribbon: Identical to the Order of Merit of 1851.

Metal: Silver and bronze.

Size: 32 mm.

Description: Obverse) the Old Head of Queen Victoria with the words VICTORIA DIAMOND JUBILEE above and the dates 1837 - 1897 below; (reverse) the Liver Bird on a shield topped with the royal crown surrounded by a wreath of oak and laurel. A scroll above the shield contained the city motto with the words FOR GOOD SERVICE and LIVERPOOL CITY POLICE around the circumference. A claw fitting and straight swivelling suspender were used.

The second medal issued in Liverpool was also prompted by Queen Victoria, this time on the occasion of her Diamond Jubilee in 1897. Official medals had been issued to officers from the Metropolitan and City of London Police in 1887 to commemorate the Golden Jubilee and the idea was taken up in a few other forces ten years later including Liverpool City. A second official medal was struck for officers from the two London forces with a bar bearing the date 1897 being awarded to recipients of the earlier issue.

The conditions for the award of the local medal in Liverpool were widened from those applicable to the Order of Merit almost 50 years earlier to reflect the fact that the Force was now well established and the qualifying length of service could be increased to give more meaning to the good service aspect. The medals were awarded to all officers who had completed 20 years approved service without *"a single black mark"* being recorded against them. There were 46 officers of the ranks of inspector and above who qualified for the silver medal and 63 sergeants and constables eligible for the bronze.

The conditions, however, were such that a few very senior officers failed to qualify and it decided that a special issue of silver medals should be made to officers of the rank of inspector or above who had served in those ranks between 20 June 1887 and 20 June 1897 irrespective of their total length of service. The Assistant Head Constable—Mr Dunning—had been with the Liverpool Police for three years and had only 15 years total police service (12 years in the Royal Irish Constabulary) thereby failing to qualify for the general medal issue but fitted the amended criteria for a special award. Similarly, Chief Superintendent Sperrin, Chief Clerk in the Head Constable's Office, but with only 18 years service was able to receive a medal. In all, standard and special silver medals were awarded to 49 officers

LIVERPOOL CITY POLICE GOOD SERVICE MEDAL

Instituted: 1900.

Ribbon: Red with a single blue diagonal stripe (silver medal) Blue with a single red diagonal stripe (bronze medal)

Metal: Silver and Bronze.

Size: 32 mm.

Description: Obverse) identical to the reverse of the Liverpool City Police Diamond Jubilee issue; (reverse) a wreath of laurel tied at the base by a bow with a central field containing an inscription with the words PRESENTED BY THE WATCH COMMITTEE, sometimes with the date of the award and the recipient's name engraved on the rim, sometimes with all details on the reverse.

After the initial presentation to commemorate the Diamond Jubilee the medals were re-designed and re-issued from 1900 onwards as a good service award for officers of all ranks. They continued to be issued in silver and bronze but the conditions were changed in 1918 with the only difference then being the qualifying length of service—20 years for the bronze medal, 25 years for the silver.

The inscription in the central field came in two styles. The words PRESENTED BY WATCH COMMITTEE were present in both styles followed by either the date of the award only with the rank, number and name of the recipient on the lower rim (for issues up to the early 1940s) or with all the information (rank, number, name and date) within the central field (later examples). Service of more than 30 years was recognised by the award of a silver bar bearing the legend SERVICE OVER 30 YEARS in raised lettering with a raised border.

Different ribbons were used for the silver and bronze medals. Initially, the silver medals were hung from a red ribbon with a single blue diagonal line running downhill left to right at an angle of 30 degrees. Bronze medals employed the same design but with the colours reversed. The design was changed during the 1930s to a more traditional pattern although the reverse colouring was retained to distinguish between the two medals. The silver medal ribbon became red with a blue central stripe, all of equal width, and a thin white line on either side of the stripe. The bronze medal ribbon was blue with a red central stripe and white lines.

The Liverpool City Police survived as a separate force until 1967 when it was amalgamated with its close neighbour at Bootle Borough to form the Liverpool and Bootle Constabulary. Seven years later, on 1 April 1974, as a result of local government re-organisation, it took over parts of the Lancashire and Cheshire forces to become the Merseyside Police.

(Right): *Inspector Harold Butcher wearing his Liverpool City Good Service Medal (left) and the Liverpool Shipwreck and Humane Society Bravery Medal (right).*

MANCHESTER CITY POLICE BRAVERY MEDAL

Instituted: February 1894.

Ribbon: Crimson.

Metal: Silver.

Size: 32 mm.

Description: *(Obverse)* the Coat of Arms of the City of Manchester inscribed above with MANCHESTER CITY POLICE and below with FOR BRAVERY; *(reverse)* a laurel wreath tied at the base with a ribbon surrounding the central area which was engraved with the words PRESENTED BY THE WATCH COMMITTEE and the name, division and number of the recipient. The medal was fitted to a scrolled swivelling suspender by means of a claw fitting and attached to the uniform by a buckle pin. There were differences in the scrolling of the suspender between the early and later issues.

The earliest medal solely awarded to police officers for bravery on a regular basis by a watch committee was introduced in Manchester in February 1894. Although it was intended primarily for award to officers from the Manchester City Police it was presented to others from neighbouring forces on a number of occasions. Some of the first awards made were to officers from three different forces at a ceremony held at Manchester Town Hall on 13 December 1894 when the Lord Mayor presented five officers with the new medal. Two officers from Lancashire County Constabulary (Constables F Schegel and J Rutter) were rewarded for *"stopping a runaway horse attached to a wagonette"* and one from the Salford Borough Police (Constable J D Roxborough) was honoured for *"rescuing a boy from drowning in the River Irwell"*. The Manchester City Force was represented by Constables C Whiting and L Keenan whose bravery in *"stopping runaway horses attached to vans"* was recognised. Constable Whiting was seriously injured and off duty for one month as a result.

Fifteen months later a further award was made to an officer from Manchester City by the Watch Committee. On 9 April 1896 Constable Lomas appeared before members of the Committee and was presented with the medal by the Chairman—Alderman Mark—for saving a boy from drowning in the canal near Princess Street. A witness to the rescue sent a cheque for one guinea as a token of his appreciation—this too was handed to the officer.

The medal was not restricted to members of the regular Force—during the air raids experienced in the Second World War it was awarded to at least one member of the Police War Reserve (Harold Norry) in 1941. At the same presentation the Watch Committee also recognised the courage of six regular officers (Constables Thomas Williams, John Craik, Herbert Davies, Frederick White, Williamson Harding and George Beardmore) on the recommendation of the Chief Constable, Sir John Maxwell. From the time of its introduction to the last award made in 1948 a total of 71 medals were presented and it is believed that four second award bars were won.

The first mention of the settlement which was to grow into the modern city came in the 4th century when it was known by the Celtic name of *"Mamucio"*. It was recorded in the Domesday Book in 1086 as *"Mamecestre"*—a Roman fort or town (*ceaster*) added to a part of the original name. It was constituted as a free borough in 1301 and granted city status in 1853. The meaning of the elements of the city coat of arms as depicted on the medal are of indicative of the history of the city and were granted by the College of arms in 1842. The design on the central shield was taken from the arms of the lords of Manchester before it was made a municipal borough in 1838 with the addition of a ship in full sail in the upper part of the shield signifying the commercial enterprise of the city's history. The globe above the shield contains a numbers of bees to recognise the fact that manufactured items from the city were exported to all parts of the world. The two supporters are a unicorn and lion each with a red rose on the shoulder. The city motto—*"concilio et labore"* contained in a scroll beneath the shield has two meanings. A precise translation means *"by council and work"* although a more meaningful interpretation is taken from the Bible—*"Let reason be the beginning of every work and let counsel go before every action"*—(Ecclesiasticus, chapter 37, verse 16)

The present Greater Manchester Police is the largest force in England outside London but experienced a disorganised start to its life as a new borough force in January 1839 when the first watch committee was formed. The existing Court Leat and Police Commissioners refused to recognise the authority of the Watch Committee and refused to disband the day police and night watchmen leading to a situation where 600 men patrolled the Borough at the same time. Within a

Police Medals of the World

few months the Government was forced to pass the Manchester Police Act 1839 introducing a new body modelled on the Metropolitan Police in London under a Commissioner—Sir Charles Shaw—appointed by Westminster. On 17 October 1839 the Force was formally founded with 200 officers. The rôle of the Commissioner ceased in 1842 and Captain Edward Willis assumed the post of Chief Constable with 316 men under his command.

The early years of professional policing were free from much of the bureaucracy which plagues present day police officers although they did not have access to many of the advantages enjoyed by their successors. The growth of scientific help available to detectives is, arguably, one of the most beneficial changes seen in the Police Service in the late 20th century. When Josiah Caminada—one of the country's leading detectives and a member of the Manchester City Police—was called upon to investigate the sudden death of an apparently drunken man (John Fletcher) in a Hansom cab in February 1889, he had little scientific aid available, an unknown cause of death and the vague description of the dead man's companion shortly before the body was found. The mystery of the cause of death was solved by an examination of the deceased's internal organs with poisoning being found responsible. Caminada was looking for a murderer. His enquiries led him to the home of a Charles Parton where he found some of Fletchers possessions and learnt that he had been killed during a bungled attempt at robbery using poison to subdue him. Charles Parton was arrested, indicted, tried on a not-guilty plea, convicted of murder and sentenced to death—all in 21 days from the time of death!—less time than it takes today to caution a boy for scrumping apples.

With the aid of detectives of the national renown of Josiah Caminada the Manchester City Police grew from its ignominious start into a highly respected professional body. It co-existed with the neighbouring Salford City Police until 1 April 1968 when the two forces amalgamated to become the Manchester and Salford Police. Six years later, in 1974, together with the borough forces at Wigan, Rochdale, Bolton and others, it became a part of the Greater Manchester Police.

NEW WINDSOR BOROUGH POLICE CORONATION MEDAL OF 1902

Instituted: 1902.

Ribbon: Red with a 6.5 mm green stripe at each edge.

Metal: Bronze.

Size: 32 mm.

Description: (Obverse) the conjoined heads of King Edward VII and Queen Alexandra acing right with the words KING EDWARD on the left edge and QUEEN ALEXANDRA on the right edge; (reverse) the Coat of Arms of the Borough of Windsor with a Kings crown above the shield. A scroll ran along the lower half of the shield containing the legend BOROUGH OF WINDSOR with the word POLICE placed outside the scroll at the very bottom. The shield and scroll were surrounded by a raised circle bearing the inscription TO COMMEMORATE THE CORONATION with the date - 1902 - at the lower edge. A plain straight swivelling suspender and claw fitting were employed. The medals were issued unnamed.

The official issue of medals to commemorate royal events dates back to the mid-16th century but it was not until the reign of Queen Victoria that they were intended for wear with uniforms. Unofficial medals were struck by a large number of bodies at the time of her coronation in 1837 but the first one produced specifically for police officers was the Liverpool City Police Order of Merit in 1851—a local issue only.

The Golden Jubilee in 1887 saw the first official issue of a medal to police officers—The Jubilee (Police) Medal 1887—although it was only made available to the Metropolitan and City of London Forces as a momento for those who took part in the parades and celebrations in London on 21 June 1887. The obverse depicted the Veiled Head of Queen Victoria with the reverse having a wreath of oak leaves surrounded by the name of the recipient's force—METROPOLITAN POLICE or CITY OF LONDON POLICE. The date—1887—was placed at the bottom edge. In the central field were the words JUBILEE - OF - HER MAJESTY - QUEEN - VICTORIA in five lines. It was cast in bronze, 36 mm in diameter and hung from a plain dark blue ribbon.

page 142

Ten years later, to mark the Diamond Jubilee, a second issue was authorised—The Jubilee (Police) Medal 1897—and was very similar in design but with the Old Head on the obverse and the date on the reverse suitably amended. The ribbon was the same. It again restricted to police officers from London although three forces in the north of England (Birkenhead, Bootle and Liverpool) issued their own unofficial award to officers who met certain qualifying criteria in relation to their length of service. Holders from the two London forces who had previously received the 1887 medal were awarded a bronze clasp with the date—1897. More than 8,000 medals were issued to police officers.

The practice of awarding medals only to officers from the Metropolis was continued at the Coronation of King Edward VII and Queen Alexandra in 1902. The medal—The Coronation (Police) Medal 1902—was struck in silver and bronze for issue according to the rank of the recipient. Almost 18,000 bronze medals were given to constables and sergeants with 61 officers receiving a silver award. Members of the London Fire Brigade (1,009), St John Ambulance Brigade (912) and the Police Ambulance Service (204) also received the medals. The obverse depicted the conjoined busts of the King and Queen with the reverse showing a crown in the lower half above a branch of oak going left and a branch of laurel going right. Above the crown were the words CORONATION - of - HIS MAJESTY - KING EDWARD VII in three lines with the date—1902—below and to the right of the crown. The name of the recipient's service was placed around the upper circumference. The medal hung from a red ribbon with a narrow dark blue central stripe.

Windsor Borough was one of only two forces to issue unofficial medals to celebrate the coronation in 1902 and repeated the exercise nine years later in 1911 at the coronation of King George V.

NEW WINDSOR BOROUGH POLICE CORONATION MEDAL OF 1911

Instituted: 1911.

Ribbon: Identical to the 1902 medal.

Metal: Bronze.

Size: 32 mm.

Description: (Obverse) the conjoined crowned busts of the King and Queen facing left with a raised circumscription which read KING GEORGE V AND QUEEN MARY - CROWNED JUNE 22 1911; (reverse) the Coat of Arms of the Borough of Windsor (a castle and a stag) with a scroll below containing the words WINDSOR BOROUGH POLICE and a circumscription reading TO CELEBRATE THE CORONATION - 1911. A plain straight swivelling suspender was used.

It was not until 1911 and the Coronation of King George V that the practice of awarding commemorative medals to police officers was extended to the whole country and not restricted to those from the Metropolis where the event actually took place. The Coronation (Police) Medal of 1911 was awarded to 2,565 officers from county and borough forces in England and Wales and 280 to Scottish constabularies. In addition awards were made to almost 20,000 members of the Metropolitan Police and 6,000 members of other services. The medal hung by a ring suspender and claw fitting from a red ribbon with three narrow blue stripes, one placed centrally and the two others towards each edge. The obverse featured the crowned bust of the King facing left; the reverse had an imperial crown at the centre within a circle of floral stylised motifs with the words CORONATION 1911 below and the name of the appropriate service above—COUNTY AND BOROUGH POLICE, for example.

The Watch Committee in Windsor followed the precedent set in 1902 and issued a further medal of their own in the Borough to celebrate this later coronation. The New Windsor Borough Police Coronation Medal of 1911 was very similar to the previous issue and used the same ribbon. The obverse obviously changed and depicted the conjoined crowned busts of the new King and Queen. The reverse again showed the arms of the Borough of Windsor although the shape of the shield was more complex and the crown which previously stood above the shield was missing. The scroll below the shield was less ornate and included the word POLICE unlike the earlier medal where it stood alone

The New Windsor Borough Police was founded in 1836 and lasted as a separate body until two years after the end of the Second World war in 1947 when it became a part of the Berkshire County Constabulary. It was the longest lasting of the borough forces in the county—Wantage, Adingdon, Maidenhead, Newbury and Wallingford all merged before the end of the 19th century. On 1 April 1968, however, the Berkshire Constabulary became a part of the Thames Valley Constabulary (Police from 1974).

The police medals issued in 1911 were the last to be awarded specifically to police officers. Further coronation medals were issued in 1937 and 1953 and jubilee medals in 1935 and 1977 and were presented to police officers but they were the same as those issued to many thousands other citizens—85,000 were awarded at the Silver Jubilee of King George V in 1935 and 129,000 to celebrate the coronation of the present Sovereign in 1953

PLYMOUTH CITY CONSTABULARY CONSPICUOUS BRAVERY AND GOOD SERVICE MEDAL

Instituted: 16 April 1930.

Ribbon: Dark red with two broad blue stripes (6.5 mm) and a central thin blue line.

Metal: Silver.

Size: 36 mm.

Description: (Obverse) the Coat of Arms of the City of Plymouth surrounded by a laurel leaf wreath topped with an imperial crown to which the suspension ring was attached; (reverse) a rectangular panel for the recipient's name and the legend PLYMOUTH CITY CONSTABULARY above and GOOD SERVICE below.

Introduced by the third Chief Constable of the combined Force—Archibald Kennedy Wilson—who was appointed in 1929 but left after only three years in 1932 to become Chief Constable of Liverpool City Police. The conditions for the grant and retention of the medal were straightforward but lengthy and have led to some confusion which persists today in relation to the penultimate (seventh) condition.

(1) The medal may be granted to a member of the Force for any act of conspicuous bravery, irrespective of length of service, and the Watch Committee shall in each case determine whether the circumstances of the act of bravery are such as to warrant the grant of the medal.

(2) Where the member of the Force has been granted the medal by fulfilment of the conditions relating to good service and subsequently performs an act of conspicuous bravery for which he would be entitled to the grant of the medal, he shall be granted a bar to the medal.

(3) Any medal so granted shall not be withdrawn except where the recipient is dismissed from the service, or is required to resign forthwith as an alternative to dismissal.

(4) The medal shall be granted to every member of the Force who has completed 17 years service, provided:

(a) He is zealous and efficient in the discharge of his duties.

(b) No default has been recorded against him during his service.

(c) If he is a constable, he is in receipt of the increment in accordance with paragraph 58 of the Police Regulations.

(5) The retention of the medal for good service shall be subject to the holder complying with the following conditions:

 (a) He shall continue to perform his duties with zeal and efficiency.

 (b) He must have no default recorded against him.

 (c) He must, if a constable, after 22 years service, be in receipt of the additional increment in accordance with paragraph 59 of the Police Regulations.

(6) The medal shall be withdrawn unless each and all of the foregoing conditions are satisfied.

(7) Where a member of the Force has been granted the medal for an act of conspicuous bravery and subsequently fulfils the conditions for good service, he shall be granted a bar to the medal.

(8) The medal shall be worn on the left breast and will rank last in order of precedence.

This last instruction was short-lived until it was pointed out in 1933 that only medals and decorations awarded by the Sovereign could be worn on the left, any unofficial awards were to be worn on the right breast only. Consequently groups to which officers were entitled for service during the Great War and earlier in India, South Africa and possibly elsewhere were separated from the local award, often forever. The police career of a Great War veteran can often remain unknown as a result and some groups are inevitably incomplete.

The coat of arms of the City of Plymouth above a banner contained the city motto—*Turris fortissima est nomen Jehova* (the name of the Lord is our strongest tower)—which is thought to refer to the siege of Plymouth between 1642 and 1646 during the Civil War. The shield of the arms shows the cross of St Andrew (the Mother Church of Plymouth) with a castle turret in each quadrant and is supported by two lions. A naval crown stands above the shield with a lion's paw holding an anchor. The arms represent the history of the city with elements from its three parts—Plymouth, Devonport and Stonehouse. The central rectangular panel on the reverse was provided for the name of the recipient to be engraved—at the officer's own expense—resulting in very few (if any) being inscribed.

The bar for gallantry was silver, of the slip-on top and plain in design with the words FOR GALLANTRY. The bar for good service mentioned in the conditions for the award of medals and bars is something of an unknown quantity. Some have speculated that it was inscribed with the legend GOOD SERVICE which would seem logical although it is doubtful if any were ever issued and this remains a matter of conjecture.

Awards for gallantry numbered 25 in total with a further nine bars granted to officers already in possession of the medal for good service. Awards for long service numbered 172. Its position as a major naval base and the largest city in Devon caused Plymouth to be the target of severe bombing between 1941 and 1943 and all awards of the medal for gallantry were made in this period. Very often the award was prompted by a more prestigious national honour granted to the officer concerned. Twenty-one officers from the Regular Force and Special Constabulary were honoured nationally for their bravery with one receiving the George Medal, 16 the British Empire Medal for Gallantry and four the King's Commendation for Brave Conduct.

John Lindsey joined the Force in November 1919 and had risen to the rank of inspector at the outbreak of war. Seventeen years later, on 18 November 1936, the Watch Committee granted him their medal for good service. Inspector Lindsey served in the city during the air raids and was the senior officer on duty when the City Hospital at Greenbank was bombed in one of the worst attacks experienced. The citation published in the *London Gazette* of 25 July 1941 announcing the award of the BEM for Gallantry clearly illustrated his courage:

> "During an air raid the City Hospital, Plymouth, was struck by high explosive bombs. Children and nurses were trapped beneath the debris which caught fire, causing dense smoke and fumes. Bombs continued to fall nearby but despite these dangers and difficulties Inspector Lindsey directed rescue operations and, under his able and courageous leadership, the police rescued nine children".

Prompted by this honour the Watch Committee awarded him a bar for gallantry to his medal on 15 October the same year. His personal record records that it was awarded *"for services during an air raid on Plymouth in March 1941"*. John Lindsey retired after 30 years service in 1949. His BEM and Plymouth City medal are in the possession of the Devon and Cornwall Constabulary but they have, over the years, become separated from any other medals to which he must have been entitled. Before he joined the Constabulary in 1919 he served in the Army for nine years and was, probably, entitled to two or three of Pip, Squeak and Wilfred, possibly others, in addition to the Defence Medal he would have been awarded for his service during the Second World War. Where these medals are is unknown and likely to remain so.

A second officer awarded the medal for gallantry—Constable 45 Daniel Crutchley—came to Plymouth from Stafford and joined the Force on 29 January 1931. He was to serve for 31 years and retire with the rank of inspector in 1962. As a constable on duty in April 1941 he won the British Empire Medal for Gallantry for his actions during an air raid.

> "A bomb demolished houses and persons were trapped in one of the basements. A large quantity of masonry and house timber, liable to collapse, was immediately over the spot at which it was necessary to begin rescue work. Regardless of this danger and the presence of coal gas, Constable Crutchley, working in a very limited space, started to remove the debris. He was partly overcome by the gas but

after a brief rest continued until, five hours later, three men were rescued. Crutchley worked ceaselessly and untiringly for a further five hours in an attempt to rescue other causalities. It was due to the efforts, courage and initiative of the Constable that the three persons were rescued alive.

(*London Gazette* 7 November 1941)

Daniel Crutchley was subsequently also awarded the Plymouth City Constabulary Conspicuous Gallantry Medal. In January 1948 he became eligible for a good service bar to his medal but there is no mention in his personal record of this ever being awarded and the medal itself has no bar fitted. He was later awarded the national Police Long Service and Good Conduct Medal in 1953 after 22 years service.

Members of the Special Constabulary do not appear to have been entitled to the medal for good service and there was, of course, the national Faithful Service Medal available to them. During the air raids, however, two won the BEM for Gallantry and three the King's Commendation for Brave Conduct—they were all also awarded the local medal for gallantry along with their regular colleagues.

In common with most borough police forces in England and Wales, the Plymouth City Police found its origins in the Municipal Corporations Act of 1935 which authorised the establishment of watch committees to introduce a means for the effective maintenance of law and order based on the example set by the Metropolitan Police in London six years earlier. In the County of Devon this milestone piece of legislation in police history led to the establishment of a number of new borough forces in 1936 including Barnstaple, Bideford, Tiverton, Torrington, South Molton and Totnes. The Devon County Constabulary which policed the rest of the County was not established for a further 21 years in 1857 following the implementation of the County and Borough Police Act 1856.

Also included amongst the borough forces introduced in 1836 was the Plymouth Borough Police, followed in 1838 by the Devonport Borough Police, both situated a few miles apart in the south-west of Devon at the mouth of the River Tamar which separates the county from Cornwall. The area between the two—Stonehouse—was an urban district of Devon with no formal policing arrangements until 1857 and the founding of the County Constabulary. Prior to 1844 West Stonehouse included an area west of the Tamar in what is now Cornwall, a situation much resented by the Cornish at the time and one which can still rouse deeply felt emotions in some quarters.

The Plymouth Borough Police was founded on 26 March 1836 with a strength of three inspectors and 27 constables under the command of the first superintendent—John Eastbridge Adams. He was to remain in post for a very short period before he resigned and was replaced on 7 October 1836 by John Sweet. His reign was to last longer but come to an ignominious end on 15 May 1838 when he was asked to resign by the Watch Committee for incompetence in his running of the Force. The period of stability the Force needed in these early years came with the appointment of the third superintendent (Lt Holman RN) who was to stay for ten years although he too left under a cloud on 15 March 1848 with his dismissal caused by money problems experienced in running the Force.

Eventually the Force settled down and developed into an efficient, well-run organisation by the turn of the century. The next milestone in the history of policing in Plymouth and the surrounding area came on 9 November 1914, three months after the outbreak of the Great War. The two borough forces of Plymouth and Devonport had both grown significantly since 1836 and it was argued in some quarters that more efficient policing would be achieved if they were to become joined, together with the urban district of Stonehouse in Devon County which was effectively being squeezed out of existence by the two boroughs, into a single police force. There was opposition in all three areas but the amalgamation duly took place.

Devonport was long considered to be a part of Plymouth and known as Plymouth Dock until the name was changed in 1824. The date of the founding of the Devonport Borough Police is not known precisely but the Force was certainly established in 1838 with a strength of two inspectors and 18 constables. William Brocklington became the first superintendent and stayed until 1853 when he resigned. At the time of the amalgamation in 1914 it was commanded by John Henderson Watson CBE KPM who went on to become the Chief Constable of Bristol City Police. The new enlarged Plymouth Borough Police was to be headed by Joseph Davidson Sowerby (13 July 1892 to 31 March 1917). The Stonehouse Division of the Devon Constabulary became a part of Plymouth with its single inspector, two sergeants and 15 constables. In 1928 the combined area was granted the city status and the Plymouth City Constabulary was born—later to be renamed the Plymouth City Police. The two terms used in the title of the Force—Police and Constabulary— were virtually interchangeable for some time before and after the amalgamation and the granting of city status.

The medal was discontinued in 1951 on the introduction of the national Police Long Service and Good Conduct Medal when the issue and wearing of local medals was prohibited although there were instances of officers being somewhat tardy in removing the ribbons from their tunics.

READING BOROUGH POLICE BRAVERY MEDAL

Instituted: 26 April 1904.

Ribbon: Royal blue with a central white stripe 4.5 mm wide.

Metal: Bronze.

Size: 36 mm.

Description: Obverse) the Coat of Arms of the Borough of Reading with the legend READING POLICE above and FOR BRAVERY below on a surrounding raised circle; (reverse) left plain for the recipient's details to be engraved. An ornate scrolled swivelling suspender was used.

The medal awarded by Reading Borough Police was of relatively simple design with the obverse showing the coat of arms of the Borough in the form of a shield containing five maidens' heads. The arms were granted in 1566 and are based on the common seal of the town which had been in use since 1365.

The central head is shown wearing a Saxon crown and is believed to represent Edward, King of the West Saxons, who reigned from 975 to 978. He was assassinated by his step-mother—Queen Alfreda—to allow her son (Ethelred the Unready) to take the throne.

One of the first recorded instances of the award of the medal was made by the Watch Committee at their meeting held on 28 January 1907 when Constable 83 Monger was rewarded for stopping a runaway horse. He was also given a gratuity of 20 shillings (£1). Exactly one year later Constable 17 Gillings was similarly awarded a gratuity of 20 shillings and the bravery medal also for stopping a runaway horse. The incidence of officers being rewarded in some way for stopping runaway horses was quite common in the early years of most police forces. The nature of the award, however, varies greatly. In some forces a commendation from the Chief Constable or Watch Committee was deemed sufficient with or without a gratuity, in others, like Reading, a local medal was awarded. In the Cornwall Constabulary, two officers received the KPM for Gallantry although the circumstances on both occasions were exceptional.

Constable Gillings was awarded a bar to his medal in January 1909 for a second act of bravery again involving stopping a runaway horse. By 1911 the gratuity given had been increased to £1 10s (£1.50) when Constable Searle was awarded his bravery medal. The last known award was made on 18 March 1941 to Constable 104 H Smith for her courage saving a lady from drowning in the River Kennet. The medal was finally abolished in 1951.

The Reading Borough Police was founded in February 1836 and survived as a separate force until 1968 when it was combined with the Oxford City Police and the county forces of Berkshire, Buckinghamshire and Oxfordshire to form the Thames Valley Constabulary (later Police). It was at the time the oldest surviving force in the newly formed police area having outlived other borough forces at Maidenhead, Adingdon, Wycombe, Wallingford, Chipping Norton and six others across the three counties.

The principle of local recognition for acts of bravery displayed in 1904 in Reading remains as relevant today as it did then. In 1996 the Tayside Police introduced a medal for award to police officers and members of the public where the act did not merit a national award but which deserved greater reward than the Chief Constables commendation—the most recent example of the principle first established in the 19th century and continued by Reading and other forces.

REIGATE BOROUGH POLICE GOOD SERVICE MEDAL

Instituted: September 1913.

Ribbon: Medium blue.

Metal: Silver.

Size: 32 mm.

Description: (Obverse) the Coat of Arms of the Borough of Reigate within an outer band containing the inscription 25 YEARS GOOD SERVICE above and REIGATE BOROUGH POLICE below; (reverse) a wreath of oak leaves with the recipient's rank and name and the date of the award inscribed in the central field. The medal hung from a plain straight suspender. It was awarded to all members of the force for 25 years good service without a blemish on their records.

The Reigate Borough Police was formed in 1864 but became a victim of defence measures deemed necessary during the Second World War which particularly affected a number of similar small borough forces along the south coast of England. The subject of force reorganisations was first raised in the 1920s by the Desborough Committee and recommended in detail for England and Wales in 1932 but no action was taken to implement the proposals. In July 1942, however, a war-time measure [Defence (Amalgamation of Police Forces) Regulations 1942] was introduced by the Home Secretary (Herbert Morrison) to amalgamate forces in areas where it was thought necessary to facilitate Naval, Military and Air Force operations. The most obvious targets were the small borough forces along the south coast of England in the counties of Kent, Sussex, Hampshire and Surrey.

The County of Kent had nine city and borough forces which were to be lost with a total authorised establishment of 560 officers of all ranks. The thought of Dover and Folkestone with 65 and 73 officers being totally separate and the area between the two boroughs being the responsibility of the Kent County Constabulary may seem incongruous today particularly in view of the position of the two towns so close to occupied Europe but the proposal to merge them and the seven others was met with fierce resistance. The objections were familiar at the time and were to be repeated long after the war ended each time the subject of amalgamations was broached by successive home secretaries—a loss of local identity and local knowledge, the destruction of small very efficient police forces and the inefficiency of large unwieldy organisations. When the proposals were first put forward there was a promise from the Home Secretary that any amalgamations would lapse when the war was over but this promise was treated with a great deal of scepticism. Many thought the measures to be another step towards the establishment of a national police force and that the mergers would prove to be irrevocable.

By early 1943 the proposed amalgamations had all taken place with varying degrees of resistance. In Surrey, the Reigate and Guildford Borough Police Forces had merged with the County Force to become the Surrey Joint Constabulary and both were never to regain their independence. With the merger the issue of the Reigate Borough Police Good Service Medal ceased.

The Police Act of 1946 required that every non-county borough police area would cease to exist and become a part of the county are— the fears of 1942 were realised. Reigate, Guildford (Surrey), Winchester (Hampshire), Salisbury (Wilts) and the nine Kent city and borough forces of Canterbury, Dover, Folkestone, Maidstone, Rochester, Gravesend, Margate, Tunbridge Wells, and Ramsgate were all gone forever.

In Sussex, the promise made by Mr Morrison to the House of Commons that *"it automatically comes to and end at the end of the war"* was kept. The three borough forces at Hastings, Eastbourne and Brighton all resumed their separate identities in 1947 and were to remain independent until 1968 when they were merged with the East and West Sussex Constabularies into the Sussex Police. Hove Borough, however, never regained its identity and merged with East Sussex in 1947 until the next round of amalgamations in 1968.

In the early years of professional policing in England and Wales there were at least 285 separate forces. This had been reduced to 183 by 1939 and 133 by April 1947. At the end of 1999 there were 43.

ROCHDALE BOROUGH POLICE MEDAL FOR BRAVERY

Instituted: 15 November 1928.

Ribbon: Red.

Metal: Silver.

Size: 35 mm.

Description: (Obverse) the Rochdale Coat of Arms and borough motto within a wreath of half oak (left) and half laurel (right) surrounded by the legend ROCHDALE COUNTY BOROUGH POLICE in a raised outer band; (reverse) a three line inscription AWARDED - BY THE - WATCH COMMITTEE followed by the rank and name of the recipient. Around the circumference were the words FOR EXTREME BRAVERY. It was suspended from a swivelling suspender with a floral design and attached to the uniform by an ornate pin buckle.

Although there was a national award for bravery available from 1909 to police officers of all ranks in the shape of the King's Police Medal for Gallantry, some forces introduced their own medal to reward them locally. Some were introduced for bravery only (Reading) whilst others were available for gallantry or long service (Plymouth). Rochdale Borough was the only force to use different medals.

The first to be authorised by the Watch Committee was the Rochdale Borough Police Medal for Bravery introduced to recognise acts of outstanding gallantry by members of the Police Force and Fire Brigade. Before the Second World War it was usual for control of the local Fire Service to rest with the Chief Constable in borough forces as a branch of the force. There was a separate and distinct rank structure and many officers spent their whole career as fire constables although they could move from one branch to another if they wished. The formation of the National Fire Service during the blitz on British towns and cities in the early 1940s changed this forever and led, ultimately, to the totally independent service which exists today.

The coat of arms depicted on the medal obverse was granted in 1857 with the devices meant to represent the two staple trades of the Borough—wool and cotton. The inner shield has a sack of wool surrounded by a cotton plant with the outer shield holding eight martlets (swallows in heraldic terms). The crest which sits above the shield consists of the iron centre of an old mill rind topped by a fleece of wool suspended by a golden hand. The motto of the borough—*credo signo* (believe in the sign)—was contained within a scroll beneath the shield.

Although most borough police forces were formed in 1836 or shortly afterwards the Rochdale Borough Police did not come into existence until 11 March 1857. The first chief constable commanded a force of 15 officers who patrolled their beat dressed in a blue swallow-tail frock coat with shiny buttons, blue trousers, a tall hat with a leather top and a brass-buckled belt. A boot allowance of sixpence (2.5 p) was paid to each officer to supplement his meagre pay. The Force was a progressive and innovative body, introducing police dogs (1898), a central criminal records office (1898), the first motorised fire engine (1908) and a primitive radio system (1927) many years before they were considered in other forces.

In 1969, in common with a number of similar borough forces in the north-west of England (Bolton and Wigan included), the Rochdale Borough Police and its 220 officers were swept up in the vogue for amalgamation and became a part of the Lancashire Constabulary. This lasted barely five years before the Manchester and Salford Police and large parts of the former Lancashire County Force, including Rochdale, were formed into the Greater Manchester Police.

This award proved to be very long-lived and wasn't formally abolished until 1969 at the time of the amalgamation with the Lancashire Constabulary.

ROCHDALE BOROUGH POLICE LONG AND FAITHFUL SERVICE MEDAL

Instituted: *14 August 1930.*

Ribbon: *Blue with a central red stripe, all of equal width (silver medal) Blue with two bands of red, all of equal width (bronze medal)*

Metal: *Silver and bronze.*

Size: *35 mm.*

Description: *(Obverse) coat of Arms of the Borough of Rochdale with the town motto and the legend ROCHDALE COUNTY BOROUGH POLICE around the circumference; (reverse) a six line inscription in the central field AWARDED BY THE WATCH COMMITTEE TO (rank and name). Around the circumference was the legend FOR LONG AND FAITHFUL SERVICE. The medals were suspended to a plain straight swivelling suspender by a claw.*

Two years later after the introduction of the medal for bravery the Watch Committee introduced another to reward officers for long service without a blemish on their records. Two types were awarded—a medal in bronze to recognise 20 years service and one struck in silver to reward 25 years. It was identical to the medal for bravery apart from the circumscription on the reverse where the words FOR LONG AND FAITHFUL SERVICE were substituted for the reference to bravery. There were some differences in the positioning of the recipient's details over the years. The most usual position was on the reverse beneath the inscription but examples exist with the naming on the lower rim. The ribbons for the bronze and silver issues differed. The bronze medal hung from a red ribbon with two blue stripes, all of equal width, and the silver from a blue ribbon with a single central red stripe 9 mm wide. Both medals were attached to the tunic by a plain trapezoidal brooch bar with a partly-scrolled lower edge.

Many officers who qualified for the award of the long service medal were veterans from the Great War who chose a career in the Police Service after demobilisation. Inspector Edward Threlfall retired from the Force on pension on 3 August 1949 after 30 years service at the age of 59 but these bare facts hide an interesting career and a distinguished record in the service of his country between 1914 and 1918. He was born in Preston two days before Christmas 1890 and took up the trade of a farrier until the outbreak of war when he enlisted in the Royal Field Artillery (75th Brigade) still as a farrier. He served on the Western Front from September 1915 and was twice decorated for bravery, once by the French Government. Both awards were published in the *London Gazette* after the Armistice.

On 7 June 1919 he was awarded the French *Medaille d'Honneur des Affaires Etrangères avec Glaives en Vermeil*. Six weeks later notification was given of the award of the Military Medal to "13703 Farrier Staff Sergeant E Threlfall, C/75th Brigade RFA (Ashton-on-Ribble)" for bravery in the field although there were no citations to accompany either entry. The full title of the French medal has two forms"the Medaille d'Honneur des Affaires Etrangères (Medal of Honour of the Ministry for Foreign Affairs) and Medaille d'Honneur du Président de la République (Medal of Honour of the President of the Republic)—and was awarded in three classes—bronze, silver and gilt (vermeil). The glaives (swords) indicate that it was awarded for services under enemy fire and take the form of two crossed swords over a wreath of oak leaves which forms the suspender. The medal was awarded to non-French nationals for acts of gallantry to the benefit of France during wartime. The medal hung from a ribbon in the colours of the French tricolour—red, white and blue stripes—of equal width and carried on the obverse the effigy of La Règublique by Dupont with the words RÉPUBLIQUE FRANÇAISE to the left and right. The reverse was engraved with the name of the recipient within a wreath of half oak and half laurel leaves.

The medal was introduced during the Second Empire (1852 to 1871) with the obverse being redesigned three times, the style of the swords once and the name changed until the pattern applicable in 1919 was adopted. The medal remains current today. All three obverse designs featured the wreath of half laurel and half oak leaves but the first carried a central circle inscribed with the name of the recipient, reason for the award and the date surrounded by the words MINISTÉRE DES AFFAIRES ETRANGÈRES. The first change retained the disc but showed only the date of the award. The final design awarded to Edward Threlfall had no central disc and was engraved in the central field with the rank and name of the recipient for military awards or simply the name for civilians.

Edward Trelfall

Within a few weeks of his return to the UK in May 1919 Edward Threlfall joined the Rochdale Borough Police, taking his oath on 14 August 1919. After no more than two months (on 25 October) he transferred to the Fire Brigade as an auxiliary fireman and stayed for four years before returning to more traditional police duty in the Detective Department on plain clothes duties. As a detective he was twice commended by the Watch Committee for *"the arrest of a man wanted by another police force"* on 11 December 1924 and again on 9 February 1928 for *"the arrest of a man charged with shopbreaking and housebreaking"*.

His ability and keenness were recognised in 1933 when he was promoted to sergeant followed five years later, on 1 January 1938, by a further advancement to inspector, the rank he held at retirement. He was awarded his bronze medal for 20 years good service on 1 September 1939 and qualified for the silver medal five years later in November 1944 but only received a ribbon to wear on his uniform to indicate his eligibility—there were no silver medals available after five years of war. He was eligible to retire after 25 years service and applied to the Watch Committee who gave their consent in November 1944. Perhaps, not surprisingly in view of the war, the Chief Constable withheld the application although his pension was secured and it was a further five years before he was allowed to retire, after 30 years service. Inspector Threlfall received his silver medal for 25 years long and faithful service six months before his retirement—five years late but well deserved.

WIGAN BOROUGH POLICE GOOD SERVICE MEDAL

Instituted: *Not known.*

Ribbon: *Dark blue with a red central stripe.*

Metal: *Silver.*

Size: *35 mm.*

Decription: *(Obverse) the Coat of Arms of the Borough of Wigan within an outer circle containing the legend FOR GOOD SERVICE (above) and WIGAN BOROUGH POLICE (below); (reverse) a laurel wreath tied at the base with a bow surrounding a central field containing an inscription with the rank and name of the recipient together with the date he joined the force. The medal has an ornamental scroll suspender attached by a swivelling claw fitting. The ribbon is attached by a brooch fitting.*

Without exception, medals issued by police forces and watch committees carried the coat of arms of the borough on the obverse or the reverse, usually the former. Where the medal was issued to commemorate a royal occasion—the Diamond Jubilee of Queen Victoria for example, or a coronation—and an image of the Sovereign was used, protocol demanded that it should always be carried on the obverse. Where there was no such image the coat of arms was usually employed. The coat of arms of a borough is a commonly used term although, in strictly heraldic language, this refers only to the devices on the shield and the full arms including the supporters, helmet, crest and mantle are correctly referred to as the achievement of arms.

Some police medals used only the shield and devices (Reading), others reproduced the full achievement and were very attractive as a result, particularly if struck in silver, with the added advantage of illustrating a number of aspects of the history of the borough. The history and development of heraldry in the United Kingdom is fascinating but very complex and dates back to the first truly heraldic shield of Geoffrey of Anjou in 1127. Coats of arms were originally awarded to a person or family and it was not until the 16th century that towns and cities began to be granted arms on a regular basis. In the early years the devices carried on the arms reflected the allegiances and interests of the town or city—the King, a local lord or the sea—but the industrial revolution of the 19th century caused a change with features more relevant to the town itself beginning to appear.

The medal issued in Wigan is a very fine award and the design of the obverse illustrates very clearly how attractive the full achievement of arms on a medal can be and how it can speak volumes about a city, town or borough. The arms used were not granted officially until 1922, surprisingly late in the light of the acknowledged importance and long history of the borough.

The shield has a three-towered Norman castle surmounted by a medieval royal crown composed of three fleur-de-lis. The castle symbolises that Wigan is a ancient town of some importance and the crown that it enjoys royal patronage. The crest of the arms shows a crowned king's head on a wreath with a lion lying down with its head to the left but looking towards the front. The king's head is not intended to depict any particular monarch although it is modelled on a portrait of King Edward III. The use of the king's head and the royal lion is very significant in heraldic terms and indicates a high level of royal favour for the town.

The terminology of heraldry originated from the Anglo-French spoken in medieval times and has developed into a complex language with terms that are not easily recognisable in modern English and with a precise and strict syntax used to describe the features concisely and accurately but leaving no room for ambiguity. The heraldic description of the arms on the Wigan medal is barely understandable today—"*On a wreath of the colours, in front of a kings head affrontee couped below the shoulders proper, vested gules, crowned and crined or, a lion couchant guardant or*". An explanation of the elements of the description can help unravel the meaning of this quaint language—"*On a wreath of the colours* (the town colours, red and silver) *in front of a king's head affrontee* (facing forward) *couped* (cut off) *below the shoulders proper* (in natural colours) *vested* (dressed in) *gules* (red) *crowned and crined* (full-haired) *or* (in gold) *a lion couchant* (crouching) *guardant* (facing forward) *or* (in gold)".

The supporters offer further evidence of Wigan's royal patronage. The use of royal insignia in armorial bearings is closely guarded and only rarely granted. There are four such insignia in the Wigan arms including the two standing lions on either side of the shield. Each lion holds a branch of mountain ash in full berry in its paw, forming a pun on the northern dialect name for the tree—the Wiggin or Wigan Tree—to add further symbolism of the full achievement of arms. The town motto—*Ancient and Loyal*—commemorates the granting of the town charter by King Charles II in 1662 and is taken from the wording where the town is described as "*an ancient borough*" and granted a "*special token of our favour for its loyalty to us*".

The Wigan Borough Police was formed in 1836 and responsible for an area of three and a half square miles with a total of six officers although it was suggested that 40 constables would be needed. The Chief Constable, John Whittle, was given an annual salary of £200, substantially more than his six constables who were required to work from 8 am until 11 pm every day except Saturday when the hours were even longer—all for £1.25 per week. John Whittle lasted barely four years before he was dismissed for drunkenness—the fate of many men in the early days of professional policing but unusual for chief constables. By the latter part of the 19th century the establishment of the Force had been increased to 50 and more than 2,500 people were taken before the Magistrates annually from a population in excess of 50,000.

In common with most borough forces, Wigan was eventually to be swallowed up by its county force—the Lancashire Constabulary—in 1969 after 133 years of independence, thirteen chief constables and with a strength of more than 150 officers. With the changes to local government boundaries in 1974 it became a division of the newly-formed Greater Manchester Police and remains so today.

THE SPECIAL CONSTABULARY

The role of the Special Constabulary in the policing of the UK has been understated and undervalued for many years, not least by the regular officers alongside whom they work. The true value of the Specials first became apparent during the Great War when large numbers of regulars were recalled to the Colours or enlisted in the Armed Forces leaving their home constabularies seriously depleted. Large numbers of Special Constables came forward to fill the gaps left by the regular officers and performed their duty admirably until the declaration of the Armistice in November 1918. Many watch committees recognised the services they had given, without the incentive of pay, by the award of medals as a token of their gratitude. National acknowledgement of the contribution of the Special Constabulary came in 1919.

Most medals awarded to members of the Special Constabulary were short-lived and all were made redundant by the introduction of the national medal in 1919. Many were issued on a single occasion only after the Great War had ended.

Although many medals were never intended to be worn with a ribbon, a small piece was often issued for wear in undress uniform to indicate possession of the medal. Examples exist of most awards where they have been adapted for wear with the ribbon although this was never officially sanctioned. Some medals were intended to be worn as watch fobs and there was no ribbon issued. Examples exist, however, where even these were worn with a ribbon although the colour and pattern had no meaning whatsoever. Clitheroe Borough in Lancashire issued an enamelled gold medal to members of its Special Constabulary even though it was a very small force and mustered a staff of only 15 regular officers when it merged with the Lancashire County Constabulary in 1947.

The list that follows is by no means complete, medals were awarded to members of the Special Constabulary in other towns and boroughs. Macclesfield (Cheshire) is an example. The medal is of the same pattern as those awarded in the Metropolitan Police, Birmingham City and Edinburgh apart from the change in the name around the circumference. The Macclesfield Borough Police was founded in 1836 and survived until 1947 when it was amalgamated with the Cheshire County Constabulary. In Scotland, a medal is believed to have been awarded to special constables in Govan Burgh although its police force had been merged into the Glasgow City Police two years before the start of the Great War. An example appeared at an auction in Australia in the late 1990s but nothing else is known about the medal. No doubt there are others waiting to be found.

SPECIAL CONSTABULARY FAITHFUL SERVICE MEDAL

Instituted: 30 August 1919.

Ribbon: White with a broad red central band and a black stripe towards each edge.

Metal: Bronze.

Size: 36 mm.

Description: (Obverse) the effigy of the reigning monarch; (reverse) a partial wreath of laurel on the right side of the medal with the legend FOR FAITHFUL SERVICE IN THE SPECIAL CONSTABULARY in a six-line inscription on the left. The medal hangs from a plain straight suspender attached by a claw fitting.

The medal is issued to all ranks in the Special Constabulary on completion of nine years unpaid service with at least 50 duties undertaken each year. Service in wartime was counted triple. Bars are awarded for each subsequent period of ten years qualifying service, each inscribed with the words LONG SERVICE and the date of the award. Members of the Special Constabulary who served in the Great War were awarded a special clasp bearing the words THE GREAT WAR 1914–1918. With the introduction of this award all local medals were discontinued.

Great Britain

ASHTON-UNDER-LYME SPECIAL CONSTABULARY MEDAL

Instituted: 1918.

Ribbon: None.

Metal: Bronze.

Size: 36 mm.

Description: (Obverse) a skeletal design with a broad circle 5 mm wide bearing the inscription ASHTON UNDER LYME SPECIAL CONSTABULARY in raised letters surrounding a central shield attached at five points to the outer band and carrying the words FOR LONG SERVICE in two lines; (reverse) left plain. The medal was issued unnamed. It was suspended by a ring fitting and a brooch bar bearing the town motto—PRO REGE LEGE ET CREGE.

The Ashton-under-Lyme Borough Police existed as a separate force from its founding in 1848 until it was merged with the Lancashire County Constabulary in 1947.

The design of the medal awarded in a number of towns and cities who rewarded members of their Special Constabulary was very similar. Likewise, the concept of issue without a ribbon was repeated elsewhere. The issue of a medal of any description by county constabularies rather than city or borough forces to regular officers or members of the Special Constabulary was uncommon with only two examples being known. Ayr County is the only known such force to reward the Special Constabulary.

The skeletal medal design awarded in Ashton-under-Lyme was adopted by a number of towns and cities and most were never intended for wear with a ribbon although some very fine ribbons were issued for wear in undress uniform.

AYR COUNTY SPECIAL CONSTABULARY MEDAL

Instituted: 1919.

Ribbon: None.

Metal: Silver.

Size: 36 mm.

Description: (Obverse) outer band bearing the words COUNTY OF AYR (above) and SPECIAL CONSTABULARY (below) and the two dates 1914 and 1919 on either side of the central shield. The shield bore the Coat of Arms of the County of Ayr; (reverse) left plain.

The medal was not fitted with any form of suspension and was never intended to be worn. The 700 plus medals awarded were presented together with certificates of service to all qualifying officers at ceremonies held in November 1919 in a number of towns in the county. Since 1975 the County of Ayr has been a part of the Strathclyde Police. The county force was formed in 1839 and took over two small borough forces in 1861 (Maybole) and 1879 (Ardrossan) before the major reorganisation of 1975.

BIRMINGHAM CITY SPECIAL CONSTABULARY MEDAL

Instituted: 1915.

Ribbon: Watered dark blue moiré with three equal central stripes of red, yellow and red. The stripes were separated by fine white lines.

Metal: Bronze.

Size: 32 mm.

Description: (Obverse) a skeletal design with a broad circle 5 mm wide containing the words BIRMINGHAM CITY CONSTABULARY 1916 in raised letters surrounding a central shield attached at five points to the outer band and carrying the words FOR LONG SERVICE in two lines; (reverse) the rank and name of the recipient. The medal was hung from a suspender with a laurel leaf design to which was attached a pin for fixing to the tunic. The medal was awarded for a minimum of two years service and it is believed than more than 2,000 were issued.

BIRMINGHAM CITY SPECIAL CONSTABULARY WATERGUARD MEDAL

Instituted: 1919.

Ribbon: Pale blue watered silk (for wear in undress uniform only).

Metal: Bronze.

Size: 36 mm.

Description: (Obverse) the Coat of Arms of the City of Birmingham with the words BIRMINGHAM SPECIAL CONSTABULARY contained within a surrounding circle; (reverse) the Foel Water Tower with 1917-1918 and WATERWORKS GUARD below in three lines surrounded by the legend BIRMINGHAM CORPORATION. The recipient's rank and name were engraved on the rim.

This was the second medal issued by the Watch Committee in Birmingham to members of the Special Constabulary who were engaged in special duties guarding the city's water supply in Worcestershire where a pipeline crosses the River Severn and in the Elan Valley in Wales. A single presentation of this medal was made on 10 June 1919 by the Lord Mayor.

BLACKPOOL BOROUGH SPECIAL CONSTABULARY MEDAL

In contrast to the plain appearance of the skeletal style of medal, some smaller borough forces awarded very attractive and individual designs to their members. The Blackpool Borough Special Constabulary struck a medal in gold for award to volunteers from the town who served between 1914 and 1919. The Blackpool Borough Police (founded in 1887) was amalgamated with the Lancashire Constabulary in 1969.

Instituted: 1919.

Ribbon: Dark blue.

Metal: Gold.

Size: 25 mm.

Description: (Obverse) the Coat of Arms of Blackpool with the word BLACKPOOL at the top and SPECIAL CONSTABULARY at the bottom in gold on blue enamel; (reverse) the legend FOR SERVICES RENDERED inscribed centrally in three lines with the rank and number of the recipient above and the name below. The meda hung from a ring suspender with a brooch bar of blue enamel edged in gold containing the dates of service, also in gold.

One recipient had previously served his country in South Africa as a trooper (30115) with the 2nd Volunteer Battalion of the 105th Imperial Yeomanry (Manchester) but was discharged in 1902 as medically unfit for military service. He held the Queen's South Africa Medal with five clasps on his discharge.

At the outbreak of the Great War he volunteered his services to the Special Constabulary and served from 1914 to 1918—the dates shown on the clasp of the medal awarded to him by the Borough.

CARDIFF CITY SPECIAL CONSTABULARY MEDAL

Instituted: 1919.

Ribbon: Blue with narrow red edges and a narrow central yellow stripe.

Metal: Bronze.

Size: 32 mm.

Description: (Obverse) the Coat of Arms of the City of Cardiff; (reverse) the words THE GREAT WAR 1914-19 centrally with CARDIFF CITY above and SPECIAL POLICE below. The recipient's rank and name were engraved on the rim. The medal hung from a ring attached to the body of the medal by a suspender which took the form of a pair of crossed truncheons.

The medal was issued by the City Corporation to all members of the Special Constabulary, irrespective of rank, who joined before 31 December 1917 and who served for at least one year. They were issued unnamed although privately engraved examples exist, a practice not uncommon where medals were not officially marked with any of the recipient's details.

CITY OF COVENTRY SPECIAL CONSTABULARY MEDAL

Instituted: 1918.

Ribbon: Half green and half scarlet with a thin central stripe in gold (for wear in undress uniform only).

Metal: Silver.

Size: 32 mm.

Description: (Obverse) the Coat of Arms of the City of Coventry with the words CITY OF COVENTRY (above) and SPECIAL CONSTABULARY (below) on a raised band around the circumference; (reverse) a laurel wreath tied at the base by a f lowing bow with the inscription FOR LONG SERVICE 1914 AWARDED TO (name of the recipient) in five lines. The medal was not intended for wear with the ribbon and was attached to the tunic by a pinned brooch bar and ring suspender.

The separate police force in Coventry was founded in 1836 and survived as an independent body until 1969 when it was amalgamated with the Warwickshire Constabulary. It became a part of the West Midlands Police on 1 April 1974.

CLITHEROE BOROUGH SPECIAL CONSTABULARY MEDAL

Instituted: 1919.

Ribbon: None officially issued.

Metal: Gold.

Size: 29 mm.

Description: (Obverse) the Coat of Arms of the Borough of Clitheroe in light and dark blue enamels with the word CLITHEROE in a white panel beneath the shield. The words SPECIAL POLICE were contained within a scroll at the bottom of the medal; (reverse) a wreath of laurel with the inscription FOR SERVICES RENDERED at the top in raised letters. There is a central plaque with the recipient's rank and name and another smaller one below containing the dates 1916-19. This medal has been seen with an unofficial dark blue ribbon.

The qualifying period for the award of medals to members of the Special Constabulary by individual forces varied but, typically, involved a minimum of one years service or more than 40 tours of duty each of more than 4 hours duration.

CITY OF DUNDEE SPECIAL CONSTABULARY MEDAL

Instituted: 1920.

Ribbon: Blue.

Metal: Frosted silver.

Size: 39 mm.

Description: (Obverse) the Coat of Arms of the City of Dundee with the dates 1914 - 1919 below; (reverse) inscribed with the words PRESENTED BY - THE - CORPORATION - OF DUNDEE - TO - (name) - SPECIAL CONSTABLE - IN ACKNOWLEDGEMENT - OF - SERVICES RENDERED in ten lines in raised letters with the exception of the recipient's name which was engraved. The medal was attached to a ring fitment by means of an ornate scrolled leaf suspender. The top ribbon bar was engraved with the number of years' service in figures —2 YEARS etc—in a thin engraved border.

Awards of the 163 medals cast were made by the Lord Provost at a special ceremony held in the city on 31 October 1920 when 244 members of the Special Constabulary were rewarded for their services between 1914 and 1919. Three groups received different awards dependent on their length of service. A typical tour of duty from 1915 to the end of the War ran from 11 pm to 3 am—recipients earned their rewards. In Dundee, special constables who failed to meet this minimum requirement were rewarded with certificates but not with the medal issued by the City Corporation. A group of eleven were awarded the National Special Constabulary Faithful Service Medal with the Great War 1914–18 bar in addition to the local medal and a certificate of service. This small group included a young boy who collected the awards on behalf of his father who had died before he could receive them A second group of 114 officers and three next-of-kin were granted the local medal and certificate of service with a third group of 116 being awarded a certificate only. The Dundee City Police was founded in 1824 but has been a part of Tayside Police since 1975.

DURHAM CITY SPECIAL CONSTABULARY MEDAL

Instituted: 1920.

Ribbon: Dark blue with a gold stripe (5 mm) at each edge.

Metal: Bronze.

Size: 25 mm.

Description: (Obverse) the Coat of Arms of Durham City encircled by a wreath of laurel with a raised outer band bearing the legend DURHAM CITY SPECIAL CONSTABLE; (reverse) inscribed with the words PRESENTED TO (name of the recipient) IN RECOGNITION OF SERVICES DURING THE GREAT WAR 1914 - 1919. A ring suspender was used with a top ribbon bar which bore the words DURHAM CITY - SPECIAL CONSTABLE in two lines.

The level of volunteering for the Special Constabulary during the Great War can often be seriously underestimated but a quick examination of one small borough force shows that volunteers came forward in large numbers. In April 1921 when the Durham City Police was amalgamated with the Durham County Constabulary the strength of the Force stood at 24 in total. Less than a year earlier more than 350 members of the Special Constabulary had been awarded medals and certificates for their help between 1914 and 1919—a huge number given the small size of the Force.

The majority of the medals were presented at a smoking concert and musical evening held in the Town Hall and attended by the civic dignitaries in October 1920. The presentation was conducted during the interval by the Mayor and his deputy (the leader of the Special Constabulary) with each recipient also being given a cigar.

EDINBURGH CITY SPECIAL CONSTABULARY MEDAL

Instituted: 1917.

Ribbon: Half black and half white with the blac towards the centre of the tunic (for wear in undress uniform only).

Metal: Bronze.

Size: 32 mm.

Description: (Obverse) very similar to the design issued by Birmingham City but with the inscription EDINBURGH CITY SPECIAL CONSTABULARY 1914 on the outer ring.

Medals were awarded to special constables from the smallest police forces in the land to the largest including Edinburgh, Glasgow and the Metropolitan Police in London. The one common feature seems to have been that the smaller forces issued the more ornate design in the more valuable material—gold and silver—compared with the simple bronze designs of the larger cities, including Edinburgh.

GLASGOW CITY SPECIAL CONSTABULARY MEDAL

Instituted: 1919.

Ribbon: None.

Metal: Silver.

Size: 25 mm.

Description: (Obverse) the Coat of Arms of the City of Glasgow and its motto LET GLASGOW FLOURISH with the dates 1814–1919 at the top; (reverse) inscribed around the circumference with the words PRESENTED BY THE CORPORATION OF GLASGOW and a five line inscription in the central field reading TO (name) SPECIAL CONSTABLE IN ACKNOWLEDGEMENT OF SERVICES RENDERED. A pinned rectangular clasp was used for fixing to the tunic inscribed with the recipient's length of service in figures — 2 YEARS, 3 YEARS etc.

One of the oldest police forces in the country issued a small, silver medal to its special constables at the end of the War as a reward for their services. It was not issued with a ribbon although it was intended for wear in similar fashion to those awarded in Edinburgh, London and a number of other cities.

GREENOCK BURGH SPECIAL CONSTABULARY MEDAL

Instituted: 1919.

Ribbon: Dark blue.

Metal: Frosted silver.

Size: 32 mm.

Description: (Obverse) the Coat of Arms of the Burgh of Greenock with the inscription BURGH OF GREENOCK in a band around the circumference; (reverse) a laurel wreath with the words GREENOCK SPECIAL CONSTABLE in two lines in the central field. The recipient's name and number were engraved in a scroll beneath the wreath. A suspender bar was employed inscribed with the recipient's length of service—2 YEARS, 3 YEARS or 4 YEARS.

A number of medals issued were very attractive, in particular those struck in silver with a frosted finish and carrying a pictorial design. As befits one of the oldest police forces in the United Kingdom (founded in 1800), the Greenock Burgh Police rewarded its special constables with a particularly fine medal.

The coat of arms of the Burgh of Greenock depicts a three-masted sailing ship at sea with two others on the horizon on either side. In front on a quay were two men rolling three barrels towards a stack of other— all reproduced in fine detail. There was only one issue of the medal made to 350 members of the Special Constabulary after the War had ended. The majority of officers had been released from duty in 1915 to enlist in the Armed Forces but those who served throughout the War (about 50) were entitled to the suspender bar showing 4 years service. The Greenock Burgh Police was very long-lived as an independent body and survived from 1800 until 1967 when it was amalgamated with the Renfrewshire and Bute Constabulary. It now forms a part of Strathclyde Police.

HARTLEPOOL BOROUGH SPECIAL CONSTABULARY MEDAL

Instituted: 1919.

Ribbon: Dark blue.

Metal: Silver.

Size: 39 mm.

Description: (Obverse) the 14th century seal of the Borough of Hartlepool showing a hart at bay in a pool with a hound on its back all surrounded by the words S'(IGILLUM) COMMUNITATIS DE HERETERPOL (Seal of the town of Hartlepool); (reverse) a number of inscriptions to illustrate the attacks on the borough by the German Navy and Air Force — the date 1916 placed centrally with the words ZEPPELIN DESTROYED surrounding it and BOMBARDMENT 1914 above and AIR RAIDS 1915-18 below. Around the circumference was the inscription BOROUGH OF HARTLEPOOL (above) and SPECIAL CONSTABLE (below). The medal hung from a plain straight swivelling suspender. They were issued unnamed.

The reference to the bombardment in 1914 commemorates the first attack on the British mainland by the Germans on the morning of 16 December of that year. Hartlepool was a major steel-making and shipbuilding town and considered by the German High Command to be a legitimate military target. The attacking fleet, made up of four battlecruisers (*Seyditz, Moltke, Vann de Tann* and *Derrflinger*), one heavy cruiser (*Blucher*), four light cruisers and two flotillas of destroyers started their attack on Hartlepool and Scarborough at 8.10 with the firing of the first shell at the coastal batteries. In the course of the next 35 minutes, they closed range to 4,000 yards and bombarded Hartlepool with 1,150 shells, killing 112 people and wounding 200 others.

The British government knew of the impending attack from decoded German naval signals but did not alert the population of either town for fear of revealing to the Germans that the code had been broken. The death and destruction caused was used by the authorities to demonize the enemy and led to a surge in recruitment in the following months.

A single issue of the medal was made in 1919 before the introduction of the national medal rendered it redundant. The Hartlepool Borough Police was founded in 1851 but ceased to exist as a separate force in 1947 when it was amalgamated with the Durham County Constabulary. It became a part of the Cleveland Constabulary on 1 April 1974.

ROYAL LEAMINGTON SPA SPECIAL CONSTABULARY MEDAL

Instituted: 1920.

Ribbon: None.

Metal: Bronze.

Size: 32 mm.

Description: (Obverse) very similar in design to the medals issued in Birmingham and Edinburgh with the only difference being the substitution of the words LEAMINGTON SPECIAL CONSTABULARY on the outer band.

LEITH BURGH SPECIAL CONSTABULARY MEDAL

Instituted: 1918.

Ribbon: Black with a broad central white stripe.

Metal: Bronze.

Size: 36 mm.

Description: (Obverse) the Coat of Arms of the Burgh of Leith with the inscriptions SIGILLUM OPPIDI DE LEITH (Seal of the town of Leith) and PERSEVERE above and below. The words LEITH SPECIAL CONSTABULARY are inscribed around the circumference; (reverse) a laurel wreath with the words FOR LONG AND CONTINUOUS SERVICE 1914-1918 in five lines in the central field. A plain straight swivelling suspender was used.

The number of volunteers who came forward to join the Special Constabulary was huge and, in some towns and boroughs far exceeded expectation. In the Burgh of Leith, no fewer than 400 people came forward. Not all qualified for the medal subsequently issued although it was produced in large numbers.

METROPOLITAN POLICE SPECIAL CONSTABULARY MEDAL

Instituted: May 1917.

Ribbon: None issued.

Metal: Bronze.

Size: 32 mm.

Description: (Obverse) very similar in design to the medals issued in Birmingham, Edinburgh and Leamington Spa but with the words METROPOLITAN SPECIAL CONSTABULARY 1914 in the outer circle; (reverse) left plain but they were commonly engraved with the name of the recipient in a wide range of styles. The medal was attached by a flat suspender with an ornate design of leaves and scrolls.

The largest issue of medals was made by the Metropolitan Police with more than 15,000 awards going to members of the Special Constabulary who had performed not less than 150 duties during the Great War and had served for at least two years.

The Metropolitan Police issued a second reward for members of its Special Constabulary to recognise those who were serving at the outbreak of war in August 1914. The Silver Service Star was authorised in 1918 and available only to officers who were serving prior to 31 December 1914 and who were still members of the Special Constabulary in 1918. It took the form of a five-pointed star with two central circles. The inner circle had the letters S and C intertwined with the word METROPOLITAN and the date 1914 in the outer circle. Qualifying officers were entitled to both medals. 8,000 stars were awarded at parades held on 16 May 1918.

The Metropolitan Police was not the only force to issue the silver star—the Hull City Police awarded one to members of its Special Constabulary for service during the Great War. The only difference between the two being the name of the force.

PERTH CITY SPECIAL CONSTABULARY MEDAL

Instituted: 1919.

Ribbon: Royal blue.

Metal: Bronze.

Size: 35 mm.

Description: (Obverse) the Coat of Arms of the City of Perth within an outer band bearing the inscription PERTH CITY POLICE (above) and SPECIAL CONSTABLE (below); (reverse) an inscription giving the reason for the award with the recipient's details engraved on the lower rim.

The period of service of members of the Special Constabulary varied greatly and some medal issues ignored this altogether although others gave some indication of the time served. In Glasgow and Greenock the total number was inscribed on the top suspender clasp but the Watch Committee at Perth decided that each year should be rewarded with a separate bar. An officer, therefore, who served throughout the War was rewarded with a medal and five bars dated from 1914 to 1918 inclusive. The date of the first years service was noted on the brooch pin and each additional year was indicated by the use of a slip-on clasp carrying the appropriate date. The Perth City Police is an old force, founded in 1811, which survived independently until it was absorbed by the Perth and Kinross Constabulary in 1964. It now forms a part of the Tayside Police.

RENFREW BURGH SPECIAL CONSTABULARY MEDAL

Instituted: 1919.

Ribbon: None.

Metal: Silver.

Size: 25 mm.

Description: (Obverse) the Coat of Arms of the Burgh of Renfrew with the inscription RENFREW SPECIAL CONSTABULARY around the circumference in blue enamel; (reverse) a six line inscription reading PRESENTED TO (name and rank of the recipient) FOR SERVICES RENDERED 1919.

The number of Scottish police forces which issued medals to their special constables was high in comparison with their English counterparts with some very small forces recognising the services the volunteers rendered. The small silver medal awarded in 1919 to all members of the Special Constabulary in Renfrew Burgh to mark their service was another never intended to be worn and no ribbon was ever issued. A separate force was maintained in the Burgh from 1856 to 1930 when it was amalgamated with the County Force and became a part of the Renfrewshire Constabulary. It is now in the Strathclyde Police area.

ROCHESTER CITY SPECIAL CONSTABULARY MEDAL

Instituted: 1919.

Ribbon: Half red and half yellow.

Metal: Bronze.

Size: 32 mm.

Description: (Obverse) the Coat of Arms of the City of Rochester in the form of a shield containing a cross with the letter r at the centre below a lion, all surmounted by a mural crown. There is an outer band bearing the legend SPECIAL CONSTABULARY; (reverse) a wreath of laurel tied at the base by a bow with an inscription in the central field which reads FOR - LONG SERVICE - AWARDED TO - (name of the recipient) - (date of joining) in five lines.

This medal was another that was not intended for wear with a ribbon although, in similar fashion to a number of others, a small piece was issued for wear on the tunic to indicate that the medal had been awarded. Examples exist, however, where the medal has been adapted and hangs from the ribbon supplied.

A single issue of this medal was made before it was made redundant by the introduction of the national medal for members of the Special Constabulary. The Rochester City Police was founded in 1837 and survived as a separate force until 1943 when it was merged with the Kent County Constabulary under wartime regulations, a temporary measure which proved to be permanent.

Great Britain

MISCELLANEOUS AWARDS

Police officers can receive medals awarded by a number of organisations and societies with special interests, the RSPCA and Royal Humane Society being amongst the better known. In the first half of the 19th century the Society for the Protection of Life from Fire introduced a medal to reward any citizen who saved the life of another from a fire and police officers have been regular recipients since although the incidence of its award has decreased. The design of the medal has been changed several times and now takes the form of a bronze medal not intended for wear although until 1984 the scarlet ribbon could be seen on the uniform of many officers.

MEDAL OF THE SOCIETY FOR THE PROTECTION OF LIFE FROM FIRE 1902 TO 1984

Instituted: 1920.

Ribbon: Scarlet.

Metal: Bronze.

Size: 40 mm.

Description: (Obverse) a depiction of a man rescuing a woman and two children from a fire; (reverse) a wreath of oak leaves with the words DUTY AND HONOR in the central field all surrounded by an outer band bearing the name of the Society around the circumference and the date 1936 at the base. A plain straight suspender was employed.

The original medal first appeared in 1836 and was amended in 1843 when the Society was granted royal patronage. Further changes were made in 1850 and 1892 until the Royal part of the title was removed on the death of Queen Victoria in 1902 and a design introduced which was to last until 1984. The prevalence of fires in cities such as Exeter before the Second World War with the fire service usually coming under the control of the local chief constable often resulted in police officers becoming involved in rescue work as the first person on the scene. Constable Mick Dooling of the Exeter City Police who was granted his Long Service and Efficiency Medal on 12 March 1931 added a bronze award from the Society for the Protection of Life from Fire in February 1936 for the rescue of a lady who had been driven to the roof of a building on fire and was in danger of falling. He was initially commended by the Watch Committee but later given the medal by the Society.

PC Dooling was typical of officers of the time—he had joined the Force in 1913 as a man of 23 after serving in the Royal Field Artillery from the age of 19. At the outbreak of war he was recalled to the Colours and saw action at the Somme, Mons, the Marne, the Aisnes and Ypres. He was seriously wounded in May 1915 and sent to Macedonia in 1917 when he had recovered from his wounds. In 1919 he re-joined Exeter City Police, his adopted home after marrying a local girl in 1912. In the course of his service until he retired on 1948, five years after he could have gone had the Second World War not intervened and forced him to put the day off, he was commended six times by his Chief Constable or the Watch Committee, three times for his conduct at the scene of a fire, the last being when he was awarded the medal.

His personal life was touched by tragedy when his wife, Lillian, died in 1936 although he had four daughters, ten grand-children and 18 great-grand-children. After his retirement he became a leading light in the local Conservative Club at Heavitree, now a part of Exeter, becoming the chairman and being awarded the Badge of Honour and Distinguished Service Award of the Association of Conservative Clubs for his work. Mick Dooling died at the aged of 78 in Exeter in 1968.

page 167

Rewards for police officers to recognise acts of courage were usually prompted by one particular event of such importance locally that special arrangements were made. In Exeter on Monday, 5 September 1887, at about 10.30 pm, a fire in the Theatre Royal resulted in the deaths of more than 180 people, the greatest single loss of life in the West Country in peacetime in a single event. The theatre had opened on October the previous year and, on the fateful night, was staging a performance of Romany Rye in front of 800 or so people. During the fourth act, one character was alone on the stage when a part of the scenery fell to the floor upsetting the stage lighting and starting a fire which very quickly spread out-of-control. Almost 300 theatre-goers in the gallery had one way out, down a narrow staircase, barely a metre wide, with poor lighting—an impossible situation, made worse by the inevitable panic, intense heat and choking smoke. Several of those who managed to escape returned to the theatre to rescue others. Two servicemen, in particular, were singled out for special praise at the subsequent inquest, one—Bombadier Samuel Scattergood of the Royal Artillery—managed to save the wife of one of the police officers on duty before he too became a victim of the flames.

Almost every police officer in the city became involved on the night and in the days following when the full extent of the tragedy became clear and the grisly process of clearing up and identifying the victims was carried out. In the report of the Chief Constable—Captain Showers— to the Watch Committee, five officers (Inspector Short, Sergeants Sullock and Gillard, Constable Symonds and Sergeant-at-Mace Wreford) received a special mention for their acts of courage at the fire. The Watch Committee acknowledged their courage and singled out Sergeant 3 James Sullock to receive the unprecedented award a Star of Silver Braid. The Star was to be worn on the left sleeve of the tunic as a permanent and visible sign of the courage displayed by the officer.

The fire at the theatre was not the only event reported by the Chief Constable to the Watch Committee on 8 October 1887. Four days earlier another officer—Constable 26 William Bastin— had attended a fire in Lower North Street in the early hours of the morning and succeeded in rescuing the lady occupant of the house. He too was awarded the new Star of Merit for his courage. When these first two awards were made there was in fact no star in existence, a design had not been considered and its introduction had not been approved by the full city council although this was rectified in early December.

A memorial to the victims of the fire stands in an Exeter cemetery alongside another, smaller gravestone erected in memory of Bombadier Scattergood by his colleagues in the Royal Artillery.

The star in silver braid worn on an officers everyday tunic proved to be less durable than intended and it was discovered that they would need replacement regularly and on each occasion that a new tunic was issued at a cost of six shillings and sixpence (32.5p) each time. In December 1888 the Town Clerk reported to the Watch Committee that a proper medal could be produced for only four shillings (20p) more than the star and would not need replacement once issued. The Watch Committee accepted his recommendation and approved the introduction of a medal to be worn in the traditional fashion on the right breast of the tunic.

Very little is known about the design of the medal apart from that which can be seen in one of the only two photographs of it known to exist—it was an eight-point star with a central medallion of unknown design, hung by a ring suspender from a ribbon which appeared to be of two colours (possibly green and white, the city colours) with a top ribbon bar which may or may not have been inscribed. When the medal was discontinued or fell into disuse is as much a mystery as the design. Records of the Exeter City Police and Watch Committee meeting minutes refer to its award on five occasions only, including the first two. The last written reference to the Star of Merit was made in October 1896 although there is no record of its award for the preceding eight years.

The last known award was made to Constable 30 George Guppy (*Pictured right*) for his courage in rescuing a local youth from drowning in the River Exe on 6 August. On 1 September 1888 the Watch Committee awarded him a Star of Merit and presented him with the Bronze Medal of the Royal Humane Society (RHS). George Guppy had joined the Exeter City Police on 27 December 1879 and served until he retired on pension at the end of January 1906 as a sergeant (promoted 1 December 1900). He was commended by the Watch Committee and Coroner on two other occasions in his service, the second four months before his retirement. A photo of George Guppy shows him wearing his medal alongside the award from the RHS.

The two other known awards were both made in 1888— to Constable 36 John Leworthy (7 April) for the rescue of a mother and child from a fire and to Constable 44 Thomas Chaplin (2 June) again for the rescue of someone from a fire.

GREAT BRITAIN (COLONIAL AWARDS)

For many years there was no pattern to the award of medals in countries of the Empire to reward officers for acts of gallantry, meritorious service or long service and good conduct. There was a blurring of the line between the duties of the military forces and the police as we understand them today in the UK and many police officers received military medals for any actions thought worthy of official recognition. These included military campaign medals and decorations intended to reward civil servants working in the Empire. In the 1930s separate medals were issued to reward such services in India and Burma and changes were made to the KPM for South Africa. In other countries—Australia, Singapore, Malta, Hong Kong and a host of others—there was no coherent, official system. The introduction of the Colonial Police Medals filled these gaps in the honours system applicable in most parts of the Empire.

COLONIAL POLICE MEDAL FOR MERITORIOUS SERVICE

Instituted: 10 May 1938.

Ribbon: Green with a dark blue central stripe flanked by a thin white line.

Metal: Silver.

Size: 36 mm.

Description: (Obverse) the head of the reigning monarch; (reverse) a police officers truncheon with the handle uppermost superimposed on a wreath in the lower two thirds of the central field. The medal carries a circumscription which reads COLONIAL POLICE FORCES FOR (left) MERITORIOUS SERVICE (right). A ring suspender is used attached to the top rim.

The second award for gallantry was the same as the medal for meritorious service apart from the substitution of the words—FOR GALLANTRY—on the right side of the reverse. Following the pattern of the KPM, thin red lines were added to the ribbon to indicate that the award had been made for gallantry, in this case on the two outer green bands. A limit of 150 was placed on the number of medals of both types which would be issued in any one year.

Silver bars of a laurel design were available for any second award of the medal, a feature most likely to occur in relation to acts for gallantry. With the introduction of these two medals the incidence of the award of the KPM decreased.

The medals were not the first in the series, they had been preceded by another very similar medal issued initially to reward junior officers for 18 years exemplary service although it was later extended to qualifying officers of all ranks.

COLONIAL POLICE LONG SERVICE AND GOOD CONDUCT MEDAL

Instituted: 1934.

Ribbon: Dark blue with a broad central green band containing two thin white lines.

Metal: Silver.

Size: 36 mm.

Description: (Obverse) the effigy of the reigning monarch; (reverse) the same as the Colonial Police Medals for Gallantry and Meritorious Service but with a different circumscription—COLONIAL POLICE FORCES FOR LONG SERVICE AND GOOD CONDUCT.

Silver bars were given after 25 and 30 years qualifying service indicated in undress uniform by silver rosettes. The name of the recipient together with his rank and number (and sometimes the force) were engraved on the rim locally which has resulted in a range of very different styles. On the introduction of this medal a number of awards which had been produced locally, often in very small numbers, were discontinued—the Ceylon and Malta Long Service Medals being two prominent examples—and allowed two anomalous situations which had arisen in Australia and Africa to be rectified.

In the early years of the British South Africa Police (BSAP) some thought was given to the question of a long service and good conduct award to police officers there for their service as early as the turn of the 20th century although the Force was young and any requirement for such a medal was a matter for the future. By the time the first officers had reached the qualifying milestone, set at 18 years, it had been decided that the most appropriate award would be one properly intended for the colonial and dominion forces but which would fit the bill with a little imagination. The unusually named medal was awarded on about 90 occasions in the BSAP from the first issue in 1916 until it was superseded by the new colonial medal in 1935.

PERMANENT FORCES OF THE EMPIRE BEYOND THE SEAS LONG SERVICE AND GOOD CONDUCT MEDAL

Instituted: 1909.

Ribbon: Maroon bearing a white central band with a narrow black stripe at the centre.

Metal: Silver.

Size: 36 mm.

Description: (Obverse) the effigy of the reigning sovereign; (reverse) the words PERMANENT FORCES OF THE EMPIRE BEYOND THE SEAS forming a circumscription with FOR - LONG SERVICE - AND - GOOD CONDUCT in four lines in the central field. The medal hung from a plain straight suspender attached with a claw fitting.

Great Britain

Rewarding police officers for long and distinguished service in other parts of the Empire was equally disjointed, many began to issue their own medals in the early years of the 20th century, in others existing decorations and medals were awarded although they were not primarily intended for police officers. In Australia, use was made of the Imperial Service Order (and Medal) although there has been some dispute over the correctness of the awards made to police officers. Such awards were rare but satisfied the needs of the time.

IMPERIAL SERVICE ORDER

Instituted: August 1902.

Ribbon: Three equal stripes of blue, crimson and blue.

Metal: Silver overlaid with gold.

Size: 61 mm high by 55 mm wide.

Description: (Obverse) a badge consisting of a circular gold plaque with the royal cypher in the centre surrounded by the words FOR FAITHFUL SERVICE in blue enamel. The badge is superimposed on a seven-point silver star topped by an enamelled crown and ring suspender; (reverse) plain.

This attractive decoration was instituted by King Edward VII to reward long and faithful service by senior grades of the administrative and clerical grades of the Civil Service at home and abroad. It was awarded for 25 years service in Britain, 20 years and 6 months in India and 16 years in the tropics. The criteria were treated with some laxity in relation to police officers with awards being made to officers of the rank of sergeant in Australia with the meaning of the term Civil Service being used in its loosest sense. When the decoration was introduced the Imperial Service Medal was also authorised for award to junior grades of the "Civil Service" under the same conditions as the Order. The criteria were also applied as freely. Several constables in Australian police forces were granted the medal for particularly meritorious service.

The medal was initially of similar design to the order but with the central medallion cast in silver and bearing a wreath and bronze star. In 1920 a circular design was adopted, cast in silver, with the effigy of the monarch on the obverse and a figure of a naked man seated and resting from his labours on the reverse. The words FOR FAITHFUL SERVICE were inscribed in the exergue. With the introduction of the series of Colonial Police Medals the award of the Imperial Service Order and Medal to police officers ceased.

page 171

Police Medals of the World

The proliferation of medals which led ultimately to the introduction of the Colonial Police Medals was complicated by the practice at the time of awarding one medal to the white officers of the police forces and another to non-Europeans, sometimes following the pattern common in Britain of rewarding one group with silver and another with bronze. In the forces of east and west Africa a separate medal was introduced exclusively aimed at non-European NCOs and men to reward them for acts of gallantry, distinguished, meritorious or long service (minimum of 15 years). The design was the same irrespective of the reason for the award. It was discontinued on the introduction of the Colonial Police Medals. The medal was awarded sparingly.

AFRICAN POLICE MEDAL FOR MERITORIOUS SERVICE

Instituted: *14 July 1915.*

Ribbon: *Sand-coloured with red edges.*

Metal: *Silver.*

Size: *36 mm*

Description: *(Obverse) the effigy of the reigning sovereign; (reverse) a crown surmounted by a lion within a wreath of palm tied at the base by an ornate bow. An outer band bore the inscription FOR MERITORIOUS SERVICE IN THE POLICE and AFRICA at the base. A ring suspender and claw fitting were employed.*

A feature of British policing taken to the colonies was the concept of the Special Constabulary, the use of volunteer officers to supplement the regular strength in times of great need, to provide local representation in isolated areas or to act as a liaison with people who might not be quite to ready to accept the services of the regular officers with all it meant. It wasn't until the reign of the present monarch that this service was marked by the issue of a medal in the way that it had been done in the UK since 1919.

COLONIAL SPECIAL CONSTABULARY LONG SERVICE MEDAL

Instituted: *1957.*

Ribbon: *Dark blue with a green broad central band containing two twin white lines.*

Metal: *Silver.*

Size: *36 mm*

Description: *(Obverse) the effigy of HM Queen Elizabeth II; (reverse) a wreath of laurel with the words COLONIAL SPECIAL CONSTABULARY outside around the circumference and the royal cypher EIIR and crown within the wreath at the top and the words FOR FAITHFUL SERVICE below.. A ring suspender was used.*

The medal is awarded to members of the colonial special constabulary in recognition of nine years unpaid service or 15 years if the officer was paid—a feature not found in the UK. After a further ten years qualifying service a bar was awarded. The larger nations of the British Commonwealth were not included in those whose special police officers were eligible for the award of the medal.

AN EVER-CHANGING WORLD

The decolonization of large parts of the world and the establishment of many independent states albeit still with Queen Elizabeth II as the head of state has resulted in a number of series of orders, decorations and medals being introduced, many of which include awards available to police officers, some exclusively so. Information on the new range of awards in a number of these countries can be hard to come by although their existence is well documented and the ribbon designs and colouring are well known.

THE BAHAMAS

Many Caribbean islands, formerly British colonies or protectorates, achieved independence in the 1960s and 70s although most remain members of the Commonwealth. The Commonwealth of the Bahamas is a group of more than 700 islands, 30 of which are inhabited, situated not far from the coast of Florida. Independence from Britain was achieved in 1973. Tourism accounts for more than half the revenue generated in the islands and it is estimated that six tourists visit each year for each of the 300,000 plus inhabitants. The Royal Bahamas Police Force has a series of four medals available to reward acts of gallantry, meritorious and faithful service and long service. The ribbons of these awards all use the national colours of black, blue and yellow in different formats.

The most prestigious of the awards—*the Police Gallantry Medal*—ranks highest of the four in the order of precedence followed by the *Police Meritorious Service Medal*. Both use a ribbon of the same basic design and colouring—a black central band bisected by a stripe of yellow and with a broad blue bands at each edge. The only difference between the two ribbons is the addition of a red stripe on the black band either side of the central yellow stripe to indicate that the award had been made for gallantry following the principle established in the UK for the award of the KPM and QPM.

The *Police Faithful Service Medal* uses the same three colours but with the blue and yellow reversed. The *Police Long Service Medal* reverses the black and blue colours of the two highest awards with the central stripe in yellow.

BARBADOS

Barbados has been fully independent since 1966 after 339 years of British rule. Although not the largest island it is the most densely populated of all Caribbean countries—605 people per square kilometre. On achieving independence a flag of blue and gold was adopted with the colours intended to represent the sea and the sand. The central gold band bears a trident (in black) which has dual symbolism—first as a link with Britain through the former colonial badge which depicted Britannia holding her trident and second using the three points to remember the three principles of democracy—government for the people, by the people and of the people. Barbados is considered to be the most British of the former Caribbean territories.

In July 1980 Barbados introduced its own series of honours and awards which included several available to police officers. The highest award is the Order of Barbados, the highest honour which is available in four classes. The fourth class is divided into two further grades—Barbados Service Star and Barbados Service Medal—awarded for meritorious work in a number of fields including the emergency services and Royal Barbados Police Force. Acts of courage performed by police officers can entitle them to one of two decorations—Barbados Star of Gallantry and Barbados Bravery Medal—with the only difference between the criteria for their award being the level of courage displayed. The Star demands that the act was one of conspicuous courage in circumstances of extreme peril and the Medal that there was an act of bravery in hazardous circumstances. The third level of honours available is reserved for members of the Barbados Defence Force, Royal Barbados Police Force, Fire Service and Prisons Service. The Services Medal of Honour is given for service of 15 to 25 years with one bar awarded for 25 to 30 years, two for 30 to 35 years and three after 35 years. The design of the medal is the same irrespective of the service but the ribbon are different. The basic colour uses the two primary colours of the national flag (blue and gold) with the police award have a green stripe running down the central gold band and a blue band at each edge.

GUYANA

The Co-operative Republic of Guyana first came to the notice of the British public in the early 1900s as the territory of British Guiana in South America, the only inroads the British Empire ever made into the continental mainland. First colonisation of the area was by the Dutch in the 17th and 18th centuries although by 1814 British control over a part of the Dutch colonies had been established and British Guiana was founded. Independence and the establishment of the present republic came in 1966 although it remains a member of the British Commonwealth.

Organised policing along the established British model for overseas territories was introduced in 1891 although the disciplinary record of the NCOs and constables of the new force was questionable—a fact reinforced by the criteria laid down when a long service medal was introduced in 1904. The *Official Gazette of British Guiana* of 19 March 1904 published the regulations for the award of the medal which required officers to be of irreproachable character and conduct and have served for at least 18 years. Although discipline at the time was harsh, the list of reasons which disqualified an officer from ever qualifying for the medal showed that there was a degree of tolerance for some offences. Six entries in the defaulter book, six cases of drunkenness recorded against him, being drunk on duty or being drunk after having been warned for duty were sufficient to deny any officer from receiving the medal. An NCO, in addition, was barred if he had been reprimanded four times or reduced in rank for an offence on a single occasion, not an uncommon occurrence in police forces in the early years of the 20th century anywhere in the British Empire.

BRITISH GUIANA POLICE GOOD CONDUCT MEDAL

Instituted: 7 March 1904.

Ribbon: Red

Metal: Silver.

Description: (Obverse) a three-masted ship in full sail heading right with the Latin inscription DAMUS PETIMUSQUE VICISSIM (we both give and seek) around the upper circumference and BRITISH GUIANA around the lower; (reverse) plain apart from the inscription FOR LONG SERVICE AND GOOD CONDUCT.

The sailing ship was the symbol of the colony and appeared on its flag in the fly of the Blue Ensign. The motto did not appear on the arms until 1906. The use of the Blue Ensign with the appropriate coat of arms was a common feature of a great many flags of overseas territories and is still evident today in Gibraltar, Anguilla, Montserrat, the Cayman Islands and the Falkland Islands and others. In the heyday of British colonialism the Blue Ensign was used in the Australian states, several Canadian provinces and many former territories which have since achieved independence. The Red Ensign was also used but to a lesser degree (Prince Edward Island, for example) and it still appears today in the Canadian Province of Manitoba and the British crown colony of Bermuda.

In common with most medals issued to police officers in overseas territories the British Guiana award is believed to have been discontinued on the introduction of the Colonial Police Long Service and Good Conduct Medal in 1934. After the Republic of Guyana was established in 1966 and the Queen ceased to be the country's Head of State, entitlement to British orders, decorations and medals was withdrawn which led, ultimately, to the introduction of a number of Guyanese honours which included three awards available to the disciplined services—the police force, prison service and fire brigade.

The medals are a part of the *Order of Service of Guyana*, introduced in 1970, which also includes three awards available for distinguished Guyanese citizens, three to reward courage and bravery and three for the military services.

The *Disciplined Services Star for Distinguished Service* (DSS) is the highest award available for distinguished service beyond the normal call of duty in the police force. Sustained and dedicated service of a high order is rewarded by the *Disciplined Services Medal for Meritorious Service* (DSM). The final award is the *Disciplined Services Medal for Long Service and Good Conduct* and awarded to officers after the completion of 15 years continuous whole-time service provided that the officer concerned does not have an entry recorded against him in the defaulters record for a period of 12 years.

Acts of courage are recognised by three awards, the highest available being the *Cacique's Crown of Valour* (CCV) for the highest acts in circumstances of great danger involving serious risk to life, followed by the *Golden Arrow of Courage* (AC) and the *President's Commendation for Brave Conduct* which takes the form of a miniature Guyana leaf in gold worn in similar fashion to the British Mention in Despatches or Queens Commendation for Brave Conduct. The word *cacique* is of Amerindian origin and describes local tribal chiefs.

JAMAICA

The largest (10,990 sq km) single island of the former British territories in the Caribbean and the most populous (2.5 million people) is Jamaica, first colonised by the Spanish but under British control from 1655 until the achievement of independence in 1962. Situated 200 kilometres south of Cuba it is remote from the rest of the former British colonies (apart from the Cayman Islands, previously a dependency of Jamaica) by several thousand kilometres. When independence was achieved a new flag was introduced to replace the Blue Ensign with its badge formerly used and adopted the colours of black, gold and green, each with a symbolism important to the islanders. Black is intended to represent the burden borne by the people, gold is indicative of sunshine and the islands natural resources (primarily bauxite) and green symbolises agriculture (mainly sugar, coffee and rum) and hope for the future. These three colours appear on the ribbons of many of the series of medals awarded to members of the Jamaica Constabulary Force, Jamaica Fire Brigade, Island Special Constabulary Force and Correctional Services Department. The medals all come under the heading of the *Medal of Honour* with three being available to each of the uniformed services—for gallantry, meritorious service and long service with good conduct. The design of the ribbons differs in most cases and red bands are added to the *Medal of Honour for Gallantry* but gold, green and black are the predominant colours used.

When independence was achieved and thought was given to a range of national emblems to reflect the islands new status, all parties agreed that the existing coat of arms dating from 1661 was of such historical importance that it should be retained with the only difference being that the motto should be changed from Latin to English—"out of many, one people". The shield at the centre of the arms has the cross of St George with five pineapples (the island's most important cash crop) on the arms, all surmounted by a helmet, mantle and Jamaican crocodile. The supporters are an Arawak man holding a bow (right) and woman holding a basket of fruit (left). The full arms appear of the obverse of all medals awarded to the uniformed services with the name of the country below. The reverse is different for each service, the Fire Brigade, for example, has a wreath of laurel with a fire-fighters helmet superimposed and the Constabulary Force a truncheon. The reason for the award (for gallantry, for meritorious service or for long service and good conduct) is inscribed around the circumference of all medals. A totally separate range of awards (seven in all) is available to members of the Jamaica Defence Force each using the same obverse as the medals available to the other uniformed services but with different reverses.

In 1979 when the Jamaica Constabulary Force celebrated its centenary a special medal was issued which hung from a ribbon of equal bands of blue, red and grey.

LESOTHO

A mountainous country entirely surrounded by South Africa, Lesotho was colonised by the British as Basutoland until the country achieved independence in 1966 as the Kingdom of Lesotho although it has had a troubled history with periods of military rule and a mutiny by police officers in the late 1990s. The monarchy has been restored under King Letsie III although he has no executive authority, is barred from any political involvement and fills a ceremonial rôle only. The Lesotho Police Service, formerly the Basutoland Mounted Police, Lesotho Mounted Police and Royal Lesotho Mounted Police, were heavily involved in the latest period of conflict with several arrested for treason and sedition. The country is experiencing a period of relative stability although the relationships between the army and the police and the monarchists and republicans is fragile.

In more peaceful times during the reign of Queen Mamohato Seeiso as regent in 1970 a series of four medals was introduced for exclusive award to members of the Lesotho Mounted Police. The design of all four was similar with the only differences being the reason for the award on the obverse and the colouring of the ribbon. The obverse depicted an effigy of Moshoeshoe the First, the founder of the Basotho nation, with the reason for the award below. The reverse carried the force crest. The highest award, the *Police Medal for Gallantry*, hung from a red ribbon with a silver rose placed in the centre. The award was available to officers of any rank in recognition of acts of conspicuous bravery. The inscription on the obverse stated simply FOR GALLANTRY.

To reward acts of meritorious service by officers of all ranks two further medals were awarded, one restricted to officers of the rank of assistant superintendent and above and another to those of the rank of inspector and below. The design of the medals was identical although the criteria for the *Medal for Meritorious Service (Officers)* were more demanding than the awards for "other ranks". The inscription on the obverse of both was FOR MERITORIOUS SERVICE.

The only difference between the two awards, apart from the criteria, was the colouring and design of the ribbon—red with two white lines in the centre for officers and green with a single central line in white for other ranks.

The fourth medal of the series was available only to officers of the rank of inspector or below and given on the completion of 18 years good service with bars awarded after 25 and 30 years qualifying service. The inscription on the obverse read FOR LONG SERVICE AND GOOD CONDUCT and the ribbon was of four bands of green, red, white and blue, all of equal width.

ST LUCIA

When St Lucia achieved independence from Britain in 1979 and adopted its new flag the colours of blue, yellow, black and white were chosen but with a motif in the centre intended to reflect the reflect the position of the island surrounded by the sea (the blue background) and the two prominent features of its topography. The double triangle design of the motif is indicative of The Pitons (two volcanic hills) and are coloured yellow (the sandy beaches) and black (the dark volcanic rocks). The island has come under both French and British control with the Gallic influence remaining strong and shown in the name of one of the divisions of the Order of St Lucia (introduced in 1986)—the *Les Pitons Medal*—where the French name for the award has been adopted. The Order has two divisions available to police officers, one for acts of outstanding bravery (the *Medal of Honour*) and another divided into two classes intended to reward meritorious service by members of the Royal St Lucia Police Force and the island's other uniformed bodies. The *National Service Cross* is awarded to commissioned officers and the *National Service Medal* is given to other ranks. Both awards are restricted, one cross and four medals being the maximum in any one year. All classes of the Order of St Lucia use the same ribbon in the national colours as seen on the flag—a black central band flanked by stripes of white and yellow with a broad blue band at the ribbons edges.

Long service by police officers, members of the Fire Service, Prison Service, Civil Service and the Teaching Service is rewarded by the *Public Services Long Service Medal* given after 15 years with a bar awarded after an additional ten years and another after a further five years.

SIERRA LEONE

Situated on the Atlantic coast of Africa, Sierra Leone was established by the British as a home for slaves freed from the clutches of slave-traders when their ships were intercepted by the Royal Navy in the late 18th century. The colony gained independence from Britain in 1961 and became the Republic of Sierra Leone in 1971 although its fortunes in recent years have been dogged by civil war. At the end of 1964 (28 December) a series of three awards was introduced to replace the three medals of the Colonial Police series of awards previously available to police officers in the colony.

The new awards closely followed the pattern of those they replaced with the effigy of Queen Elizabeth on the obverse and a design on the reverse depicting a pair of scales and a truncheon with the words SIERRA LEONE POLICE FORCE and the reason for the award at the circumference—FOR GALLANTRY, FOR MERITORIOUS SERVICE or FOR LONG SERVICE. They were discontinued in 1971 when Sierra Leone became a republic.

The ribbons of all three awards were in the national colours of royal blue, white and a light green as seen on the new flag of the independent state. The *Police Medal for Meritorious Service* had five equal bands of white, green, blue, green and white with the *Police Medal for Gallantry* following the pattern of the QPM and CPM by the addition of a red line (on the white bands) to indicate that the medal was awarded for an act of courage. The ribbon of the *Police Medal for Long Service* differed slightly from the colouring of the previous awards by the inclusion of yellow stripes. The basic colour was green with white bands at the edges with a narrow blue band separating the two. The central green band was bisected by a narrow band of yellow. The criteria for the award of all three medals mirrored that of the CPM they replaced.

SOLOMON ISLANDS

The influence of the British Empire stretched far and wide, from the West Indies to Africa, India and a number of small islands in the Pacific Ocean. When these states achieved independence they were usually very quick to establish an honours system of their own to reinforce their new found status. The Solomon Islands are situated in the Pacific Ocean south west of Papua New Guinea and are made up of several hundred islands totalling almost 290,000 square kilometres and supporting a population of more than 400,000. Independence from Britain was achieved on 7 July 1978 and an honours system introduced in 1981 which included two awards available to police officers of the Royal Solomon Islands Police, one exclusively. The ribbons of all four new awards adopted the national colours—green, yellow and blue—in a variety of designs.

The medal available exclusively to police officers—the *Royal Solomon Islands Police Long Service and Good Conduct Medal*—is awarded on completion of a minimum of 18 years continuous service with bars granted on the achievement of 25 and 30 years service in total. Prior to the granting of independence in July 1978 officers were entitled to the CPM for Long Service and qualifying service for that award was allowed to count towards the new medal provided that it had not been awarded. The ribbon of the medal is green with royal blue bands at the edges, the two colours separated by stripes of yellow.

The second award available to police officers is also given to any members of the disciplined forces of the Solomon Islands for valuable service characterised by resourcefulness and devotion to duty which included long service marked by exceptional merit, ability or exemplary conduct. The medal ribbon is royal blue with green bands at the edges, the two separated by lines of yellow.

In addition to these two continuing awards, there have been two medals issued to mark the achievement of independence and the tenth anniversary of the milestone, both awarded to police officers. The *Independence Medal* was widely distributed and used the national colours on the ribbon with an additional band of white, a colour which appears on the national flag (and those of several other countries in the southern hemisphere) in the form of the southern cross constellation. The broad central band in white is flanked by bands of yellow with a green band at the left edge and one of royal blue on the right.

On the tenth anniversary of independence a special medal was struck for award to members of the country's disciplined forces. *The 10th Anniversary Medal for the Disciplined Forces* hung from a ribbon with a royal blue central band flanked by bands of green, red and yellow.

TRINIDAD AND TOBAGO

The former colonies and territories in the Caribbean retained the Queen as the head of state when they achieved independence and did not go as far as declaring themselves a republic—with one exception. Trinidad and Tobago followed the norm for the region for 14 years after independence was achieved in 1962 but finally made the break and became the Republic of Trinidad and Tobago on 1 August 1976. The country remains a member of the Commonwealth. The Commonwealth has approximately 50 members although those which are republics or which have a local monarch as the head of state now far outnumber those within the realm of Queen Elizabeth II. From 1962 to 1976 police officers in Trinidad and Tobago were entitled the Colonial Police Medals for Gallantry, Meritorious Service or Long Service with Good Conduct but this entitlement ceased when the republic was established.

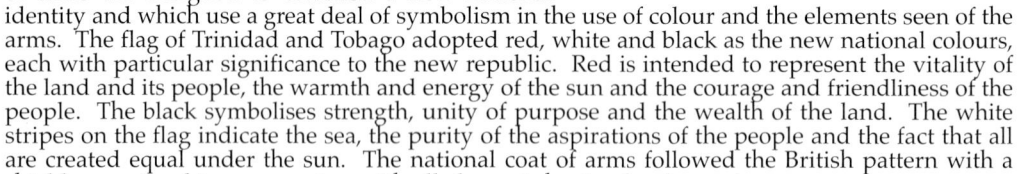

Before independence is achieved, a flag and coats of arms are designed to establish a new national identity and which use a great deal of symbolism in the use of colour and the elements seen of the arms. The flag of Trinidad and Tobago adopted red, white and black as the new national colours, each with particular significance to the new republic. Red is intended to represent the vitality of the land and its people, the warmth and energy of the sun and the courage and friendliness of the people. The black symbolises strength, unity of purpose and the wealth of the land. The white stripes on the flag indicate the sea, the purity of the aspirations of the people and the fact that all are created equal under the sun. The national coat of arms followed the British pattern with a shield, a crest and two supporters with all elements having local meaning.

Two elements of the national coat of arms have a particular relevance to the series of medals introduced by the Republic of Trinidad and Tobago—the humming birds on the shield and the mound on which the two supporters stand. The shield is in the national colours and has in the upper third two humming birds as a reminder of the fact that the islands are home to more than 17 species of these stunning birds and were known locally by the Carib people as the "Land of the Humming Bird" when they were first discovered by Columbus in 1498. The two supporters—a scarlet ibis and cocrico, the two national birds of the Republic—stand on a mound with a representation of the three peaks of the southern mountain range known as the "Three Sisters" which Columbus used as his inspiration to name the island of Trinidad. Both these features—humming birds and the three peaks—are remembered in the name of two medals in the Trinidad and Tobago honours system.

The highest award is the *Trinity Cross* with the *Humming Bird Medal* also available as the third highest award. There is also the *Chaconia Medal* named after the Republic's national flower, also known as the wild poinsettia The chaconia was chosen partly because it blooms each year at the end of August, very often on Republic Day itself. A feature of the Trinidad and Tobago honours system is the use of the national colours on the ribbons of every award made by the State in the form of a broad red band with a central black band flanked by lines of white. At each edge of the ribbons is a band in one of a number of colours depending upon the award. The gold *Trinity Cross* has the outer bands in gold, the *Chaconia Medal* in light green and the *Humming Bird Medal* in dark blue, the colours remaining constant for the two latter awards although they are both available in gold, silver and bronze. The Humming Bird Medal is awarded for loyal and devoted service to the community of Trinidad and Tobago or to reward acts of gallantry or other outstanding humane action and, as such, has been awarded to officers of the Trinidad and Tobago Police Service. The Chaconia Medal is not awarded to police officers.

The award most frequently made to police officers is the *Public Service Medal of Merit* available in gold, silver and bronze for a number of reasons with the class of the award indicated by the outer bands of the medal ribbon—purple, light blue or silver. The gold award (purple edges) is given for outstanding and meritorious service with the silver medal (light blue edges) being given for long and meritorious service. The bronze medal with silver edges to the ribbon is awarded for long service with good conduct of at least 12 years. The obverse of the medal depicts the full achievement of arms of Trinidad and Tobago and has an irregular shape following the outline of the arms. It uses a simple ring suspender. Recipients of all four awards are entitled to the use of post-nominals—TC (Trinity Cross), CM (Chaconia Medal), HBM (Humming Bird Medal), or MOM (Medal of Merit).

HONG KONG

By the time the People's Republic of China, home of the worlds oldest continuous civilisation, assumed control of Hong Kong on 1 July 1997 the colony had been an anachronism for many years, one of the last remaining remnants of the British Empire, with no validity in the world in the last years of the 20th century. When the British first took control of Hong Kong island in January 1841 it was populated by a few fishermen and charcoal burners living around the coast. As the new colony expanded to cope with the shipping which quickly began using the port, opium dens, gambling houses and brothels appeared with an inevitable adverse effect on the maintenance of law and order.

The first attempt at the establishment of an official, paid and disciplined police force came in May 1844 although it was none too successful and the character of many of the first officers was dubious. One year later the first steps in the reform of the force and its establishment as an efficient, disciplined, well-run and effective body were taken with the appointment of Charles May as the commander. In 17 years he transformed the original force and made a significant impact of the levels of robbery, murder and piracy which were almost out-of-control when he took over command.

The first medal made available to Hong Kong police officers was introduced before the force was 18 years old and inspired by the Constabulary Medal (Ireland) awarded by the Irish Constabulary, the model used by Charles May for Hong Kong.

HONG KONG POLICE MEDAL FOR MERIT

Instituted: 3 May 1862.

Ribbon: Differed according to the class of the medal.

Metal: Gold, silver and bronze.

Size: 36 mm.

Description: (Obverse) the effigy of the reigning monarch; (reverse) the words HONG KONG - POLICE FORCE - FOR MERIT in three lines within a wreath of laurel.

The medal was available in five classes with different ribbons for each, the class been dependent upon the length of service of the recipient and the type of service thought worthy of official recognition. The gold medal was reserved for the first class award and hung from a maroon ribbon—it was given in small numbers for only the most exceptional displays of courage in the course of duty. The second class medal was cast in silver with a yellow ribbon and awarded where the level of courage displayed by the recipient or the act of service performed was not thought sufficient to merit the gold medal. The yellow ribbon was used for the third and fourth class awards (both bronze) with the addition of one or two black stripes respectively placed centrally to indicate the class of award. The fifth class medal, also cast in bronze, was restricted to members of the Police Reserve and hung from a green ribbon with two black stripes. The Medal for Merit was replaced by the Colonial Police Medal series in 1938.

Hong Kong in the 19th century was a dangerous place, apart from the levels of violent crime which were still high, natural disasters and disease took their toll of the population which by the 1880s had grown to more than 150,000. The worst of these disasters came in 1894 when the colony was struck by an outbreak of bubonic plague, the black death of Europe which killed 25 million people in the 14th century, one third of the total population. From the early 1890s it had been spreading along the trade routes of southern China and reached epidemic proportions by 1894 in Canton, less than 100 kilometres from Hong Kong. The first case was diagnosed in Hong Kong on 8 May and 20 more sufferers found in a nearby hospital two days later—the nightmare had started. In the space of the following three months more than 2,500 people died although this was almost insignificant in comparison with the million who died in India and the ten million who were to fall to the disease as it spread from southern China to many parts of the world in the next 20 years. The one positive effect of the plague in Hong Kong if there could be such a thing was the discovery of the bacillus responsible, the result of the work of doctors in the colony in 1894.

The effect of the plague on the work of the Hong Kong Police was immense, the maintenance of order amongst the panic-stricken populace, the enforcement of quarantine, the disposal of bodies and the movement of those stricken all these duties fell to the officers assisted by elements from the Royal Navy, Royal Engineers and a detachment of 300 men from the Shropshire Light Infantry. When the epidemic has been contained the authorities in Hong Kong issued a special commemorative medal as a token of thanks for those involved in the crisis including police officers. Doctors and nursing staff were also rewarded. The more senior staff from all the services were given medals in gold (45) with 400 in silver being awarded to the remainder.

HONG KONG PLAGUE MEDAL

Instituted: 1894.

Ribbon: Red with two narrow yellow stripes towards the centre and yellow edges.

Metal: Gold and silver.

Size: 36 mm.

Description: (Obverse) the scene of a Chinese man lying on a trestle table being tended by a woman and supported by a man who is warding off the figure of Death with his left hand. The date 1894 is in a scroll in the exergue and the name of the colony in Chinese characters is on the left of the medal; (reverse) the words FOR - SERVICES - RENDERED - DURING - THE PLAGUE - OF - 1894 in seven lines in the central field surrounded by an outer band inscribed with the words PRESENTED BY THE HONG KONG COMMUNITY. A simple ring suspender was used.

The first police officers in Hong Kong were primarily European (including a contingent from Edinburgh) or Indian with some Chinese and their area of responsibility was concentrated on the commercial and European residential areas. The Chinese population were neglected and relied upon a second body paid for by prominent citizens unlike the Hong Kong Police which was financed by the colony authorities.

The District Watch Force was a purely Chinese body with responsibility for the policing of the Chinese areas although they had a range of powers and patrolled in uniform. In 1868 a medal was introduced to reward members of the Watch for meritorious conduct in much the same was as the Medal of Merit was made available to members of the Hong Kong Police although it was issued in a single class only.

Hong Kong

HONG KONG DISTRICT WATCH FORCE MERIT MEDAL

Instituted: 1868.

Ribbon: Dark green with a central stripe in dark red.

Metal: Silver.

Size: 31 mm.

Description: (Obverse) the words GREAT BRITAIN HONG KONG in four Chinese characters above a watchman's lamp superimposed on a cutlass and truncheon; (reverse) a wreath of laurel with the words DISTRICT (upper) WATCHMANS FORCE (across the centre) and FOR MERIT (lower) in the central field in circular form. A large suspender ring was used.

As the 19th century drew to a close and Queen Victoria celebrated her golden and diamond jubilees a new group of official medals was introduced to mark these special occasions and awarded to a wide range of members of the public as souvenirs including many who had not attended the ceremony but who had been chosen for their particularly noteworthy work during the year. The practice of issuing medals to celebrate royal events was far from new, the first official example being produced in 1547 to commemorate the accession to the throne of King Edward VI. Coronation medals first appeared in 1603 when James I was crowned and they have been issued continuously since.

These medals were never intended to be worn and there were several different designs produced by private individuals and local authorities, many of which were offered for sale to the general public. The golden jubilee of Queen Victoria marked the first occasion when an official medal was instituted and awarded to the likes of police officers and which was intended to be worn. To celebrate the diamond jubilee, special medals were produced in parts of the British Empire, a practice continued in 1902 when King Edward VII was crowned. In Hong Kong a total of approximately 6,000 were produced and awarded to military personnel and police officers serving in the colony.

HONG KONG CORONATION MEDAL 1902

Instituted: 1902.

Ribbon: Red with a broad central band in royal blue flanked by bands of white.

Metal: Silver and bronze.

Size: 36 mm.

Description: (Obverse) the conjoined busts of King Edward VII and Queen Alexandra facing right with their names inscribed around the circumference; (reverse) the origina coat of arms of the colony—a circular picture of a three-masted sailing ship and a Chinese junk with two figures (one Chinese, one European) shaking hands in the foreground—all surrounded by two concentric inscriptions around the lower circumference—SIR HENRY A BLAKE GCMG GOVERNOR (inner) and TO COMMEMORATE THE CORONATION OF THEIR MAJESTIES THE KING AND QUEEN (outer). The words HONG KONG were inscribed at the upper circumference.

The first half of the 20th century in Hong Kong was marked by turmoil in neighbouring China, a burgeoning population and the effects of the two world wars which included four years of occupation by Japan. In 1945 the new commissioner was faced with a police force that needed rebuilding, almost from scratch, to face new challenges which included a civil war raging in China, the subsequent establishment of a communist government there, hundreds of thousands of refugees, increased levels of crime, terrorism and more natural disasters. At the end of a particularly anxious period in the late 1960s which included riots, bombings and the murder of five police officers by communist militia from the Chinese side of the border, the title "Royal" was added to the Force name in recognition of the courage and dedication of all its officers. The Royal Hong Kong Police grew in reputation and established itself as a professional, efficient and reliable body.

There was, however, a dark cloud on the horizon which threatened to change the Force forever—the end of the lease giving the British control of the colony. Shortly after the British first took possession of the island in 1841 it was ceded to them in perpetuity at the Treaty of Nanking which also led to the establishment of the foreign concessions in Shanghai, Tientsin and other cities on mainland China. Further territory was acquired culminating in an agreement from China to lease the territories to Britain for 99 years—expiring in 1997. In 1984 Britain agreed to hand over sovereignty to China on 1 July 1997 provided that certain conditions were met. Negotiations were hard and prolonged but, on the agreed date, the hand-over took place and Hong Kong became a part of the People's Republic of China as a special administrative region. The Royal Hong Kong Police ceased to exist.

When the change was inevitable plans were made to mark the end of the Force's existence by the introduction of two special commemorative medals, one for regular officers and another for members of the Hong Kong Auxiliary Police who had worked alongside their colleagues for many years. The two medals were authorised by the Commissioner of Police but not issued to officers in the usual sense, they were available for purchase to anyone who had served between 1844 and 1997. It is estimated that only a small proportion of those eligible (40,000) were willing to hand over the H$1,000 requested.

ROYAL HONG KONG POLICE COMMEMORATION MEDAL

Instituted: 1996.

Ribbon: Magenta with a broad dark blue central band flanked by narrow stripes of old gold.

Metal: Silver.

Size: 38 mm.

Description: (Obverse) the crest of the Force—a wreath of laurel leaves surmounted by a crown with a central disc bearing the first coat of arms of the colony with the Force name in a banner below; (reverse) a wreath of laurel leaves tied at the base with a bow enclosing a pair of crossed tipstaves with the dates 1844 and 1997 to the left and right. A ring suspender was used.

The medal offered to members of the RHK Auxiliary Police was very similar in design with the only difference being the substitution of the name ROYAL HONG KONG AUXILIARY POLICE in the banner below the crest on the obverse. The tradition of voluntary police officers in Hong Kong dates back many years under a variety of names—Special Constabulary, Police Reserve and Auxiliary Police included. At the time of the hand-over of sovereignty there were almost 6,000 members of the RHK Auxiliary Police (98% Chinese) with 1,000 reporting for duty each day. The training of these officers was regular and intensive—the equivalent of 26 days each year—and the officers are an integral part of current policing.

Although Hong Kong was the most well-known of the Chinese cities where foreign powers had great influence, it was not alone. The cities of Shanghai (*see under France, p75 et seq.*) and Tientsin (Tianjin)—further north and approximately 200 kilometres from Beijing—were subject to concessions granted to Britain, France, American and other western powers.

In Shanghai the foreign concessions were merged and policing arrangements became the responsibility of the international community. In Tientsin this never happaned and the British concession remained independent. The British concession in Tientsin was granted in 1860 and managed to survive after the city was occupied by the Japanese on 30 July 1937 until the British forces withdrew on 31 August 1940. The concession was formally ended in January 1943 when still under Japanese control. Today Tientsin is China's third city with a population in excess of seven million and has been granted the status of an autonomous municipality along with Beijing and Shanghai. The European influence is still very much in evidence particularly in the architecture where it is possible to see the effects of the different styles adopted by the concession holders. The residents of each concession were not subject to Chinese law and each European power made its own policing arrangements within its area of influence. The British concession was the responsibility of the British Municipal Council Police who issued a long service medal to officers.

BRITISH MUNICIPAL COUNCIL POLICE (TIENTSIN) LONG SERVICE MEDAL

Ribbon: *White with a yellow band towards each edge.*

Metal: *Gilt.*

Size: *38 mm.*

Description: *(Obverse) a circular medal with the seal of the British concession in the centre above the words LONG SERVICE all surrounded by an outer band inscribed with BRITISH MUNICIPAL COUNCIL POLICE around the upper two-thirds of the circumference and TIENTSIN at the lower edge. A plain straight suspender bar was used attached by a claw fitting.*

Police Medals of the World

HONG KONG SPECIAL ADMINISTRATIVE REGION OF THE PEOPLE'S REPUBLIC OF CHINA

When the People's Republic of China resumed responsibility for Hong Kong, all entitlement held by officers to medals from the Colonial Police Medal series ceased although it was quickly replaced by a new series instituted by the new regime which included four medals available exclusively to police officers. One of the first awards introduced was a group of three medals to reward acts of courage by citizens of Hong Kong (including police officers). The Medal for Bravery is available in three classes dependent on the level of courage displayed. By the end of the year 2000, 29 awards had been made, seven in gold (five posthumous), seven in silver and 15 in bronze. The design of all three classes is the same although coloured enamel is used which differs for each. The ribbon colour is also different for each class.

The central disc of the medal has three conjoined heads facing left, two male (one Chinese, one European) and a female with an outer band made up of two narrow wreaths bound together. The central medallion is in the metal of the appropriate award with the wreaths and the ribbon in red (gold), purple (silver) or bronze (bronze). The ribbons are in the pentagonal style familiar on eastern European awards.

POLICE MEDAL FOR DISTINGUISHED SERVICE

Instituted: 1 July 1998.

Ribbon: Five equal stripes of white (three) and red (two).

Metal: Silver.

Size: 35 mm.

Description: *(Obverse) the new crest of Hong Kong (a five-petal bauhinia flower) surrounded by an outer band bearing its full official name in Chinese characters around the upper two-thirds of the circumference and HONG KONG in English at the bottom edge; (reverse) a wreath of laurel encircling an inscription in two Chinese characters all within an outer band bearing the name of the medal in Chinese characters (upper) and English around the circumference.*

The most prestigious award exclusively available to police officers is restricted to the most senior police officers only and awarded for especially meritorious service to the community.

The second of the series of awards is available to officers of all ranks and awarded in recognition of meritorious service marked by exceptional resourcefulness, devotion to duty or ability and ordinary duty in demanding or dangerous circumstances.

POLICE MEDAL FOR MERITORIOUS SERVICE

Instituted: 1 July 1998.

Ribbon: Dark green with a broad central band in dark blue flanked by thin red lines.

Metal: Silver.

Size: 35 mm.

Description: (Obverse) the same as the previous award; (reverse) similar to the previous award apart from different Chinese characters in the central field and the name of the medal in the outer band.

The two remaining awards are both long service awards, one for officers of the regular force and the other for members of the Auxiliary Police.

POLICE LONG SERVICE MEDAL

Instituted: 1 July 1998.

Ribbon: Dark blue with a broad central band in green flanked by thin lines in red.

Metal: Silver.

Size: 35 mm.

Description: (Obverse) the same as the two previous awards; (reverse) a wreath of laurel with a vertical truncheon (handle uppermost) with the end superimposed on the base of the wreath (very similar to the Colonial Police Medal series) within an outer band bearing the name of the medal in Chinese characters (upper) and English (lower) around the circumference.

The medal intended for officers of the Auxiliary Police is similar to that for regular officers with the only differences being the substitution of the name around the circumference of the reverse and the ribbon which is dark blue with a broad central band in green bisected by a pair of thin red lines.

The one blot on the reputation of the Royal Hong Kong Police (RHKP) appeared in the early 1970s when allegations of corruption amongst officers came to a head. The paying of bribes to officials in the immediate post-war years was widespread and accepted as a fact of life by most inhabitants of the colony. After the disruption of the 1960s and the return of stability, many sections of the populace began less tolerant of corruption and demanded action by the government. In 1973 a senior police officer was implicated, the people took to the streets and a commission of inquiry was held under the direction of a senior high court judge. The outcome was the establishment of a wholly independent body charged with rooting out corrupt officers. The newly-appointed members of the Independent Commission Against Corruption (ICAC) went about their task with gusto aided by wide-ranging powers of investigation and arrest.

Many police officers were arrested and prosecuted although the catalyst for the establishment of the Commission—Chief Superintendent Peter Godber—escaped the colony and was never brought to justice. The work of the Commission left many scars although the reputation of the RHKP recovered and it was handed to the authorities from China in good order with its reputation restored. The work of the ICAC was continued after Hong Kong was handed back to China and the value of its work has been recognised by the new regime with the introduction of a medal for meritorious service to acknowledge this.

The design of the medal is similar to those awarded to other disciplined bodies with the exception of the colouring of the ribbon—red with a narrow dark blue stripe towards each edge and a broader band offset to the right of centre—and two different Chinese characters on the reverse.

INDIA AND BURMA

Apart from the countries where the indigenous people were few and easily subdued and the majority of those policed were immigrants (or criminals) the British Empire held sway over nations with huge populations, a multiplicity of religious beliefs and ancient cultures. As British rule was imposed, the legal and policing systems of Britain were introduced into countries as diverse as Canada, Burma, India, Mauritius, Sri Lanka, the West Indies, a number on the continent of Africa and the islands of the Seychelles. The most populous and complex of these nations by some margin was India with five major religions, 15 main languages, 700 minor ones and dialects and a proportion (50 million) of its current population living in tribal communities. It is currently the worlds second most populous country after China—the one billionth Indian citizen was born in May 2000.

British influence in India began in the 17th century but it wasn't until the early 1800s that the whole country was firmly under British control after almost 100 years of fighting with the French and local rulers.

India remained a country of a number of independent states although the local rulers were under strong British influence. The area under control was very different from the India of today and included Pakistan, Bangladesh and Burma which was ruled as a province of India from 1886. The culture, religion and traditions of the people were generally not subject to any interference with one of the few exceptions being the imposition of British ideas in relation to law and policing.

Modern style policing was established by the British in 1669 and expanded as control over India increased until 1861 when the basis of the present day service was introduced in all states and main cities. In the late 1920s and early 1930s much thought was given to the introduction of ways to reward police officers in many parts of the Empire for acts of bravery or meritorious service to compliment the system in operation in the Armed Forces. The position of India as the "Jewel in the Crown" of the Empire led to the introduction of a medal which was to be available to Indian police forces and fire brigades in recognition of any such outstanding service.

INDIAN POLICE MEDAL

Instituted: 23 February 1932.

Ribbon: Crimson with bands of dark blue and silver grey towards the edges.

Metal: Bronze.

Size: 36 mm.

Description: (Obverse) the head of the reigning Sovereign; (reverse) a wreath of laurel with an imperial crown at the top and a panel across the centre bearing the words FOR DISTINGUISHED CONDUCT. Within the wreath are the words INDIAN (above the panel) and POLICE (below). A plain straight suspender was employed attached by a claw fitting.

This design was retained until 1942 when a change was made to differentiate between the two reasons for the award by the additional of a central silver stripe on the ribbon to denote that the medal was given for gallantry. In 1944 this was taken a stage further with a redesign of the medals reverse. The wording in the panel across the centre was changed to read either FOR GALLANTRY or FOR MERITORIOUS SERVICE. Bars were available for any second award (bronze with a laurel design) and it was possible for one won for gallantry to be worn with a medal awarded for meritorious service and vice-versa although instances of this occurring were very few.

In total almost 1,100 medals for gallantry were won with an additional 21 first bars. The medals were issued unnamed although many were engraved locally with the recipient's details.

When India gained independence from Britain in 1947 the Indian Police Medal was retained for a few years during the transition period when India was a dominion until it became a republic in 1950 and the medal was formally discontinued. To celebrate the full independence of India and the establishment of republic status a special medal was issued and awarded to all police officers who were serving on 26 January 1950—independence day.

POLICE INDEPENDENCE MEDAL 1950

Instituted: 1950.

Ribbon: Red with a central orange band flanked by two dark blue stripes.

Metal: Cupro-nickel.

Size: 36 mm.

Description: (Obverse) the Indian emblem with the words INDEPENDENCE MEDAL above and the date 26TH JANUARY 1950 below; (reverse) the chakra within a wreath of lotus above the word POLICE. The medal hung from a plain straight suspender attached by a claw fitting.

Two further medals to celebrate anniversaries of the achievement of independence were issued in 1973 (25 years) and 1997 (50 years) and awarded to members of the Indian armed forces and police service who were serving on the 15th of August of each year, the date on which India became a dominion, the first step towards true independence.

A central feature found on the majority of Indian medals is the national emblem—the replica of the *Lion of Sarnath* taken from the Lion Capital erected in Uttar Pradesh in the third century BC by Emperor Ashoka to mark the spot where Buddha is said to have first proclaimed his gospel of peace and emancipation to the four corners of the universe. The four lions (one hidden from view) symbolise power, courage and confidence and stand on a circular plinth. The plinth is carved with four animals depicting the guardians of the four directions—a lion to the north, elephant to the east, a horse to the south and a bull to the west. The plinth rests on a lotus in full bloom to represent life and creative inspiration. A motto in Hindi script reads "*satyameva jayate*" (truth alone triumphs). The "*chakra*" featured on the reverse of the medal symbolises the *khadi* spinning wheel and is a powerful image of the road to independence by its association with Mahatma Gandhi. It has appeared on very few Indian medals since 1950 but is familiar as the centrepiece of the flag of the Republic of India.

Hindi is the most important Indian language and the official language of government although it is spoken by only 20% of the population, mainly in the north of the country. Most medals issued in India are dual language with the name in Hindi script and English although, in recent years, the English has been replaced by the anglicised translation of the Hindi script. For a number of years there has been a movement to adopt Hindi as the official Indian language to replace English but this has led to resistance from the southern states where very few people speak Hindi and wish to retain English as the official language. The problem is never likely to be satisfactorily solved. The country's banknotes provide an example of the difficulties faced by the government—those over 5 rupees use 13 different scripts, a situation with no easy remedy.

Following independence the Indian Police Medal was replaced by two national awards, introduced in March 1951, exclusively available to police officers and members of the fire service following the example of the King's Police and Fire Service Medal in the UK. The awards were gilded circular medals which hung from a plain straight suspender bar attached by a claw fitting. One was available to reward acts of gallantry and a second was given for meritorious or distinguished service although of limited issue. The medal for gallantry could be awarded posthumously.

PRESIDENT'S POLICE AND FIRE SERVICES MEDAL FOR GALLANTRY

Ribbon: Halved dark blue and white with a central red stripe.

Description: (Obverse) the President's flag (pictured right) on a shield with the words PRESIDENT'S POLICE AND FIRE SERVICES MEDAL around the upper circumference and INDIA in the lower separated by a pair of five-pointed stars; (reverse) the national emblem placed centrally with the words FOR GALLANTRY at the lower circumference and a wreath around the remainder.

This medal was awarded for conspicuous gallantry in saving life and property, in the prevention of crime or the arrest of criminals. It was available to all members of any police force in India irrespective of rank or length of service who perform an act of bravery thought worthy of presidential recognition. The award made to recognise distinguished service was similar, differing only in the inscription of the reverse which read FOR DISTINGUISHED SERVICE and the colouring of the ribbon which lacked the central red stripe.

The Presidential standard is quartered dark blue and red with an emblem in each depicting an aspect from Indian culture representing the national ideals: the lions of Sarnath (national unity), an elephant from the Ajanta frescos (patience and strength), scales from the Red Fort in Old Delhi (justice) and a vase of lotus flowers from Sarnath (prosperity).

Again following the precedent set in the UK, new, separate medals (in gold) were introduced for the police and fire services both awarded in the name of the President with second awards also being introduced to acknowledge acts of courage or distinguished service which did not meet the stringent standards required by the premier award. The ribbons of the two higher awards were unchanged.

PRESIDENT'S POLICE MEDAL FOR GALLANTRY

Description: *(Obverse) a five-pointed star with a surrounding inscription which reads PRESIDENTS POLICE MEDAL in English (lower) and Hindi (upper); (reverse) the national emblem surrounded by a wreath with the inscription FOR GALLANTRY in Hindi script (above) and English (below) outside the wreath around the circumference. A plain straight suspender bar is used attached by a claw fitting.*

The award of the medal brings with it a monthly allowance of 200 rupees which was also a pension or widow's allowance if the recipient died. Recipients are also entitled to a further allowance which is unusual by British standards, with no equivalent, the right to free second class rail travel.

The second gallantry award is also a national medal available to all officers from any force without regard to rank or length of service but it is not issued in the President's name. It is given for acts of conspicuous gallantry although the criteria are not as restrictive as the higher award. Special allowances are similarly paid to the recipient with the monthly sum, however, being reduced to 100 rupees.

POLICE MEDAL FOR GALLANTRY

Ribbon: *Red with four narrow stripes of dark blue, silver, dark blue and silver at each edge.*

Description: *(Obverse) a circular medal showing the national emblem placed centrally with the motto of the Republic in Hindi script below. The words POLICE MEDAL are inscribed at the circumference in English (lower) and Hindi (upper); (reverse) a wreath towards the circumference bisected by a central bar bearing the words FOR GALLANTRY with INDIAN above and POLICE below, very similar to the earlier British medal.*

Members of Indian police forces are also eligible for other military and civil awards for bravery in addition to those available exclusively for police officers. One of the most recently formed, and most demanding, police forces in India is the Indo-Tibetan Border Police (ITBP), established in October 1962 to guard the politically sensitive border with Chinese occupied Tibet in the Himalayas. The Force is responsible for a border length of 2,115 kilometres with its forward posts situated at altitudes of 9,000 to 18,000 feet where they are subject to the full fury of blizzards, landslides and avalanches, the dangers of high altitudes and temperatures which rarely rise above -40° Celsius. In addition to the normal border policing duties of preventing and detecting any illegal immigration and smuggling, officers of the Force are often involved in anti-terrorist activity. These activities have resulted in the deaths of several officers and the award of national decorations for bravery other than the two police medals.

Assistant Commissioner Ashok Kumar Rana had been a member of the ITBP for 13 years when he was caught up in an encounter with Afghan mercenaries on 2 November 1998 in Jammu-Kashmir. He killed three of the terrorists but was fatally wounded in the action. For his courage he was posthumously awarded the Shaurya Chakra Indias third highest peacetime decoration for gallantry. He had previously been awarded the Police Medal for Gallantry on two separate occasions.

SHAURYA CHAKRA

Instituted: 4 January 1952.

Ribbon: Dark green with three orange bands.

Metal: Bronze.

Size: 35 mm.

Description: (Obverse) a circular medal with the chakra at the centre surrounded by a wreath of lotus; (reverse) the name of the medal in Hindi along the upper edge and in English at the bottom. The central field is left blank. The medal was originally known as the Ashoka Chakra but renamed in 1967.

A second officer—Inspector Raj Kumar—also lost his life in Jammu-Kashmir in an encounter with terrorists on 5 May 1997 and was posthumously awarded the Sena Medal, the fourth highest Indian bravery decoration. The inspector had served with the ITBP for almost 20 years when he was killed at the age of 44.

SENA MEDAL

Instituted: 17 June 1960.

Ribbon: Red with a narrow white central stripe.

Metal: Silver.

Size: 35 mm.

Description: (Obverse) a bayonet pointing upwards; (reverse) a soldier standing with the name of the medal in Hindi script above. It hangs from a plain straight suspender attached by a scrolled ring fitting. The Sena Medal is not exclusively a gallantry award and is also given for exceptional devotion to duty and meritorious service.

By mid-2000, officers of the Indo-Tibetan Border Police had been decorated for gallantry on 51 separate occasions since the founding of the Force in 1962, usually as a result of encounters with terrorists sponsored by foreign governments along the sensitive and dangerous border. The President's Police Medal for Gallantry has been awarded three times and the Police Medal for Gallantry on 44 occasions. A further four civil bravery awards have been made to officers serving in one of the most demanding police environments in the world.

India

To reward distinguished or meritorious service two further medals are available although there are restrictions on the number awarded in any one year. They are both a form of long service medal although the criteria are such that there is no automatic entitlement to either, the recipients must have performed their duty over and above the standards normally expected of police officers.

PRESIDENT'S POLICE MEDAL FOR DISTINGUISHED SERVICE

Ribbon: Half white, half dark blue.

Description: (Obverse) the same as the President's Police Medal for Gallantry; (reverse) similar to the gallantry award but with the inscription moved to a position inside the wreath surrounding the chakra and amended to read FOR DISTINGUISHED SERVICE in Hindi script (above) and English (below). The method of suspension remained the same.

Considering the size of the country and the number of police officers in the Indian police forces, this medal is awarded in very limited numbers—about 125 in any one year although the precise number can vary. It is presented at special ceremonies held each year on Independence and Republic Day (26 January) in recognition of especially distinguished police service. All police officers are eligible but they must have at least 21 years service to be considered. Most awards go to senior officers, including 51 to the ITBP.

The second award is given in far greater numbers—fixed at 740 annually—and is similarly presented at the ceremonies held on Independence and Republic Day. All police officers, irrespective of their rank, are eligible, provided that they have achieved more than 15 years service and performed their duties in a noticeably meritorious fashion. 259 have gone to officers from the ITBP.

POLICE MEDAL FOR MERITORIOUS SERVICE

Ribbon: *A broad central band in red with a slightly narrower dark blue band on either side and white edges.*

Description: *The design is the same as the Police Medal for Gallantry but with the substitution of the words FOR MERITORIOUS SERVICE in the central bar of the reverse.*

In addition to the four medals described there are two others available for more specific reasons, both with no restrictions on the numbers awarded in any one year. The first is the *Prime Minister's Medal for Lifesaving* (ribbon—yellow with one black (left) and one white (right) stripe in the centre) instituted in 1958 and intended to reward police officers for outstanding work in saving life and to encourage others to give help and assistance to those in trouble more readily than was the case at the time of its introduction. The medal has been awarded to officers from the Indo-Tibetan Border Police on 54 occasions.

The second of the two medals is effectively given in recognition of service in areas of India where police officers perform their duties under particularly difficult circumstances and it is thought that they deserve special reward. The medal was introduced in 1962 and made available to all officers with an aggregate of one years service in the specified areas effective from 1 January 1959. Changes to the regulations were made in 1988 to extend the eligible areas of the country to include the Punjab, Sikkim, the border with Tibet, the Nicobar Islands and most north-eastern states—areas often associated with unrest between India and its neighbours.

POLICE (SPECIAL DUTY) MEDAL

Instituted: 23 February 1962.

Ribbon: Two sets of vertical bands of red, yellow and green separated by white lines and with white edges.

Metal: Cupro-nickel.

Size: 39 mm.

Description: (Obverse) the Indian emblem within an ornate wreath; (reverse) a representation of the Himalayas and the word GANGOTRI below and to the left. The name of the medal in Hindi script (POLICE KATIN SEVA PADAK) lies in the upper circumference. The medal hangs from an ornamented straight suspender attached by a claw fitting. Bars inscribed with the medal name in English and the area of service are issued.

A similar medal is awarded to qualifying members of the Special Constabulary with the ribbon being of the same design but with the repeated group of colours being brown, orange and green.

A number of Indian medals are made by independent manufacturers and bought by individual eligible police officers or their force and presented to them. This is not true of the four senior awards available to police officers but a common practice for most others. This can lead to great variation in the quality of the medal and the colour of the ribbon.

Each Indian state and most major cities have their own police forces with a number of other agencies lending support in specialised areas or where there are national implications—the Border Security Force, Railway Police, Central Reserve Police Force and others. The state of Uttar Pradesh borders Nepal in the north-east and is one of the less volatile areas of this part of the country although the Uttrakhand Division is a designated area for eligibility for the Police (Special Duty) Medal as a result of its position at the border with China.

The area covered by the Uttar Pradesh State Police is huge—294,411 square kilometres—with responsibility for the policing of 160 million people. It is the largest single police force in the world with more than 200,000 officers. From the time of its formation in 1860 until the end of the 20th century, more than 22,500 police officers have lost their lives in the State and the courage of the police officers there has been recognised on no fewer than 572 occasions since independence—the President's Police Medal for Gallantry has been awarded 94 times and the Police Medal for Gallantry on 478 occasions. In addition the President's Police Medal for Distinguished Service has gone to 129 officers and the Police Medal for Meritorious Service to a further 1,442.

page 193

Police Medals of the World

A further medal awarded to acknowledge service in difficult conditions is available to any member of the Indian armed services and police officers for service at high altitude posts along India's northern border, which includes officers from the police force of the Uttar Pradesh.

HIGH ALTITUDE SERVICE MEDAL

Instituted: 1986.

Ribbon: Medium blue with a series of white chevrons.

Metal: Cupro-nickel.

Size: 35 mm.

Description: (Obverse) the Indian emblem with the legend UCCHH TUNGTA MEDAL on the right and same in Hindi script on the left; (reverse) a Himalayan mountain scene. The medal hangs from a plain straight suspender attached by a claw fitting.

The history of India since independence has been troubled by border disputes and wars with Pakistan. The borders between the two countries have never been formally acknowledged by either and the tension there has erupted into armed conflict three times—in 1948, 1965 and 1971. An official statement by the Indian government declares that the external boundaries of India are neither settled nor authenticated. Campaign medals were awarded to all those who took part or were caught up in the two most recent wars, including police officers. The cause of the disputes dates back to the partition of the sub-continent into India and West and East Pakistan, a decision that was never going to work. Although the tension in the east was eased by the establishment of Bangladesh (East Pakistan) as a separate sovereign state, the west continues to be a potential flashpoint.

During the wars with Pakistan members of the Indian police forces played an active rôle and were rewarded with the campaign medals introduced when the conflicts were over.

RAKSHA MEDAL (1965 WAR WITH PAKISTAN)

Instituted: 26 January 1967.

Ribbon: Orange with a dark blue central stripe with another of red to the left and one of pale blue to the right.

Metal: Cupro-nickel.

Size: 36 mm.

Description: (Obverse) the Indian emblem placed centrally; (reverse) an image of the rising sun with a partial wreath below and the name of the medal in Hindi and the date—1965—above. A plain straight suspender was used attached by a claw fitting.

page 194

SANGRAM MEDAL (1971 WAR WITH PAKISTAN)

Instituted: 17 January 1973.

Ribbon: Maroon with three narrow white stripes even spaced.

Metal: Cupro-nickel.

Size: 35 mm.

Description: (Obverse) the Indian emblem placed centrally with the name of the medal in English (right) and Hindi (left) at the circumference; (reverse) an image of the rising sun above a partial wreath. A plain straight suspender was used attached by a claw fitting.

The Sangram Medal was awarded to all those who played a part in the war in operational areas between 3 December 1971 and 20 December 1972. Recipients included members of the military, paramilitary forces, civilians and police officers.

In 1973 after the end of the second war with Pakistan, a special medal was issued to members of the Indian armed forces, reserve forces, territorial forces, civil defence, the police service and a number of other organisations concerned with state security who suffered a wound as a direct result of enemy action. Although intended primarily for those wounded in the war it was made available to anyone wounded in any type of military, terrorist or counter-insurgency operation effective from August 1947 when the first formal steps towards India's independence were taken.

WOUND MEDAL

Instituted: 1973.

Ribbon: White with a broad red central band.

Metal: Silver.

Size: 35 mm.

Description: (Obverse) the Indian emblem with the words WOUND MEDAL in English on the right and in Hindi script on the left; (reverse) a representation of the chakra within a circle. The medal hangs from a ring suspender. The medals are named on the lower rim.

Police Medals of the World

In the latter quarter of the 20th century, members of the Indian military and its police forces have become involved in operations where existing medals were not suitable to recognise their contribution. A peace-keeping operation conducted in north and east Sri Lanka was the catalyst for the introduction of a special award to acknowledge such service and recipients including large numbers of police officers although they were mostly awarded to members of the army, navy or air force.

SPECIAL SERVICE MEDAL

Instituted: 1986.

Ribbon: Blue-grey with a red band at each edge.

Metal: Cupro-nickel.

Size: 35 mm.

Description: (Obverse) the Indian emblem placed centrally with the name of the medal in English (above) and Hindi (below) all within a wreath and a stylised sunburst at the outer circumference; (reverse) the two outer representations of a sunburst and wreath are repeated with a central image of a dove flying above a mountain range. The medal hangs from a straight suspender attached with a claw fitting. Bars (in Hindi) indicate where the "special service" was performed.

The majority of Indians are Hindu or Muslim and as such they frown on the consumption of alcohol although it is tolerated and available in every state (except one)—at a price. Gujerat is the only totally dry state but another at the south-eastern tip of the sub-continent has a history of prohibition which was relaxed only recently. Tamil Nadu was less affected by the days of the British Empire than many states although the main city—Madras—was the site of the East India Company's first settlement. It remains a stronghold of the Tamil culture. Prohibition was introduced under British rule in 1937 in a small area of the State and gradually extended over the following eleven years until it was all subject to the ban. After independence prohibition continued under 1971 when it was suspended although the manufacture and sale of alcohol was controlled by the state authorities. There is currently a policy of selective prohibition in force.

Apart from religious objections there are sound medical reasons why the manufacture and sale of alcohol should be controlled by the state—the prevalence of cheap, very dangerous concoctions which can, and frequently do, lead to blindness and death. Every year hundreds of Indians die or lose their sight as a result of drinking these poisons. All are banned and the Tamil Nadu Police are enthusiastic in their enforcement of the prohibition laws. There are seven of these illicitly produced alcohols with the most dangerous being methyl alcohol (wood alcohol) which is added to illicit arrack (produced from the fermentation of fruit, molasses and a variety of other foods) to boost the alcohol content. Death from methyl alcohol poisoning can be caused by as little as 30 ml and half this amount has been known to cause blindness. Anything from 60 to 240 ml would kill most adults within 24 to 36 hours.

The authorities in Tamil Nadu have recently (1995) introduced a special police medal for award to officers for outstanding service in curtailing the manufacture, sale or transportation of these illicit liquors. Recipients usually have more than five years service and are also given a one-off payment of 10,000 rupees. The medal is bronze, 35 mm in diameter and has on the obverse an effigy of Gandhi, the father of the modern state. From its inception up to the end of 1999 the medal was awarded on ten occasions only.

India

Although French ambitions in India were thwarted by the British they maintained footholds in four areas until as late as 1954 when they were handed over to the Indian authorities as the French colonies in the far east unravelled with the loss of the three countries in Indo-China. Although India took over the administration of the territories in 1954, a treaty was not signed until 1956 and the formal transfer was delayed until August 1962, the French being the last of the European coonists to leave the sub-continent. Two of the French enclaves were in Tamil Nadu (the other two are in Andhra Pradesh and Keral) with the largest of the four being Pondicherry, the capital of the territory. After the territories were handed over to India they stayed together as the Union of Pondicherry under central government control although hundreds of miles separate them, they are all relatively small and lie in three separate states. When the movement towards independence was under way in India, a movement which affected the French territories, the authorities there instituted a special medal for award to members of *La Force Publique* (the body responsible for maintaining public order) for acts of courage, devotion to duty and faithful service. The medal became redundant after the French left India.

LA MÉDAILLE D'HONNEUR DE LA FORCE PUBLIQUE DE L'INDE

Instituted: *12 August 1943.*

Ribbon: *Off white, very slightly pink with a broad central band in dark green and red lines at the edges. The white bands either side of the central band are bisected by blue lines.*

Metal: *Silver (first class) and bronze (second class).*

Size: *28 mm.*

Description: *(Obverse) a bust of a former governor-general of the French territories in India—Joseph Dupleix—with his surname below and the words ETABLISSEMENTS FRANÇAIS DANS LINDE; (reverse) plain apart from the inscription FORCE PUBLIQUE across the centre in a rectangular panel and MÈDAILLE (above) and D'HONNEUR (below) around the circumference. An ornate suspender taking the form of two leaves was used.*

Joseph Dupleix holds a special place in the memory of French involvement in India and almost succeeded in achieving a French empire in India. He was governor-general of the French territories when war broke out between Britain and France in 1744 as a result of the War of Austrian Succession. Fighting broke out in India despite French attempts to maintain neutrality there and Dupleix took control of Madras from the British which he succeeded in holding until the Treaty of Aix-la-Chapelle (1748) which ended the war returned the city to Britain who were to hold it until the achievement of independence. Dupleix spent the following six years attempting to force the British East India Company out of the country but merely succeeded in virtually bankrupting the French East India Company, the counterparts and rivals of the British. He was recalled to Paris in 1754 and died nine years later an impoverished and discredited man, an opinion which has since been reviewed and which resulted in his appearance on the medal.

Police Medals of the World

The British policy of "divide and rule" and general tolerance of local religions, customs and traditions once domination of the sub-continent had been achieved resulted in a hotchpotch of 562 separate states at the time independence was achieved. Each was ruled by a king although they were generally known by different names according to the local language and predominant religion of the area—maharana, maharaja or rana (Hindu) and nizan or nawab (Muslim) included. Several of these "princely states" as they were commonly known, awarded their own series of medals to reward meritorious service and acts of courage or to commemorate royal occasions. Medals were made available to police officers in a few of the states for any of these reasons although the historical record is far from complete and available information is very limited. The structure of the police forces in the states was organised broadly on the lines of British overseas territories although there were significant local influences. Some states issued no medals, others a single award, some two and one—Travancore (now in Kerala)—issued three. The existence of many medals is known only from the ribbon, the piece itself having never been seen or definitely identified outside the old states.

The princely state of Patiala (now a part of the Punjab) awarded one medal exclusively to police officers—the *Police Medal* (ribbon—dark blue with crimson bands at the centre and towards each edge). Jodhpur (now in Rajasthan in the north-west bordering Pakistan) issued two medals, both available to police officers only—one for meritorious service and the *Police Medal for Bravery* (ribbon—five equal bands of green, yellow, red, white and pink).

The partition of India which resulted in the establishment of Pakistan (1947) and later Bangladesh (formerly East Pakistan, independent in 1971) saw the old princely state of Bahawalpur become a part of the state of Punjab in the Islamic Republic of Pakistan which borders Rajasthan in India. The Police Medal (*Tamgha Polis*) was introduced during the reign of Sadiq Khan Muhammed V although the precise date is not clear. He was three years old when he succeeded to the throne of Bahawalpur and given limited authority on his 18th birthday although it was not until 1924 that he was given full ruling power. It is likely that the medal was introduced shortly afterwards and the effigy on the obverse would tend to support this view. The reign of Sadiq Khan Muhammed V ended in 1947.

BAHAWALPUR POLICE MEDAL

Ribbon: Dark blue with three stripes of red, yellow and red (each 1 mm) towards the edges.

Metal: Silver.

Size: 36 mm.

Description: (Obverse) the crowned effigy of the Nawab facing left with a pair of palm fronds at the lower circumference and an inscription in Farsi script at the circumference either side of the effigy which reads THE RULER OF THE GOD GRANTED KINGDOM OF BAHAWALPUR (left) BY THE GRACE OF GOD MUHAMMAD ABBASI V (right); (reverse) a wreath of palm leaves tied at the base with a bow containing the inscription POLICE MEDAL in Farsi script in the central field. A ring suspender was used.

The state was founded in 1748 by Nawab Bahwal Khan Abbasi I whose family ruled for more than 200 years until it became a part of Pakistan in 1947. Although Urdu is the official language of Pakistan, Farsi (Persian, the language of Iran and Afghanistan) was once widely understood from the Middle East to India in countries where Islam was the predominant religion. It takes its name from the region of Fars in Iran and means the area where Persian is spoken.

BURMA

India's neighbouring country of Burma was administered as a province of India from 1886 until 1937 when it was separated and treated as a separate state. It came under total British control after the last of three bloody wars with the third ruling Tibeto-Burman dynasty in 1824, 1852 and 1885. Burma was occupied by the Japanese in the Second World War and the moves towards complete independence began during the invasion when the Burmese Independence Army (BIA) gave positive help and support to the invaders. Although the BIA changed sides and helped the Allies re-occupy the country, independence was inevitable and Britain agreed in 1947. Elections were held but the winner and prime minister elect was assassinated, setting the scene for the violence, torture, killing and disregard for human rights which was to plague the country for the following half century.

During its days as a province of India, police officers there were entitled to the Indian Police Medal in a similar fashion to their colleagues in India proper. In 1937 a new, separate medal was introduced for all ranks of the police, frontier police and fire brigades, both European and Burmese, to acknowledge acts of gallantry or distinguished service.

BURMA POLICE MEDAL

Instituted: 14 December 1937.

Ribbon: A wide blue central band flanked by broad black stripes with white edges.

Metal: Bronze.

Size: 36 mm.

Description: (Obverse) the effigy of King George VI; (reverse) the same as the first issue of the Indian Police Medal—a laurel wreath topped by the Kings crown with a panel across the centre containing the legend FOR DISTINGUISHED CONDUCT with BURMA (above) and POLICE (below) in the central field. It hung from a plain straight suspender attached by a claw fitting.

The reverse remained the same throughout its life and it was not redesigned to follow the pattern of the Indian Police Medal in 1944 to distinguish between awards made for gallantry (53) and distinguished service (80). Similarly there was no amendment to the colouring of the ribbon. In addition to the 133 awards where the reason for the award was known eight further medals were issued but unclassified. In 1948 when Burma was granted independence the award of the medal was discontinued. In 1962 a military coup took place and Burma (known officially as the Union of Myanmar) became effectively isolated from the outside world, a situation which has only very recently begun to ease and only to a limited extent.

IRELAND AND NORTHERN IRELAND

The current policing structure of Ireland is a result of the Anglo-Irish War of 1919–1921 which led to the establishment of the Republic of Ireland in the south (policed by the Garda Síochána na h-Éireann) and the six counties of Ulster (policed by the Royal Ulster Constabulary—RUC) in the north which remained a part of the United Kingdom. The first body of police to be founded in Ireland was in the City of Dublin with the rest of the country being the responsibility of baronial police, a group of ill-disciplined men who were answerable to the local magistrates. Between 1812 and 1818 when he was Chief Secretary for Ireland, Sir Robert Peel first developed his ideas for a uniformed civil police force organised on a national basis. After he became Home Secretary in 1822 he introduced the Irish Constabulary Act on 5 August that year which established the Constabulary Police, the first organised police force in the British Isles, seven years before the founding of the Metropolitan Police.

Chief Constables were appointed for each barony with a strength of 16 constables and sub-constables under their command in turn under the authority of an inspector general in each of the four provinces. By 1841 the Constabulary of Ireland boasted a strength of 8,600 police officers providing professional policing arrangements which were, in effect, a model for Britain and subsequently much of the Empire and Commonwealth.

The three major cities in Ireland—Dublin, Belfast and Londonderry—each had their own separate police force, established in 1836 although the Belfast Borough Police (Belfast Bulkies) was merged with the national force in 1865 after a period of serious sectarian violence followed shortly afterwards by the Londonderry Borough Police (Horney Dicks) in 1869 when an enquiry into the deaths of two apprentice boys in riots during a visit by Prince Arthur highlighted serious shortcomings in the organisation and efficiency of the Force. The Dublin Metropolitan Police survived until 1925 after the Anglo-Irish War when it was merged with the Garda.

Irish society in the first half of the 19th century and in the early years of professional policing was disorderly, volatile and could be very violent with fighting on a large scale occurring between the large number of secret societies which abounded at the time. In 1834 one particularly bloody encounter involving more than 3,000 people resulted in the deaths of 200 of them. The potential for violence associated with the distillation of illicit alcohol and the steady rise of republicanism meant that the work of the Irish Constabulary was demanding and dangerous. In 1842 it was decided that a special medal should be introduced to recognise acts of gallantry and meritorious service performed by the officers.

CONSTABULARY MEDAL (IRELAND)

Instituted: 1842.

Ribbon: Light blue.

Metal: Silver.

Size: 36 mm.

Description: (Obverse) the Irish harp with the front in the form of a female figurehead topped by St Edward's crown and a half wreath of oak leaves (left) and shamrock (right) below. The name of the Force IRISH CONSTABULARY—is inscribed around the lower circumference and REWARD OF MERIT appears above the harp; (reverse) a wreath of laurel and shamrock with the date and the recipient's rank, number and name engraved in the central field.

Prior to the introduction of the medal, officers whose actions were thought to merit some form of recognition were granted a sum of money from the Reward Fund. The issue of a medal was one stage in a process of rewards involving half-chevrons, full chevrons and, finally, the medal to denote various degrees of distinguished service or exceptional acts.

For a lesser act of service which was still worthy of note an officer was awarded a half-chevron and for a more distinguished act a full chevron of merit. After five full chevrons had been won the officer was awarded the Constabulary Medal although it could also be given for a single exceptional act. Half-chevrons counted towards the total necessary for the award of the medal. The chevrons were originally of blue lace and worn on the left cuff with a silver badge of merit. From 1867 the lace was replaced by a band of black patent leather although the silver badge was retained. In 1872 this rather complex system was abolished and the medal was awarded only for gallantry. The colour of the medal ribbon was also changed from light blue to green.

Before the abolition of the chevrons, officers who had won them, and the medal, were eligible for a monetary reward on their discharge from the Constabulary. Head constables received the sum of £6 for each chevron and constables or sub-constables the sum of £4. Holders of the Constabulary Medal were entitled to a gratuity of £35 (head constables) or £25 (constables and sub-constables). The sums were also payable to the widow or children of any chevron or medal holder who died in service. The first Constabulary Medal awarded went to a Sub Inspector Cox in 1848 and the last four were presented in 1922.

The exact number of medals awarded is not known although it is reasonably thought that there were more than 300 with the largest number in any one year being about 180 in 1920 at the height of the Anglo-Irish War. In addition there were awards of the KPM for Gallantry to members of the Irish Constabulary and Dublin Metropolitan Police who were not eligible for the Constabulary Medal.

The demanding nature of the work of members of the Irish Constabulary and the potential for extreme violence is well illustrated by examples of the circumstances in which medals were awarded.

In 1867 the growth in the republican movement culminated in an organised rebellion (the Fenian Rising) which was a series of co-ordinated attacks on isolated police stations. On 13 February 1867, at the height of the attacks, Sub-Constable William Duggan was carrying official despatches to his district headquarters in County Kerry by horse when he was attacked by a group of armed rebels who called on him to hand over his despatches and surrender. He refused and forced his way through the group using his sword to defend himself. The group fired at him and severely wounded him but he survived and was subsequently awarded the Constabulary Medal for gallantry although he was unable to attend the presentation ceremony held in September that year. He never fully recovered and was retired on pension in May 1868. A total of nine Constabulary Medals were awarded during the uprising and the conduct of the officers led Queen Victoria to grant the Royal prefix to the Force's title as a mark of her appreciation for their courage and professionalism. The Royal Irish Constabulary (RIC) became the first police force in the British Empire to be granted this honour.

The republican movement was not the only cause of violence in Ireland in the 19th century, the call for land reform led to the killing or burning out of a number of landlords in some parts of the country. On 11 September 1887 a large group of "moonlighters" attacked a house in County Clare which was defended by a detachment of officers from the Royal Irish Constabulary. In the heavy fighting that followed Head Constable Whelehan was killed but all the attackers subsequently arrested. The constables who were defending the house, 13 in all, including Constable James Garvey, were all awarded the Constabulary Medal for their courage. The term "moonlighting" was coined during this period in recognition of the fact that the burnings were usually a night-time activity and lit up the sky for miles around the buildings under attack.

Awards of the Constabulary medal were not all the result of violent encounters with dissidents—acts of courage in saving life were also recognised. Head Constable John Giles from County Clare was rewarded for his part in the rescue of the crew of the French merchantman *Leon XIII* which had run onto rocks in a severe storm off the coast of Clare and sank. He was also granted the Médaille d'Honneur des Affaires Étrangères by the French government for his actions.

The addition of the prefix "Royal" to the name of the Irish Constabulary necessitated changes to the obverse of the Constabulary Medal. Apart from the change to the inscription of the Constabulary name at the lower circumference to ROYAL IRISH CONSTABULARY, the central design of harp, wreath and crown was amended. The female figurehead at the front of the harp was replaced by a plain design, the half-wreath of oak leaves and shamrock became a full wreath and the Tudor crown was used. The precise date of the changes is not known.

Irish police officers were not awarded either of the two medals issued to celebrate the jubilees of 1887 or 1897 but the visit of Queen Victoria in 1900 was marked by a bronze medal presented to officers of the RIC and Dublin Metropolitan Police who were involved in security and policing of the various events connected with the visit. In all, 2,285 medals were awarded.

VISIT TO IRELAND MEDAL 1900

Instituted: 1900.

Ribbon: Dark blue.

Metal: Bronze.

Size: 36 mm.

Description: (Obverse) an effigy of Queen Victoria; (reverse) a female figure representing Hibernia holding a bunch of flowers in her left hand beside a wall looking left over the sea at Kingstown (Dun Laoghaire) where the Royal Yacht can be seen. The date — 1900 — is in the exergue.

Following his coronation in 1902, King Edward VII made a visit to Ireland the following year and a further medal was granted under the same terms as the early version. The only differences in the design of the medals was the use of an effigy of the new Sovereign on the obverse and the change of the date to 1903 on the reverse. A pale blue ribbon was used and the number awarded increased to 7,750.

VISIT TO IRELAND MEDAL 1903

Instituted: 1903.

Ribbon: Pale blue.

Metal: Bronze.

Size: 36 mm.

Description: As the 1900 medal above.

The next medal issued to celebrate a royal occasion was the Coronation (Police) Medal 1911 with 585 being presented to members of the RIC although a further specific medal was awarded when King George V paid a visit to Ireland on 7 to 12 July that year. This medal was awarded in greater numbers (2,500) and cast in silver unlike the two previous royal visit medals of 1900 and 1903 which were bronze.

VISIT TO IRELAND MEDAL 1911

Instituted: 1911.

Ribbon: Dark green with thin red stripes towards the edges.

Metal: Silver.

Size: 36 mm.

Description: (Obverse) the crown bust of King George V facing left; (reverse) the Imperial crown at the centre with a surrounding band bearing an ornate design and the words CORONATION 1911 around the upper circumference and the dates of the visit JULY 7 - 12 at the base. A floral emblem is inscribed on the circumference between the two sets of words. A ring suspender is used.

This was the last medal issued to members of any Irish constabulary before the Easter Uprising in 1916 and the Anglo-Irish War which saw the partition of the island, the founding of the Irish Free State, the disbandment of the RIC and the establishment of the two present-day police forces. The last of the Constabulary Medals awarded to officers from the RIC were earned during the war and authorised in March 1922, eight months after the truce which ended the conflict. One example of an engagement where several medals were won clearly illustrates the intensity of the conflict.

In the early hours of 28 May 1920 a group of about 100 armed insurgents attacked the RIC barracks at Kilmallock, County Limerick from three sides using bombs, rifles and handguns. The barracks were defended by two sergeants and eight constables who refused every entreaty to surrender made by the attackers. Petrol bombs were thrown onto the roof of the barracks which was soon well ablaze and eventually fell in and killed one of the sergeants and Constable Morton whose charred bodies were found later. The reaming sergeant—Tobias O'Sullivan—and remaining constables fixed bayonets and succeeded in breaking out to safety. One officer—Constable Hoey—was shot in the stomach and badly wounded although he survived. The attack was called off at about 7 am when the raiders thought they had inflicted sufficient damage. All surviving constables were promoted to sergeant and Sergeant O'Sullivan to head constable—all were awarded the Constabulary Medal. Sergeant O'Sullivan, then a district inspector was murdered on 20 January 1921 as he left his police barracks.

At the end of the war Ireland was partitioned into the Irish Free State (later the Republic of Ireland or Eire) and the Province of Ulster (Northern Ireland) comprising the six counties in the north which remained a part of the United Kingdom. In the south policing arrangements became the responsibility of the Civic Guard, later to be given its Irish name of the *Garda Síochána na h-Éireann* (the Guardians of the Peace in Ireland). In the north the Royal Ulster Constabulary was formed from the remnants of the RIC.

ROYAL ULSTER CONSTABULARY

The RUC differs from every other police force in the UK by being the only one that is armed in the normal course of its duties, the result of its rôle in protecting the State from armed subversion from within and without its borders. No sooner had the partition of Ireland taken place than it was apparent that the movement for a united country was never going to give up its struggle although for many years outbreaks were sporadic and never reached the intensity seen in the last 30 plus years.

When the Police Long Service and Good Conduct Medal was introduced in 1951, RUC officers were amongst those eligible for its award but in 1982 a further medal was authorised to acknowledge the special conditions of policing in Ulster particularly since the start of the current IRA campaign in 1968-69. Eligibility for the new medal was made retrospective to 1 January 1971. It was awarded for 18 months continuous service but given immediately to recipients of a gallantry decoration or Queen's Commendation.

ROYAL ULSTER CONSTABULARY SERVICE MEDAL

Instituted: 1982.

Ribbon: Green with three narrow central stripes of blue, black and red.

Metal: Cupro-nickel.

Size: 36 mm.

Description: (Obverse) the effigy of Queen Elizabeth II wearing the St Edward crown; (reverse) the badge of the RUC—an Irish harp above a half-wreath of oak leaves and shamrock within a belt containing the name of the Force (ROYAL ULSTER CONSTABULARY) topped by St Edward's crown — and the words FOR SERVICE around the lower circumference.

During the Anglo-Irish war, before the RUC was formed, the Protestant community reacted to attacks by the IRA on the Royal Irish Constabulary by taking the first steps towards the formation of the Ulster Special Constabulary (USC). After the truce which ended the conflict the USC came under the control of the Northern Ireland Government and was involved in security duties for many years. Originally there were three classes of constable—Class A who were full-time and enlisted to serve alongside regular officers, Class B who were part-timers organised under their own command structure and Class C who were mainly a reserve force. In 1925 the USC was reorganised and reduced in number to leave the Class B officers who fulfilled a security rôle guarding premises and manning roadblocks. The B Specials as they became known gained a certain notoriety, particularly during the IRA campaign of 1956-62, and were subsequently disbanded in April 1970 following the Hunt Report. They were effectively replaced by the RUC Reserve. As a mark of appreciation for their work a special version of the *Special Constabulary Faithful Service Medal* was issued to all officers who had served at least 15 years. The medal differed only in the inscription on the reverse which was amended to read FOR FAITHFUL SERVICE IN THE ULSTER SPECIAL CONSTABULARY. When the *Royal Ulster Constabulary Service Medal* was introduced for regular officers in 1982 a further change was made to the Special Constabulary medal to reward members of the RUC Reserve for 15 years service. The reverse was again amended to reflect the change in name to RUC Reserve.

Many officers from the RUC have been decorated for gallantry and devotion to duty since the founding of the Force all culminating in the award of the George Cross to the Constabulary itself on 23 November 1999 as a mark of the Queen's respect for all the officers there, past and present.

In November 2001 the award of the GC to the RUC was recognised by a change to the colouring of the ribbon for the Service Medal—the addition of a blue band at each edge to represent the GC. At the same time the name of the Constabulary was changed to the "Police Service of Northern Ireland". In due course this will, no doubt, be reflected in the design of the medal.

George Cross

The highest gallantry award for civilians, as well as for members of the armed forces in actions for which purely military honours would not normally be granted.

Instituted 24th September 1940

A plain bordered cross with a circular medallion in the centre depicting the effigy of St. George and the Dragon.

The Gallantry Series

Name ....

Address ....
....
....

We value your custom.
FREE Medal Email Newsletter
FREE 8 Postcard set. RRP £4.95p
FREE Ads/Wants/Offers/Exchange
FREE Subscription. Send email
NOW
free@britishweb.net
Nothing to pay. All FREE inc. p&p

www.britishweb.net
Gambia Properties for sale.
Car importing from Europe.
Military Books/Medals
FREE Lottery Systems
Learning Courses + ECDL

Ireland

GARDA SÍOCHÁNA NA H-ÉIREANN

Considering the circumstances which led to the establishment of the Irish Free State and subsequently the Republic of Ireland, coupled with the activities of the republican groups there and in Ulster, the fact that the Garda is an unarmed service is somewhat surprising. The choice, however, was quite deliberate and is also reflected in the name. The use of "police", "force" and "constable" were purposely avoided to give the fledging service a better chance of being accepted by the population of the new country which was for so long riven by disorder, strife and bloodshed.

Less than two years after the formation of the Garda, an offer was made to present a gold medal for bravery to the officer who had performed the most heroic act of bravery in any one year. the benefactor, Walter Scott, a Canadian with a lifelong interest in the police and an admirer of the performance of the Garda since its founding under difficult and dangerous conditions, made the offer to the Garda Commissioner, General O'Duffy, when they met at an international police conference in New York. The Commissioner accepted the offer and a medal was designed and produced in 18 carat gold ready for the first presentation in 1924. The recipient of this medal was Garda James Mulroy for his actions in May 1923.

After the first presentation it was suggested that two further classes of award should be available—silver and bronze—to reward acts of bravery which would not reach the standard necessary for the award of the gold medal. Mr Scott agreed to the suggestion and donated a further sum to finance these extra awards. Since its creation about 250 medals of all classes have been awarded. They are presented annually at a ceremonial parade attended by the Minister of Justice.

WALTER SCOTT MEDAL FOR VALOR

Instituted: 1923.

Ribbon: Three equal bands of green, white and orange for all classes.

Metal: Gold, silver and bronze.

Size: 44 mm.

Description: (Obverse) An ornate medal in the shape of a Celtic cross. The top and bottom arms bear the name of the medal WALTER SCOTT MEDAL (upper) FOR VALOR (lower) with the eagle and shield of the United States in the left arm and the Irish harp in the right. A central medallion bears the stylised letters GS; (reverse) the central medallion shows the Great Seal of New York City with the initials NY below. On the arms of the cross are the emblems of the four Irish provinces of Ulster, Leinster, Munster and Connaught. The full title of the Garda is contained within a broken band around the circumference between the arms. The medal hangs from a ring suspender. The top ribbon bar is inscribed with the rank, name and number of the recipient and usually the date of the award in a small shield below the bar.

The acts of courage for which the Walter Scott Medal is awarded vary greatly but the criteria for its award are demanding and it is a coveted, highly regarded medal. Confrontation with armed criminals, life-saving and, inevitably, actions involving terrorists have resulted in officers being honoured for their courage.

The medal has an elaborate design with a number of devices intended to reinforce the strong link which existed between Ireland and the US, in particular New York City. Included is the emblem of the Province of Ulster, still separate from the Republic and not within the Garda's area of responsibility.

page 205

Although the Garda had a troubled start, it developed into a respected and professional law enforcement agency which gained the respect of the community it served in a very short time. On the 50th anniversary of its founding, a special commemorative medal was issued as a token of this respect.

GOLDEN JUBILEE COMMEMORATIVE MEDAL 1922–1972

Instituted: 1972.

Ribbon: Yellow with a blue central band, all of equal width.

Metal: Gilt.

Size: 34 mm.

Description: (Obverse) A central medallion with an ornamental circle enclosing the stylised initials GS (taken from the Garda badge), surrounded by a pentagon made up of ten five-pointed stars joined by lines; (reverse) a fluted pillar to symbolise the sure and steadfast nature of law enforcement in Ireland entwined by a banner which bears the words LUBHAILE ORGA (Golden Jubilee) and the dates 1922 - 1972. A ring suspender is used.

LONG SERVICE MEDAL

Instituted: 1972.

Ribbon: Green with a central white band, all of equal width, and a green stripe placed centrally on the white band.

Metal: Silver.

Size: 34 mm.

Description: (Obverse) A representation of a full sunburst with twenty-two rays, eleven narrow and eleven wide, overlain by a central circular medallion showing the scales of justice and an outer band bearing the words GARDA SÍOCHÁNA; (reverse) the words SEIRBHÍS FHADA (long service) in the lower half below a stylised shamrock formed from extension of the first and last letters of the word seirbhis. A ring suspender is used.

Ireland

The dawn of the new millenium led to the introduction of a special medal for award to every serving officer of the Garda irrespective of rank or length of service.

GARDA MILLIENNIUM MEDAL

Instituted: *1 January 2000.*

Ribbon: *Blue with a broad central band of yellow flanked by narrow lines of red, white and red.*

Metal: *Gilt.*

Size: *35 mm.*

Description: *(Obverse) a representation of the scales of justice with the date of the start of the millenium in Roman numerals (MM) in the left balance and the dove of peace bearing an olive branch in its beak in the right. Below the base of the scales is the year 2000 and around the upper circumference the name of the Garda in Irish AN GARDA SÍOCHÁNA; (reverse) left plain apart from a narrow wreath around the circumference.*

The rôle of police officers is most usually thought of as a local matter but, as the 20th century unfolded, they were called upon to perform their duties in unfamiliar parts of the world, in unfamiliar circumstances and in the face of dangers previously unknown to most of them.

In 1950 the Korean War became the first real test of the raison d'être of the United Nations and brought together military forces from a number of countries. The conflict also saw the introduction of a United Nations medal awarded to all those who took part, the first in what was to become a series of similar awards which was extended from 1951 to apply to a large number of peacekeeping, observation and supervisory rules in all parts of the world since. The design of the medal remains the same irrespective of the operation with the differences being indicated by the colouring of the ribbon. Where police officers were involved they were often awarded medals by their country but were also entitled to a UN medal in addition.

In 1989 Garda officers first became involved in these operations with a contingent being sent to Namibia to supervise the truce there and the subsequent elections. They were all entitled to the medal awarded by the United Nations but the Irish government instituted their own award in recognition of the work done supervising members of the Namibian Police Service, accompanying them on patrol and curbing or investigating any possibility of abuse by the local officers in the difficult times.

The *Peacekeepers Medal* was not intended to be awarded for this occasion only and is available to any Garda officer who takes part in any official UN operation whenever and wherever it might be.

PEACEKEEPERS MEDAL

Instituted: 1990.

Ribbon: White with a dark blue central band a pale blue edges.

Metal: Gilt.

Size: 27 mm.

Description: (Obverse) A circle bearing the stylised letters GS placed in the lower half with the dove of peace holding a branch of olive in its beak flying above. The words SEIRBHÍS THIAR LEAR (Service Overseas) lie around the upper circumference; (reverse) plain apart from the name of the Garda around the upper circumference, DON TSÍOCHÁIN NA NÁISIÚIN AONTAITHE (Peacekeeping with the United Nations). The medal hangs from a plain straight suspender with a slight downward bow attached to the top as an integral part of the disc.

The importance of police officers as distinct from the military in peacekeeping operation has long been recognised by the UN and, in some circumstances, their use is the only true option available.

In January 1998 the UN decided to establish a group of 180 civil police officers to act as monitors in the Danube Region of Croatia to supervise the actions of the local police with particular importance being given to the return of displaced persons and refugees. Their duties were to include monitoring police operations, accompanying local officers on patrol, investigating human rights abuses and an overall supervisory and guiding rule. Officers from the Garda were amongst the contingent. The UN issued a separate medal for award to all those involved.

ITALY

Policing in Italy is the responsibility of three distinct organisations—the *Carabinieri*, the *Guardia di Finanze* and the *Polizia di Stato* (State Police). Their jurisdictions are essentially separate although there is a degree of overlap and duplication. The most senior of the three is the Carabinieri, the premier regiment of the Italian Army, which is very similar in its structure and operational responsibility to the Gendarmerie Nationale in France.

L'ARMA DEI CARABINIERI

The Carabinieri was formed as a part of the army of Savoy in 1814 and their duties extended to the whole of Italy in 1861 under the control of the Ministry of Defence although its duties are very similar to those of the civil police in many respects. The duties include riot control, dealing with public disturbances, crime investigation and a variety of other matters required by local conditions. They also provide escorts for government officials and visiting dignitaries. As army personnel, members of the Carabinieri are rewarded with military decorations for acts of bravery and devotion to duty and are also eligible for awards intended to reward long service

The award of medals in Italy covers the two most recent periods of the country's history since it was fully unified in 1870 into what we know today (with some noticeable exceptions).

In 1900 King Umberto I was assassinated and succeeded by King Vittorio Emanuele III who reigned until he abdicated shortly after the end of the Second World War but before the Republic of Italy was declared in 1948 after a referendum of the people held two years earlier. The vote was close, a majority of one million from a vote of more than 24 million saw the end of the monarchy. King Umberto II who had succeeded his father only a month earlier was sent away to exile and an interim leader appointed until the constitutional questions could be debated, a process which took two years. The first medal issued in the Kingdom of Italy after unification in 1870 to reward long service was introduced in 1900 and made available to members of the Royal Army including the Carabinieri.

CROCE ANZIANITÀ DI SERVIZIO NELL'ESERCITO (SORMONTATA DA CORONA)

Republic version.

Instituted: 8 November 1900.

Ribbon: Three bands of bright green, white and bright green, all of equal width.

Metal: Silver-gilt.

Size: 36 mm by 52 mm including the crown.

Description: (Obverse) a Maltese cross with a central medallion bearing the entwined letters—RI (Repubblica Italiana); (reverse) the Roman numerals XL (40) in the centre of the medallion. A large royal crown was originally fixed to the upper arm of the cross.

This award was effectively a long service cross available to officers of the Royal Italian Army for 40 years service. A similar gold-coloured (silver-gilt) award but without the crown above the cross was awarded also only to officers on completion of 25 years service with the numeral in the centre of the medallion on the reverse amended to read XXV. A silver medal of the same design (apart from the numeral on the reverse) was awarded to all "other ranks" in recognition of 16 (XVI) years service. An amendment to the regulations was made in June 1912 when 25 years service by "other ranks" was rewarded with a cross surmounted by a crown similar to the officers' 40 year cross but cast in silver. The ribbon for all four medals was the same.

Italy was a European colonial power although with far fewer territories under its control than Britain and France—primarily in Africa. Towards the end of the 19th century the country joined the scramble for colonies in Africa and brought Libya, Eritrea and the southern part of Somalia under its control. The Second World War, Mussolini's invasion of Ethiopia and his army's defeat by the Allies in 1941, however, saw the end of Italian colonialism. Policing in all three colonies was performed by a branch of the Italian Army although they were a separate body organised on similar lines to the Carabinieri. They were also awarded their own long service medal—*Anzianità Polizia Africa Italiana*—which was the same as that available to the Carabinieri and with the same criteria for its award but with a different ribbon—a white central band flanked by broad stripes of blue and green.

In February 1953, five years after Italy had become a republic, the design of the crosses was altered to reflect the new status and all references to royalty were removed. The initials on the obverse of the medallion were changed to RI (Repubblica Italiana) and the royal crown used on the two most senior crosses removed and replaced by five-point star worn on the ribbon. The name of the award was also changed to read *"Croce per Anzianità di Servizio Militare"*. The awards are currently available according to rank and length of service. Officers and NCOs are rewarded with three crosses—gold (silver-gilt), marked XL and with a star on the ribbon for 40 years service, gold (silver-gilt) and marked XXL for 25 years service and silver marked XVI for 16 years service. Other ranks have two crosses available—silver, marked XXL and with a star on the ribbon for 25 years service and silver marked with XVI for 16 years service. The ribbon of all five medals remains the same as the one introduced in 1900—green, white and green, all of equal width.

A further medal to reward long service was introduced for award to army personnel in 1936 but only made available to officers and NCOs to recognise periods in a position of command. The length of service necessary to qualify differed between the two groups with officers being required to serve for longer periods than the NCOs. The medals were produced in gold, silver and bronze with the qualifying periods being 30, 20 and 15 years for officers and 20, 15 and 10 years for NCOs.

MEDAGLIA AL MERITO DI LUNGO COMANDO NELL'ESERCITO

Republic version.

Instituted: 16 July 1936.

Ribbon: Alternating stripes of dark blue (ten) and white (nine), all of equal width.

Metal: Gold, silver and bronze.

Size: 36 mm.

Description: (Obverse) the effigy of Vittorio Emanuele III facing right with the words AL MERITO DI LUNGO COMANDO around the upper two-thirds of the circumference; (reverse) a wreath around the circumference—half laurel (left) and half oak leaves (right) with a Roman gladius pointing upwards from the base of the wreath to the middle of the central field.

In 1953 the effigy of the King was removed from the obverse and replaced by the emblem of Italy current today—a wreath of half laurel and half oak leaves with a device in the centre of a star and toothed wheel above a banner bearing the words "Repubblica Italiana". The regulations were also amended to bring the qualifying period for officers and NCOs into line, the period applicable to NCOs being adopted. Stars were also introduced for wear on the ribbons to indicate the length of service which was otherwise not apparent from the ribbon alone—in gold for 20 years and in silver for 15 years. The ribbon worn alone indicates the award of the bronze medal after ten years service in a command position.

Awards for bravery are available to members of the Carabinieri from a number of sources, not simply the army. Since the founding of the Corps in 1814 many thousands have been awarded medals in gold, silver and bronze for military, army, civil and navy valour, four different groups available to the Carabinieri. The medals were introduced in the Kingdom of Italy but changed after 1948 to reflect the country's new status as a republic.

MEDAGLIE AL VALOR MILITARE

Ribbon: Medium blue.

Metal: Gold, silver and bronze.

Size: 36 mm.

Description: (Obverse) the emblem of the Republic of Italy with the words AL VALORE MILITARE around the circumference; (reverse) a wreath of half laurel and half oak leaves with the central field available for the recipient's details.

The two higher classes awarded (silver and gold) are indicated by a motif on the ribbon in undress uniform, the bronze medal carries no additional emblem. The Medal for Military Valour has been awarded to members of the Carabinieri on at least 9,000 occasions—more than 100 gold, 3,000 plus silver and almost 6,000 bronze. The medals are available to any branch of the Italian Armed Forces. A separate award is issued in the name of the Army but issued in far lesser numbers to the Carabinieri.

In addition to the military awards there is another available for civil valour and this has been issued to members of the Carabinieri in numbers which rival those for military valour—more than 5,000 of all classes since the Corps was formed. The medal itself is very similar to the award for military valour but with a wreath on the reverse of a slightly different design and the words AL VALORE CIVILE around the upper circumference of the obverse around the Italian emblem. The ribbon is in three equal bands in the country's colours of green, white and red.

The two other arms of the Italian policing structure—the Guardia di Finanze and the Polizia di Stato (State Police)—each have their own long service medal available but they share with the Carabinieri the award of the medal to reward time in a command rôle although the reverse of both was changed and the colours of the ribbons of all three differed. The Guardia di Finanze, a part of the Italian Armed Forces, has no direct comparison in the UK although it is an integral part of the Italian policing structure but with a special remit.

GUARDIA DI FINANZE

The role of the Guardia di Finanze (GdiF) is clearly defined and it is concerned with much more than the investigation and prevention of revenue offences than its name would suggest although this forms the most important part of its remit. It is also responsible for combating illegal immigration and smuggling, performing the duties of the customs service and immigration authorities in the UK.

The medal available to the armed forces to recognise a number of years in a command position was also awarded to officers and NCOs from the GdiF with similar criteria applicable. It was introduced at the same time as the award available to the Carabinieri and the obverse was also changed in 1953 to remove the image of Vittorio Emanuele on the obverse. There were, however, two differences—the colour of the ribbon and the design on the reverse. The ribbon was made up of alternating stripes of medium blue (six) and white (five) and the reverse included the units emblem hanging from the top of the wreath. When the changes were made in 1953 the gladius was omitted and the GdiF emblem moved to the lower half of the central field and enlarged. The name of the recipient is sometimes found in the upper part of the central field.

In addition to the medal shared with other units, officers of the Guardia were eligible for their own award for meritorious service. It was introduced in 1905 and is still current today with the only major changes coming after the demise of the monarchy.

CROCE AL MERITO DI SERVIZIO NELLA REGIA GUARDIA DI FINANZE

Instituted: 26 September 1905.

Ribbon: Green with three yellow stripes in the centre and at each edge.

Metal: Gold.

Size: 29 mm.

Description: (Obverse) a plain cross moline with a central medallion bearing an eagle with outspread wings and the cross of Savoy (white on a red enamel background) in the centre; (reverse) plain apart from the words AL MERITO DI SERVIZIO in four lines on the medallion.

The cross was awarded to officers of the Guardia on completion of 25 years service and to NCOs and other ranks after 20 years. It was also available as a reward for acts of courage although very rarely bestowed for a single act and used more to acknowledge several gallant deeds. In 1907 an amendment to the regulations was made and a silver cross introduced for award to NCOs and other ranks after 16 years service. The next major change came in 1929 when the whole system of reward came under scrutiny and the two existing medals replaced by four to reward periods of meritorious service ranging from 16 to 40 years. The basic design of the cross was unchanged but a royal crown was added to indicate truly long service. The crown was large and attached to the

page 212

upper arm of the cross with a ring suspender to which was attached the ribbon which was the same for all awards. After the amendments to the regulations were made, the Cross was available to officers of all ranks;-

- (a) gold surmounted by a crown for officers after 40 years,
- (b) silver surmounted by a crown for NCOs and other ranks after 25 years,
- (c) gold for officers after 25 years, and
- (d) silver for NCOs and other ranks after 16 years.

In 1954, after the monarchy had been voted into obscurity and a republic declared, the design of the Cross was changed to remove all references to royalty. The royal crown which surmounted the Cross on the two most senior awards was abolished and the medallion in the centre of the obverse amended and replaced by the initials RI (Repubblica Italiana). The colouring of the ribbon remained the same. The two most senior awards are now indicated by a star of the appropriate colour worn on the ribbon.

The GdiF existed in some form long before the unification of Italy and is an integral part of Italian policing. Visitors to the country are unlikely to come into contact with them although officers have the power to stop anyone within a certain distance of a cafe, restaurant or shop and demand to see the receipt for the goods or services which must, by law, have been provided. If you know the owner of the restaurant, however, or are a good customer who tips well you could well have two receipts—one for the finance police and another for you with a substantial difference in the number at the bottom.

POLIZIA DI STATO

The civil police in Italy undertake the majority of normal policing duties as we know them in the UK and the current national Polizia di Stato grew from a disparate set of forces in the cities, towns and regions of Italy dating from before the unification and have been known by a number of different names. The range of medals available to officers of the State Police differs from the two previous organisations and they have no entitlement to any army awards.

They share the medal awarded to officers and NCOs for meritorious service in a position of command with the Carabinieri and GdiF although there are differences in the colouring of the ribbon and design of the obverse. The ribbon has 19 stripes of equal width, the same as the Carabinieri medal but of crimson and white. The motif on the obverse in the lower half of the central field shows the emblem of the force—an eagle with outstretched wings holding a mural crown above its head and a shield on its breast bearing the initials RI. It was not introduced into the police until 1965 when the old system dating from the early days of the 20th century was reviewed.

The very first medal for the civil police was instituted when they were known as the "Corps of Town Guardians".

MEDAGLIE AL MERITO DI SERVIZIO NEL CORPO GUARDIE DI CITTÀ

Instituted: 8 July 1906.

Ribbon: Five equal stripes of blue, green, white, red and blue bordered by white lines.

Metal: Gold and silver.

Size: 36 mm.

Description: (Obverse) a female figure representing Italy seated upon a lion which she is stroking with her left hand. In her right hand she holds a parchment bearing the words DOVERE ABNEGAZIONE CORAGGIO (duty, self sacrifice, courage). A representation of the ruins of the Roman Forum is in the background; (reverse) a wreath of laurel (left) and oak leaves (right) with the words AL MERITO - DI - SERVIZIO in three lines in the central field.

The medal was awarded to officers on completion of 20 years good service and to guards for 15 years. In 1926 the name of the police was changed the Corps of Public Security Agents and the regulations for the award of the medal amended to reflect this, it became the *"Medaglie al Merito di Servizio nel Corpo Agenti di Pubblica Sicurezza"*. Changes were made to the design of the medal in 1930 but they were of such a minor nature that they are not evident from its appearance.

The establishment of the Republic of Italy caused a further name change for the police and more very minor alterations to the medal although the basic design remained. The most obvious difference is on the reverse where the wreath and bow at the bottom were changed slightly. The medal was renamed the *Medaglie al Merito di Servizio Corpo Guardie di Pubblica Sicurezza*. In 1965 the most radical change was made when the medal was discontinued and replaced by a long service cross of totally new design.

CROCE D'ANZIANITÀ DI SERVIZIO NEL CORPO GUARDIE DI PUBBLICA SICUREZZA

Instituted: 14 July 1965.

Ribbon: The same as the previous medals.

Metal: Gold and silver.

Size: 39 mm.

Description: (Obverse) a Maltese cross with the police emblem (eagle, crown and shield) between the arms and a central medallion bearing the initials RI; (reverse) identical apart from the Roman numerals XXV or XVI in the medallion.

The gold medal is awarded to officers on completion of 25 years service and the silver to NCOs and guards after 16 years. If an officer serves for 40 years he is entitled to wear a gold star on the central white band of the ribbon to indicate these extra years and the same principle applies to NCOs and other ranks when they complete 25 years service with the star being of silver in their case.

COMMEMORATIVE MEDALS

In addition to any of the medals previously mentioned, members of all three organisations can be awarded any of the commemorative medals issued in Italy. Such medals are well known in the UK and issued to celebrate royal occasions, they are also frequently issued in former colonial countries to celebrate their independence and anniversaries of these important days. In Italy, they have been introduced after natural disasters in recognition of the work of the emergency services at such times. The most well known such award in the UK is the medal instituted after the earthquake in Messina, Sicily in 1908 when more than 80,000 people lost their lives in a few minutes.

MESSINA EARTHQUAKE COMMEMORATIVE MEDAL

Instituted: 1908.

Ribbon: Green with white edges and a central white band.

Metal: Silver.

Size: 32 mm.

Description: (Obverse) the profile of King Vittorio Emanuele III facing left with the words VITTORIO EMANUELE III RE D'ITALIA around the circumference; (reverse) a wreath of oak leaves with an inscription which reads MEDAGLIA COMMEMORATIVA - TERREMOTO CALABRO SICULO 28 DICEMBRE 1908 in six lines.

The medal was awarded in large numbers to many people who helped with the immediate aftermath and the work which went on for many months and years afterwards as the authorities struggled to cope with the killed and injured, the threat of disease, the homelessness and the rebuilding of the town. The British involvement was provided by the Royal Navy, Royal Marines and the Merchant Navy who became heavily involved in the relief operations. Almost 5,000 medals were awarded to Britons. A special medal in gold, silver and bronze was awarded to anyone who rendered especially meritorious service—the ribbon was also green and white but lacked the central white band.

Of all western European countries, Italy is more prone to earthquakes than any. The country sits at the point where three tectonic plates meet—the Eurasian, African and Arabian all moving in different directions—with a number of mini plates complicating the issue. Italy has Europe's only active volcanoes within its territory—Etna and Strómboli—and the sleeping giant of Vesuvius towering over the Bay of Naples threatening do once more what it did to Pompeii and Herculaneum in 79 AD. Strómboli is in constant eruption but is an island many miles from the mainland, Etna erupts regularly and causes immense damage to Sicily but Vesuvius offers the greatest threat.

Its last eruption was in 1944, the next one is many years overdue, pressure within is building day by day, week by week, month by month and the potential for death and destruction is frightening. Volcanism and earthquakes are linked, in 1980 the potential was demonstrated in southern Italy on 23 November when an earthquake struck the regions of Campania and Basilicata around Naples causing huge damage but surprisingly little loss of life. 300,000 people were made homeless and the relief operation involved many members of the Carabinieri and Polizia di Stato. A special medal was struck to recognise the aid given and effort put in by everyone involved. The earthquake was linked with the activity deep below the region and Vesuvius—it will happen again in one form or another.

In the north-east of the country, close to the border with Slovenia, the Adriatic mini plate is in constant conflict with the two large tectonic plates in the area and has the potential for great destruction. On 6 May 1976 an earthquake measuring 6.9 on the Richter scale struck the areas of Friuli and Udine, north-east of Venice, resulting in the deaths of almost 1,000 people and damage over a wide area. A medal was specially struck to recognise the efforts of everyone who came to help, including the Carabinieri and Polizia di Stato.

MEDAGLIA COMMEMORATIVA PER LE OPERAZIONE DI SOCCORSO ALLE POPOLAZIONI CALPITE DAL SISMA DEL 1976 (FRIULI)

Instituted: 1976.

Ribbon: Four equal alternative stripes of blue and yellow.

Description: (Obverse) two hands reaching each other against a background showing a church bell-tower cracked in half and in danger of falling, representative of the help given to the injured.

In 1991/92 Mount Etna in Sicily erupted once more although the nature of the eruptions is such that there is rarely any loss of life. As the volcano is in virtually constant eruption there is not the same danger of the pressures inside building up to the extent that they are under Vesuvius. When Etna plays up there is no explosive eruption although the lava flows cause widespread damage to the fertile fields around and threaten towns and villages on its slopes. It's a little incongruous to call a volcano placid but the nature of Etna eruptions gives the civil authorities time to plan and build diversions for the lava flows and effect evacuations of threatened towns and villages. It's possible to walk to within a few hundeed metres of the summit as little as four months after the eruption ended (*pictured right, September 1992*). As the lava approaches houses it is not unknown for occupants to leave out a little wine and food for the God of the mountain in an effort to have their house spared. In 1991 concrete blocks were dropped into the path of the lava and succeeded to diverting the flow sufficiently to save many properties. When Vesuvius next erupts, the explosions will be massive with no chance of escape for anyone caught in the path of the fast-moving, superheated cloud of gasses that will envelope and destroy all in its path. When the emergency in Sicily was over a specially struck medal was awarded to all those who played a part in the efforts to limit the damage caused by Etna. The *Medal of Merit for Intervention in the Etna Emergency 1991/92* was awarded to members of the Carabinieri and Polizia di Stato who had performed valuable duty there.

In recent years the idea of striking a new medal each time a natural disaster strikes Italy has been questioned and a general medal authorised to cover most eventualities—the *Commemorative Medal for Participation in Public Calamity Rescue*.

MEDAGLIA COMMEMORATIVA PER LA PARTECIPAZIONE AD OPERAZIONE DI SOCCORSO ALLE POPOLAZIONI CALPITE DA PUBBLICHE CALAMITÁ

Instituted: 1976.

Ribbon: In the Italian national colours with a broad central band of red flanked by narrower bands of white and green

Description: (Obverse) a stylised scene from a flood with rushing water in the foreground and a hand protruding for help. In the background to the left is a forest on fire and a cloud of smoke extending across the top of the disc with a bolt of lightning. In the very centre is a five-point star.

Officers from the Carabinieri and Polizia di Stato will be called upon to help at the scene of the next major natural disaster in Italy—where it occurs and when are obviously not known, the fact that it will happen isn't in dispute

MALAWI

The Republic of Malawi first came to the attention of Europeans after the travels of Dr Livingstone and was first known as British Central Africa once colonisation started in the late 19th century. It was declared a British protectorate in 1891—known as Nyasaland—and remained under British control until independence was granted on 6 July 1964.

The first police force in Nyasaland was established in 1896 but was little more than a tax collecting unit with the additional responsibility of obtaining African labour for employment in estates owned by European settlers. A more professional force was established in the 1920s and assumed more traditional policing duties across the Protectorate. By the end of the 1920s, the presence of supporting British troops was reduced and the police force grew and expanded over the next 30 years to a body with more than 3,000 officers—European and African—which was in place when British rule was relinquished.

In the period of British rule, officers in Nyasaland were entitled to the colonial police series of medals but, with the granting of independence, these awards ceased and a further series of local medals was introduced, starting with one issued to celebrate the event.

INDEPENDENCE MEDAL

Instituted: 29 May 1964.

Ribbon: Three equal stripes of black, red and green.

Metal: Cupro-nickel.

Size: 36 mm.

Description: (Obverse) the crowned effigy of Queen Elizabeth II; (reverse) the Coat of Arms of Malawi with the words MALAWI INDEPENDENCE (top) and 6TH JULY 1964 (below) around the circumference. A ring suspender was employed.

This medal was the first awarded by the newly independent state and issued to all members of the security forces, including the police, who were serving when independence took effect. The coat of arms on the reverse was first granted to the Protectorate of Nyasaland on 11 May 1914 and showed a few changes from the unofficial arms used before. The original arms used a coffee tree as the central feature but the crop never lived up to its expectations as a major influence in the colony and was dropped from the arms when they were officially authorised. At the time of independence, the arms featured a shield with a leopard in the centre above a sun and below a series of waves—the supporters were a lion (left) and a leopard (right).

The Republic of Malawi is landlocked but Lake Malawi (formerly Lake Nyasa) runs for almost the length of the country, certainly more than two-thirds, more than 500 kilometres, and is represented on the coat of arms by the emblem indicating waves.

Two years after independence was achieved, Malawi gained the status of a republic and a special medal was authorised and issued in similar circumstances to the Independence Medal of two years earlier. Police officers were amongst the recipients.

REPUBLIC MEDAL

Instituted: 6 July 1966.

Ribbon: Five equal stripes of green, red, black, red and green.

Metal: Silver.

Size: 36 mm.

Description: (Obverse) the head of the President —Dr Hastings Banda; (reverse) the Coat of Arms of Malawi with the inscription REPUBLIC OF MALAWI (above) and 6TH JULY 1966 (below) around the circumference. A ring suspender was employed.

Two special police medals were instituted in 1967 for award exclusively to police officers, the first for meritorious police service worthy of special recognition and the second as a long service award.

The Presidential Police Medal is awarded to recognise valuable service characterised by devotion to duty or exceptional resourcefulness and can include long service where the recipient has displayed special ability, merit or exemplary conduct. In normal circumstances not more than three awards are made in any one year although this can be exceeded for very special reasons.

PRESIDENTIAL POLICE MEDAL

Instituted: 28 October 1967.

Ribbon: Royal blue with white stripes in the centre and at each edge.

Metal: Cupro-nickel.

Size: 36 mm..

Description: (Obverse) the head of the President with the legend PRESIDENT KAMUZU BANDA; (reverse) the badge of the Malawi Police consisting of a bird of prey with outstretched wings in front of a sun rising above the waves and the legend FOR MERITORIOUS SERVICE. An ornate scrolled suspender was used. A slip-on bar bearing the word POLICE was issued with the medal.

In addition to the Presidential Police Medal, awarded for meritorious service, a long service and good conduct medal was available to police officers of all ranks on completion of 18 years service without a major blemish on their record. The medal was very similar with the only difference being the substitution of the words FOR LONG SERVICE AND GOOD CONDUCT and the omission of the central white stripe on the ribbon. A further period of 18 years service is marked by the award of a silver bar bearing the badge of the Malawi Police.

Acts of bravery performed by any citizen of Malawi is recognised by the award of the Republic of Malawi Cross and Republic of Malawi Medal—both available to police officers although the award of the Cross was very rare and the Medal was the appropriate award in most circumstances.

REPUBLIC OF MALAWI MEDAL

Instituted: 28 October 1967.

Ribbon: Seven stripes of green (four) and white (three)—all of equal width.

Metal: Silver.

Size: 36 mm.

Description: (Obverse) the head of the President; (reverse) a charging lion against the background of Mount Mlanje with the words REPUBLIC OF MALAWI (above) and FOR BRAVERY (below) around the circumference. A plain, straight suspender bar was used.

In 1994 a full multi-party election was held in Malawi and a new president elected—Bakili Muluzi. The medals introduced by Dr Banda during his 30 years of office remain although the effigy of the Head of State on the obverse has changed to reflect the new regime.

MALTA

The islands which form the Republic of Malta in the Mediterranean Sea are familiar to most Britons for one of two reasons. Either they are an ideal holiday destination, perfect for a little winter sunshine or they are the gallant little islands that resisted the worst the Luftwaffe and Italian Air Force could throw at them in the early years of the Second World War. For the courage and fortitude of the Maltese people the islands were awarded the George Cross, Britain's highest decoration for bravery for civilians, as a mark of King George VI's admiration for their suffering.

The award of a decoration to a place rather than an individual was not without precedent—the town of Ieper (Ypres) more commonly known in the UK as "Wipers" was awarded the Military Cross at the end of the Great War for all it had suffered between 1914 and 1918.

The British government was not alone in awarding medals to places—in 1948 the town of Cherbourg on the Cotentin Peninsula of France was awarded the *Croix de Guerre avec Palme* by the French government for the help given by the town and its occupants to the American First Army in the weeks and months following D-Day on 6 June 1944 which allowed the Americans to unleash the full might of their military resources against the occupying Germans. The full citation is inscribed on a plaque on a side wall of the Hòtel de Ville tucked away in a quiet street rarely frequented by visitors or locals.

In 1919 the city of Leningrad (now St Petersburg) was awarded the Soviet Order of the Red Flag for the defence of the city during the civil war which followed the October Revolution. The order was instituted on 16 September 1918 with a variety of designs produced by the individual Soviet republics. In August 1924 a single design was adopted, the one in use in the Russian Republic, for the whole of the Soviet Union. It was awarded to individuals of the armed forces, citizens, military units and places for conspicuous bravery most usually in wartime but often in peaceful times where the level of courage displayed merited high official recognition. The award became redundant with the break-up of the Soviet Union.

Probably the most decorated town of all is Verdun, awarded more than 30 orders and medals by many countries in recognition of the suffering of its people, *les poilus* and the French nation during the Great War. Britain awarded the Military Cross, France the Legion d'Honneur, Russia the Cross of St George and Italy the Gold Medal for Military Valour with others—Greece, Romania, Latvia and the United States among them—awarding a variety of decorations, orders and medals. Italy also awarded the same medal to at least four of its own cities—Florence, Turin, Cagliari and Vittorio Veneto—during the Second World War.

The award by the United States differed from the others in that the country bestowed its highest decoration for gallantry—the Medal of Honor—usually reserved to reward acts of courage of the very highest degree, the equivalent of Britain's Victoria Cross and not given lightly. The horrors and sacrifice of the Great War, however, led to the award of the honour to the town of Verdun by special resolution of Congress as a mark of the respect of the American people for the suffering of all those who took part in the defence of Verdun and everything it symbolised. For more than 70 years this was the only such award of the Medal of Honor to a place until the 50th anniversary of the Second World War when a second was presented to mark the attack on Pearl Harbour in Hawaii in 1941 by the Japanese, an act which brought America into the conflict.

The impact of the Great War on all western nations was profound and, in the years immediately following the Armistice, governments across Europe attempted to find some appropriate way to recognise the sacrifices made by ordinary men and women. In the UK, France, Belgium, Italy and Romania these attempts centred on the honouring of the body of the unknown warrior buried in Westminster Abbey in the UK, under the Arc de Triomphe in Paris and in the national monument to King Vittorio Emanuel II in Rome. The United States added their respects to these warriors by granting each the Medal of Honor by virtue of special acts of Congress.

In the United States a similar award was made to the unknown American buried in the Memorial Amphitheater of Arlington National Cemetery at the end of the Great War. Unlike the UK and France where there is a single unknown warrior to represent all those who died in all wars, in the US further unknown Americans were buried at the end of the Second World War, the Korean War and the Vietnam War. Each was awarded the Medal of Honor by the President in the name of Congress on behalf of the American people.

The islands of Malta thus hold a special position in the annals of the history of warfare and the award of medals for courage. The Republic of Malta consists of a number of islands, three of which are inhabited—Malta, Gozo and tiny Kemmuna situated in the strait between the two larger ones—with a total area of 320 square kilometres and a population of about 350,000.

Their position in the Mediterranean is of such strategic importance to more powerful nations that they have in turn been dominated by the Phoenicians, Romans, Greeks, Carthaginians, Arabs, Sicily, Spain, France and finally the British who wrested control from the French in 1800. In 1814 the Treaty of Paris formally recognised the islands as a British crown colony, a situation which persisted until full independence was gained in 1964. Each of the occupying powers left its mark on the culture of the islands and in the Malti language which reflects a host of differing influences. The written language as seen on the second of the two long service medals is a relatively recent innovation and was not developed until the early years of the 20th century. In 1921 English was made the official language of administration and remains one of the two official languages on the islands. In the same year the first medal for award to police officers on the islands was introduced.

MALTA POLICE LONG SERVICE AND GOOD CONDUCT MEDAL 1921–1934

Instituted: 1921.

Ribbon: Medium blue with a white central stripe.

Metal: Silver.

Size: 36 mm.

Description: (Obverse) the effigy of King George V; (reverse) a Maltese cross placed centrally surrounded by a wreath of laurel and a circumscription which read MALTA POLICE at the top and FOR LONG SERVICE & GOOD CONDUCT around the lower two-thirds. The medal hung from a ring suspender and claw fitting.

There are two different effigies of King George V on the obverse of the medal, one showed a full bust of His Majesty wearing the Imperial crown and coronation robes, the other the bare coinage head designed by Bertram Mackennal. The medal was replaced by the Colonial Police Long Service and Good Conduct Medal in 1934.

The medal was awarded on completion of 18 years service with exemplary conduct and good character and it is estimated that 99 awards were made although this cannot be known precisely and there is a suspicion that there were more. It was available to officers of any rank although those of officer rank must have served the 18 year qualifying period as a constable or NCO to be eligible, irrespective of their final rank.

In 1990 the Maltese government introduced a series of orders and medals to award its citizens for acts of service to the State, bravery and long and efficient service in any of its disciplined services, including the police. The design of the medal is the same for the three disciplined services of Malta (Armed Forces, Police and Prison Services) but with different ribbons for each.

MALTA POLICE
LONG AND EFFICIENT SERVICE MEDAL 1990

Instituted: 1990.

Ribbon: White with a thin blue stripe in the centre and two wider blue bands towards the edges.

Metal: Cupro-nickel.

Size: 36 mm.

Description: (Obverse) the Coat of Arms of the Republic of Malta; (reverse) a Maltese cross placed centrally surrounded by a wreath of laurel and a circumscription in Maltese which reads GHAL SERVIZZ TWIL U EFFIÜJENTI (For Long and Efficient Service). The medal hangs from a plain straight suspender attached by a claw fitting.

Police officers are eligible for the medal on completion of an aggregate of 18 years efficient service with irreproachable character and conduct throughout. After an additional seven years service a first bar is awarded with a second available after a further five years. The bars are of plain cupro-nickel with a mural crown in the centre.

The first awards of the medal were made to members of the Armed Forces. Apart from a single presentation made to the Police Commissioner in 1992, the first awards to police officers were not made until July 1995 on the 181st anniversary of the founding of the Force. On 12 July 1995, 131 officers were presented with the medal alone, 61 with a medal and one bar to reward 25 years service and 47 officers from constable to commissioner with a medal and two bars to signify a total of 30 years service with the Force.

Acts of bravery performed by police officers from Malta are recognised by the award of the *Medal for Courage and Bravery*, available to any citizen of the Republic, not only members of the disciplined services.

MIDALJA JA GHALL-QLUBIJA

Instituted: 1975.

Ribbon: Half red and half white moirÈ.

Metal: Silver.

Size: 40 mm..

Description: (Obverse) the Emblem of the Republic of Malta superimposed on a representation of the rays of the sun; (reverse) a geographical representation of the islands of Malta with the inscription GHALL-QLUBIJA below, all superimposed on a representation of the rays of the sun. A scrolled top ribbon bar bears the date 1975.

The shield which forms the basis of the emblem of Malta is based on the silver and red flag of the islands which has been in use for centuries. The shield is flanked by a wreath of palm (right) and olive (left) representing tradition and peace which have long been associated with Malta. The mural crown located above the shield is indicative of the islands fortifications and also denotes a city state. The name of the Republic (in Maltese) is in a scroll below the shield. The award of the George Cross is remembered by its inclusion in the upper left of the shield, the same position as it appears on the flag.

MAURITIUS AND SEYCHELLES

The two republics of Mauritius and Seychelles, both members of the British Commonwealth, are situated in the Indian Ocean 2,000 and 1,500 kilometres east of Africa respectively. The two countries were probably first discovered by Arab sailors in the 15th century with European interest starting with visits by the Portuguese in the early 1500s although it was not until the French took possession of Mauritius in 1715 and Seychelles in the 1770s that large scale settlement began. Their history was linked from those times and Seychelles were governed as a dependent territory of the larger island until the islands became a separate British crown colony in 1903.

REPUBLIC OF MAURITIUS

The island of Mauritius is of volcanic origin, covers an area of 1,864 square kilometres and supports a population of approximately 1.25 million with a unique blend of races, cultures and religions. The multiracial society has people of European, African, Chinese and Indian origin, the result of three hundred years of population movement encouraged by the French and British for commercial reasons. The island was initial settled by the Dutch in the late 17th century but abandoned by them in 1710 and taken as a French possession in 1715. The name of the island was given in honour of Prince Maurice van Nassau of the Netherlands. Development of the island by the French started in earnest in 1735 with the establishment of a naval base and ship-building centre at Port Louis to take advantage of its strategic position on the route from Africa to India. The total population of the island at the time was barely 1,000 but this was increased over the following 30 years to more than 20,000 by the use of slaves (more than 15,000).

During the Napoleonic wars, the Isle de France as it was known, was an important base for the French and a thorn in the side of the British commercial fleet. In 1810 a strong British force defeated the French garrison and captured the island. In 1814 it was ceded to Britain and entered a period of great social and economic change, arguably the most profound being the abolition of slavery in 1835. To make up the shortfall in available labour following the abolition of slavery and the development of the islands agriculture, particularly the growing of sugar cane, thousands of workers were brought in from Indian, followed by Chinese traders laying the foundations of the current multicultural society. Mauritius remained under British control until 12 March 1968 when independence was granted followed 24 years later by the establishment of a republic.

Policing in Mauritius during the period of British rule was based on the principles adopted across most crown colonies and it became one of the very first to award medals to police officers to recognise good service and, in some instances, acts of courage or particularly meritorious service. An early reference to a medal for police officers appears in the *Mauritius Government Gazette* of 11 May 1872 where the criteria for its award were laid down. The entry refers to a good conduct medal being formerly given out of the Police Reward Fund which was established on 8 September 1871 giving the probably date of the medal's introduction although there was no specific reference made to a medal in the gazette.

MAURITIUS POLICE GOOD CONDUCT MEDAL

Instituted: Believed 1871.

Ribbon: Three different types - see below.

Metal: Silver and bronze.

Size: Oval, 40mm by 33mm.

Description: (Obverse) crossed tipstaves surmounted by an imperial crown with a banner below containing the words PAX NOBISCUM (peace be with us) all surrounded by an outer band inscribed POLICE DEPARTMENT (above) and MAURITIUS (below); (reverse) a pair of palm fronds tied at the base by a bow with the words FOR GOOD CONDUCT in three lines in the central field. A large ring was used for suspension.

There is a degree of uncertainty about the ribbons for the two medals. Three designs are known and it is thought that different ribbons were used for the bronze and silver awards at some time. It is known with a degree of certainty that the silver medal hung from a blue ribbon with two narrow white stripes towards each edge. Similarly it is thought that the bronze medal came with a ribbon that was half white and half dark blue. The third ribbon was white with a blue central band, all of equal width, which was possibly the original bronze medal ribbon. When the change was made is not clear and the combinations of medals and ribbons is equally uncertain.

The initial criteria for the award of the bronze medal to NCOs or constables demanded that they should have performed their duties in a satisfactory manner for a period of at least five years and been free of any adverse report for the last three. They were also granted a gratuity of £3. Similar satisfactory service for a further period of five years without any report being made against them for the whole period entitled the officer to the award of the silver medal and a gratuity of £5. The bronze medal was given up on the award of the silver one. If an officer who had been granted either medal found himself the subject of an adverse report, the medal was immediately withdrawn although it could be re-instated after a further three years (bronze) or five years (silver) of good conduct.

There was no provision in the first ordinance for the award of either medal for anything other than the appropriate length of service with good conduct. On 30 May 1876, the regulations were amended and included a provision for the award of either medal by the Governor of the island to recognise an act of especially meritorious or distinguished conduct irrespective of the length of service of the officer concerned. The amendments to the ordinance also increased the qualifying periods of service for the two medal to 10 years for the award of the bronze and an additional eight years for the silver. The periods of rehabilitation for officers who were deprived of their medal for an indiscretion were reduced to two and three years respectively.

The new ordinance defined for the first time examples of the highly meritorious conduct which would entitle an officer to a reward or gratuity and, under the new proviso, the award of a bronze or silver medal. Four examples were given. The first was defined as *"having traced out and apprehended or having joined in apprehending persons suspected to have been concerned in murder, larceny or other heinous crime, when more than ordinary intelligence has been displayed, or more than ordinary exertion or danger has been incurred in the duty"*. The second condition involved the recovery of stolen property by the exercise of more than ordinary intelligence, exertion or danger. The two remaining examples were concerned with the saving of life or property in dangerous circumstances or at a risk to the officer's life.

The regulations for the granting of the medals were tinkered with again in 1896 with the period of service necessary for the award of both medals again being amended but only for officers who were not subject to the earlier ordinance. The period of service required for the bronze medal was set at five years once more and the gratuity changed to 30 rupees. A further seven years service without an entry in the default book was rewarded with the grant of the silver medal and a gratuity of 50 rupees. The proviso giving the Inspector General the power to recommend an officer for the award of either medal without having the necessary period of service remained but the criteria were altered to include officers who had displayed *"special zeal and devotion to duty"* with no further examples given of the behaviour expected.

In common with most medals awarded in the police forces of the British Commonwealth the two medals in Mauritius were discontinued on the introduction of the Colonial Police Long Service and Good Conduct Medal in 1934. After independence was granted in 1968 the Queen remained as Head of State until a republic was declared on 12 March 1992. During this period the design of the long service medal was altered by the substitution of the words MAURITIUS POLICE FORCE for COLONIAL POLICE FORCES on the inscription around the right circumference of the reverse. The obverse carried the effigy of the Queen wearing the Tudor crown with the word QUEEN (left) and ELIZABETH II (right) at the circumference. The ribbon colour was altered to dark blue with two central red stripes very similar to the Coronation Medal of 1911. The medal was discontinued in 1992 and subsequently replaced by one from the range of honours introduced into the Republic with the highest award being the intriguingly named *Order of the Star and Key of the Indian Ocean*. The ribbons of the range of awards followed a similar style with a basic colour and four central lines in the colours of the national flag—red, blue, yellow and green. The *President's Police Long Service and Good Conduct Medal* is mauve with the four central lines, the same as the long service medal awarded to officers from the Prison Service and two higher honours available to members of all the disciplined forces, the *President's Distinguished Service Medal* and *President's Meritorious Service Medal*.

REPUBLIC OF SEYCHELLES

The area of the Indian Ocean covered by the Republic of Seychelles exceeds one million square kilometres although the land mass of the 115 islands is less than 450 square kilometres. The largest by some distance is Mahe (153 sq km) which is home to more than 80% of the total population of approximately 80,000. Geographically the islands are of two types, the 76 coral islands which average 1.5 metres above sea level with the highest point rarely exceeding 9 to 15 metres and the granitic main islands (including Mahe) which are very different, rising to altitudes of 600 to 1,000 metres above sea level. On the coral islands settlements are small with a typical number of inhabitants being less than 100. The islands are thought of as an unspoilt tropical paradise (they lie just south of the equator) and live up to the image in most respects with white sandy beaches and luxuriant tropical vegetation. The islanders have developed these virtues whilst seeking to retain the island's natural beauty and unique wildlife and have encouraged an elite class of tourism.

Occupation of the islands by the western colonial powers started in the 1770s with the arrival of French planters and their slaves although Arab traders and Portuguese explorers visited them as early as the 16th century. The French ruled Seychelles for 40 years during which time they developed a spice trade in competition with the Dutch East Indies using slave labour. The islands were also a transit point for the movement of slaves between Africa, India and other countries. Conflict with the British started in the late 1700s with the islands changing hands seven times in the following eleven years until they were occupied for the final time by the British in 1811. In 1814 they were formally handed over to their new rulers at the Treaty of Paris and administered as a dependency of Mauritius.

In 1903 the islands were split from Mauritius and became a separate crown colony which lasted until 1976 when independence from Britain and the establishment of the First Republic were achieved although remaining a part of the British Commonwealth. In 1993 the Third Republic was established which remains in power today.

Policing arrangements in Seychelles during the period of British rule followed the pattern established in many countries and were allied to those of Mauritius although they were two separate bodies. Early references to the award of medals for good conduct to officers of the Seychelles Police Force appear in the *Seychelles Government Gazettes* of January 1890, March 1891 and January 1892 when a total of ten bronze medals were handed out. The criteria for the award of the medals (bronze and silver) were very similar to Mauritius and the medals themselves were almost identical in design with the only differences being the substitution of the word SEYCHELLES around the lower circumference of the obverse and the colouring of the ribbon—orange with a dark blue central stripe although there is a suggestion that it was crimson. The award of both medals in Seychelles ceased on the introduction of the Colonial Police Long Service and Good Conduct Medal.

NAMIBIA (SOUTH WEST AFRICA)

The Republic of Namibia was of very little interest to the European colonial powers until the end of the 19th century when it was annexed by Germany and quickly renamed German South West Africa. It was considered to be an inhospitable place caught between the cold South Atlantic and the Kalahari Desert with no mineral resources worth the time, money and effort to find. It stayed in German hands until the Great War when the defeat of their forces by the South Africans caused it to come under their direct control with a mandate from the League of Nations. From then until independence was achieved in 1990 it was known as South West Africa and effectively treated as a province of South Africa. Policing was carried out by the South African Police and it wasn't until 1981 that a separate force was established although it was run on very similar lines and staffed by officers from the old order.

At the end of 1981, a series of four medals was produced for the new forces officers to reward outstanding, distinguished and faithful service in addition to a special single issue award of another to celebrate the establishment of the South West African Police.

MEDAL FOR THE ESTABLISHMENT OF THE SOUTH WEST AFRICAN POLICE

Instituted: December 1981.

Ribbon: Orange with two blue bands.

Metal: Gilt.

Size: 36 mm.

Description: (Obverse) a multi-pointed circular star with a representation of Needle Rock against a rayed background in the centre surrounded by an outer band containing eleven motifs; (reverse) plain apart from the badge of the Force. A plain triangular suspender is used.

The medal was awarded to every member of the South African Police (including reserves) serving in the territory on 1 April 1981 when the Force first started to function as an independent body. A total of 1,287 medals were issued.

Every medal in the series depicted the badge of the Force on the reverse although the four others each also carried an inscription with the name of the medal in Afrikaans. The obverse of all five carried emblems depicting features of the local landscape and topography with an unusual species of plant, unique to the area, appearing on two.

Namibia

The Star of Outstanding Service, the highest of the remaining four awards, was given in recognition of outstanding service which could include acts of bravery. It was awarded on very few occasions. Recipients of the honour were entitled to the use of the post-nominal letters—SOE. Following the precedent set in South Africa to overcome the difficulties caused by the existence of two official languages—English and Afrikaans—the post-nominals were in Latin—SOE being an abbreviation of *Stella Officii Egregii*, the Latin name for the medal.

STAR OF OUTSTANDING SERVICE

Instituted: December 1981.

Ribbon: A neck ribbon in red with a white band (4 mm) at each edge and a gold central band (4 mm)

Metal: Silver gilt and red enamel.

Size: 36 mm.

Description: (Obverse) a Maltese cross with a large central medallion leaving only the points of the cross visible in red enamel. At the centre of the medallion is Franke Fort surrounded by an outer band carrying a design of interwoven leaves; (reverse) the Force badge surrounded by the name of the star in Afrikaans. A plain straight suspender was used.

Franke Fort was used during the German occupation and was the scene of a particularly heroic action by a handful of German soldiers who held a large force of Herero tribesmen at bay during the uprising in 1904, the last attempt at that time by the local Herero and Nama people to rid themselves of the colonial power. The rebellion was brutally crushed.

The second highest award was awarded for two reasons, first as a reward for particularly meritorious service by an officer of any rank and, second, after not less than 30 years faithful service. It too carried with it the right to the use of post-nominals—SOO (*Stella Officii Optimi*).

STAR FOR DISTINGUISHED SERVICE

Instituted: December 1981.

Ribbon: Blue with a gold central stripe (2 mm) and two white bands (4 mm).

Metal: Silver gilt and blue enamel.

Size: 36 mm.

Description: (Obverse) a circular disc containing a star with 22 points around a central medallion bearing a representation of the Bogenfels (a well-known natural rock arch on the Atlantic coast) surrounded by an outer band with a design of leaves in the form of a series of arches; (reverse) the Force badge with the name of the medal in Afrikaans—SWA POLISIESTER VIR VOORTREFLIKE DIENS.

Police Medals of the World

Faithful service was marked by the award of two decorations, one on the achievement of 20 years service and another after ten years. The higher of the two awards was called a star although it was, in reality, of very irregular shape.

STAR FOR FAITHFUL SERVICE

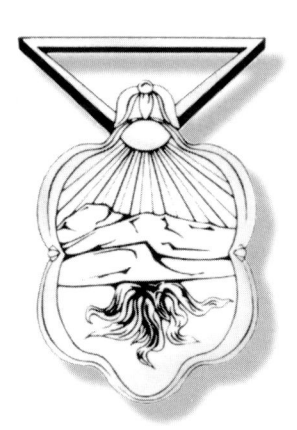

Instituted: December 1981.

Ribbon: Green with band of silver, orange and silver (all 3 mm) on either side of the broad green central band (8 mm)

Metal: Silver.

Description: (Obverse) a stylised view of the countryside with the dunes of the Namib Desert in the centre with the sun shining down on it and the Welwitschia plant in the foreground all within a frame at the stars edge; (reverse) the Force badge and the name of the medal SWA POLISIESTER VIR TROUE DIENS around the top half. A plain triangular suspender was cast with the medal protruding from the upper lobe.

The *Welwitschia Mirabilis* is a truly remarkable plant found only in the Namib Desert. It is one of the strangest and largest plants known to science and is thought by some to be the longest-lived—Carbon 14 dating tests have shown that it lives for over 750 years and may exceed 1,000. It is found in dry desert areas where rainfall may never exceed 25 mm a year and where rainless years are frequent. The leaves grow throughout the plants life and can reach a length of over three metres with the whole plant often having a circumference of more than four metres. The root system can go down more than 18 metres to obtain water from old river beds and it fully deserves its description as a living fossil.

The last of the series of medals—the *Medal for Faithful Service* (right)—is cast in bronze and awarded for at least ten years faithful service. It is circular and has a very similar design on the obverse—sun, desert and plant—as the Star for Faithful Service. The reverse is identical. The ribbon has nine stripes of green (four) and brown (five) with the central brown stripe being just over twice the width of the other eight.

When Namibia achieved independence in 1990 the medals became effectively redundant and their award ceased.

THE NETHERLANDS

The Netherlands is a country which issues a range of medals to its police officers and these have included some to celebrate royal events, mirroring the situation in the UK, although national official medals were always awarded to all sections of the community who assisted in preparing for the event or who were on duty in any capacity on the actual day never solely to police officers. In addition to these official medals, however, individual police forces occasionally issued their own medals to mark the occasion, one of the very first being the Amsterdam Municipal Police to celebrate the inauguration of Queen Wilhelmina which took place in the city on 6 September 1898 with the national celebrations starting the day before and continuing until 9 September.

The Dutch monarch is not crowned in a church as they are in the UK and the use of the term "coronation" is incorrect, a situation which is the direct result of the split of the Netherlands from Spain in the 16th century and formally established when the first truly Dutch king—Willem I—ascended to the throne in the early 19th century. A national festival is held in celebration.

POLITIEKRUIS VOOR DE INHULDIGINGFEESTEN VAN 1898

Instituted: 11 September 1898.

Ribbon: 29 mm wide in watered half red and half black (the colours of Amsterdam).

Metal: Gold and bronze.

Size: 38 mm.

Description: (Obverse) a cross with a central medallion bearing the left facing head of Queen Wilhelmina surrounded by three thin circles. Between the arms of the cross are wreaths of laurel and oak leaves giving the appearance of a round medal. On the arms of the cross the date of the coronation is given starting with 5 - 9 on the upper arm and SEPT on the lower with the year on the horizontal arms—18 (left) and 98 (right); (reverse) left plain apart from the legend HULDE - VAN - AMSTELS BURGERIJ - AAN DE - POLITIE (an award from the citizens of Amsterdam to the police) in five lines.

The *Police Cross for the Inauguration Festival of 1898* was presented to police officers only, with the medal presentation being held on 19 January 1899. The single gold medal produced was presented to the Mayor of Amsterdam with the 1,250 produced in bronze being distributed between municipal police officers from Amsterdam (1,153), the Amsterdam County Constabulary (61) and representatives from the municipal police forces of Arnhem, The Hague, Harlem, Rotterdam, Utrecht and Leeuwarden. A miniature was produced but never issued.

Police Medals of the World

Other royal occasions in the Netherlands have been marked by the issue of an official medal, a practice still current today. Three years after she ascended to the throne, Queen Wilhelmina married the German Duke Hendrick von Mecklenburg-Schwerin with the *Wedding Medal 1901* being issued for award to a wide cross-section of the Dutch people, including police officers, who played a part in the celebrations.

HUWELIJKSMEDAILLE 1901

Instituted: 7 February 1901.

Ribbon: *A central gold stripe 8 mm wide with a white stripe (3 mm) on either side and thin stripes (2 mm) of gold and orange at each edge.*

Metal: *Bronze.*

Description: *(Obverse) the conjoined heads of Queen Wilhelmina and Hendrick facing left; (reverse) the intertwined initials W and H surmounted by a crown within a wreath of laurel.*

The issue of medals by the City of Amsterdam to its police officers continued throughout the long reign of Queen Wilhelmina, the second being issued to celebrate her silver jubilee in 1923. The *Police Cross for the Jubilee Celebrations 1923* was awarded to every officer from the Force who was on duty on 5 and 6 September.

POLITIEKRUIS VOOR DE HULDIGINGFEESTEN 1923

Instituted: *1923.*

Ribbon: *20 mm wide, half red, half black (the colours of the City of Amsterdam).*

Metal: *Bronze.*

Size: *25 mm.*

Description: *(Obverse) a four armed cross with a central medallion bearing the uncrowned head of Queen Wilhelmina facing left. On the arms of the cross are the words JUBILEUMFEESTEN (jubilee festival) - 1923 - AMSTERDAM - 1898. The central medallion is surrounded by a wreath of laurel which overlaps the upper and lower arms but passes under the two side arms; (reverse) left blank.*

Fifteen years later, on the 40th jubilee of Queen Wilhelmina's reign, the Amsterdam Jubilee Commission introduced a further medal (the *Police Cross for the Jubilee Festival of 1938*) for issue to police officers on duty at the celebrations which, on this occasion, lasted from 5 to 11 September 1938.

POLITIEKRUIS VOOR DE HULDIGINGFEESTEN 1938

Instituted: 1938.

Ribbon: 20 mm wide, orange (occasionally found with a red—black ribbon similar to the 1923 cross).

Metal: Bronze.

Size: 28 mm.

Description: (Obverse) a five armed cross with a central medallion bearing the crowned effigy of Queen Wilhelmina and the circumscription WILHELMINA KONINGIN DER NEDERLANDEN (Wilhelmina Queen of the Netherlands). On the arms of the cross is the legend AMSTERDAM - 1938 - FEESTEN - JUBILEUM - 1898; (reverse) blank apart from the hallmark.

The last medal of the group of four issued to officers of the Amsterdam Municipal Police to commemorate royal occasions served a dual purpose—first to celebrate the golden jubilee of Queen Wilhelmina on 31 August 1948 and, secondly, at the formal inauguration of her daughter (Queen Juliana) on 6 September when Wilhelmina stepped aside to allow Juliana to ascend the throne. The *Police Cross for the Coronation Festival 1948* was presented to all officers on duty at either of the two events.

POLITIEKRUIS VOOR DE KRONINGSFEESTEN 1948

Instituted: 1948.

Ribbon: Orange, 24 mm wide.

Metal: Bronze.

Size: 25 mm.

Description: (Obverse) a four armed cross with a central medallion bearing the crowned head of Queen Wilhelmina facing left and the words KRONINGSSTAD 1948 - AMSTERDAM - 1898-1948 - COMITE on the arms of the cross. The medallion was surrounded by a broad ring passing under the arms of the cross; (reverse) left blank apart from the hallmark.

The practice of awarding medals to police officers in a city police force in celebration of a royal event was not limited to Amsterdam; in 1936 when Princess Juliana became engaged to Prince Bernhard the city authorities in The Hague followed the example set in Amsterdam and produced a special commemorative medal. *The Police Medal for the Engagement Celebrations* was awarded to large numbers of local people who had assisted in the week long celebrations in the city from 8 to 15 September 1936, including officers from the city police.

POLITIEPENNING VOOR DE VERLOVINGFEESTEN 1936

Instituted: 1936.

Ribbon: Half yellow, half green, the colours of The Hague.

Metal: Bronze.

Description: (Obverse) the Coats of Arms of Juliana and Bernhard superimposed on a wreath of laurel; (reverse) plain apart from the legend 8-15 SEPT 1936 VAN DE HAAGSCHE BURGERIJ (from the citizens of The Hague).

The principle of individual police forces awarding medals to its officers was not confined to celebrations of royal events; there is one instance of a local authority rewarding officers for their actions during an industrial dispute. The event occurred in 1903 at Amersfoort during the Dutch general strike by railway workers. When the action was over, the local city authorities struck a special medal for officers of the local police force to thank them for their action. *The Police Medal for the Railroad Strike 1903* was awarded in very small numbers.

POLITISMEDAILLE
VOOR DE SPOORWEGSTAKING 1903

Instituted: 1903.

Ribbon: Half red, half white.

Metal: Bronze.

Description: (Obverse) the Coats of Arms of Amersfoort (a red Greek cross on a white shield) with the legend TROUWE PLICHTBETRACHTING (faithful in duty) and APRIL 1903 around the circumference; (reverse) plain apart from the inscription HULDE VAN DE AMERSFOORTSCHE BURGERIJ (with thanks from the citizens of Amersfoort).

The Netherlands

In 1966 another royal wedding medal was awarded when Crown Princess Beatrice van Oranje-Nassau (the daughter of the reigning Queen Juliana) married the German diplomat Claus von Amsberg in Amsterdam. It was an official national medal, however, not restricted to police officers from Amsterdam, and awarded to all Dutch citizens who had played an active part in the preparations for the ceremony or who were on duty on the day. With the Second World War and occupation of the Netherlands by the Nazis being still being a recent and vivid bad memory for many Dutch people and the source of much animosity towards the Germans, the wedding was sadly marked by the outbreak of civil disorder in Amsterdam. The resources of the Amsterdam Police were stretched to such an extent that the Commissioner was forced to call on the Military Police and Dutch Marines to help restore order.

HUWELIJKSMEDAILLE 1966

Instituted: 10 March 1966.

Ribbon: Orange with a thin blue line at each edge and thin stripes of green and white together towards the edge on both sides.

Metal: Cupro-nickel.

Description: (Obverse) the conjoined heads of Princess Beatrice and her husband facing left; (reverse) the intertwined initials C and B with the date of the wedding - 10 MAART 1966 - around the circumference.

When Crown Princess Beatrice succeeded her mother, Queen Juliana, to the throne in 1980 another official national commemorative medal was issued to those who had played an active part in the planning for the event or who were on duty on the day to ensure that there was no repetition of the scenes of 1966 at her marriage. *The Inauguration Medal 1980* was of a simple but attractive design and the latest in the line of similar such medals issued to record royal occasions.

INHULDIGINGSMEDAILLE 1980

Instituted: 30 April 1980.

Ribbon: Orange with three thin dark blue lines at the centre.

Metal: Cupro-nickel.

Description: (Obverse) the bare head of Queen Beatrice; (reverse) the letter B surmounted by a crown with the date of the wedding below with the inscription BEATRIX KONINGEN DER NEDERLANDEN (Queen of the Netherlands) around the circumference.

The history of the police service in the Netherlands is complex and the structure has been changed a number of times, most recently in 1994 when the present system of a number of regional forces (*Regiopolitie*) was established to replace the Rijkspolitie (State Police) and more than 100 municipal forces. The basis of the structure replaced in 1994 was laid down in 1813 when each town and city was required to organise its own policing arrangements. One year later a military force modelled on the French Gendarmerie—the *Koninklijke Marechaussée* (Royal Constabulary)—was formed to police the rural areas. In 1855 a further force—the *Rijksveldwacht* (County Constabulary)—was formed with a jurisdiction which overlapped that of the Marechaussée in some areas but which was intended to police smaller urban areas and those which did not have their own municipal police. There was some confusion until the 1930s when areas of responsibility were more clearly defined.

The occupation of the Netherlands by the Nazis between 1940 and 1945 resulted in the next major change to the policing structure when the municipal forces and County Constabulary were merged to form the *Rijkspolitie*. At the end of the war the municipal forces were re-established and the State Police retained—until 1994—but the County Constabulary had gone forever. As a part of the Dutch Army the Marechaussée was unaffected by the most recent change and is now the oldest arm of the Dutch policing system. Amongst the municipal forces only Amsterdam and possibly Rotterdam and Utrecht are thought to have issued long service and good conduct medals to their officers.

GEMEENTEPOLITIE AMSTERDAM MEDAILLE (25 & 40 JAAR DIENST)

Instituted: 19 May 1971.

Ribbon: 30 mm wide, royal blue with a 5 mm central black stripe.

Metal: Cupro-nickel and gilded cupro-nickel..

Size: 38 mm.

Description: (Obverse) the emblem of the force taking the form of an eight-pointed star with a central field containing a sword pointing upwards superimposed upon a lawbook with a green enamel wreath of laurel in the lower half. The Force motto VIGILAT UT QUIESCANT (we keep watch while you sleep) is contained in a scroll below the central field; (reverse) the coat of arms of the City of Amsterdam in red and black enamel in a small shield offset to the upper left and the date of the award. A small ring suspender was employed.

The silver medal was awarded to all members of the Amsterdam Police for 25 years loyal devotion to duty and the gilt medal after 40 years service. The latter medal had a gilt crown attached above the ring suspender and carried a gold-coloured figure 40 on the ribbon when worn in undress uniform. Service in the Dutch Armed Forces, the Justice Department and a number of other similar agencies could be counted in the necessary qualifying period. Until 1986 it could only be awarded to operational police officers but this was changed to include administrative, scientific and technical personnel in August of that year by the Mayor of Amsterdam who was responsible for the award of the medal. The Amsterdam Municipal Police has existed in some form since the early 19th century but the last force was formed in 1948 when the effects of the German occupation were changed. It ceased to exist in 1994 when the State Police and municipal forces were amalgamated into the regional forces and the medal became obsolete.

The only truly national long service medal issued to Dutch police officers was available to members of the County Constabulary only—the *Rijksveldwacht*—which existed from 1855 to 1940 when it was disbanded under the German occupation. The *Medal for Faithful Service with the County Constabulary* was awarded for 25 years faithful and honest service and came with a magnificently illustrated citation document.

MEDAILLE VOOR TROUWE DIENST BIJ DE RIJKSVELDWACHT

Instituted: 7 April 1909.

Ribbon: 37 mm wide with the flag of the Netherlands (horizontal stripes of red, white and blue, each 10 mm wide) repeated several times and with two vertical orange stripes of equal width (4 mm) towards each edge.

Metal: Silver.

Size: 35 mm.

Description: (Obverse) a cross of four arms with rounded edges with a central shield bearing the national emblem of the Netherlands - a lion. The top arm of the cross is mostly hidden behind the royal crown but the words VOOR - TROUWEN - DIENST (for - faithful - service) are inscribed on the three others. Branches of laurel are between the arms of the cross; (reverse) the same design as the obverse apart from the substitution of an ornate letter W in the centre.

Police officers in the Netherlands have had the right to belong to a civil trade union for many years, the first such organisation being founded on 22 February 1887 in Amsterdam and formally recognised by the government on 1 March 1904. The General Dutch Police Union (*Algemeene Nederlandsche Politiebond*—ANPB) was followed by a number of others representing the various forces in the Netherlands until 1946 when several were merged to form the body which exists today—the *Nederlansche Politiebond*—Dutch Police Union (NPB). In 1937 at least 15 separate unions were active in the Netherlands, including eleven operating at national level.

Shortly after it was formed the ANPB introduced a medal to reward officers from any established police force in the country for faithful service of 10, 20 or 30 years provided that they were members of the Union. Over the years, officers from city and municipal forces, the County Constabulary, the State Mines Police, Foresters Corps, police forces from the Dutch East Indies, Marechaussée and Corps of Military Police joined the Union and were awarded medals. As military personnel, members of the last two forces were later forbidden from joining the civil trade union by the Ministry of War although there are records of awards being made to officers several years after the ban was introduced. Three versions of the *General Dutch Police Union Medal for Faithful Police Service* were awarded—bronze after ten years service, silver after 20 years and silver-gilt after 30 years.

MEDAILLE VOOR TROUWEN POLITIEDIENST VAN DE ALGEMEENE NEDERLANDSCHE POLITIEBOND

Instituted: *28 August 1888.*

Ribbon: *Three vertical stripes in the national colours—red, white and blue—each 4 mm wide with a yellow stripe (2 mm) at each edge.*

Metal: *Bronze, silver and silver-gilt.*

Size: *21 mm.*

Description: *(Obverse) a circular medal with a shield bearing the appropriate number of years service in Roman numerals and the words JAAR TROUWE DIENST (years faithful service). Above this is a scroll containing the words ALTIJD WAAKZAAN (always on guard) with a cockerel standing on the scroll; (reverse) left blank apart from the inscription ALGEMEENE NEDERLANDSCHE POLITIEBOND between two small six-pointed stars.*

The medal was replaced on 21 August 1913 by a cross although the criteria for its award remained unchanged. The ribbon was also re-designed to identify awards made for 20 and 30 years service—silver and silver-gilt medals were worn with a line of the appropriate colour at the ribbon's edge. *The General Dutch Police Union Cross for Faithful Police Service* was discontinued on 29 January 1946.

KRUIS VOOR TROUWEN POLITIEDIENST VAN DE ALGEMEENE NEDERLANDSCHE POLITIEBOND

Instituted: *21 August 1913.*

Ribbon: *A white central stripe (8 mm) with 3 mm stripes on either side—red (left) and blue (right). At each edge is a yellow band 4 mm wide.*

Metal: *Bronze, silver and silver-gilt.*

Size: *23 mm.*

Description: *(Obverse) a cross with rounded edges and a central medallion bearing the Coat of Arms of the Netherlands. The upper arm has the length of service in Roman numerals and the word JAAR (years). On the three other arms are the words TROUWE POLITIE DIENST. A wreath of laurel lies between the arms of the cross; (reverse) left plain apart from the inscription ALG on the upper arm and NED POL BOND across the centre.*

The Netherlands

One of the oldest of the Dutch medals, the *Officer's Cross* (a shortened version of the official name), is essentially a military decoration awarded to officers for 15 years service in any branch of the armed forces including the reserve forces. After the formation of the Rijkspolitie in 1948 its senior officers (Lieutenant to General) were included in those entitled to the Cross although the Force was a civil body responsible to the police and judicial authorities.

OFFICIERSKRUIS

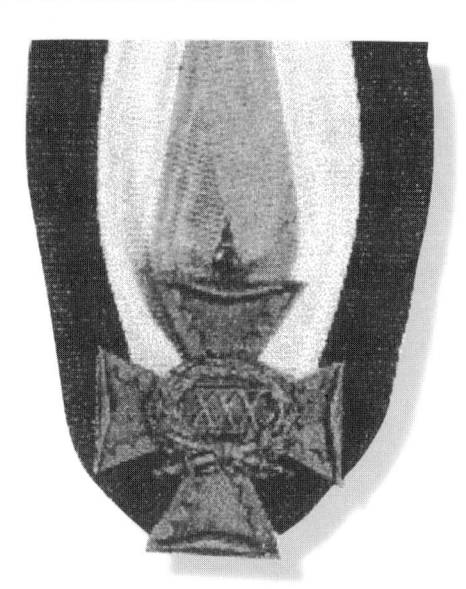

Instituted: *19 November 1844.*

Ribbon: *Three equal stripes of gold, white and blue.*

Metal: *Gilded white metal.*

Description: *(Obverse) a Maltese cross with a central medallion showing the number of years service in Roman numerals within a wreath of laurel tied at the base; (reverse) plain.*

The first award has the Roman number XV in the central medallion but this is changed each time a further five years qualifying service is achieved. Originally it consisted of the medallion only showing the officer's total service but was changed to its current design at the end of 1866. In undress uniform a gilt Roman numeral is worn on the ribbon. There is an alternative unofficial name for the Cross—the *Jeneverkruis* (gin cross)—in recognition of the practice of toasting the award in the officers' club.

Police Medals of the World

The Dutch Police Service has a similarity with the UK in the use of voluntary officers very like the Special Constabulary although there are differences in the powers of regular and volunteer officers in the Netherlands. The Police Reserve Corps (*Reservepolitie*) was founded in 1948 but became a victim of the reorganisation of 1994 and was disbanded. A similar body—the *Vrijwillige* (Voluntary Police)—but with reduced powers and the right to carry arms removed—was established as a replacement. Unfortunately it has not met with the same degree of enthusiasm as the Reserve Corps and is operating well below its anticipated strength with its future in doubt. At the completion of ten years service with the Reserve Corps, volunteers became entitled to the award of the *Volunteers Medal for Public Order and Safety*.

VRIJWILLIGERSMEDAILLE OPENBARE ORDE EN VEILIGHEID

Instituted: 1958.

Ribbon: Watered grass green with an orange line towards each edge.

Metal: Bronze.

Size: 40 mm.

Description: (Obverse) a circular medal with five castle battlements representing a wall across the middle and rays of light behind to symbolise the country protected by the wall against a snake which is found at the bottom of the medal. On the wall are the words PATRIAE SER - VIRE LIBER - TAS (to uphold peace in the country) in three lines; (reverse) the Coat of Arms of the Dutch monarchy with the motto of the Orange-Nassau family - JE MAINTIENDRAI (I shall uphold).

On its introduction, the medal was simply named the *Volunteers Medal* until June 1998 when the present title was substituted. It is awarded for a minimum of ten years service in a number of voluntary organisations apart from the police including the Ambulance Service, the Fire Department, the Army National Reserve Corps, life-saving organisations, the Dutch Red Cross and other first aid societies. After the initial award, further periods of five years service were recognised by the award of a clasp bearing the total numbers of years in Roman numerals—XV, XX, XXV etc. The longest known period of service recognised by the award of a clasp is 40 years (XL). A small version is available for wear on the ribbon in undress uniform. Only one clasp (the latest awarded) is worn.

The 50th anniversary of the Voluntary Police in both its forms was marked by the issue of the *Voluntary Police Commemorative Medal 1948–1998*. It was awarded to former and serving officers of the voluntary forces and those who played an active part in the celebrations although they may not have been in the Voluntary Police.

HERINNERINGSMEDAILLE VRIJWILLIGE POLITIE 1948–1998

Instituted: 26 May 1998.

Ribbon: Dark blue with two narrow (2 mm) stripes of ochre and § white towards each edge.

Metal: Bronze.

Size: 35 mm.

Description: (Obverse) the emblem of the Regional Police—a law book topped by a flame and the circumscription VRIJWILLIGE POLITIE (Voluntary Police); (reverse) plain apart from the dates 1948–1998.

Before the introduction of the national award in 1958 the Amsterdam Police issued a medal for members of the city's volunteer corps although it existed for two years only and was awarded on only 43 occasions before it was replaced by the national medal. The Wearable Medal for Faithful Service with the Police Volunteer Corps was awarded in three classes—bronze, silver and gold— to recognise service of 10, 15 and 20 years respectively.

DRAAGMEDAILLE VOOR TROUWE DIENST BIJ HET KORPS VRIJWILLIGE POLITIE

Instituted: 1956.

Ribbon: Three equal bands of red, black and red.

Metal: Gold, silver and bronze.

Description: (Obverse) the Coat of Arms of the City of Amsterdam; (reverse) the words VOOR TROUWE DIENST (for faithful service) and KORPS VRIJWILLIGE POLITIE (volunteer police corps) with a space for the date of the award to be engraved.

Acts of courage by Dutch police officers are rewarded by national medals available to any member of the community in similar fashion to the UK, there are no gallantry awards specifically for the police. The practice of recognising bravery by Dutch citizens goes back to 1822 when the first version of the *Medal for Humane Action* was instituted. It has undergone a number of changes since its introduction although the current medal has remained the same since 1912. The medals are awarded for any humane action, although life-saving is the most prevalent, characterised by courage, brave conduct and self-sacrifice. The level of courage involved is denoted by the material of the medal—gold, silver or bronze.

EREPENNING VOOR MENSCHLIEVEND HULPBETOON (1912 TO PRESENT)

Instituted: 11 April 1912.

Ribbon: Orange-yellow with a red central stripe.

Metal: Gold, silver and bronze.

Size: An oval medal 33 mm wide and 61 mm high.

Description: (Obverse) a portrait of the statue of "Charity" with the circumscription VOOR MENSCHLIEVEND HULPBETOON (for humane action); (reverse) the inscription DE KONINGIN AAN (The Queen to) and the recipient's engraved name.

The current medal is the fifth design since 1822. The first three were not intended for wear although there are examples where they have been adapted and can be seen with a ribbon in the Dutch national colours—red, white and blue—in horizontal stripes of equal width. On 24 May 1897 when the medal was redesigned for the fourth time it became wearable with the same ribbon seen today. The design, however, was very different.

EREPENNING VOOR MENSCHLIEVEND HULPBETOON (1897 TO 1912)

Instituted: 24 May 1897.

Ribbon: The same as the current medal. When worn in undress uniform gold and silver medals are indicated by a gold or silver crown worn on the ribbon.

Metal: Gold, silver and bronze.

Size: 34 mm.

Description: (Obverse) the head of Queen Wilhelmina facing left; (reverse) the inscription VOOR MENSCHLIEVEND HULPBETOON AAN (for humane action to) in three lines followed by the recipients name.

The Dutch were one of the great colonial powers, rivalling Britain, France and Spain in their exploration of the unknown regions and domination of any they found and were able to conquer. The greatest Dutch influence was in the far east where present day Indonesia was known as the Dutch East Indies until independence was granted in 1949 after a five year war. The policing of the islands from the time they were first colonised in the 17th century rested with the Royal Maréchaussée, a part of the Dutch Army and therefore eligible for military medals for any acts of courage or meritorious service although very few were ever awarded. There were no medals issued exclusively for police officers.

The other major area of Dutch influence was in South America and the West Indies although conflict with the British resulted in many places changing hands until some form of political stability was reached in the 19th century and tension between the two powers in overseas territories eased.

At one time the Netherlands ruled the three countries—Guyana, French Guyana and Surinam—on the north-east coast of South America along with large areas of Brazil. Rivalry with the British and a number of disputes over the territory ended in 1667 when the British relinquished all control over what is now Surinam to the Dutch in exchange for a small settlement under their control on the east coast of North America—Nieuw Amsterdam, later to be renamed New York. The Dutch stayed in Surinam until independence was granted in 1975 after a period as an autonomous region of the Kingdom of the Netherlands (from 1954) but their influence remains and they are the main aid supplier to the new country although this was suspended for a period in protest at the abuse of human rights in Surinam. The country is large by European standards—165,270 square kilometres—with a population of 425,000. One third of Surinamese actually live in the Netherlands and the ethnic mix of the country is very diverse. For a period up to independence the Dutch government awarded a medal to officers from the Surinam Police Corps for faithful service of twelve, twenty and twenty-five years.

Police Medals of the World

MEDAILLE VOOR TROUWE DIENST VAN HET POLITIECORPS SURINAME

Ribbon: *Four equal stripes of yellow, red, white and blue.*

Metal: *Bronze, silver and silver-gilt.*

Description: *(Obverse) a circular medal with the Coat of Arms of Surinam; (reverse) a Roman numeral with the number of years served—XII, XX or XXV surrounded by the words POLITIE SURINAME (Surinam Police Corps) above and VOOR TROUWE DIENST (for faithful service) below.*

The coat of arms consists of an oval shield with a three-masted schooner at sea supported by two natives holding a bow in their hands. The medal came with a certificate signed by the Governor of Surinam.

The Netherlands is perhaps the country closest to the UK in the range of medals awarded to police officers and this includes honours included in the Orders of Knighthood of the two countries. In the UK police officers of all ranks are regularly appointed to the Most Excellent Order of the British Empire (CBE, OBE and MBE) and were awarded the BEM before it was abolished. In the Netherlands a similar situation occurs with many officers being admitted to the two equivalent Dutch orders—the Order of the Dutch Lion (*Orde van den Nederlanschen Leeuw*) and Order of Orange-Nassau (*Orde van Oranje-Nassau*). The Orders were founded in 1815 and 1892 respectively, although they were both amended when the honours system was reviewed in the mid 1990s. Honours are granted on "Queens Day"—30 April, the birthday of the former Queen Juliana—known colloquially as the *lintsesregen* (rain of awards) as a result of the ever-growing list of awards made and the nature of many of the recipients. Awards of the Order of Orange-Nassau are the most common and come in six classes although they once included a Medal of Honour associated with the Order but discontinued in 1994 and replaced by the current sixth grade award.

ORDE VAN ORANJE-NASSAU—EREMEDAILLE

Instituted: *4 April 1892.*

Ribbon: *Orange with lines of white and blue at the edges.*

Metal: *Gold, silver and bronze. The class is shown by a replica of the medal in the appropriate metal worn on the ribbon.*

Description: *(Obverse) a circular medal with the badge of the Order in the centre—a Maltese cross with ball finials superimposed on a wreath of laurel and a central medallion bearing the Dutch lion and the words JE MAINTIENDRAI on an outer band; (reverse) the ornate initial W in the centre with an outer band bearing the words GODE ZY MET ONS (God be with us). The disc is surmounted by a royal crown.*

page 244

NEW ZEALAND

The present New Zealand Police was founded as a national service modelled on the British policing system in 1886 and drew together the officers of the Armed Constabulary and a number of provincial police forces which existed in Auckland, Otago, Wellington, Canterbury and other places. Policing in New Zealand was first established in 1840 when magistrates were given authority to appoint constables in their area of responsibility. In October 1846 this arrangement was formalised and each provincial council was required to maintain a police force to preserve the peace, a requirement that was fulfilled across the country by 1853. This system provided adequate policing cover until the early 1860s when the discovery of gold in the provinces of Otago and Canterbury led to an increase in crime and violence putting a strain on the resources of law and order available. The upsurge in crime and disorder led to the establishment of the Armed Constabulary, the forerunner of today's national force. When the provinces were abolished in 1877 the provincial police forces that existed were merged with the Armed Constabulary until 1886 when the national, civil police force was founded by Act of Parliament.

At the time the new policing arrangements were established a long service and good conduct medal was introduced as a reward to all officers on completion of fourteen years service and made retrospective to include all qualifying members of the constituent forces.

NEW ZEALAND POLICE MEDAL

Instituted: 1886.

Ribbon: Crimson with a central dark blue stripe flanked by a white stripe on either side.

Metal: Silver.

Size: 38 mm.

Description: (Obverse) the St Edward crown resting on a cushion and a crossed sword and sceptre with the initials NZ below separated by a star with three others to the sides and above symbolic of the Southern Cross constellation. Around the circumference was a wreath of oak leaves (left) and palm fronds (right) tied at the base by a bow; (reverse) plain apart from the inscription FOR - LONG SERVICE - AND - GOOD CONDUCT in four lines. A ring suspender was used originally but this was changed to straight one attached by a claw fitting.

The ribbon was plain crimson when the medal was introduced but changed in 1919 (partly because of its similarity to the VC) to the design described above which is retained today. The period of service required for the award of the medal was unusually low at fourteen years and bars were available for each subsequent period of seven years with the bar showing the total length of service. The additional qualifying time for the bars was changed from eight years to seven in 1963. They are inscribed in the style—22 YEARS SERVICE—with the appropriate numeral—21, 22, 28, 35 or 38 years. When the ribbon was worn alone the award of any bars was indicated by the wearing of a five-point star in silver or silver-plate. The star was apparently chosen in preference to the rosette more usually seen on British medals to emphasise that the NZ Police was not a military or paramilitary body.

The manufacturer of the medal changed frequently and the detail of the design was amended on a number of occasions in the method of suspension, design of the palm fronds and the removal of the star between the initials NZ being the most noticeable. The medal was an unofficial but accepted reward for service in the New Zealand Police until official recognition was granted in 1976 when the whole honours system in the country was made subject of a review.

NEW ZEALAND POLICE LONG SERVICE AND GOOD CONDUCT MEDAL

Instituted: 1976.

Ribbon: The same as the previous medal.

Metal: Silver.

Size: 38 mm.

Description: (Obverse) the crowned head of Queen Elizabeth with the circumscription ELIZABETH II DEI GRATIA REGINA F.D.; (reverse) the same as the obverse of the medal replaced but with the removal of the initials below the cushion and the addition of the words NEW ZEALAND POLICE (above) and LONG SERVICE AND GOOD CNDUCT (below) around the circumference outside the wreath. A plain straight suspender is used attached to the upper rim of the medal.

Bars awarded to accompany this medal are plain with a crown placed centrally and remain the same irrespective of the number of years served and bars awarded. When the new medal was introduced it could only be given to holders of the previous award on the surrender of that medal. This policy lasted for barely four months before the instruction was rescinded.

Awards to recognise acts of bravery by police officers in New Zealand are made nationally in much the same way as they are in the UK with the officers being eligible for the range of civilian awards. Until 1975 the awards were the same in both countries with officers eligible for the George Cross, George Medal, Queens Police Medal for Gallantry, Queens Gallantry Medal or Queen's Commendation for Brave Conduct dependent upon the level of bravery displayed and the other factors which are considered.

In 1976 changes to the New Zealand honours system were proposed with a view to the introduction of a wholly local range of awards. New awards were introduced in the years following until 1999 when approval was granted by the Queen for the new range of awards for New Zealand. These new awards included replacements for the GC, GM, QPM, QGM and Queen's Commendation available to police officers.

The highest honour now available to a New Zealand police officer for bravery is the *New Zealand Cross*, the equivalent of the George Cross, awarded to recognise acts of great bravery in situations of extreme danger. Police officers are rewarded as civilians but there is a higher standard expected of them due to their training, skills and qualifications coupled with a knowledge that the nature of the work is such that the possibility of dangerous situations occurring can reasonably be expected. It is not a new award but a re-designed version of one introduced in 1869 during the Maori Wars of 1860–72 as the equivalent of the Victoria Cross which, at the time, was not available to local volunteer forces or members of the Armed Constabulary. The Governor of New Zealand, Sir George Bowen, was concerned that acts of courage by these forces would not be recognised in the same manner as other troops and authorised the New Zealand Cross by Order-in-Council. He had awarded five crosses before London was informed and received a strong, official rebuke for over-stepping his authority when it became known what he had done. As the awards had already been made Queen Victoria had little option but to ratify the Order-in-Council and give official blessing to the Cross. It was retained as an official medal for many years but was awarded on only 23 occasions before it was withdrawn, the last occasion being in 1910. It is one of the rarest of all bravery medals.

Five members of the Armed Constabulary were awarded the New Zealand Cross—Private Solomon Black,

Sergeant Arthur Carkeek, Captain George Preece, Sergeant Richard Shepherd and Samuel Walker, an Irish born doctor who served with the Constabulary as a surgeon for eight years and took part in 34 engagements against the Maori. He was decorated for attending the wounded whilst under fire in March 1869. Sergeant Shepherd was awarded his cross for the bravery he displayed in defending a narrow path leading to a Maori encampment against superior forces at Otauto on 13 March 1869. He was badly wounded during the action by a bullet which passed through his mouth and neck but held his position until reinforcements arrived. Of the seven men (including Sergeant Shepherd) who were involved, three were killed and the others wounded.

Bravery which merits an honour at the second level is recognised by the silver New Zealand Bravery Star, a new award given for acts of outstanding bravery in situations of danger. At the third and fourth levels of bravery the silver New Zealand Bravery Decoration and bronze New Zealand Bravery Medal are awarded, both new medals. All four honours bring with them a right to the use of post-nominals and all are engraved with the name of the recipient. The ribbons of all awards are basically bright blue, plain for the New Zealand Cross, but with the addition of two, three or four stripes of red ochre to indicate the level of the award on the three others. The use of red ochre is an acknowledgement of the country's Maori tradition where it is considered to be a powerful, spiritual colour. All four awards carry an inscription on the reverse in both English and Maori—FOR BRAVERY—MŌ TE MĀIA.

The enforcement of traffic law and responsibility for road safety in New Zealand fell for many years to a group of officers (Traffic Safety Service) under the control of the Ministry of Transport who were not entitled to the award of the Police Long Service and Good Conduct Medal although there was some similarity in the duties performed. Police officers were not authorised to issue tickets for motoring offences and officers of the MOT had only limited powers of arrest but a responsibility for traffic matters. In 1970 a special medal was authorised for award by the MOT to Traffic Officers, Traffic Instructors, Road Safety Officers and Parking Meter Officers of the MOT to correct this omission in the NZ honours system.

LONG SERVICE AND GOOD CONDUCT (TRAFFIC ENFORCEMENT) MEDAL

Instituted: 28 September 1970.

Ribbon: Light blue with a central white line flanked by black stripes.

Metal: Silver.

Size: 38 mm.

Description: (Obverse) the crest of the NZ Ministry of Transport; (reverse) the words FOR - LONG SERVICE - AND - GOOD CONDUCT - TRAFFIC - ENFORCEMENT in six lines above a pair of fern fronds. The suspender bar is in the shape of a pair of silver fern fronds

The medal was awarded on completion of 15 years service with additional periods of ten years recognised by the award of a bar, also in silver, bearing the total numbers of years—25 or 30. One anomaly of the award was its semi-official status—it was never accorded any place in the order of precedence for the wearing of medals and honours although this was rectified in 1988 when an official replacement medal was authorised.

The length of service necessary to qualify for the new medal was reduced by one year to bring the criteria into line with those applicable to long service awards for the Police Service, Fire Service, Prison Service and military personnel. The bar was re-designed and the extra periods of service amended to fall into line with the other medals. The new bars were silver with a crown placed centrally.

TRAFFIC SERVICE MEDAL

Instituted: 22 December 1988.

Ribbon: *The same as the previous award.*

Metal: *Silver.*

Size: *38 mm.*

Description: *(Obverse) the effigy of Queen Elizabeth wearing the St Edward crown circumscribed by the words ELIZABETH II DEI GRATIA REGINA FID DEF; (reverse) a pair of fern fronds topped by a crown with the words THE - NEW ZEALAND - TRAFFIC SERVICE - MEDAL in the central field in four lines. A plain straight suspender was used.*

In 1992 the two bodies were amalgamated under the control of the New Zealand Police although the early years of the merger were not particularly happy partly because of the reluctance of police officers to assume responsibility for traffic matters. Additional friction was caused by the decision to grant officers and NCOs from the MOT an equivalent rank in the Police Service with responsibilities for which they lacked the necessary training, experience or qualifications. The situation eased with time and as specialist traffic units were established and older officers retired. The Traffic Service Medal was discontinued shortly after the amalgamation although holders are still entitled to wear it. In time, some former MOT officers will become entitled to the NZ Police Long Service and Good Conduct Medal and sport the ribbons of both.

In addition to the national awards made available to police officers there were two locally awarded medals which crop up from time to time albeit very infrequently indeed. In the early 20th century New Zealand experienced a period of industrial unrest which started with a six-month long miners' strike in the gold mining town of Waihi during which a regular police officer was shot and one of the striking ringleaders beaten to death. The strike ended in defeat for the miners but the resentment of the workers simmered until further disputes broke out at coal mines in Huntly and the wharves at Wellington and Auckland in late 1913. Prime Minister William Massey was determined to end the power of the unions finally and established two groups of special constables, made up in the main of farm workers, to crush the strikers. The decision to use special constables was taken partly out of a distrust of the loyalty of regular officers following an attempt to form an association (later prohibited) to improve the police conditions of service.

The most feared, and ruthless, of the two bodies was the Mounted Special Constabulary, dubbed Massey's Cossacks, who took to their task of fighting the strikers with a gusto that earned them a hatred and notoriety which was to persist for years. The Special Foot Constabulary were equally as ruthless but less reviled although reports of drunkenness, the indiscriminate discharge of firearms and the beating of strikers and public alike abounded. Although the commemoration of the bitter and divisive industrial disputes would seem to be an unlikely reason for the issue of a medal, Auckland City Council in the far north of North Island produced two, one to each of the two bodies. Both medals are scarce, those awarded to the Foot Special Constabulary especially so, and there is very little documentation about either.

MOUNTED SPECIAL CONSTABULARY MEDAL 1913

Instituted: 1913.

Ribbon: None.

Metal: Bronze.

Size: 29 mm.

Description: (Obverse) a figure of a mounted constable holding a baton in his right hand within an outer circle bearing the legend SPECIAL CONSTABULARY (upper) and MOUNTED (lower) around the circumference, the two inscriptions separated by two stars; (reverse) the shield from the coat of arms of Auckland flanked by laurel branches above a scroll bearing the motto ADVANCE all within an outer band inscribed AUCKLAND NOV 1913. A small ring was attached to the top of the disc although the medal was never intended to be worn with a ribbon. The medals are usually inscribed with the name of the recipient on the reverse.

The medal awarded to members of the Foot Special Constabulary has an identical reverse but the word FOOT at the lower circumference of the obverse and a standing figure of a constable in the centre holding his baton in a fashion which has been described as positively obscene.

In common with a great many countries, in recent years New Zealand has contributed to a number of peacekeeping missions conducted under the authority of the United Nations with civilian police officers being amongst those who have served. One of the most recent of these UN missions and one of the closest to New Zealand has been in East Timor in an attempt to solve the long standing dispute between the East Timorese people and Indonesia.

New Zealand has sent members of its Defence Force, Police Service and civilian advisors since the mission was opened in 1999 and has marked their contribution with the introduction of a special medal, the first occasion in the country in which a specific award has been made. Prior to this, any involvement by NZ personnel has entitled them only to the appropriate UN medal.

EAST TIMOR MEDAL

Instituted: 25 April 2000.

Ribbon: A broad dark green central band flanked by narrow red stripes, wider black bands and white edge stripes.

Metal: Silvered alloy.

Size: 36 mm.

Description: (Obverse) the effigy of Queen Elizabeth with the words ELIZABETH II QUEEN OF NEW ZEALAND around the circumference; (reverse) the head of a kiwi facing right overshadowing a map of East Timor with the words EAST TIMOR below and a branch of olive above. A plain straight suspender is used.

The mission saw the involvement of more than 1,500 civilian police officers from 41 countries including contingents from New Zealand. The first deployment of NZ police officers was made in June 1999 to act as advisors to the Indonesian Police in providing a secure environment for the ballot and supervising the security of the ballot boxes. Following the outcome of the ballot and the overwhelming desire of the East Timor people for independence, two further deployments were made to help maintain law and order as the transition took place. The third deployment comprised a team of ten officers including two trainers to help develop the newly formed East Timorese Police.

The medal is awarded to members of the NZ Defence Force, police officers and civilian personnel who serve in the operational area for one day or more, seven days afloat or at least 30 days of continuous or aggregated service of a temporary nature after 19 June 1999. The first investiture took place in the NZ Parliament, Wellington on 28 March 2001. More than 2,000 awards have been made including several to police officers.

In addition to East Timor, New Zealand has a small presence—two officers—working in Bougainville on a community policing project to train local officers to a standard which will enable them to re-establish basic law and order on the island. Prior to these two most recent deployments, officers from New Zealand had served in UN missions in Cyprus, Namibia, Vanuatu and Cambodia. There were no special medals introduced to mark these events.

COOK ISLANDS POLICE

The Cook Islands are a group of 24 coral atolls and volcanic islands spread over more than six million square kilometres of the Pacific Ocean lying 3,500 kilometres north-east of New Zealand with a population of approximately 18,000. They were claimed for the Crown in 1901. They achieved self-government in 1965 but remain in free association in New Zealand and, until 1986, relied upon that government to defend them as a part of the ANZUS alliance although they now look to France to provide surveillance in their territorial waters as a part of the friendship treaty signed between the two countries in 1991.

The policing arrangements on the islands follow the British constabulary model in most respects including the adoption of a long service and good conduct medal to reward police officers there for their service. In 1947 the unofficial medal awarded in New Zealand was introduced into the islands without any changes and this included the initials NZ on the obverse which was ultimately thought to be inappropriate if the identity of the islands was to be safeguarded. In 1963 amendments were made which resulted in a design that was more distinctive although the medal itself was unchanged. The most significant change was to the ribbon—white with a narrow central dark blue stripe flanked by white lines and broader bands of red—to represent the Cook Islands' flag. A top brooch bar was also added which bore the words COOK ISLANDS in relief. The medals were engraved on the lower rim with the recipient's full name and date he joined the Force. The medals were awarded after only eight years service.

When the position of the New Zealand medal was formalised in 1976 the Cook Islands Government considered that the time was right to look at changes which could be made to the medal awarded in the islands. In 1981 a design was approved by the Queen's Cook Islands representative and the first 14 issues were made. These medals were of silver-plated plastic although this was only meant to be a temporary measure with the use of brass as the basic metal being introduced for awards made thereafter. The obverse carried the police badge in the form of a partial wreath of palm fronds joined at the base with a pair of crossed adzes in the centre and a crown at the top. A chief's stool is superimposed over the adzes with the words POLICE COOK ISLANDS below. The suspension bar is of a somewhat unusual shallow V shaped design.

NIUE, TOKELAU AND WESTERN SAMOA

In addition to the Cook Islands, New Zealand currently has one other associated territory (Niue) and a dependent territory (Tokelau) and once had responsibility for a third (Western Samoa) which it controlled under a United Nations Trusteeship until it was granted independence in 1962. The authority for the entitlement of police officers in these three countries to the New Zealand Police Medal and its replacement is somewhat unclear although there is no doubt that the entitlement exists and a number of medals were awarded.

The island of Niue lies almost 3,000 kilometres NNE of New Zealand and was originally annexed in 1901 along with the Cook Islands but granted self-government in 1974. It is a small island (264 sq km) with a population of approximately 2,000. Before the NZ Police Medal became obsolete in 1976, nine medals, two first bars and one second bar had been awarded. The only difference to the medal awarded in New Zealand was the addition of a top clasp inscribed NIUE in similar fashion to those first awarded in the Cook Islands. Police officers in Niue are currently entitled to the replacement medal introduced in 1976.

Tokelau consists of three islands with a total area of slightly under 11 square kilometres and a population of approximately 1,500. The islands lie 600 km further north than Niue and have been under New Zealand control since 1925. A single police officer from the islands was awarded the NZ Police Medal in 1955. The medal was not altered in any way.

The six islands which make up the current independent state of Samoa were initially under German control although they were taken under New Zealand authority shortly after the outbreak of the Great War. Full independence was achieved in 1962. In 1933 the entitlement of officers from the Samoan Constabulary to the NZ Police Medal was raised and it was initially suggested that a special medal should be struck for them. A design for a medal was even put forward but rejected and authority was eventually given to the award of the NZ medal, thirteen years after the question was first raised. From then until independence in 1962 a total of 15 medals, five first bars and three second bars were awarded. During the fourteen year period officers were rewarded for each ten years satisfactory service with the issue of a small silver five-point star which they wore on the right side of their tunics.

The design for the special medal proposed in 1946 had the badge of Western Samoa as carried on the British Blue Ensign (the colony's flag) consisting of a beach scene with three palm trees placed in the upper half with the words SAMOAN CONSTABULARY above and beneath a line across the centre of the medal a further inscription FOR LONG SERVICE AND GOOD CONDUCT. There was no suggestion for the design or colouring of the ribbon or what should be shown on the obverse. The idea went no further than a hand-drawing. After independence was achieved regulations were introduced by the new government for the award of a long service medal but not pursued.

PAPUA NEW GUINEA

Papua New Guinea (PNG) is an interesting country with a population of more than four million and covered mostly by dense tropical forests much of which is still isolated. The island of New Guinea was first colonised by the Dutch in 1824 although it had come to the interest of Europeans 300 years earlier when the Portuguese made the first contact. It was of little importance to European colonists until the Dutch sought to expand their interests in the East Indies and settled the western half of the island in what is now part of Indonesia (Irian Jaya). The north of the eastern half was occupied by the Germans in 1884 with the British declaring the south of the eastern half as their territory four days later although total annexation did not happen for a further four years. In 1906 British New Guinea was renamed Papua and control handed to Australia which had achieved independence from Britain shortly before (1901). Policing of the colony was the responsibility of the Royal Papua Constabulary (RPC) with officers there being eligible for British medals and awards for any acts of courage or particularly meritorious service.

On the outbreak of the Great War the German territory in the north was taken over by Australian troops and control formally passed to Australia as a mandated territory by the League of Nations in 1920. Policing of the former German colony became the responsibility of the New Guinea Native Constabulary and remained so until the entry of Japan into the Second World War and the occupation of part of the colony and mandated territory. One consequence of the Japanese invasion was the demise of the New Guinea Native Constabulary as a separate force leaving the RPC responsible for policing the whole of the eastern half of the island. The Japanese advance was stemmed by allied troops south of the Owen Stanley range of mountains and the work of police officers from the new combined force was primarily involved in assisting allied troops. The emergency highlighted the difference which existed between the methods of acknowledging acts of courage by officers from the two different forces which existed before the start of the Second World War. As a mandated territory officers from the New Guinea Native Constabulary were not entitled to British awards and an attempt to rectify this was first introduced in 1930 with a badge available to any native member of the Constabulary who performed an act of conspicuous bravery involving a risk to his life in the course of his duty.

NEW GUINEA NATIVE CONSTABULARY VALOUR BADGE

Instituted: 1930.

Ribbon: Not intended to be worn with a ribbon.

Metal: Silver plated brass.

Size: 38 mm.

Description: (Obverse) a circular badge with the words NEW GUINEA POLICE FORCE around the upper circumference and NATIVE CONSTABULARY around the lower. The legend FOR BRAVERY was inscribed in two lines in the central field; (reverse) left blank.

At the height of resistance to the Japanese advance a proposal was put forward to regularise the situation between the two sections of the Police Service and introduce a replacement valour badge which would be available to all officers irrespective of whether they served in Papua or the mandated territory of New Guinea. The criteria for the award of the badge were unchanged and the design was very similar to the previous award.

PAPUA AND NEW GUINEA NATIVE POLICE VALOUR BADGE

Instituted: 30 June 1940.

Ribbon: Not intended to be worn with a ribbon.

Metal: Sterling silver.

Size: 38 mm.

Description: (Obverse) a circular badge with the words PAPUA-NEW GUINEA around the upper circumference and NATIVE POLICE around the lower. The legend FOR BRAVERY was inscribed in two lines in the central field; (reverse) two palm trees in the upper half with a punched number below. The word NATIVE was removed in 1953.

It is believed that 28 officers were awarded the badge in 1945 and 1946 although large numbers of unissued badges were later sold to collectors. The situation of awards made to police officers is confused by the fact that some were awarded British honours (one George Medal and five BEMs) and there was a further award (Papua New Guinea Loyal Service Medal) available which was intended for civilians and not members of the RPC although 24 were awarded to them between 1942 when it was first awarded and October 1944 when it was formally established and the eligibility of police officers finally made clear—they were not entitled to it.

The end of the Second World War and the return of normality did not see the end of the bravery badge although there were no awards after 1946. The position of the mandated territory of New Guinea was decided after 1945 when the eastern half of the island and several offshore islands became the Territory of Papua and New Guinea (PNG).

In 1963 the Dutch East Indies (the western half of the island) was incorporated into Indonesia and, ten years later, PNG was granted self-government. Full independence was achieved in 1975.

In the 1960s, before independence was under consideration the Valour Badge was discontinued and replaced by a medal with very similar criteria but intended to bring the reward for local officers for acts of courage more in line with that available for western officers. Eleven officers were awarded the medal between 1965 and 1975.

ROYAL PAPUA AND NEW GUINEA CONSTABULARY POLICE VALOUR MEDAL

Instituted: 1965.

Ribbon: Green with a central band of blue flanked by bands of red.

Metal: Bronze.

Size: 36 mm.

Description: (Obverse) the Red-plumed Bird of Paradise facing left with the name of the Force in a scroll on which the bird is perching and the words POLICE VALOUR MEDAL around the upper circumference; (reverse) two palm trees to the left and right with the words FOR BRAVERY in two lines between them. A plain straight suspender was used.

Police officers in PNG, before the introduction of the Colonial Police Medal for Gallantry in 1938, had been entitled to the award of the King's Police Medal although it was awarded to an officer of the Native Constabulary on a single occasion only. Senior Sergeant Gaiberi had served for more than 40 years when he won the medal following a disturbance in 1930 in which five police officers were faced by a angry group of villagers numbering almost 500 who refused to believe that the deaths of 18 of their number were accidental. Sergeant Gaiberi died before he could receive his medal although it was presented to his widow. He was buried with great honour.

In line with most former colonies, Papua-New Guinea issued a special medal to celebrate independence which was awarded to distinguished current residents or former residents of the country and persons serving in a number of organisations on the day of independence if they had given outstanding or meritorious service. This included 3,464 officers of the RPNGC. In total, more than 12,000 were awarded.

INDEPENDENCE MEDAL

Instituted: 2 September 1975.

Ribbon: Red flanked by narrow stripes of gold, white and black.

Metal: Cupro-nickel.

Size: 36 mm.

Description: (Obverse) the crowned head of Queen Elizabeth II surrounded by the words ELIZABETH II DEI GRATIA REGINA FD; (reverse) the national emblem (the Red-plumed Bird of Paradise facing forward) with the words PAPUA NEW GUINEA above and INDEPENDENCE 1975 below. A ring suspender was used attached to the top of the disc.

On the tenth anniversary of the achievement of independence a second medal was issued and awarded to those who had contributed to the development of the country after 1975, a group which included members of the Royal Papua New Guinea Constabulary. The medal was designed by superintendent David Pringuer from the Force. 10,500 medals were awarded.

TENTH ANNIVERSARY OF INDEPENDENCE MEDAL

Instituted: 1985.

Ribbon: White flanked by stripes of black, orange and yellow.

Metal: Cupro-nickel.

Size: 36 mm.

Description: (Obverse) the crowned head of Queen Elizabeth II surrounded by the words QUEEN ELIZABETH PAPUA NEW GUINEA; (reverse) the national emblem with the words INDEPENDENCE 1975 - 1985.

A further commemorative medal was issued in 1988, on this occasion in celebration of 100 years of the Constabulary. It was awarded to officers of all ranks who were serving on the anniversary.

ROYAL PAPUA NEW GUINEA CONSTABULARY CENTENARY COMMEMORATIVE MEDAL

Instituted: 7 July 1988.

Ribbon: Navy blue with a central white stripe (2 mm) flanked by narrow (2 mm) stripes of yellow, black and red.

Metal: Rhodium plated cupro-nickel.

Size: 36 mm.

Description: (Obverse) the badge of the Constabulary placed centrally with an outer wreath of laurel leaves and the dates 1888 - 1988 at the lower circumference; (reverse) the words ONE HUNDRED - YEARS OF - COMMUNITY SERVICE in four lines in the central field and Constabulary name around the circumference. A ring suspender was used.

The badge of the Constabulary is in the form of a wreath of laurel topped by a Queen's crown enclosing a bird of paradise flying left with the Force name in two banners across the lower half. The medal was awarded to selected officers who had served for a continuous period of 20 months or more on the anniversary date and to others who had given distinguished service or support at the discretion of the Commandant.

The bird of paradise depicted is one of a group of birds of such beauty that they were said to have come from paradise when knowledge of them and samples of their skins first arrived in Spain in the 16th century. They are found only on the islands around New Guinea and some are so extraordinary that it took some time before scientists accepted that the skins they were seeing were real. One of the most unusual is the King of Saxony Bird of Paradise, a small bird, only 20 or so centimetres long, with black and yellow plumage and two long plumes trailing from its head that are twice the body length. Each plume has up to 40 small flag-like feathers, brown on the inside and bright blue on the outside. It was first described in 1894 from a specimen found in a Paris market but for several years ornithologists refused to believe it was real and thought it had been manufactured for the fashion trade in the city.

Papua New Guinea is also home to the only poisonous birds currently known to science although their recent discovery (1992) suggests that there may well be others. To date six species have been identified with toxins in their plumage very similar to that found on the arrow poison frogs of South America. An ornithologist who was bitten by a captured Hooded Pitohui made the unpleasant discovery when he put his injured hand to his mouth and was surprised to find his lips going numb and a burning sensation around his mouth. The local people were less surprised, they knew all about the "rubbish bird" and avoided them.

The toxic effect of touching the plumage is thought to be a defensive mechanism for the birds and possibly their eggs which are preyed on by tree-dwelling snakes. Although the origin of the toxins is not known with any degree of certainty it is thought to come from the bird's diet of ants, millipedes, termites and other insects. The plumage of all six known species is bright and vivid, perhaps a warning to predators that they have an unpleasant taste, a feature common amongst insects but not thought to exist in birds where brightly coloured plumage was always considered to be found in males as an aid to winning a mate.

Police Medals of the World

The species on the badge of the RPNGC and the RPNGC Police Valour Medal of 1965 is the Red-plumed Bird of Paradise, a large bird (45 cm) with brown plumage, a yellow nape and head, bright green throat feathers and long red plumes extending well beyond its tail. None of the birds of paradise are common and the number of species is not known accurately, some have never been seen in the wild by ornithologists and are only known to exist from one or two skins collected by local people with no supporting data at all.

Papua New Guinea is an independent country although it is a member of the British Commonwealth and the British monarch remains as the head of state. The effigy of Queen Elizabeth II appears on the obverse of the long service and good conduct medal awarded to police officers which was introduced at the achievement of independence when eligibility for the Colonial Police Medal was withdrawn.

LONG SERVICE AND GOOD CONDUCT MEDAL

Instituted: 1975.

Ribbon: Fifteen equal stripes of white (eight) and blue (seven).

Metal: Cupro-nickel.

Size: 36 mm.

Description: (Obverse) the head of the Queen wearing the St Edward crown with the legend PAPUA NEW GUINEA (left) and QUEEN ELIZABETH II (right) around the circumference; (reverse) plain apart from the inscription FOR - LONG SERVICE - AND GOOD - CONDUCT in four lines. A plain straight suspender bar is used.

page 258

The next medal is included as a curiosity although there is evidence that it did exist and was presented to three people on a single occasion reported in early 1900 although there is some confusion over the sequence of its introduction, presentation and subsequent withdrawal from use just over a year after it was first announced.

BRITISH NEW GUINEA GOOD CONDUCT MEDAL

Instituted: 27 October 1899.

Ribbon: Crimson with a dark blue central band.

Metal: Silver.

Size: 36 mm.

Description: (Obverse) the Veiled Head of Queen Victoria with no inscription; (reverse) a wreath of laurel surmounted by an imperial crown with the words BRITISH - NEW GUINEA - GOOD CONDUCT - MEDAL in four lines in a banner in the central field. The medal was suspended from a bar with curved ends attached by a plain claw fitting.

The medal was intended for members of the Armed Native Constabulary of British New Guinea of any rank as a reward for acts of bravery or to NCOs and constables on completion of twelve years service with good character and without having served a term of imprisonment. Bars inscribed with the place and date of the act were given where the award was made for gallantry and were also available for any second or subsequent act of bravery. A second award for meritorious service bearing the words MERITORIOUS SERVICE MEDAL on the reverse in place of the legend LONG SERVICE MEDAL was proposed and a specimen produced although it was never introduced.

Notice of the medal was given on 16 December 1899 with the publication of regulations dated 31 October. The medal had been approved four days earlier. In April 1900 notification of the first (and only) award to the Force Commandant and two local NCOs was published, giving the date of the award as 30 October 1899, the day before the regulations were dated. On 24 January 1901 a further notice was published in the *British New Guinea Government Gazette* directing that regulations were suspended until further notice. Nothing more was heard and the medal never appeared again. An interesting tale, factually correct, but with questions which will remain unanswered.

Papua-New Guinea is the most linguistically diverse country in the world, more so even than India, the second most populous country in the world with a population which has recently topped one billion. There are more than 750 separate local languages in PNG and an official language—Pidgin English—that has an interesting origin and is often amusing to western ears. Pidgin (also spelt pigin, pigeon or pidjin) is usually based on a western European language, very often English but also using French, which evolved as a method of communication between groups without a common tongue, most commonly the colonists or settlers and the local people. The multiplicity of languages in Papua New Guinea led, inevitably, to the development of Pidgin there which became one of the official languages.

The vocabulary of Pidgin is limited and the grammar greatly simplified—it is a method of spoken communication with the need for complex rules and literature much reduced. In Papua New Guinea, a policeman is a "polisman", the police station the "polis stesin" and the post office is the "pos opis". The derivation of the language is not hard to understand and there are some amusing aspects—no smoking, for example, is "no ken smok", to be dismissed or sacked is "autim long wok", Europeans are referred to as either "mastamisis" or "ol waitman" and to ask someone's name you say "kolim nem bilong yu".

POLAND

It is all too easy in the west to think of Poland in terms of its recent past and forget that it was once a large and powerful kingdom with territory that stretched from the Baltic to the Black Sea and included Lithuania, large areas of Belorussia and a substantial part of the Ukraine. The country has suffered over the centuries as a result of its position and has been conquered, partitioned and reduced in size many times—on one occasion in the late 18th century, it disappeared as a separate state completely after war with Prussia and Russia, a familiar tale.

The recent history of policing in Poland falls into four distinct periods starting with the declaration of the Second Republic on 7 October 1918. This lasted for barely 20 years until the country was invaded once more, this time by Nazi Germany, on 1 September 1939 heralding the start of the Second World War. Occupation lasted for six long years only to be followed by a period of communist government when the country was effectively occupied by the Soviet Union until 1989 when democracy returned. Poland suffered more than most during the War with the greatest loss of life (more than six million), the longest period under occupation and the greatest damage caused. In all this time, however, there was never any collaboration with the invaders and no Polish unit ever fought alongside the Nazis, unlike every other occupied country.

The first truly Polish police force was established on 24 July 1919 shortly after the Second Republic came into existence and was organised along traditional lines with its primary purpose being to fight crime. After the invasion by the Nazis in 1939 many thousands of Polish police officers died and almost 12,000 were captured by the Soviet forces and ended up in prison camps which very few left alive. In the spring of 1940 more than 6,000 were murdered by the Red Army and buried in mass graves, a truth which only came to light after 1989 and the end of communist rule. The officers who survived the invasion from the west by the Nazis and east by the Soviets were offered the opportunity to continue their work under German administration but few took up the offer and those who did helped the Polish underground in their resistance of the occupiers—many died as a result. The total number of Polish police officers who died at the hands of the Germans and Soviets between 1939 and 1944 is estimated at more than 20,000.

Although there was a range of long-standing orders, decorations and medals available to members of the Polish Armed Services it was not a Polish tradition to award long service medals. Service by the military, police or any other of the Polish disciplined forces in a particular area or in particular circumstances was recognised by the award of a badge worn below any medals that had been won. A year's service on the northern front, for example, was rewarded with the Northern Front Badge.

There were no special service medals available to police officers although the military principle of awarding badges was followed. The first true long service medal was introduced in 1938 but was short-lived due to the outbreak of war, the Nazi occupation and the subsequent communist government which introduced its own system of rewarding long service. *The Long Service Medal* was not an exclusively police award and was also made available to the armed forces, fire service and many national or local government servants.

MEDAL ZA DLUGOLETNIA SLUZBE

Instituted: 8 January 1938.

Ribbon: Claret with a broad white central band.

Metal: Silver and bronze.

Size: 35 mm.

Description: (Obverse) a circular medal with the Polish eagle emblem placed centrally surrounded by a wreath opening out at the top into ears of wheat. The words ZNA DLUGOLETNIA SLUZBE (for long service) are inscribed around the lower circumference; (reverse) a spray of laurel leaves in the lowerhalf with the Roman numerals X (bronze, 10 years) or XX (silver, 20 years) above. A ring suspender was used.

The ribbon for both classes was the same with the difference when worn in undress uniform being signified by the use of the appropriate Roman numerals in silver or bronze placed centrally. A third class of medal was authorised—in gilt for thirty years service—but never produced or awarded following the outbreak of war. Only service from 11 November 1918 was counted.

Ten years after the achievement of independence a special commemorative medal was authorised to mark the occasion. The *Medal to Commemorate Ten Years of Independence* was awarded to all Polish citizens who had served in the armed forces between 1918 and 1928 and to others who had served at least five years in a range of government institutions, including the police.

MEDAL 10-LECIA ODZYSKANIA NIEPODLEGLOSCI

Instituted: 27 September 1928.

Ribbon: Light blue.

Metal: Bronze.

Size: 35 mm.

Description: (Obverse) the head of Marshal Jozef Pilsudski, the architect of Polish independence after the Great War, facing left; (reverse) a figure representing a ploughman caring for an oak tree and removing a weed with the years 1918–1928 below. A ring suspender was used.

Police Medals of the World

Acts of courage performed by police officers at the risk of their lives in defence of the law, state frontiers, human life or property was recognised by the award of the *Cross of Merit for Bravery* introduced in 1928 and retained throughout the different régimes since—it remains current today.

KRZYZ ZASLUGI ZA DZIELNOSC

Instituted: 7 March 1928.

Ribbon: Maroon a pale grey stripe near each edge and a diagonal (upper left to lower right) stripe of green and dark blue.

Metal: Silver with maroon enamel.

Size: 40 mm.

Description: (Obverse) a Maltese cross with ball finials, the arms are enamelled in maroon and bear the words ZA - DZEIL - NOSC (for bravery) on the three upper ones in gold with the spaces between the arms carrying five rays. The central medallion has the letters RP (Rzeczpospolita Polska—Polish Republic) at the centre on a white background surrounded by a ring of enamel and a further gold-coloured band. .

During the War the award of the cross was maintained by the government in exile in London although production was returned to Poland in 1945 under the communist régime with the initials in the central medallion being amended to read PRL—*Polska Rzeczpospolita Ludowa* (Polish People's Republic). The dark blue and green diagonal stripe used to indicate the award was for bravery was altered in 1945 to a central vertical band.

The award is a specially produced variant of a pre-existing medal which dated from 1923. It was introduced in three classes (gold, silver and bronze) and was awarded freely to a wide cross section of the Polish people for achievements in sport, business, art, science, charitable work and even for long marriage or to women for bearing many children.

Poland

The concept of rewarding couples who had remained together for 50 years (provided they had at least one child) or who had a certain number of children with a medal may seem strange to people in the UK but it is not unique to Poland. In France, the long-established (since 26 May 1920) *Médaille de la Famille Française* is awarded in three classes to the mothers of 4 or 5 children (bronze), 6 or 7 children (silver) or in gold to those with more than eight.

The award of the *Cross of Merit* in Poland to recognise the achievement of 50 years of marriage to the same person was discontinued in 1960 and a special medal —*Medal for Long Marital Life*— instituted to couples who celebrated their golden wedding anniversary. Although it was introduced during the period of the communist régime the medal remains current today.

MEDAL ZA DLUGOLETNIE POZYCIE MALZENSKIE

Instituted: *17 February 1960.*

Ribbon: *Pink with a central white stripe.*

Metal: *Silver.*

Size: *35 mm.*

Description: *(Obverse) a cross with six arms with squared ends and the spaces between them carrying an ornamental design. The central medallion shows two crossed roses in silver on pink enamel; (reverse) the letters PRL in the centre (changed to PR in 1990) with the words ZA DLUGOLETNIE POZYCIE MALZENSKIE (for long marital life) around the circumference.*

As the outcome of the Second World War became inevitable so did the future of the Polish people—they were to become part of the Soviet sphere of influence and faced what turned out to be a further 45 years of occupation by a foreign power in all but name. The name and rôle of the former Polish State Police were also changed—they became the People's Militia (*Milicja Obywatelska*) with similar objectives to the former organisation in principle but with little or no freedom to select their own officers and an overriding responsibility to the security of the state rather than the people.

The majority of orders, decorations and medals that were available during the Second Republic were continued after 1945 under the new rulers although a number of new awards were authorised. After the demise of the communist régime in 1990 and the establishment of the Third Republic authorisation was given for recipients of communist awards to continue wearing them with one exception. Wearing the *Medal for the Struggle in the Defence of the People's Rule* was not acceptable to the people or the new rulers.

MEDAL ZA UDZIAL W WALKACH W OBRONIE WLADZY LUDOWEJ

Instituted: 22 November 1983.

Ribbon: Red with a white stripe at each edge and a green band towards the edges.

Metal: Silver.

Size: 38 mm.

Description: (Obverse) an eagle with outstretched wings superimposed on a banner and a pair of crossed laurel sprays all superimposed over a downward pointing sword. The words MANIFEST PKWN 1944 appear below the eagles and banner. The emblem is taken from the heading of a document produced in 1944 at the time that the new communist Polish government was established in 1944. The words of the inscription in full mean MANIFEST OF THE POLISH COMMITTEE OF NATIONAL LIBERATION; (reverse) a shield with the initials PRL superimposed on a map of Poland and the inscription UCZESTNIKOM WALK W OBRONIE WLADZY LUDOWEJ (to participants in the struggle in defence of people's rule) around the circumference.

The struggle referred to occurred in the 1940s and 50s as the new government sought to exert its authority under the watchful eye of Stalin in the Soviet Union using methods which would have brought his approval. Very similar to the period of terror under Stalin, all opposition to the Polish government was put down ruthlessly and many died, disappeared or, if they were lucky, sent into exile. The medal was awarded to any Polish citizen who supported the government and actively assisted in the repression. Most recipients were soldiers, members of the People's Militia, the political police or communist party members. There is little wonder that this medal was not authorised for wear when the communist era came to an end.

Poland

Two medals awarded to police officers during the communist era were discontinued in 1990 with the change to democratic rule and the replacement of the Peoples Militia by the State Police although holders are permitted to wear the ribbons and medals on appropriate occasions. Neither award has been replaced. The first was a form of long service award available to members of the Militia and security services in recognition of 10 (bronze), 20 (silver) or 30 (gold) years service. The *Decoration for Service to the Nation* replaced two previous decorations issued after 10 and 20 years which were both pinback medals worn on the right side of the uniform.

ODZNAKA W SLUZBIE NARODU

Instituted: 12 May 1974.

Ribbon: Blue flanked by bands of red and white.

Metal: Gold, silver and bronze.

Description: *(Obverse) a circular medal with the Polish eagle superimposed on a sword (point downwards) and a partial wreath of oak leaves around the circumference. At the base, superimposed over the point of the sword is a small tablet with the appropriate number of years service in Roman numerals—X, XX or XXX. The lower part of the wreath is over-written with the words W SLUZBIE (left) and NARODU (right)— in the service of the nation; (reverse) the initials MSW (for Ministerstwo Spraw Wewnetrznych—Ministry of the Interior) with a sprig of eight laurel leaves above and below. Around the circumference are the words POLSKA RZECZPOSPOLITA LUDOWA (Polish Peoples Republic). A simple ring suspender is used.*

The second of the two awards (*Decoration of Merit for the Protection of Public Order*) was issued in recognition of particularly meritorious service in the field of the preservation of public order, law enforcement and general service to the state. It was available to members of the public in addition to the Militia and security services. It could also be given to groups of people, official bodies and organisations. It was also awarded in three grades—gold, silver and bronze—with the class being dependent on the level and quality of the service being recognised.

ODZNAKA ZA ZASŁUGI W OCHRONIE PORZĄDKU PUBLICZNEGO

Instituted: 15 October 1971.

Ribbon: Dark blue with a broad red central band and a white stripe towards each edge.

Metal: Gold, silver and bronze.

Description: (Obverse) a circular medal with a stylised Polish eagle in a shield superimposed on a twelve-point star with rounded ends; (reverse) the name of the medal in four lines placed centrally with a sprig of three laurel leaves above and below. The initials PRL are inscribed at the base. A simple ring suspender is used.

With the demise of the communist government and establishment of the new police service in Poland, the medals available to officers has been restricted to the Cross of Merit which can be awarded for bravery and distinguished or meritorious service. Whether any long service awards are introduced remains to be seen but Polish history and tradition suggests that they might.

PORTUGAL

The history of the Republic of Portugal in the 20th century was volatile, starting with the overthrow of the monarchy in 1910 which was followed by 16 years of parliamentary democracy which was marked by restlessness amongst the military, a desire in some quarters to restore the monarchy, a civil war and the most unstable parliamentary régime in western Europe. In the space of the 16 years there were 44 changes of government. The patience of the military finally ran out in 1926, a bloodless coup was mounted and western Europe's most long-lived dictatorship was established. The authoritarian system under Prime Minister Salazar lasted until 1974 and the latter years saw the economy grow at a rate which was exceptional for what was, at the time, western Europe's poorest country. The oil crisis and a period of inflation in 1973 coupled with the cost of three colonial wars took their toll and precipitated a second revolution.

Most of 1974 and 1975 was typified by political and social instability although the revolution itself had met with little resistance from any quarter and was broadly welcomed by the people. A new constitution was approved in early 1976 which led, ultimately, to the establishment of the stable government of modern Portugal.

Apart from the special force responsible for border duties, there are three arms to the Portuguese Police Service—the *Policia de Seguraça Pública* (Public Security Police—PSP), the *Policia Judiciaria* (Judicial Police) and the *Guarda Nacional Republicana* (National Republican Guard) which operates in a rôle very similar to the Carabinieri in Italy and the Gendarmerie Nationale in France.

Officers from all policing agencies in Portugal are eligible for three different medals awarded in recognition of distinguished service, merit or long service. There is a further medal awarded for good conduct which is available only to officers from the PSP. The highest award is the *Distinguished Service Medal* awarded for individual or collective acts of outstanding service, leadership or bravery which result in a mention in official documents.

MEDALHA DE SERVIÇOS DISTINTOS DA SEGURANÇA PÚBLICA

Instituted: 12 May 1982.

Ribbon: Half black, half white.

Metal: Gold and silver.

Size: 45 mm.

Description: (Obverse) a Greek cross with the ends of the arms widening out to form a partial triangle with a central medallion bearing the Coat of Arms of Portugal within an outer band inscribed with the words REPÚBLICA PORTUGUESA; (reverse) the same shape but with the central medallion having the inscription MEDALHA DA SEGURANÇA PÚBLICA and the date 1926 in the outer band. In the central disc are the words SERVIÇOS DISTINTOS above two branches of laurel. A simple ring suspender is used attached to the upper arm of the cross.

The criteria for the award of the two classes available differ only in the nature of the document which contains the official mention of the act which merits the award of the medal. The gold award is given if the act merits a mention in the national *Diàrio da República* (similar to the *London Gazette* in the UK) and the silver if the mention is recorded in police despatches only. The award of either class of medal brings with it an unusual benefit - the gold award cancels all disciplinary matters which are preventing a promotion and the silver the cancellation of all disciplinary matters for the preceding ten years.

Police Medals of the World

The second medal is awarded in four classes according to the rank of the recipient, a common feature of the Portuguese honours system. The regulations which apply to the award of the *Medal of Merit* are complex although the basic requirements are for qualities of devotion to duty, self-sacrifice, good character, ability and the performance of duty with dignity and morality over a period which depends on length of service which differs with rank. Officers can also qualify for the medal by receiving commendations from three different sources—the Minister of the Interior (one), the commanding general of their particular force (three) or their immediate commanding officer (five).

MEDALHA DE MÉRITO DA SEGURANÇA PÚBLICA

Instituted: 12 May 1982.

Ribbon: Three blue and two silver stripes, all of equal width.

Metal: Gold, silver and enamel.

Description: (Obverse) the Coat of Arms of Portugal as a central medallion with an outer band bearing the name of the country—REPÚBLICA PORTUGUESA—in gold letters on a blue background. The medallion is superimposed on a silver star with only the points visible which are themselves superimposed on a wreath of laurel in gold; (reverse) the same basic design but with the central medallion showing a police sword (point upwards) within a wreath of laurel and the words SEGURANÇA PÚBLICA (left and right) and MÉRITO (below) in the outer band also in gold on blue. A simple ring suspender attached to the point of the upper arm of the star is used.

The first class award is made to officers of the rank of captain and above with at least 20 years service and is signified by the use of a device on the ribbon in the form of a six-point star in gold on a blue background within a wreath of laurel in gold. The second class award is available to junior officers with at least 12 years service and is indicated by the same emblem worn on the ribbon but with the star in silver. For the third and fourth class awards made to NCOs (ten years service) and constables (five years service) the gold laurel wreath on the medal in changed to silver and a simple star in gold or silver is worn on the ribbon.

There is one other idiosyncrasy relevant only to members of the PSP. For officers from that force, irrespective of the class, the star worn on the ribbon has five points rather than six for historical and heraldic reasons.

page 268

The third of the three medals available to officers from all branches of the Portuguese Police Service was introduced shortly after the 1926 revolution although the design was changed in 1982 when the regulations were renewed. The *Long Service Medal* is of more simple design than the two higher awards—a circular silver piece first awarded after ten years service but with stars available to indicate each subsequent ten years. There is a proviso in the regulations that recipients should have held a command rôle or worked a proportion of their time on active duties rather than being office bound and this requirement will disqualify many officers in administrative rôles. For the first award after ten years, two-thirds of the officer's time must have been spent on active duties and for the awards after 20 and 30 years this is reduced to half.

MEDALHA DE ASSIDUIDADE DA SEGURANÇA PÚBLICA

Instituted: 30 November 1929.

Ribbon: Five black and four white vertical stripes, all of equal width.

Metal: Silver.

Size; 38 mm.

Description: (Obverse) a female head symbolic of the Republic facing right with the words REPÚBLICA (left) and PORTUGUESA (right) in the upper circumference; (reverse) a circular band of oak leaves with the words SEGURANÇA PÚBLICA at the upper circumference and ASSIDUIDADE and the bottom. Inside the band are the five words PÁTRIA (fatherland) DEVER (duty) DEDICAÇÃO (dedication) HUMANIDADE (humanity) ALTRUÍSMO (altruism) and the date—1926.

When the regulations were renewed in 1982 the design of the medal was changed. The inscription around the circumference of the obverse was amended by the addition of the words SEGURANÇA PÚBLICA on the right of the figure. The reverse was wholly re-designed to show a winged female figure holding a pair of palm fronds in her left hand and a trumpet in her right with a snake entwined around her legs in the left half and the words taken from the original version moved to the right. The date of the revolution in 1926 was retained at the lower rim. The class of the medal was indicated by an open buckle-shaped silver bar with a star placed centrally—one for ten years, two for 20 and three for 30 years qualifying service.

Police Medals of the World

Officers from the PSP have available a second award which was also introduced in 1929 but amended when the regulations were renewed in1982. The *Exemplary Service Medal* is not awarded to officers from the Judicial Police or Republican National Guard. It is awarded in three classes indicated by the metal used for the medal—copper after eight years, silver after 15 years and gold after 25 years with each new medal replacing the earlier award.

MEDALHA DE COMPORTAMENTO EXEMPLAR DA SEGURANÇA PÚBLICA

Instituted: 30 November 1929.

Ribbon: Alternate equally sized horizontal stripes of black and white.

Metal: Gold, silver and copper.

Size: 38 mm.

Description: (Obverse) a female head symbolic of the Republic facing right with the words REPÚBLICA (left) and PORTUGUESA (right) in the upper circumference; (reverse) a palm frond placed in the left third with the words MEDÁLHA DA SEGURANÇA PÚBLICA COMPORTAMENTO EXEMPLAR 1926 in seven lines to the right of the frond. A simple ring suspender was used.

When the regulations were renewed in 1982 the design was amended in similar fashion to the Long Service Medal with the only difference being in the wording on the reverse which was changed to read COMPORTAMENTO EXEMPLAR in two lines with the date—1926—retained towards the lower rim.

The rôle of the Portuguese police during the century of instability and change had changed little apart from the natural evolution of policing methods in Europe and some restriction in their powers and duties in the late 1960s shortly after Prime Minister Salazar had suffered a stroke and left office. Police officers in Portugal today have fewer powers than most European countries although they are an efficient, competent body.

RHODESIA 1965–1980

The Republic of Rhodesia existed between December 1964 when the President—Ian Smith—made his unilateral declaration of independence (UDI) from Britain and April 1980 when Robert Mugabe became the first black prime minister (later president) of the country which was soon to become known as Zimbabwe. Britain reacted swiftly by declaring the actions illegal and imposed economic sanctions which were adopted by the United Nations in 1968. The sanctions were widely ignored by western and some British companies and, at first, the new country flourished but the clamour for black majority rule increased until the two most prominent African political parties chose the path of guerrilla warfare to achieve their aims. The economy faced collapse and the emigration of white Rhodesians forced Ian Smith to look for a compromise and a way to avoid the inevitable collapse of his regime. An internal settlement and the holding of elections which resulted in black rule, at least on paper, were tried without much success until after the general election in Britain in 1979 which brought Margaret Thatcher and the Conservatives to power. Early in 1980 after long and difficult discussions which went on for 14 weeks a multi-party election was held in Rhodesia and saw the end of white rule.

Settlement of Rhodesia began in earnest in 1889 with the formation of the British South Africa Company (BSAC) under royal charter granting authority to do almost anything including the establishment and maintenance of a police force. The Union Jack was raised over Fort Salisbury (Harare) on 12 September, the start of decades of British rule. Administration of the country remained in the hands of the BSAC until 1923. In 1953 the colony of Southern Rhodesia, its northern namesake and Nyasaland were formed into the Federation of Rhodesia and Nyasaland although it lasted barely ten years before independence was granted to Zambia and Malawi in 1964 and events set in train which were to lead to UDI.

The police force established by Cecil Rhodes remained under the control of the BSAC until a major reorganisation in 1896 which included a change in name to the British South Africa Police (BSAP). When true independence was achieved in 1980 it became the Zimbabwe Republic Police Force although the effect on the Force was relatively minor at the time apart from the resignation of a number of white officers.

Until the declaration of independence, officers from the BSAP were entitled to the award of the colonial police series of medals but this all ceased in 1964. As the war with the guerrilla movement intensified and the involvement of police officers increased this led to a need for a system of honours to reward acts of courage and meritorious service. The introduction of a formal structure of medals and awards began in 1969 and expanded the following year. It was based, to a degree, on the British system it replaced.

The first medal to be authorised was available to any member of the regular forces, including the police and police reserve. It was issued in large numbers (more than 28,000) and was awarded for three months service for regular forces and for fourteen days under operation command or in contact with insurgents for reserve officers. Due to these criteria, it is commonly found in groups with any one or more of the other medals introduced in the country the following year. The medal was always issued engraved on the rim with the name, rank and number of the recipient.

RHODESIA GENERAL SERVICE MEDAL

Instituted: 1969.

Ribbon: A broad band of red to the left with one of light blue to the right separated by a narrow band consisting of stripes of dark blue, yellow and dark blue.

Metal: Cupro-nickel.

Size: 36 mm.

Description: (Obverse) the head of Cecil Rhodes; (reverse) the Coat of Arms of Rhodesia. An ornate curved suspender bar attached by a claw fitting was used.

The coat of arms depicted on the obverse of this medal and four others subsequently introduced for award to police officers was taken from the original arms of Southern Rhodesia (granted in 1924) before the federation with Northern Rhodesia (now Zambia) and Nyasaland (now Malawi) and incorporated features from the personal arms of Cecil Rhodes. The dominant feature of the shield is the pick (facing upwards) which represents mining and agriculture in the country. Above this is a lion flanked by a thistle, both taken from Rhodess personal arms. The supporters (sable antelope) are indicative of the country's wildlife and the motto in the banner below the shield—"*sit nomine digna*"—means "may she be worthy of the name".

Shortly after the introduction of the Rhodesia General Service Medal, a series of awards was authorised including some exclusively available to regular police officers and members of the Police Reserve for gallantry, meritorious service and long service and good conduct.

Rhodesia

POLICE CROSS

Instituted: 1970.

Ribbon: Dark blue with two vertical white bands.

Metal: Gold on silver.

Size: 48 mm.

Description: (Obverse) a Maltese cross with the arms in blue enamel bordered with gold and a central medallion in white bearing the crest of the BSAP in gold, surrounded by an outer band bearing the name of the medal and reason for its award; (reverse) left plain for the inscription of the recipients name and rank. A large ring suspender was used.

The Police Cross was the highest decoration available to police officers and was awarded for conspicuous gallantry or distinguished service with the reason being given on the outer ring of the central medallion although awards for gallantry were also indicated by the addition of two red lines to the white bands of the ribbon following the style of the Queen's Police Medal which were made redundant by the declaration of UDI and which the Police Cross effectively replaced. The award for gallantry ranked higher in the order of precedence. Very few of either were awarded—five for gallantry and 33 for distinguished service—and provision was made for the award of bars although none were ever authorised.

In common with all decorations under the regime the Police Cross was available without regard to rank although awards for distinguished service were most commonly made to senior police officers who had attained the rank of senior assistant commissioner in a very similar fashion to the British medal it replaced. Recipients were entitled to use the letters PCG or PCD after their name.

At the same time that the Police Cross for Conspicuous Gallantry was introduced, a second medal was made available to officers for gallantry in the face of the enemy, irrespective of their rank. It was awarded on only 22 occasions. There was a provision for the granting of a bar for any second or subsequent award but none were ever issued. Recipients were entitled to the use of the post-nominals PDG.

POLICE DECORATION FOR GALLANTRY

Instituted: 1970.

Ribbon: Green with a broad dark blue central band flanked by white lines and with thin red lines positioned in the centre of both green bands.

Metal: Silver.

Size: 36 mm.

Description: (Obverse) the Coat of Arms of Rhodesia; (reverse) a wreath of laurel with a truncheon (handle upwards) in the centre but overlapping the wreath at top and bottom and an outer band bearing the words FOR GALLANTRY around the lower circumference.

The equivalent medal given for meritorious police service was awarded more freely than the Decoration for Gallantry and went to 227 officers of all ranks although the majority were from the junior or middle ranks. The award carried with it a right to the use of the letters PMM after the name of the recipient.

POLICE MEDAL FOR MERITORIOUS SERVICE

Instituted: 1970.

Ribbon: Green with a central blue band flanked by yellow lines.

Metal: Silver.

Size: 36 mm.

Description: (Obverse) the Coat of Arms of Rhodesia; (reverse) the same as for the Decoration for Gallantry but with the substitution of the words FOR MERITORIOUS POLICE SERVICE around the circumference.

For unblemished police service of at least 18 years a further medal was awarded to officers of all ranks. Further periods were rewarded with bars made available to recognise 25 and 30 years service. In total, 2,577 officers received a medal, 460 a first bar and 58 achieved 30 years service and were awarded a second bar.

POLICE LONG SERVICE MEDAL

Instituted: 1970.

Ribbon: Purple with a green central band flanked by yellow lines.

Metal: Silver.

Size: 36 mm.

Description: (Obverse) the Coat of Arms of Rhodesia; (reverse) the same as the two previous award but with the words FOR LONG SERVICE AND GOOD CONDUCT.

The regular police were supported by the Police Reserve who performed almost identical duties and who were rewarded with their own medal in recognition of this service. Reserve officers qualified after nine years with the A reserve or 15 years with the Field Reserve although at times of real need there was very little difference in the duties they performed. In all more than 3,250 officers received the medal.

POLICE RESERVE LONG SERVICE MEDAL

Instituted: 1970.

Ribbon: Purple with a central red band flanked by yellow lines and with a yellow line at each edge.

Metal: Silver.

Size: 36 mm.

Description: (Obverse) the Coat of Arms of Rhodesia; (reverse) the words FOR FAITHFUL SERVICE in the centre with POLICE RESERVE around the upper circumference and two floral branches around the base.

The elections held in 1980 were conducted under the strict supervision of independent bodies including police officers from the UK. Those who served for a period of fourteen days between 1 December 1979 and 20 March 1980 were awarded a specially commissioned medal.

RHODESIA MEDAL

Instituted: 1980.

Ribbon: Pale blue with a central band of red, white and blue stripes.

Metal: Rhodium plated cupro-nickel.

Size: 36 mm.

Description: (Obverse) the crowned bust of Queen Elizabeth II; (reverse) a sable antelope facing left with the name of the medal—THE RHODESIA MEDAL—around the upper circumference and the year—1980.

With the establishment of an independent Zimbabwe, the issue of the series of medals introduced by Ian Smith's régime in the Republic of Rhodesia ceased. Zimbabwe introduced a medal in its own right to celebrate the achievement of independence for distribution to a great many people, including police officers from the UK who had been sent to supervise the conduct of the elections.

The crest of the BSAP reproduced in the central medallion of the Police Cross shows a lion (facing left) charging from a protea bush. It has a spear embedded in its chest, another in front of it and two shields and more spears under its feet. The Force motto—PRO REGE, PRO PATRIA, PRO LEGE—is written in a banner below. The use of the lion emblem in this form on a medal was first seen on the reverse of the British South Africa Company's Medal issued in 1896 although the original idea went back to the South Africa Medal of 1854. The reverse of that medal showed the British lion drinking at a waterhole in front of a protea shrub. When the BSA Company's medal was proposed it was decided to use the lion but concern was raised that it did not appear to be doing anything very definite and it had its tail between its legs—an undignified pose for such an animal and not the image that the British lion was meant to present. The design was changed and the lion made more aggressive and brave, still attacking despite its wounds, the British lion at its best.

BRITISH SOUTH AFRICA COMPANY'S MEDAL

Instituted: 1896.

Ribbon: Yellow with three dark blue stripes.

Metal: Silver.

Size: 36 mm.

Description: (Obverse) the Old Head of Queen Victoria; (reverse) the charging lion emblem with the inscription MATABELELAND 1893 above and BRITISH SOUTH AFRICA COMPANY below. A very ornate suspender using roses, thistles, shamrocks and leeks entwined together was employed attached by a claw fitting.

The medal was issued to reward troops who took part in the suppression of the Matabele rebellion three years earlier. Further issues of the medal were made with the inscription on the reverse changed to either RHODESIA 1896 or MASHONALAND 1897 and a series of clasps was made available to recipients of the first issue. Many years later, in 1927, it was decided to issue a further medal for the campaign in Mashonaland in 1890 although there was no inscription on the reverse although the name and date were inscribed on the clasp also authorised. Officers of the BSAC police force, the forerunners of the BSAP, were amongst those who were awarded the medal. The practice of medals being awarded by a company rather than the Crown with the effigy of the Sovereign on the obverse may seem somewhat unusual today but it was not an unusual practice in the 19th century when many of these companies operated with official sanction under a royal charter—the Royal Niger Company (1899) and Honourable East India Company (1851) were the two most prominent such organisations.

RUSSIA AND THE SOVIET UNION

The impact of this vast country on the history of the 20th century is impossible to measure. The 19th century Russian poet—Fedor Tiuchev —remarked that it could not be understood with the mind and commentators invariably describe it as a country that has to be experienced, no description, however well-written, could ever do it justice or explain why it is such an enigma to those of us in the west. Before its break-up, the Union of Soviet Socialist Republics (USSR) accounted for nearly one sixth of the total land area of the earth, stretched for more than 10,000 kilometres from east to west, almost 5,000 from north to south and was only slightly smaller than the whole of the continent of Africa. Current popular understanding of the country in the west is based on the cold war, the iron curtain and a nuclear third world war being a real possibility, particularly during the 1960s and 70s. It never happened and the Soviet Union fell apart towards the end of the 20th century it had dominated since the revolution in 1917.

The revolution ended centuries of rule by the Romanov family in Russia—autocratic, almost feudal rule, which was inefficient and insensitive to the needs of the people and which was, with the benefit of hindsight, almost inevitably destined to end as it did. The concept of policing in Imperial Russia is as far removed from the western model, even that of the times, as it is possible to get but a police force did exist and officers were rewarded for long service and good conduct many years before any similar such system was available in the UK.

IMPERIAL RUSSIA

MEDAL FOR EXEMPLARY POLICE SERVICE

Instituted: 17 December 1876.

Ribbon: Red with a yellow stripe at each edge, worn in the Russian style.

Metal: Silver.

Size: 36 mm.

Description: (Obverse) the effigy of the reigning Tsar with the legend BY THE GRACE OF GOD (name) EMPEROR AND TSAR OF ALL THE RUSSIAS around the circumference all within a wreath a three laurel leaves which forms the outer edge of the medal; (reverse) the wreath of laurel is continued with the words FOR EXEMPLARY POLICE SERVICE in four lines in the central field. All inscriptions are in the Cyrillic script.

The medal was awarded to police officers as a reward for exemplary service of at least five years in Russian cities or ten years in the rural areas. It was introduced in the reign of Tsar Alexander II in 1876 and the last issue made by Nicholas II, an incompetent and autocratic ruler who was crowned in Moscow on 26 May 1896 and reigned until February 1917 when he was persuaded to abdicate after the first of the two uprisings that year. The later October Revolution which brought the Bolsheviks to power led to civil war and, ultimately, the execution of the former tsar, his wife and children in June 1918.

SOVIET UNION

Under the communist régime which ruled after the revolution, the issue of medals to all sections of society, including police officers, ran riot with regular awards being made to celebrate anniversaries of the founding of the state and state organisations, significant episodes in Soviet history and to reward meritorious or distinguished service and long service with good conduct. The image of a senior officer from the armed forces of the Soviet Union with his uniform festooned with medals is almost a caricature in the west but we cannot ignore the fact that there was a huge number of medals awarded for a wide variety of reasons, some of which have no direct comparison in the UK and which are hard to understand but were typical of the communist era.

Policing in the Soviet Union as we understand the term in the west was the responsibility of the Ministry of Internal Affairs (MVD) and performed by the Militia. Initially controlled centrally, the Militia was reorganised on a regional basis in 1956 and control devolved to municipal, district or provincial authorities. The organisation most commonly associated with Soviet policing—the KGB—was a national internal security body with little relevance to the everyday policing performed by the Militia. Members of the Militia and KGB were eligible for the commemorative medals, including the more unusual examples.

After the devastation of the Second World War, work was urgently needed to restore the basic infrastructure of the USSR and bring the coal mines and iron and steel industries of the south back to full production to help rebuild the country. After this had been achieved in 1947 and 1948 all workers and engineers were given specially produced medals in recognition of their work. Many thousands of both awards were issued. A further similar award was made in 1956 to reward everyone who took an active part in the reclamation of long-untilled and virgin lands of Siberia, the Urals and Kazakhstan. Included amongst the recipients were many described as volunteers and those who were there to make sure that these volunteers did not escape!—the Militia and KGB.

The concept of rewarding workers with medals for their part in similar such enterprises was retained by the Soviet authorities until the 1970s with the award of the Medal for the Construction of the Baikal-Amur Railroad in 1976 and the Medal for the Development of the Oil and Gas Fields of Western Siberia in 1978. About 25,000 of these medals were awarded.

MEDAL FOR DEVELOPING THE OIL AND GAS FIELDS OF WESTERN SIBERIA

Instituted: 28 July 1978.

Ribbon: Green with a pale blue broad central band flanked by lines of dark blue and white.

Metal: Brass.

Size: 32 mm.

Description: (Obverse) an industrial scene with two oil drilling platforms, pipes and storage tanks behind a hammer and sickle emblem offset to the right. The name of the medal in Cyrillic script lies around the circumference with a small five-point star at the base; (reverse) a five-point star superimposed on a five-point rayed badge with the letters CCCP across the centre. Sprigs of oak leaves (left) and laurel (right) are below the stars.

In addition to these special issue commemorative medals, two series were also available to Soviet citizens and members of the military, including the Militia, to celebrate the founding of the Soviet armed forces after the October Revolution in 1917 and the defeat of Nazi Germany in the Great Patriotic War of 1941–1945. A new medal in each series was issued every ten years with each being of a different design and hanging from a different ribbon. After the break-up of the Soviet Union both series were continued although the new medals were not officially approved.

MEDAL TO COMMEMORATE THE 20TH ANNIVERSARY OF THE ESTABLISHMENT OF THE SOVIET ARMED FORCES

Instituted: 24 January 1938.

Ribbon: Grey with a red line at each edge.

Metal: Silver and red enamel.

Size: 32 mm.

Description: (Obverse) a circular silver medal with an enamelled red star in the centre with the points reaching the perimeter and the Roman numerals XX at the base; (reverse) an image of a soldier of the Red Army firing his rifle with the dates 1918–1938 to his right. A simple ring suspender is used.

The medal was awarded to serving officers of the Red Army, the Militia and KGB and also to those who had served for 20 uninterrupted years before 1938. It was the first of the series with more than 37,000 being issued.

The second in the series, issued shortly after the end of the Second World War on 22 February 1948 with the horrors of that conflict still fresh in the minds of the people, showed the conjoined heads of Lenin and Stalin on the obverse, facing right, with the Roman numerals XXX at the base. The ribbon was white with a broad central band in red and with red edges. Later medals in the series showed members of the various branches of the armed forces and a selection of the latest weaponry developed by the USSR as the anniversaries became due.

MEDAL TO CELEBRATE VICTORY IN THE GREAT PATRIOTIC WAR 1941–1945

Instituted: 7 May 1965.

Ribbon: Red with stripes of green, black and white to the right edge.

Metal: Brass.

Size: 32 mm.

Description: (Obverse) a figure of a soldier standing above a partial wreath of laurel holding a sword in his right hand and carrying a child in his left with the dates 1945 (left) and 1965 (right) on either side; (reverse) a small five-point star placed centrally with the Roman numerals XX behind on a background of rayed lines. An inscription in Cyrillic script lies around the circumference.

The medal was awarded in vast numbers to civilians, veterans and members of the armed forces (including the Militia) alike to mark the anniversary of the victory over Nazi Germany. Further medals in this series were issued after each succeeding ten years, all with a different design and different ribbons. The theme of each showed figures celebrating the victory.

Although police officers were eligible for the award of medals from these two series a special medal was produced for award to members of the Militia only in commemoration of the organisation's 50th anniversary. It was given to officers with 25 years good service.

MEDAL TO CELEBRATE 50 YEARS OF THE SOVIET MILITIA

Instituted: 1 November 1967.

Ribbon: Blue with a red band towards each edge and three red lines on the central blue band.

Metal: Cupro-nickel.

Size: 32 mm.

Description: (Obverse) the Soviet five-point star superimposed by a shield bearing the inscription 50 YEARS (in Cyrillic script) and a small hammer and sickle on the top. A partial wreath of laurel lay around the lower circumference.

page 280

Russia and the Soviet Union

To reward long service and good conduct Militia officers were entitled to medals awarded in three classes after 10 (third class), 15 (second) and 20 (first) years service with the medal itself being of the same design although of different materials and with the use of enamels on the first class award.

MEDAL FOR EXEMPLARY SERVICE IN THE MILITIA FIRST CLASS–20 YEARS

Instituted: 14 September 1957.

Ribbon: Red with green stripes (3 mm) at the edges and a single central yellow stripe (3 mm).

Metal: Silver and red enamel.

Size: 33 mm.

Description: (Obverse) a circular medal with the Soviet red star in red enamel placed centrally with a small hammer and sickle in silver in the centre. A second star with rayed arms lies behind the red star and the whole is surrounded by laurel branches; (reverse) plain apart from a small star at the very top above an inscription in Cyrillic script which read FOR 20 YEARS EXEMPLARY SERVICE. Along the lower circumference were the initials MVD (for Ministry of the Interior) and CCCP.

The second class award (15 years) was also of silver but with the central Soviet star in gilt and the third class award (10 years) was of gilded bronze only. In addition to the different metals used, the class of the award was indicated by the number of yellow stripes at the centre of the ribbon— one for first class, two for second class and three for the third class award.

Particularly meritorious police service was rewarded by a separate medal which was introduced earlier than the long service award. It was available in one class only and given for acts of courage and sacrifice in the defence of public order, fighting crime or other circumstances thought sufficient to merit official recognition. It was awarded to members of the Militia and citizens alike.

MEDAL FOR DISTINGUISHED SERVICE IN PRESERVING PUBLIC ORDER

Instituted: 1 November 1950.

Ribbon: Red with a broad dark blue central band containing two thin red lines.

Metal: Cupro-nickel.

Size: 33 mm.

Description: (Obverse) the Coat of Arms of the USSR with the letters CCCP below; (reverse) a small star at the top above an inscription in Cyrillic script in five lines which read FOR DISTINGUISHED SERVICE IN THE PRESERVATION OF PUBLIC ORDER.

A special medal awarded for saving the life of a person from drowning was available to all Soviet citizens, members of the rescue services and foreign nationals. The criteria were wide and the medal was given for courage, bravery and selflessness while rescuing a person from drowning, for outstanding vigilance and resourcefulness which prevents drowning and for excellent organisation of sea rescue operations. Members of the Militia were eligible for the award.

MEDAL FOR RESCUING A DROWNING PERSON

Instituted: 16 February 1957.

Ribbon: Pale blue with a thin white central line and a group of three thin white lines towards each edge.

Metal: Bronze.

Size: 33 mm.

Description: (Obverse) a figure of a swimmer taking the rescued person to safety and the words FOR LIFE SAVING in Cyrillic script at the upper and lower circumference; (reverse) a branch of laurel with the hammer and sickle emblem above and the initials CCCP below.

RUSSIAN FEDERATION

After the break-up of the Soviet Union in 1991 the design of medals available to citizens of the Russian Federation and other former Soviet republics was changed and all communist symbols removed. One of the first, introduced in 1992, was a direct replacement for the Medal for Rescuing a Drowning Person although the criteria were widened to include all instances of life-saving whatever the circumstances—fire, flood, accidents. The medals are all numbered on the reverse.

MEDAL FOR SAVING LIFE

Instituted: 2 March 1994.

Ribbon: White with a burgundy stripe at each edge.

Metal: Silver.

Size: 32 mm.

Description: (Obverse) a circular medal containing a cross patée with concave rayed arms and convex ends with the Russian emblem of a double-headed eagle with outstretched wings placed in the centre. The emblem has a shield at its centre showing St George, the patron saint of Moscow and Russia for many centuries; (reverse) a partial wreath of palm leaves with a two line inscription.

The Life Saving Medal is effectively a lower grade of the highest order available in the Russian Federation to reward citizens and members of the armed forces alike for acts of bravery and self-sacrifice in the course of saving life, the protection of public order, fighting crime or at the scenes of fires, floods, accidents and natural disasters. The order itself is awarded in a single class only.

ORDER OF COURAGE

Instituted: 2 March 1994.

Ribbon: Burgundy with a white stripe at each edge.

Metal: Silver.

Size; 40 mm.

Description: (Obverse) a cross patée with concave rayed arms and convex ends containing the Russian emblem in the centre; (reverse) the words BRAVERY (in Cyrillic script) along the horizontal arms.

The Medal for Distinguished Service in Preserving Public Order previously mentioned and awarded under the Soviet government was discontinued in 1991 but re-introduced by the new Russian Federation although the design was changed to remove the Soviet emblem. The criteria for its award were left unchanged.

MEDAL FOR DISTINGUISHED SERVICE IN PROTECTING PUBLIC ORDER

Instituted: 2 March 1994.

Ribbon: The same as the former Soviet medal.

Metal: Silver.

Size; 35 mm.

Description: (Obverse) a five line inscription giving the name of the medal in Cyrillic script within a wreath of oak leaves; (reverse) left blank apart from a number.

When the new order in Russia becomes more firmly established and more pressing priorities have been addressed the range of medals available to police officers will increase although it is unlikely that the range will be as wide as it was under the Soviet régime. Other former Soviet states have started to issue their own range of awards although, similarly, at present it is limited but very likely to increase in the coming years.

SARAWAK

Sarawak is one of three separate territories which make up the Federation of Malaysia although it is more than 700 miles from the mainland on the north coast of the island of Borneo (part of Indonesia) and encircles the Sultanate of Brunei to which it once belonged. It was a British Crown Colony from 1946 until it achieved self-government in 1963 and joined Malaysia. For the previous 122 years it had been ruled by three members of the same family with the exception of the Japanese occupation during the Second World War between 1942 and 1945. The first Rajah—Sir James Brooke—was an English adventurer and military officer who visited Sarawak in 1839 and assisted the Sultan of Brunei to put down a rebellion by native Iban tribes (the original head hunters) and was given the territory to rule as the Rajah by the Sultan as a gesture of gratitude in 1841. He was to rule until 1863 when he returned to England and handed the government of the territory to a nephew—Sir Charles Brooke—who assumed the title on Sir Jamess death in 1868.

Quite apart from his place in history as the first white rajah of Sarawak, James Brooke had one of the world's most attractive and striking butterflies named after him in 1855. The Rajah Brooke's Birdwing was discovered on Borneo and named in his honour by the naturalist A R Wallace. It is a large butterfly with the male having a wingspan of 16 to 19 centimetres and striking colouring—deep velvety black with a band of metallic green triangles on the forewings, white on the hindwings and a contrasting red band around the neck. The female is larger but a dull brown and white.

The name Sarawak means hornbill country in the local dialect after the large, striking bird found there, which is also revered by the native population as a symbol of marital devotion taken from its nesting habits. The birds are thought to mate for life and nest in holes in trees. When the female is ready to lay she enters the nesting hole and is sealed in by her mate with a mixture of mud and saliva which hardens like concrete, leaving a hole big enough only for her bill. She is fed by the male through this hole until the young are ready to leave the nest and she can leave her prison. This adaptation is thought to serve as a protection against predators, in particular tree snakes, who would be unlikely to risk the dangers posed by her large and very sharp bill.

The authority of the Brooke family as rulers of Sarawak was formally recognised by the governments of the United States (1850) and Britain (1864) and it was enlarged by purchase and conquest over the following half-century. Sir Charles had a long reign, until 1917, when he was succeeded by his eldest son, Charles Vyner Brooke, a much less decisive and autocratic man who introduced measures intended to bring self-government to the territory in 1941. The occupation by the Japanese thwarted his plans and he ceded the territory to Britain at the first available opportunity after the War on 1 July 1946, end more than a century of white rajah rule.

During the reign of the second Rajah in 1908 a medal was introduced to reward members of the Sarawak Rangers and Sarawak Police Force for long service. The medal was presented annually on the Rajah's birthday to all men (not officers) on completion of 18 years service in either body provided that they had no serious crime recorded against them in that time. If the standards of discipline in Sarawak were similar to those in the UK then the term "a serious crime" could include such grave sins as being late for duty, failing to report even a trivial matter to a superior officer or insubordination, which itself covered a multitude of very minor matters. The award of the medal was accompanied by an increase in pay.

SARAWAK GOVERNMENT GOOD SERVICE MEDAL

Instituted: 16 June 1908.

Ribbon: Three equal stripes of black, yellow and red.

Metal: Bronze.

Description: (Obverse) a bust of the Rajah facing right with the words VYNER BROOKE RAJAH around the upper circumference; (reverse) the legend SARAWAK GOVERNMENT around the upper circumference and two tied branches of laurel at the bottom with GOOD SERVICE MEDAL in three lines in the central field.

When Sir Charles Brooke died in 1917 and the title passed to his son, Charles Vyner Brooke, the medal continued to be issued without any change to the design or conditions of its award. In 1924 a penal code modelled on that of British India was introduced and changes made to the honours system of the country. The single long service medal was replaced by three separate issues for the police, military and other government officials—customs officers, clerks etc. The criteria for its award were unchanged but provision was made for a bar to be available for each additional period of ten years qualifying service. Police officers who enlisted before 1924 were given the choice of receiving either medal.

SARAWAK POLICE SERVICE GOOD SERVICE MEDAL

Instituted: 16 December 1924.

Ribbon: A central yellow stripe with a black stripe to the left and one of red to the right, both half the width of the yellow.

Metal: Bronze.

Description: (Obverse) a bust of the Rajah facing right with the words VYNER BROOKE - RAJAH around the upper circumference; (reverse) an ornamental scrolled tablet in the lower half inscribed with the words GOOD SERVICE MEDAL in three lines, the tablet superimposed on a branch of laurel. In a band around the circumference were the words SARAWAK POLICE SERVICE.

The medal continued to be issued until 1946 when the territory was ceded to Britain as a Crown Colony and its award ceased. Between 1924 and 1941, annual awards were few, no more than eleven in any one year, but, on 20 June 1946, a final presentation of the medal was made to 62 officers before it passed into history. As a British Crown Colony, police officers in Sarawak became eligible for the Colonial Police series of medals until it joined the Federation of Malaysia when they were subject to the honours system of that country.

During the reign of Vyner Brooke, one further medal was available—the Sarawak Conspicuous Bravery Medal—although it was issued sparingly and is a very rare award. It was cast in matt silver and featured the same obverse as the Police Good Service Medal. The reverse had two branches of palm leaves in the upper half, the words FOR CONSPICUOUS BRAVERY in the three lines below and SARAWAK GOVERNMENT around the lower circumference. The ribbon was black, red and yellow. When the unique reign of the white rajahs ended in 1946 these interesting medals were rendered redundant.

SINGAPORE

The island which makes up the Republic of Singapore supports a population of more than three million in an area of only 239 square miles. It was virtually uninhabited before Sir Stamford Raffles, an official of the East India Company, set up a trading post there in 1819 after recognising the island's potential resulting from its strategic position. Within seven years it had become Britain's primary colonial centre in South East Asia. Total British rule lasted until 1959 when it was granted self-government although control of defence and foreign policy was retained by London. It joined the Federation of Malaysia briefly in September 1963 but left at the invitation of the Malay government following a period of political friction and became a separate independent state on 9 August 1965. Singapore is a member of the Commonwealth.

Before self-government was granted in 1959 police officers in Singapore had been eligible for the Colonial Police Long Service Medal since 1948 and they retained this entitlement until December 1961 when the local Singapore Police Long Service Medal was introduced to replace it.

PINGAT BAKTI SETIA

Instituted: 29 December 1961.

Ribbon: Dark blue with stripes gold (3 mm) near the edges and stripes of silver (3 mm) towards the centre.

Metal: Silver.

Size: 36 mm.

Description: (Obverse) the Coat of Arms of Singapore with shield, supporters and motto and the words POLIS NEGARA SINGAPURA around the upper circumference; (reverse) a lion's head above a wreath of laurel and the words PINGAT (medal) BAKTI (service) SETIA (faithful) around the circumference. The medal hangs from a ring suspender.

The medal was awarded to officers below the rank of assistant superintendent for 18 years service with good character and exemplary conduct. Bars were awarded on the completion of 25 and 30 years qualifying service. Officers who had already been awarded the Colonial Police Long Service Medal were not eligible for the new medal but they were still entitled to the bars available for further service. The bars of the local medal were of silver and carried the motif of padi sheaves. In undress uniform the award of bars was signified by silver rosettes worn on the ribbon.

The motif in the centre of the shield on the coat of arms shows a moon (the nation) pursuing five ideals—democracy, freedom, prosperity, justice and health—represented by the five stars. The lion supporter represents the name of the country (lion-city) and the tiger its relationship with Malaysia.

At the time of the introduction of the local long service medal for regular officers, a second medal was instituted to replace the Colonial Police Special Constabulary Long Service Medal which had previously been available to members of the Special Constabulary (Reserve) Unit or Special Constabulary (Active) Unit of the Singapore Police. Nine years unpaid service was required by volunteers of the Reserve Unit and fifteen by the Active Unit with bars available to both for each subsequent period of ten years service. The British medal had been introduced into Singapore in December 1957 but was replaced by the *Singapore Special Constabulary Long Service Medal* four years later.

POLIS KHAS PINGAT BAKTI SETIA

Instituted: 29 December 1961.

Ribbon: Dark blue with stripes of gold and white together towards each edge.

Metal: Silver.

Size: 36 mm.

Description: (Obverse) the Coat of Arms of Singapore with shield, supporters and motto and the words POLIS NEGARA SINGAPURA around the upper circumference and POLIS KHAS (special) at the bottom; (reverse) the shield of the Singapore Coat of Arms consisting of a crescent and five stars surrounded by a wreath of laurel and the words PINGAT BAKTI SETIA around the circumference. The medal hangs from a ring suspender.

Both medals remained in use after independence was achieved until late 1974 when the government of Singapore, now a republic, introduced a range of honours which included replacement medals for regular police officers and the Special Constabulary. The new medals differed in one respect only—the substitution of the word REPABLIK (republic) for NEGARA (state) on the circumscription of the obverse. The ribbons were also retained unchanged. The regulations for the award of the new Singapore Police Long Service and Good Conduct Medal, however, were subject to a number of changes. The period of service needed to qualify for the medal was reduced to 12 years from 18 and it was available to officers of all ranks including assistant superintendents and above who were excluded from the previous award. Service in the Armed Forces or with the Royal Malaysian Police when Singapore was a part of the Federation of Malaysia could be counted towards the qualifying period. Bars were available after 20 and 30 years service and were similar in design to the replaced medal. Holders of the Colonial Police Long Service Medal or the Singapore Police Long Service Medal were not entitled to the award of the new medal but could continue to count their service towards the two bars available for either.

In 1994 a single medal was introduced to replace the long service awards to both regular and volunteer officers. The new medal became available to all members of the Singapore Police Service—regular police officers, members of the Special Constabulary, Vigilante Corps, Central Narcotics Bureau and the Prison Department alike. The qualifying period of 12 years service for the award of the medal and provision for the award of bars after 20 and 30 years were retained. In working uniform the award of bars was indicated by a silver star worn on the ribbon.

SINGAPORE POLICE SERVICE LONG SERVICE AND GOOD CONDUCT MEDAL

Instituted: 1 April 1994.

Ribbon: The same as the original medal.

Metal: Silver.

Size: 36 mm.

Description: (Obverse) the Coat of Arms of Singapore with shield, supporters and motto and the words PERKHIDMATAN POLIS SINGAPURA around the circumference; (reverse) the lion's head above a small wreath of laurel and the words PINGAT BAKTI SETIA around the circumference. A ring suspender is used.

In addition to this award a method of recognising good, efficient and faithful service by junior officers with five years service was also introduced in 1994.

SINGAPORE POLICE SERVICE GOOD SERVICE MEDAL

Instituted: 1 April 1994.

Ribbon: Dark blue with golden yellow central band, all of equal width.

Metal: Silver.

Size: 36 mm.

Description: (Obverse) the Coat of Arms of Singapore with shield, supporters and motto and the words SINGAPORE (left) POLICE (right) and SERVICE (bottom) at the circumference; (reverse) a wreath of laurel with the words FOR GOOD SERVICE in three lines in the centre. A ring suspender is used.

Singapore is somewhat unusual in that a long service medal is awarded by the State to police officers additional to those exclusively available to police officers. The *State Long Service Medal* is available to large numbers of public servants including members of the armed forces, police officers, customs and immigration staff and all civil servants (teachers etc) irrespective of rank or position on completion of 25 years faithful service to Singapore. The medal is awarded in the name of the President and presented on Singapore's national day—9 August. Two types have been produced, the first from 1961 to 1995 and the second from 1996 to the present. It remains current. All recipients are entitled to use the initials PBS (the name of the medal in Malay—Pingat Betia Setia) after their name. The two versions of the medal were very different with the only common features being the name and criteria for their award.

PINGAT BETIA SETIA 1961–1995

Instituted: 1961.

Ribbon: White with five thin maroon lines towards both edges.

Metal: Silver.

Description: (Obverse) a five-point star with a central medallion bearing the crescent moon and five stars; (reverse) the name of the medal in Malay in the central disc. A ring suspender was used attached to the point of the top arm of the star.

PINGAT BETIA SETIA 1996

Instituted: 2 August 1996.

Ribbon: Grey with a broad central band in red and a red stripe towards each edge.

Metal: Silver gilt.

Size: 40 mm.

Description: (Obverse) a multi-lobed design with a central shield bearing the symbol of the crescent moon and five stars encircled by a scalloped design; (reverse) a central disc showing the full Achievement of Arms of Singapore and the name of the medal in Malay around the upper circumference. A ring suspender is used.

The award of medals issued by the state and available to police officers is not restricted to the long service awards, particularly outstanding efficiency, competence, industry, devotion to duty or competence can result in the officer concerned receiving one of a number of medals which can be awarded to any citizen or state servant. One of the very highest honours available in Singapore has been awarded to senior police officers on a few occasions in similar fashion to the honours bestowed on the highest ranks in the UK. The *Distinguished Service Order* ranks fifth in the order of precedence and has been given to the highest ranking officers, albeit rarely. It is awarded in recognition of an act or series of acts of distinguished conduct in the service of Singapore. Different awards although with the same name are awarded to members of the Singapore Armed Forces and other citizens which includes police officers.

DARJAH UTAMA BAKTI CHEMERLANG

Ribbon: White with a broad maroon central band and two maroon stripes towards each edge. Worn as a neck ribbon

Metal: Gold and enamels.

Description: (Obverse) a shield as a centrepiece in red enamel with the crescent moon and five stars in white. It is surrounded by an outer band in white bearing the name of the award in red all within a wreath of laurel (green) above a banner bearing the state motto; (reverse) plain apart from the name of the recipient and the date awarded. A simple ring suspender is used.

Lesser awards are also made to police officers, usually on National Day, and reward a wide range of services to Singapore. The most basic of these awards although it ranks above the long service awards is the *Efficiency Medal* given to recognise exceptional efficiency, outstanding devotion to duty or work of special significance. Two versions have been produced, the second coming as a result of the review of the honours system in 1996.

PINGAT BERKEBOLEHAN 1969–1995

Ribbon: Maroon with a white central band and a white line near each edge.

Metal: Bronze.

Description: (Obverse) a circular medal with the crescent moon and five stars with the name of the medal in Malay around the upper circumference.

PINGAT BERKEBOLEHAN 1996

Ribbon: Red with a pair of green lines either side of the centre and green edges.

Metal: Silver.

Description: (Obverse) a four-point star with concave arms superimposed on a circular disc with a central medallion bearing the motif of crescent moon and stars.

The highest award a police officer might receive apart from those given to the most senior ranks or to recognise an act of courage is the *Public Service Star* awarded to persons who have rendered valuable public service to the people of Singapore or who have distinguished themselves in the fields of arts and letters, sport, science, business, the professions or the labour movement. Police officers have been awarded this star on a number of occasions.

BINTANG BAKTI MASYARAKAT (FIRST ISSUE)

Ribbon: White with a broad central band in mauve bisected by a narrow white line.

Metal: Silver.

Description: (Obverse) a five-point star with ball finials and a large central medallion bearing the five stars seen on the Singapore Coat of Arms above a banner bearing the state motto MAJULAH SINGAPURA. A ring suspender attached to the top point of the star is used.

BINTANG BAKTI MASYARAKAT (CURRENT ISSUE)

Ribbon: Mauve with a broad central band in white containing two pairs of narrow red lines.

Metal: Gold and white enamel.

Description: (Obverse) a circular medal in gold with a five-point star with concave arms as a central medallion and a disc placed centrally bearing the five stars and crescent moon of the Coat of Arms. A circular wreath lies behind the star at its points with the background to the star and wreath being of white enamel. The name of the medal in Malay is inscribed around the lower circumference.

A similar award made for similar reasons is given to any person who performs any commendable rather than valuable public service in Singapore. The original version of the *Public Service Medal* used the same ribbon as the Public Service Star and was a circular bronze medal with the obverse carrying the same design as the central medallion of the Star. When the medal was re-designed in 1996 the colouring of the ribbon was changed to its own distinctive pattern.

PINGAT BAKTI MASYARAKAT (CURRENT ISSUE)

Ribbon: Mauve with a broad central band in white and a thin red line on either side.

Metal: Silver.

Description: (Obverse) A lobed design with a circular central medallion superimposed on a cross with three straight arms and an upper arm in the form of a cross moline. The central medallion carries the five stars and crescent moon with a banner below the disc containing the name of the medal in Malay.

Singapore medals are awarded in a single class with one exception—the *Public Administration Medal*—which is issued in gold, silver and bronze and given to any public officer (including members of the Singapore Police Service) for outstanding efficiency, competence and industry. Recipients can receive more than one class of the award and are entitled to wear them all together. The simple circular design of the original medal was replaced in 1996 by a more ornate version in similar fashion to many Singapore awards.

PINGAT PENTADBIRAN AWAM (FIRST ISSUE)

Ribbon: White with four narrow lines of red in the centre.

Metal: Gold, silver and bronze.

Description: (Obverse) the shield of the Coat of Arms of Singapore with a banner above bearing the state motto and a pair of laurel branches tied at the base with a bow around the lower circumference.

PINGAT PENTADBIRAN AWAM (CURRENT ISSUE)

Ribbon: White with a red band at each edge, a central red band and two thin red lines either side of the middle band.

Metal: Gold, silver and bronze.

Description: (Obverse) a cross with the arms in the shape of a pentagon in white enamel and the shield from the Coat of Arms placed in the centre superimposed on a second star with narrow arms.

Methods of recognising acts of courage by police officers in Singapore after the republic was established have undergone several changes. The first medal available was not an exclusively police award—the *Conspicuous Gallantry Medal* was awarded very sparingly such was the level of courage required in circumstances of the most extreme danger. Between its introduction and 1998 only 14 were awarded, including four to police officers.

PINGAT GAGAH PERKASA

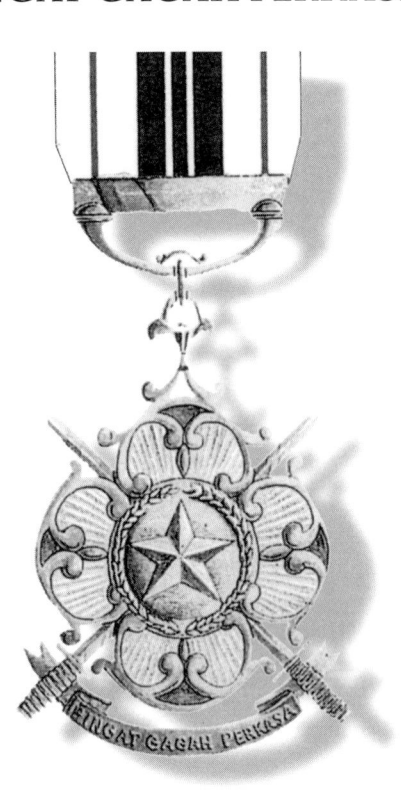

Instituted: 1962.

Ribbon: White with a broad central band in dark blue with two thin white lines and a red line towards each edge.

Metal: Gold

Description: (Obverse) an ornate medal of irregular shape in the basic design of a cross with lobed arms. The central medallion containing a five-point star within a circular wreath is superimposed on two crossed swords with a banner below attached to the sword handles bearing the name of the medal in Malay; (reverse) the central medallion has the full Achievement of Arms of Singapore in the upper half with space below for the recipient's details. The method of suspension was equally ornate.

In 1974 a new medal was introduced exclusively available to police officers and intended to reward them acts of distinguished and gallant conduct in circumstances where there was danger to the life of anyone. It could be awarded posthumously and silver bars were available for any second or subsequent act of courage of the required standard. In undress uniform the award of a bar was indicated by small silver star worn on the ribbon. The first ten awards of the *Police Gallantry Medal* were made in June 1975 followed by two more in 1978, the only awards before it was renamed.

PINGAT POLIS PERKASA

Instituted: 22 October 1974.

Ribbon: Dark blue with a red central stripe and white bands at the edges.

Metal: Silver.

Description: (Obverse) the Coat of Arms of Singapore with the legend POLIS REPABLIK SINGAPURA around the circumference; (reverse) the police crest consisting of the shield taken from the arms with the moon and five stars within a wreath of laurel above a banner bearing the name of the Force and a circumscription which reads PINGAT POLIS PERKASA. A ring suspender was used and the name of the recipient was inscribed on the rim.

The view of Singapore in the west is one of a country with few problems of law and order that the efficient police service cannot cope with comfortably, aided by severe punishments provided by the government and handed out by the judiciary. The work of a police officer, though, in any country, including one such as Singapore, is potentially dangerous with the threat to an officers life being very real. One recipient of the Police Gallantry Medal in 1975—Detective Anthony Eng—was in danger of being shot with his own gun when he attempted to arrest a notorious gunman after an attempted armed robbery. The robber ran off when the officer arrived at the secne but managed to ambush him and take his gun from him. The gun was held to the officer's head but the gunman slipped as they were going down a flight of stairs giving Detective Eng the opportunity to retrieve his gun. The gunman pulled out his own gun and tried to fire but was shot and killed by the police officer.

The name of the medal was amended in 1988 to the Police Medal for Valour (Pingat Polis Keberanian) but discontinued after the 1996 review of the honours system and replaced by the *Medal for Valour*, available to any citizen (including police officers) for an act of courage where a person's life was in danger.

PINGAT KEBERANIAN

Instituted: 2 August 1996.

Ribbon: White with a brown central band flanked by two thin brown lines.

Metal: Silver-gilt.

Description: (Obverse) an eight point star on a base of a sixteen-point star with a central medallion supporting a pair of crossed swords and a shield bearing the five stars and crescent moon. Below the medallion is a banner with the name of the medal in Malay; (reverse) the Coat of Arms of Singapore. A ring suspender is used.

Police Medals of the World

In addition to the national and exclusively police awards for bravery, efficiency, competence and long service available to police officers two medals were introduced to recognise service in the period when Singapore was a part of the Federation of Malaysia and in the twelve months after it left to become an independent state during which time a period of tension with its much larger neighbour existed. Any member of the armed forces or police, including volunteers serving on 15 September 1963 was awarded the *Uniformed Services Malaysia Medal*—the first of the two medals introduced.

PINGAT PERKHIDMATAN ANGGOTA BERUNIFORM MALAYSIA

Instituted: 7 September 1964.

Ribbon: Half white, half red.

Metal: Bronze.

Size: 36 mm.

Description: (Obverse) the shield at the centre of the Coat of Arms of Singapore consisting of the moon and five stars with the words MAJULAH SINGAPURA around the circumference and a palm frond at the top; (reverse) the Singapore lion encircled by the inscription SEPTEMBER 16TH 1963 and an outer band of hibiscus buds.

Following the breakaway from Malaysia and the establishment of a separate state on 9 August 1965 there was a period of tension with its neighbour and police officers were amongst those who were placed on active service for certain prescribed periods until the situation became more stable. These officers were subsequently awarded the *Defence Medal* together with members of the armed forces. The operative period for qualification for the medal lasted for one year from 9 August 1965 when the confrontation with Malaysia came to an end. The medal was awarded to members of the regular force, the Special Constabulary, the Vigilante Corps, the Port of Singapore Authority and Singapore Airport Auxiliary Police Forces.

PINGAT PERTAHANAN

Instituted: 22 June 1970.

Ribbon: Yellow with stripes (each 1 mm) of red, white and red either side of the central yellow part and blue stripes at each edge..

Metal: Cupro-nickel.

Size: 35 mm.

Description: (Obverse) the full Achievement of Arms of Singapore; (Reverse) the flag of Singapore surrounded by a wreath of palm fronds and an outer band bearing the medals name in Malay. A ring suspender was used.

page 294

Since the Second World War the rôle of the United Nations in peacekeeping duties in the worlds trouble spots has increased year upon year and police officers from many countries have often been called upon to support the local forces, supervise the transition to more democratic forms of government or keep the peace following war or periods of unrest. The issue of special medals for service overseas has become a feature of a number of countries including Australia, Fiji and the Republic of Ireland amongst others. Officers from the Singapore Police Force have served overseas on a number of occasions and have been rewarded with their own medal, the *Singapore Police Overseas Service Medal*. They are also entitled to the appropriate United Nations medal.

PINGAT SEBERANG LAUT PERHIDMATAN POLIS SINGAPURA

Instituted: 16 August 1993.

Ribbon: Three bands of dark blue, light blue and dark blue, all of equal width..

Metal: Silver.

Description: *(Obverse) the Coat of Arms of Singapore with the name of the police force in English - SINGAPORE POLICE SERVICE - around the circumference; (reverse) a globe of the world (Europe, Africa, Asia and Australasia with the words FOR OVERSEAS SERVICE around the circumference. A simple ring suspender is used.*

The medal is awarded to any police officer, including members of the Special Constabulary and Vigilante Corps, who have been involved in operations where there was a threat to life and limb for a period of at least 96 hours or in operations involving peacekeeping, the restoration of law and order or the provision of humanitarian aid for a period of four days or more outside Singapore. Any second or subsequent entitlement to the medal is indicated by a silver bar. Officers from Singapore have been involved in a number of operations including the UN Transitional Assistance Group (UNTAG) in Namibia in 1990 and the UN Transitional Authority in Cambodia (UNTAC) between March 1992 and September 1993.

SOUTH AFRICA

History in South Africa falls into three distinct periods—the years before 1910 when the Union of South Africa was formed, the time from then until 1961 when the country left the Commonwealth and became a republic and the period which began in 1994 with the election of Nelson Mandela as President and the introduction of black majority rule. South Africa rejoined the Commonwealth as one of the first acts of the new régime. A legacy of the years before 1910 and the original colonisation of the country by Dutch settlers and the British is the existence of two of thirteen official languages of the country—Afrikaans and English. Afrikaans (also known as Cape Dutch) is descended from 17th century Dutch but has evolved into a language in its own right, sufficiently different to be considered a different language rather than a dialect or version of one language. The differences are more profound than those between English and American or Australian or between Dutch and Flemish. The impact of the differences can be seen in the inscriptions on the earliest medal instituted for award to police officers in the Union of South Africa in 1923.

POLICE GOOD SERVICE MEDAL

Instituted: 5 June 1923.

Ribbon: Green with a dark blue central stripe (9 mm) flanked by bands of white (5 mm).

Metal: Silver.

Size: 36 mm.

Description: (Obverse) the Coat of Arms of the Union of South Africa with the words POLICE SERVICE above and POLITIE DIENST below; (reverse) plain apart from the inscription FOR FAITHFUL SERVICE and VOOR TROUE DIENST, both in three lines. A plain straight suspender was used attached with a claw fitting.

The medal was awarded after 18 years service although there was provision for acts of gallantry or particularly distinguished service to be recognised. In these circumstances a silver bar was worn inscribed MERIT—VERDIENSTE. The medal was issued in large numbers (more than 11,500) before it was withdrawn in 1963 and replaced by the South African Police Medal for Faithful Service as a part of the honours system introduced by the government of the new Republic.

The language used for the non-English inscriptions was High Dutch but the adoption of Afrikaans as the official language in South Africa in 1925 led to amendments to the inscriptions on the obverse and reverse of the medal. The first change was made in 1932 with the obverse being changed to read POLIESIE DIENS and the inscription of the reverse amended to VIR GETROUE DIENS. A further amendment was made in 1951 when the wording became POLISIEDIENS and VIR TROUE DIENS. All medals with inscriptions subsequently issued in South Africa used Afrikaans, not the High Dutch of the early years.

The coat of arms of the Union of South Africa depicted on the obverse were first granted on 17 September 1910. The central shield was quartered with each of the four elements being indicative of the history of the Union from the days when the Boers and British were rivals for influence and power in the region. The upper left quarter depicted the figure of Hope, taken from the arms of the Colony of Good Hope, a settlement which was occupied by the Dutch, British and Dutch again until 1806 when the British again assumed control which they were to retain until the establishment of the Union of South Africa in 1910. The upper right quadrant contains two wildebeest from the colony of Natal. In the lower half are an orange tree (Orange Free State) to the left and a Boer wagon (Transvaal) on the right. The shield was topped by a lion with its right paw resting on the fasces (a bundle of rods surrounding an axe, the Roman symbol of authority). The two supporters are a springbok (left) and an oryx (right).

Acts of great courage or meritorious service were rewarded by the same King's Police Medal available to police officers in the UK and other Commonwealth countries until 1937 when two new bi-lingual medals were introduced for award in South Africa only—the South African King's Police Medal (the Queen's medal after 1952) for gallantry and meritorious service. When the country left the Commonwealth in 1961 the South African Queen's Police Medal was no longer available and all awards to police officers came from the honours system introduced there on 20 May 1963.

The new system had four medals to reward acts of bravery, distinguished service and faithful service. The highest honour was available only for the most outstanding acts of bravery and could be awarded posthumously—of the first three awarded, two were posthumous. In all, only eleven awards were ever made, six posthumously. The honour brought with it the right to the use of the post-nominal letters—PCF, an abbreviation of the Latin phrase *Prefecturae Crux Fortitudinus*.

SOUTH AFRICAN POLICE CROSS FOR BRAVERY (SUID-AFRIKAANSE POLISIEKRUIS VIR DAPPERHEID)

Ribbon: A neck ribbon (44.5 mm) - dark blue with an old gold central band (6.5 mm) flanked by bands of white (3.5 mm).

Metal: Gold.

Description: (Obverse) a cross with broad stepped arms and a large central medallion with no motif other than two pairs of crossed lines within an outer band of blue enamel bearing the inscription VIVIT POST PUNERA VIRTUS (virtue lives after death) all within a wreath of laurel (green enamel); (reverse) the Coat of Arms of the Republic of South Africa and the words VIR DAPPERHEID to the left and FOR BRAVERY to the right. A ring suspender was used.

The second highest honour in the new series doubled as an award for distinguished service and for gallantry with bars available for any second or subsequent award. Recipients were entitled to the use of the post-nominal letters—SOO—*Stella Officii Optimi*.

page 297

Police Medals of the World

POLICE STAR FOR DISTINGUISHED SERVICE (POLISIESTER VIR VOORTREFLIKE DIENS)

Ribbon: White with three stripes of green, white and red at the left edge and orange, white and dark blue at the other.

Metal: Silver gilt with green enamel.

Description: (Obverse) a six-point star with rayed arms superimposed by another, smaller star with a circular band interwoven between the arms. The inner star carried a motif of a winged torch with a flame at the top and a pair of scales of justice; (reverse) the shield of the coat of arms with the words DISTINGUISHED SERVICE in a tablet above and VOORTREELIKE DIENS below. The suspender bar was integral with the medal attached between the top two arms of the larger star by an ornate design. The bars were plain with the emblem of a flame in the centre.

On 1 May 1979 the criteria for the award of the star were changed and it was no longer available for acts of gallantry. It became an award for officers of the general staff only and was issued with a breast star, a neck ribbon and a chain for wear at appropriate formal occasions.

The two other medals introduced in 1963 were both a form of long service medal although the criteria for the first were more strictly defined and required at least 30 years exemplary service with irreproachable character or particularly meritorious service. It was awarded in substantial numbers and officers who were honoured for meritorious service who later qualified after serving for 30 years were entitled to wear a bar which was of silver and carried a circular motif in the centre.

POLICE STAR FOR MERIT (POLISIESTER VIR VERDIENSTE)

Ribbon: Orange with a narrow white central band flanked by dark blue bands of equal width.

Metal: Silver and blue enamel.

Description: (Obverse) a six-point star with rayed arms and an inner circle of white enamel superimposed by a triangle (apex uppermost) of purple enamel containing a motif with two forearms joined at the fingertips from where a flame emerges; (reverse) the badge of the South African Police (SAP) within an outer band. The plain suspender bar was integral with the top of the medal body and joined by a triangular piece bearing a motif.

The badge of the South African Police consists of an eight-point star with the national coat of arms placed in the centre surrounded by an outer band with the Force name in Afrikaans (above) and English (below)

page 298

South Africa

The fourth medal was a purely long service award available to officers of all ranks on completion of 18 years exemplary service. After a further 15 years, making 33 in all, officers were awarded a bar inscribed with the initials TDFS (Troue Diens Faithful Service) in ornate lettering. If the officer concerned had previously been awarded the old Good Service Medal (1923 to 1963) he was awarded the new medal after an additional 15 years service, not a bar.

MEDAL FOR FAITHFUL SERVICE

Ribbon: Dark blue with a central gold band.

Metal: Bronze.

Description: (Obverse) a circular medal with the shield of the national coat of arms surmounted by the lion all within a wreath of laurel; (reverse) the badge of the South African Police and the words TROUE DIENS (above) and FAITHFUL SERVICE (below) around the circumference.

On 1 May 1979, the length of service necessary for the award of the Medal for Faithful Service was amended to ten years with officers who went on to complete 20 years or more becoming eligible for a new award.

STAR FOR FAITHFUL SERVICE

Ribbon: Gold with a green band placed centrally and a narrow green band towards each edge. A purple stripe appeared on the two broadest gold bands.

Metal: Silver.

Description: (Obverse) a circular medal containing an eight-point star and a central medallion with a motif of four groups of three aloe plants in red and green enamels arranged to form a cross; (reverse) the badge of the SAP with the words TROUE DIENS (above) and FAITHFUL SERVICE (below) at the circumference.

The changes made to the honours system in 1979 simplified the award of long service medals with awards being made after ten years (Medal for Faithful Service), 20 years (Star for Faithful Service), 30 years (Star for Merit) and 40 years (bar to the Star for Faithful Service). Each award had its own distinctive ribbon and any bars awarded were also different. The 1979 review also introduced two further honours, bringing the total available to officers of the South African Police for gallantry, distinguished, meritorious or faithful service to seven.

The system of honours introduced in 1963 made no special provision for senior officers to be rewarded for distinguished service or leadership in the especially trying and demanding environment of South Africa in the 1970s. The amendments to the regulations governing the issue of the Star for Distinguished Service went some way towards addressing this need but another, higher, award was also introduced.

STAR FOR DISTINGUISHED LEADERSHIP

Ribbon: Old gold with a dark blue central band flanked by white stripes.

Metal: Gold and enamel.

Description: (Obverse) a Maltese cross with a second cross superimposed between the arms of the first and a diamond shaped central medallion bearing a motif representative of three aloe flowers and leaves in blue and white enamels.

The basic award came in three parts with an ordinary breast medal for everyday wear, a neck ribbon with a chain for use in the appropriate circumstances and a breast star when the award was worn around the neck. The breast star was a rayed four-point affair with the central medallion bearing the same motif as the medal and the neck medallion being the same as the standard medal but larger. The chain which was used at only the most formal of occasions was attached by a diamond shape bearing the badge of the SAP. The chain consisted of a series of links each embossed with the aloe plant motif. The Star was awarded only to the most senior members of the Force hierarchy and general staff. Recipients were entitled to the use of the post-nominal letters—SED (*Stella Excellentis Ductis*). The star was awarded on two occasions only.

The second of the two new honours was the equivalent of the Queens Police Medals in many ways with the criteria for award being very similar. It was available for outstanding service and gallantry and brought with it the right to the use of the post-nominals—SOE (*Stella Officii Egregrii*).

POLICE STAR FOR OUTSTANDING SERVICE (POLISIESTER VIR UITMUNTENDE DIENS)

Ribbon: A multi-coloured ribbon with a central band of old gold flanked by bands of white, dark blue, white, old gold and green.

Metal: Silver gilt and enamel.

Description: (Obverse) a very ornate eight-point star shape with the four most prominent arms in the form of a fan and the intermediate arms being narrower. The circular central medallion carried the aloe flower motif found on the previous award on a white enamel background; (reverse) the Coat of Arms of South Africa with the words STELLA OFFICII EGREGRII at the top and on each side and S A POLICE below the arms. The medal hung from a V-shaped suspender which was an integral part of the main body.

South Africa

Between the two revisions of the honours system applicable to the South African Police in 1963 and 1979 there was a special medal introduced to acknowledge the performance of all officers specifically engaged in anti-terrorism work on or at any time after 26 August 1966. The medal was awarded to any member of the SAP or any person acting in support of the Force who was involved in combat with terrorist or who sustained any injury (including fatal wounds) or who executed their duties in such a fashion that they displayed exceptional zeal, vigilance, ingenuity, ability or leadership.

POLICE MEDAL FOR COMBATING TERRORISM (POLISIEMEDALJE VIR DIE BEKAMPING VAN TERRORISME)

Instituted: *1974.*

Ribbon: *White with two broad and two narrow red bands.*

Metal: *Silver.*

Description: *(Obverse) a six-point star with three long and three short points superimposed on a band bearing motifs of a series of crossed aloe leaves; (reverse) the badge of the SAP with an outer band bearing the words BEKAMPING VAN TERRORISME - COMBATING TERRORISM. It is also engraved with the rank, name and number of the recipient. The V-shaped suspender was attached to the medal by a shield bearing a representation of three aloe flowers and four leaves.*

If an officer who had been awarded the medal subsequently qualified again they were granted a silver bar decorated with a shield depicting the aloe plant motif. In undress uniform, the award of the bar is indicated by a small silver shield bearing the aloe plant motif worn in the centre of the ribbon. A maximum of two bars only could be awarded irrespective of the number of qualifying periods the officer had served. More than 21,000 medals and 16,000 bars were awarded.

In February 1985 a further change was made to the honours system with the introduction of an award for bravery which was to rank second only to the Cross for Bravery in the order of precedence. It was awarded to officers of the SAP who performed an act of conspicuous gallantry, or an outstanding act of courage in which they endangered their lives in the performance of their duty in the fight against terrorism or in the protection or saving of life or property threatened by a terrorist attack. It could be awarded posthumously. Before the cross was replaced in June 1989 it was awarded on only 29 occasions, seven posthumously.

SILVER CROSS FOR GALLANTRY (SILWERKRUIS VIR DAPPERHEID)

Ribbon: White with a broad (16 mm) dark blue central band and a red stripe placed centrally on each of the outer white bands.

Metal: Sterling silver and gold.

Description: (Obverse) a Maltese cross with a central medallion in gold containing the badge of the SAP within a wreath of laurel; (reverse) an image in relief of the monument to the SAP at Berg-en-Dal which was erected in recognition of the heroism of members of the Zuid Afrikaansche Republick Politie (SA Republic Police) at the battle of Dalmanutha in 1900. The words DAPPERHEID (left) and GALLANTRY (right) are inscribed on the arms of the cross.

Recipients were entitled to the use of letters after their name with English (SCG) and Afrikaans (SKD) versions authorised, a departure from the usual practice in South Africa where Latin was used. The letters are the initials of the cross in the relevant language—*Silwerkruis van Dapperheid* in Afrikaans. Any second or subsequent award was acknowledged by the issue of a silver bar which carried a small Maltese cross in the centre and on the ribbon in undress uniform.

The use distinctive devices on ribbons to indicate second awards is not unique to South Africa although it is, arguably, more widespread there than elsewhere. This is particularly true of medal available for the SAP, the South African Prisons Service and National Intelligence Service. Whereas in the UK a silver rosette is the usual indicator of a second award for most medals, in South Africa a prominent motif from the individual medal is used. The Prisons Service Medal for Merit, for example, has the national coat of arms as the centrepiece of the obverse and this is used on a ribbon to indicate a second award. Also in the Prison Service a second award of the Decoration for Valour is shown by a gold miniature of the obverse of the medal which has an unusual shape.

The Police Silver Cross for Gallantry was a short-lived award and the regulations which introduced it were repealed in June 1989 at the same time that the Police Cross for Bravery and the award for gallantry of the Police Star for Outstanding Service were also both discontinued. All three medals were replaced a single award available in three classes and cast in different metals to indicate the class of the award and degree of courage required. They became the three highest awards for bravery in the South African Police. The basic design was very similar to the Silver Cross for Gallantry.

The Police Cross for Bravery (Gold) was awarded only in the most exceptional circumstances to reward outstanding acts of bravery in extremely dangerous circumstances. The ribbon was royal blue with a central band of old gold (4 mm) flanked by white stripes. The second award—the Cross for Bravery (Silver)—demanded a lower but still very high degree of courage with the recipient honoured for performing an exceptional deed of bravery in very dangerous circumstances. The ribbon was royal blue with two bands of white either side of the central blue band each with a stripe of old gold. The final award was produced in lower grade silver and known simply as the Cross for Bravery. It was awarded to performing acts of bravery in dangerous circumstances, with no further qualification of the criteria give. The ribbon was basically royal blue with a central band (4 mm) of old gold and three lines of white on either side.

The history of policing in South Africa from the time of the establishment of the first Dutch settlement at the Cape in 1655 to the present day is very complex. The expansion of Dutch influence, wars with the local people, the involvement of the British, the Boer War and involvement in the policing of Namibia and Zimbabwe in the troubled times of the past have all left their mark. The basis of the present South African Police Service was laid on 1 April 1913 when most of the large number of municipal and regional forces which existed were disbanded and amalgamated into the South African Police, one of two national organisations. Further changes took place after the Great War and responsibility for policing the whole country finally fell to the SAP on 1 April 1936.

In 1988, to celebrate the 75th anniversary of the founding of the SAP a commemorative medal was introduced and awarded to permanent and temporary members of the Force and members of the Reserve Police Force who were serving on 1 April 1988. Other officers who had given particularly meritorious service also received the medal. The awards were also issued named, engraved on the reverse with the recipients number, rank and name below the Force badge. Provision was made in the regulations for the award of a bar to any officer still serving on the Forces centenary—in 2013.

SOUTH AFRICAN POLICE 75TH ANNIVERSARY MEDAL

Instituted: 1 April 1988.

Ribbon: A dark blue central band flanked by gold lines and light blue edges.

Metal: Bronze.

Description: (Obverse) the figures 75 surmounted by a motif of an aloe plant with the Force motto SERVAMUS ET SERVIMUS along the upper circumference and the dates 1913 - 1988 at the bottom; (reverse) the badge of the South African Police. A plain straight suspender bar was used.

Following the multi-racial elections in 1994 and subsequent developments, the honours system was subject to a further review and all awards to the South African Police changed.

The old coat of arms depicted on many of the old medals was retained by the new government after 1994 although a change was inevitable. This change came on 26 April 2000 with the adoption of new arms with no elements in them from colonial days. They are quite complex with two series of features placed in the form of two arcs, one placed above the other. In the lower arm, the most prominent feature are four elephant tusks to symbolise wisdom, strength, moderation and eternity enclosing a shield containing two human figures taken from South African rock art, partially encircled by two sheaves of wheat. The motto contained in a banner below the shield is written in the Khoisan language—!ke e: /xarra //ke—and means "unity in diversity".

The Khoisan language is now extinct but belonged to the fascinating group of click languages found in many parts of southern Africa. The symbols in the words stand for the different clicking sounds made in the speech, all with different meanings, which were an inherent part of the language. In the motto the letters "ke" are preceded by an exclamation mark in the first word and two slashes in the other giving the basic letters two pronunciations and two separate meanings - they are two totally different words although, to western eyes, they are the same.

The upper arc of the arms depicts a secretary bird in flight with a spear and a knobkierie as its legs to represent strength, growth, speed and the protection of the nation against its enemies. A rising sun above the bird is meant to indicate the rebirth of South Africa. There are other elements, each with their own meaning and the adoption of the new arms finally severed the ties with the days of empire and the country's troubled past.

SOUTH AFRICAN RAILWAYS POLICE

The South African Railways Police was an independent body which worked alongside the South African Police for 52 years with responsibility for railways, harbours and airports. It was founded on 1 July 1934 but merged with the other service in 1986 to form a single body with jurisdiction over all aspects of policing in the Republic. From its inception the Force awarded medals to its officers for bravery, distinguished and meritorious service and long service and good conduct. In total, 13 different medals were made available although this included some replacements and redesigns. The first medal issued was in recognition of long service and good conduct and authorised when the Force was founded in 1934 although the first award was not made until 1946.

RAILWAYS AND HARBOURS POLICE LONG SERVICE AND GOOD CONDUCT MEDAL

Instituted: 1934.

Ribbon: A central green band (9 mm) flanked by bands of white (4.5 mm) and blue (6 mm).

Metal; Silver.

Description: (Obverse) the Coat of Arms of South Africa with the words S.A.R. AND H. POLICE around the upper circumference and S.A.S.- EN HAWE POLISIE at the bottom; (reverse) plain apart from the words FOR FAITHFUL SERVICE and the Afrikaans version VIR TROUE DIENS, both in three lines. A plain straight suspender was used attached by a claw fitting.

Although the medal was primarily to reward good service of at least 18 years it was also awarded to recognise acts of bravery or particularly meritorious service without the service qualification. In these cases, a bar was attached to the ribbon inscribed MERIT—VERDIENSTE. The inscription on the obverse acknowledged the original name of the Force as the South African Railways and Harbours Police although was amended and the wording changed in 1960 to S.A.S. - POLISIE at the top and S.A.S POLICE at the bottom. Very few medals of the original design were awarded.

It remained the only medal awarded until 5 August 1966 when it was discontinued and a series of four replacements introduced with the various reasons for its award being recognised by separate medals. The highest honour was awarded to recognise acts of conspicuous bravery by any officer of the Force irrespective of rank. The Cross brought with it the right to the use of the post-nominals—IF (*Insigne Fortitudinis*). In South Africa, English and Afrikaans were both official languages and the names of the medals issued were very different, resulting in the use of different post-nominals if the usual convention was adopted. To overcome this problem the authorities turned to Latin for a compromise acceptable to all.

South Africa

POLICE CROSS FOR VALOUR

Ribbon: A neck ribbon in old gold with black lines at each edge and a central white band flanked by two black lines.

Metal: Silver gilt and enamel.

Description: (Obverse) a circular medal with a Maltese cross superimposed on a four-point star and a central medallion depicting the lion and bundle of sticks from the South African crest surrounded by a wreath of oak leaves.

The second award was also given for gallantry although of a lesser degree than was required for the Cross of Valour but which displayed particular ingenuity, proficiency or perseverance. It was also awarded for particularly distinguished service which did not necessarily involve and act of bravery. Recipients were also entitled to the use of letters after their name, also in Latin, in this case—SMO (*Stella Muneris Optimi*).

DECORATION FOR DISTINGUISHED SERVICE

Ribbon: White with a central band in old gold flanked by black stripes and with stripes of green and black at each edge.

Metal: Silver gilt and green enamel.

Description: (Obverse) a circular medal with a five-point star superimposed on another with broader, rayed points and a central medallion depicting a hand holding two lightning bolts on a background of green enamel within a wreath of oak leaves.

Particularly meritorious or exceptional service without involving an act of gallantry was rewarded by the third medal in the series. It served a dual purpose and was also given to officers on completion of 30 years exemplary service with irreproachable conduct. Those to whom it had previously been awarded for meritorious service and who subsequently qualified on the grounds of time served were issued with a bar. There was no entitlement to post-nominals. All three medals could be issued on more than one occasion, any second or subsequent awards being indicated by a bar worn on the ribbon.

STAR FOR MERIT

Ribbon: White with a broad central band in old gold flanked by stripes of dark blue and with black lines at each edge.

Description: (Obverse) a circular medal with five-point star superimposed on a rayed disc with a central medallion containing a motif of two hands cupping the flame of life within a wreath of oak leaves.

The final issue of the series of four was a faithful service medal with no requirement for particularly outstanding service or acts of courage. It was basically available to any officer who had completed 18 years service, which need not be continuous, on 1 January 1966. It was a replacement for the Good Service Medal with a number of conditions attached to the regulations for its award resulting from the multi-purpose nature of the previous medal. The earlier award was not given to an officer who had achieved the rank of inspector or above before the completion of his 18 years—this proviso was removed from the new regulations. Any officer who had been awarded the earlier honour for an act of gallantry or for outstanding service was also entitled to the new medal if he completed his 18 years service after 1 January 1966. Finally, officers who had received the Good Service Medal on the grounds of time served only and who went on to complete a further 15 years were awarded the new medal in addition. Recipients of the newer medal who served for an additional 15 years were awarded a bar to their medal.

MEDAL FOR FAITHFUL SERVICE

Ribbon: Old gold with a broad central stripe in white flanked by red lines and with a black line at each edge.

Description: (Obverse) a circular medal with a central medallion depicting a Boer covered wagon within a wreath, all superimposed on a rayed disc.

In 1980 the series of medals was reviewed and expanded to eight different awards to cover the whole range of police activity and included for the first time two orders which were available only to members of the Force general staff. One medal from the previous series was retained without any change to its appearance although its name was amended from the Decoration for Distinguished Service to the Decoration for Outstanding Service and the criteria were widened slightly. The highest award remained the Cross for Valour although it was completely redesigned.

POLICE CROSS FOR VALOUR

Ribbon: A neck ribbon in old gold.

Metal: Gold.

Description: (Obverse) two Maltese crosses, one with narrow arms superimposed on another with broader arms both lined with enamel and with an enamelled central medallion of a sprig of three acorns within two branches of oak leaves. Recipients were also given a small gold bar decorated with a miniature double Maltese cross emblem to wear in civilian clothing. A plain straight suspender was employed.

The second award in the new series was available only to officers from the general staff who had distinguished themselves through their leadership and who had provided particularly meritorious service which contributed to the security of the state or had rendered outstanding service to a head of state.

It was an elaborate decoration for a police officer whatever the rank, with no counterpart in the UK. This gold decoration came with a neck ribbon in plain bronze green, a collar chain and a breast star with the method of wear being dictated by the occasion. The collar chain was made up of a series of circular discs each with a motif in the shape of a pair of branches of oak leaves and was worn on only the most formal of occasions. The medal itself was of a simple design with two eight pointed stars, one superimposed on the other and with a smaller similar star in the centre. It was attached to the collar chain, when used, by an eight-point star containing the South African coat of arms. Recipients were entitled to the use of the initials SEE (*Stella Eximmi Emperii*) after their name—these words also appeared on the breast star in gold on enamel around the edge of the central medallion.

The second of the decorations available only to members of the general staff was of an equally plain design—a simple eight-point star—and could also be worn with a collar chain or a neck ribbon of bronze green with two bands of old gold at the edges. The Star for Distinguished Devotion was granted in similar circumstances to the previous award although the criteria are somewhat less demanding. The post-nominal letters—SDE stand for *Stella Diligentiae Egregiae*, the name in Latin. All other medals in the series were available to all officers irrespective of their rank and included a replacement for an award from the previous series.

STAR FOR MERIT

Ribbon: Old gold with a central stripe of orange red (2 mm) flanked by bands of white (3 mm) and bronze green (5 mm).

Metal: Silver gilt.

Description: (Obverse) a octagonal medal with an outer band (also octagonal) of oak leaves and an eight point star superimposed on both. The central medallion displayed a motif of two hands cupping the flame of life. A plain straight suspender and ring fitting were used, attached to the top of the disc by a scrolled fixture.

It served a dual purpose and was awarded in recognition of an act of personal heroism, for particularly meritorious service or on the completion of at least 30 years exemplary service with the Force. Any second or subsequent award was indicated by a bar bearing the emblem seen in the centre of the full-size award.

The design on the obverse of the Star for Merit was repeated on the Star for Faithful Service, a silver award introduced to reward officers for 20 years exemplary service although the ribbon was different—bronze green with a central white band (6 mm) flanked by stripes of orange red (2 mm) and silver (4 mm). Should an officer serve for another 20 years, a bar was issued inscribed with the initials TDFS (Troue Diens Faithful Service) in ornamental lettering.

The next medal in the series was a bronze medal issued on the completion of ten years service which need not have been continuous but must have been exemplary and with irreproachable conduct. The octagonal shape of the two previous awards was used for the Medal for Faithful Service but the design on the obverse was changed to a representation of the South African coat of arms. The ribbon was old gold with a narrow orange red stripe at each end and a central band of bronze green flanked by black lines.

The final medal of the series followed the example set by the South African Police and was awarded for service in anti-terrorist operations. It was issued to any officer who had been involved in combat with terrorists or who had suffered any wound or injury which arose from terrorist action in the course of their duty. Police officers were not the only recipients of the award. Anyone who was working in support of the police in an operational area on counter insurgency duties for a period of 60 days was also entitled to the medal. The period of service could be accumulated and bars were available for subsequent qualifying service.

The Medal for Combating Terrorism was circular, smaller than the previous three, and depicted a sword pointing upwards partially superimposed on a wreath of laurel. The ribbon was predominantly white with broad green bands in the centre and at each edge. The white bands had narrow lines of red, dark blue and red

After the Force was merged with the South African Police, all officers became eligible for the honours and awards of that organisation and any service they had accumulated prior to the merger was counted. The Force ceased to exist on 30 September 1986 and all medals were rendered redundant.

SOUTH AFRICAN BLACK HOMELANDS

Between 1962 and 1994 four independent and six non-independent homelands were created in South Africa with varying degrees of autonomy granted although none ever achieved any form of international recognition and all were re-incorporated into South Africa on 27 April 1994 after the multi-party elections which saw the end of apartheid and the appointment of Nelson Mandela as president. The states each had an ethnic and linguistic basis although only two (Ciskei and QwaQwa) had a continuous area, most were scattered pockets of land often with some distance between them. One unwelcome side effect of the establishment of the homelands was the withdrawal of South African citizenship from anyone with the appropriate ethnic or linguistic background who was declared to be a citizen of the new republic, reinforcing the racial separation of apartheid. The homelands were given all the trappings of independence—a government, their own flag and coat of arms, responsibility for health, education and roads and a separate police force each of which subsequently introduced a series of medals to reward the local officers in a similar fashion to those available in the Republic of South Africa. In total seventy medals were introduced in the ten homelands—Kwazulu, Lebowa, KwaNdebele, QwaQwa, Venda, Transkei, Bophuthatswana, Ciskei, KaNgwane and Gazankulu.

The officers of the new forces were mostly drawn from the SAP, many of whom had previously been awarded medals during their service with that force. They were entitled to continue wearing these awards alongside any from their new force. When the ten forces were disbanded in 1994 this same entitlement was extended to any awards received in their time with the Homelands forces. It is possible to see medals awarded by the SAP, a Homelands force and the new South African Police Service worn alongside each other.

Most of the medals awarded in the homelands used the coat of arms of the Homeland as a centrepiece with any inscriptions being in the local language alongside English and/or Afrikaans and they provide an interesting reminder of the multi-cultural make-up of modern South Africa. The coats of arms and flags used in the Homelands were all withdrawn from use in 1994.

The medals were produced in gold, silver gilt, silver, silver-plate and bronze, made extensive use of enamels and, in some instances, semi-precious stones. The designs were often very ornate and used a great deal of symbolism with the reasons and the criteria for their award broadly following the pattern used by the SAP. The numbers authorised varied between forces with one—KaNgwane—only issuing one but with two others—Ciskei and Venda—each producing ten different awards. A full descriptive sample of one award from each force follows.

BOPHUTHATSWANA POLICE MEDAL FOR COMBATING TERRORISM

Ribbon: White with a green central band and a red stripe towards each edge.

Metal: Silver.

Size: 38 mm.

Description: (Obverse) a circular medal with semi-circles cut from each side to give the form of a stylised Tswana shield. The obverse featured a motif of ten spears, five pointing upwards and five down; (reverse) a leopard. A straight suspender was used bearing a leaf pattern.

The Republic of Bophuthatswana was made up of seven territories dispersed over a wide area of north-central South Africa close to the border with Botswana. It was home to the Tswana people to whom the name meant that which binds. The Homeland was originally created in the 1960s with a territorial assembly, became a self-governing state in 1972 and was declared a republic on 6 December 1977. The Republic instituted seven medals in all, including the one described, one for bravery, one for outstanding leadership, three for differing periods of faithful service and one issued to celebrate the declaration of republic status. The criteria for the award of the Medal for Combating Terrorism were very similar to those of the SAP.

CISKEI POLICE CROSS FOR DISTINGUISHED LEADERSHIP

Ribbon: Yellow with a blue central band flanked by white stripes and with a blue stripe towards each edge.

Metal: 18 ct gold.

Size: 50 mm.

Description: (Obverse) a cross patée with the space between the arms containing a roundel in ivory and a blue semi-precious stone at the centre of each. The central medallion showed the Coat of Arms of the Republic of Ciskei within an outer band carrying the words AMAPOLISA ASECISKEI (above) and CISKEI POLICE (below) in gold on blue enamel; (reverse) the police badge and the words UBUNKOKHELI (above) and LEADERSHIP (below) around the circumference.

Without doubt, this was the most ornate decoration awarded in any of the Homelands police forces. It was worn from a neck ribbon in most normal circumstances but, if the occasion was appropriate and demanded full dress, it was worn with a neck chain made up of series of kite-shaped links in blue enamel carrying an oxs head in gold. The decoration also had a breast badge associated with it to be worn on the left breast pocket at suitable times. The badge had the same central medallion (although the enamel of the outer band was green, not blue) superimposed on a gold four-point rayed star and a light blue diagonal cross.

Ciskei was a small republic on the Indian Ocean coast of South Africa and one of only two with contiguous territory. It was mainly inhabited by Xhosa-speaking people. It was first granted a degree of self-government in 1961 and became a republic on 4 December 1981. The Republic's name in the Xhosa language means this side of the Kei referring to the Great Kei River which ran along its north border. A second Xhosa-speaking people lived in another republic on the far side of the river—Transkei (across the Kei)—separated by the river and a strip of South Africa containing the city of Port Elizabeth.

The Republic issued ten awards to its police officers, four decorations (including the one described), a cross for bravery, three for differing periods of good service, one for combating terrorism and an independence medal.

The Coat of Arms of Ciskei which appears on all but two of the medals awarded has a number of elements. The shield is that traditionally used by the people of Ciskei and is quartered diagonally with a bull's head in the upper part (symbolising that cattle farming was the main source of income of the people) and a milkwood tree in the lower (to represent acceptance of the rule of God). Behind the shield are a crossed assegai and knobkierie (symbols of a chief's authority) with two leopards as supporters. Above the shield standing on four ivory rings is the Republic's national bird, the blue crane, representing the will of the people to be steadfast and courageous. A motto in the Xhosa language—SIYAKUNQANDWA ZIINKWENKWEZI (we will be stopped by the stars)—lies below the shield.

GAZANKULU POLICE STAR FOR DISTINGUISHED LEADERSHIP

Ribbon: Sand coloured with a central red band and a blue stripe towards each edge.

Metal: Gilt with red and blue enamel.

Size: 52 mm.

Description: (Obverse) two ten-point stars, one (with long rays) superimposed on the other. A central medallion with a blue enamel centre bearing the image of a lion in red enamel holding an antelope horn, surrounded by a wreath of blue and red enamel and a second outer band carrying a motif of six pairs of spoons taken from the Coat of Arms of Gazankulu; (reverse) the badge of the Gazankulu Police with a circumscription in three languages - VURHANGERI BYO HLAWULEKA (above), UITNEMENDE LEIERSKAP (right) and DISTINGUISHED LEADERSHIP (left).

The lion holding the horn is a symbol of power and the spoon motif which consists of a pair of spoons joined at the handles by a chain is representative of the peace and hospitality of the people. The difference is the design and style of the awards made for the same reason by Ciskei and Gazankulu could not be more marked. Gazankulu was not declared a republic although it was a self-governing state independent of South Africa. The four separate territories which made up the state were situated in the north-east corner of South Africa close to the borders with Zimbabwe, Mozambique and Botswana and home to the Bantu-speaking Tsonga people and the Shangaan who originally came into the area from Mozambique in the mid-19th century.

Gwazankulu issued a set of seven awards—a cross for bravery, stars for distinguished leadership and distinguished service, three for faithful service of varying lengths and a medal to commemorate the establishment of the Homeland. The establishment medal was little more than an alternative term for the independence medal issued in the four Homelands which were declared republics although this status was never recognised outside South Africa.

KANGWANE POLICE ESTABLISHMENT MEDAL

Ribbon: Red with a blue central band and yellow edges.

Metal: Silver.

Size: 38 mm.

Description: (Obverse) a simple circular medal with the badge of the KaNgwane Police (a seven-point Brunswick star with the Coat of Arms of KaNwane in the centre) on the obverse above a banner bearing the word SIMUNYE; (reverse) the Coat of Arms of KaNgwane and the date 86.06.01 above (the date the Homeland was established).

This was the only medal issued in the KaNgwane Homeland and awarded to commemorate its establishment on 1 June 1986. It was one of the smallest of the Homelands and made up of two separate areas, mostly of high veldt along the northern and western borders of the Kingdom of Swaziland—a truly independent state wholly surrounded by South Africa. The purpose of establishing KaNgwane was to provide a homeland for any Swazi people living outside the Kingdom of Swaziland.

KWANDEBELE POLICE LONG SERVICE MEDAL—30 YEARS

Ribbon: Yellow with a broad central band in green and a black stripe at each edge.

Metal: Silver gilt

Size: 38 mm.

Description: (Obverse) a lion's head; (reverse) the Coat of Arms of KwaNdebele. The suspender bar which was fixed to the top of the medal disc directly took the form of a pair of ox horns.

This medal was one of a series of three awarded for different periods of faithful service, the two others being given after ten years (bronze) and twenty years (silver). The reverse of all three awards was the same but the obverse showed the head of a lynx on the bronze medal and a leopard on the silver. The ribbons were also different in each case although both used a combination of green, yellow, white and black. The only other medal known to have been struck in the Homeland was the Establishment Medal although provision was made for the institution of four other awards—the Gallantry Cross (in gold and silver), the Medal for Most Distinguished Service (gold), the Medal for Distinguished Service (silver) and the Commendation Medal. It is thought that these four awards were never struck.

NwaNdebele was a self-governing state established in 1979 as a homeland for the Ndebele people—it was never granted the status of a republic. Many inhabitants were forcibly expelled from nearby Bophuthatswana and the state became little more than a group of twelve camps which housed more than 40 per cent of the population.

KWAZULU POLICE STAR FOR FAITHFUL SERVICE—20 YEARS

Ribbon: Silver with two bands of green.

Metal: Silver-plated with green enamel.

Size: 38 mm.

Description: (Obverse) an eight-point star with an octagonal central medallion in green enamel bearing the Coat of Arms of KwaZulu; (reverse) the badge of the KwaZulu Police with the inscription FAITHFUL SERVICE below. The triangular suspender bar was attached to the medal by means of a plaque bearing an elephant's head facing forwards.

The status of the eight awards of the KwaZulu Police is uncertain although there is evidence that they were all produced. KwaZulu was a non-independent black state and was the legal home to all of South Africa's Zulus although it consisted of eleven widely dispersed areas in the Province of Natal in the south-east of South Africa centred on the old capital of the Zulu empire (Ulundi) before the final battle of the Anglo-Zulu wars in 1879. The name was retained after the Homeland was abolished in 1994 and it now forms a part of the Province of KwaZulu/Natal.

The elements of the KwaZulu Coat of Arms reflect the people's past and the position of the King. The full arms are not used on the medal—the crest and motto are missing—and consist of the central shield and both supporters. The shield is taken from the royal regiment of Zulu tribes and has the royal sceptre in the centre, point upwards, with nine spear thongs on either side. The supporters, a lion and a leopard, each hold a spear to symbolise the will of the people to defend themselves.

LEBOWA POLICE STAR FOR DISTINGUISHED SERVICE

Ribbon: *White with a green band at each edge and two central orange stripes*

Metal: *Silver gilt.*

Size: *38 mm.*

Description: *(Obverse) circular with a central medallion bearing the image of a flame surrounded by ten points of a star; (reverse) the Coat of Arms of Lebowa. A plain straight suspender bar is used.*

The flame depicted in the central medallion is the crest of the Coat of Arms and symbolises spiritual power. The other features shown on the full Arms on the reverse have a quartered shield with two having a depiction of water and rain to represent the importance of water in farming and cattle-rearing, the two staple industries of the Sotho people. The plant and oxs head shown in the other two quarters reinforce this. The supports (leopards) each with an aloe plant behind are indicative of nature.

Lebowa was a non-independent state made up of a number of separate territories in the Transvaal in the north-east corner of South Africa. It was first established in 1962 and replaced by a legislative assembly in 1971 but granted self-government the following year.

The Star for Distinguished Service was of identical design to a second award although, in this case, it was cast in silver and sported a different ribbon. The Star for Excellent Service was awarded where the standard of service was less than that required for the premier award but still worthy of official recognition. Four other medals were produced in Lebowa, three to recognise 10, 20 and 30 years long service and the Establishment Medal. Two others were authorised—the Cross for Gallantry and the Star for Distinguished Leadership—but there is no evidence that either was ever struck although the ribbons for both were made.

QWA QWA POLICE FAITHFUL SERVICE MEDAL —TEN YEARS

Ribbon: Sand coloured with two red bands each having a thin black line outside.

Metal: Bronze.

Size: 37 mm.

Description: (Obverse) a circular medal with an eight-point star (four large and four small arms) with a central medallion bearing a ponys head in black enamel on a yellow disc within a white outer band with 16 black points around the central part; (reverse) plain apart from the inscription VIR TROUE DIENS and FOR FAITHFUL SERVICE in two lines in the upper half. The suspender was attached to the top of the medal disc.

The pony which appeared on the medal and as a full figure on the national flag was meant to symbolise the sure-footed progress of the people on an often difficult path and was chosen as it represented the most natural means of transport in the country. Although approval had been given for the issue of six medals, only three were ever produced and there is some doubt if the three others ever reached the design stage.

Qwa Qwa was the smallest of all the homelands with an area of less than 655 square kilometres in the Drakensberg Mountains close to Lesotho. It was granted self-government in 1974 but never achieved full independence. It was home to the Basuto people although it never contained more than a small minority of the people in South Africa.

TRANSKEI POLICE INDEPENDENCE MEDAL

Ribbon: A bright green with narrow band of white and brown at each edge.

Metal: Bronze.

Size: 38 mm.

Description: (Obverse) the Armorial Bearings of Transkei; (reverse) plain apart from the word UZIMELE across the centre with the date 26-10-76 below.

The Republic of Transkei was one of the first black states to be founded with self-government being introduced in 1959 followed by a declaration of independence in 1976. It was a large state made up of three territories, one very large, on the south-east coast of South Africa. It was almost completely surrounded by South Africa apart from the Indian Ocean coastline and a small area to the north which touched Lesotho. It was established, along with Ciskei, as a homeland for the South African Xhosa-speaking people and granted independence when they lost their South African citizenship under apartheid.

The Independence Medal was not an exclusively police medal although members of the Force received it. The position of the group of medals awarded in Transkei is somewhat confused and changes were made to those available a year before independence was granted. A system of rewarding long service had been in place before 1976 with awards for 18 and 30 years although this was brought into line with other black states and South Africa and the required periods of service were amended to 10, 20 and 30 years. Four rewards for more specific acts were authorised although there is some doubt whether they were all manufactured. The Gallantry Cross was the highest award followed by the Distinguished Service Decoration, Medal for Efficient Service and Medal for Combating Terrorism.

The Transkei Armorial Bearings appeared on several of the medals authorised in particular the series of long service awards. The central shield carried three elements—a bull's head to stress the importance of cattle farming, a cogwheel to represent industry and a head of the mealie plant symbolising agriculture. The crest was made up of a wicker basket flanked by two aloe plants with two leopards as supporters. In common with all other homelands coats of arms it was withdrawn from use in 1994.

VENDA POLICE MEDAL FOR FAITHFUL SERVICE (TEN YEARS LONG SERVICE)

Ribbon: Half pale blue, half brown.

Metal: Bronze.

Size: 38 mm.

Description: (Obverse) a young boabab tree; (reverse) the badge of the Venda Police with the words U FULUFHEDZEA MUSHUMONI (above) and FAITHFUL SERVICE (below). The fixed straight suspender was attached to the medal disc by a pair of crossed elephant tusks.

Located just south of the border with Zimbabwe in the Transvaal, the Republic of Venda covered an area of only 7,000 square kilometres and was home to a population of almost 600,000, who spoke their own, little known language (Venda). In 1962 the area was designated first as a homeland for the Venda-speaking people with a degree of self-government granted in 1973 followed by full independence in 1979.

The police badge consists of a six-point star with the coat of arms of the Republic of Venda in the centre with an outer band bearing the Force name in English at the bottom and in the local language at the top—HAPHOLISA A VENDA. The Coat of Arms was first introduced as a shield, crest and motto in 1972 and expanded following independence into a full achievement of arms including two supporters (elephants). The full bearings were reproduced on all the medals awarded in Venda in one form or another, either as a part of the badge or alone. The central shield bears an elephants head symbolising power and the crest of a tribal drum is indicative of the unity of the Venda people and was chosen for its use by the chief to summon local people to receive important messages. The motto—*Shumela Venda*—means "inspire always for Venda".

The Republic of Venda issued ten medals ranging from the Gallantry Cross in gold to the Independence Medal which was not exclusively available to police officers although large numbers received it. When Venda first became independent, a uniformed service was established with responsibility for all state security functions—police, prisons and military. Before long it became apparent that the single service did not function as efficiently as separate services and the national force was divided into three distinct units, including the new Venda Police Force. A series of medals had been produced for officers of the national service and these were taken over by the new police force on its formation although changes were made to the detailed design in many cases. By the time it was disbanded in 1994 the Venda Police issued a Gallantry Cross in gold and silver (two separate awards), a Distinguished Service Decoration, a Star for Outstanding Service, three medals to reward faithful service of 10, 20 and 30 years, a Medal for Combating Terrorism in addition to one in commemoration of the establishment of the new Venda Police Force and the Independence Medal instituted in 1979.

SPAIN

Although the policing structure of Spain is broadly similar to that of other western European countries, the establishment of seventeen autonomous regional governments, each with its own parliament, between 1979 and 1983 led to a fundamental difference. The desire for independence amongst some sections of the Spanish people is not a new phenomenon, the first stirrings came as early as the mid to late 1800s. The independence movements met with some success and the two most well-known and active groups—the Basques and Catalans—were granted autonomous status during the Second Republic (1931 to 1936) with provision being made for the third region (Galicia) to join them. The start of the Spanish Civil War (1936 to 1939), however, and Franco's subsequent victory resulted in the repression of all independence movements and the imposition of central control from Madrid.

The desire for independence though, primarily based on fundamental cultural and linguistic differences, persisted and bred the terrorist movement in the Basque country—ETA—which sought to achieve its aims by violence. The death of Franco in 1975 and the return of Spain to democracy gave the independence parties a boost and a real hope that their aims might be achieved through the democratic process although ETA continued their own campaign of violence. In 1979, after referendums held in both regions, agreement was reached to establish fully autonomous communities in the Basque country and Catalania. Regional parliaments were elected the following year and given control of local services which included responsibility for policing arrangements. The Basque Autonomous Police (*Cuerpo de la Policìa Autonoma del Paìs Vasco—Ertzaintza* in the Basque language)—a force some 7,350 officers strong—assumed the rôle previously undertaken by the Policia Nacionale in the region. In 1986 a medal was introduced for award to officers of the force in recognition of especially meritorious police work.

MEDALLA AL RECONOCIMIENTO DE LA LABOR POLICIAL (ERTZAIN-LANAGATIKAKO ESKERRONA ADIERAZTEKON)

Instituted: 27 February 1986.

Ribbon: Plain white, green or red accordingly to the division of the medal.

Metal: Gold with red, blue and green enamel.

Description: (Obverse) the badge of the Basque Police (a shield containing the Basque coat of arms above a dark blue enamel semicircle divided into five segments) surrounded by a wreath of oak leaves (below) and laurel (above); (reverse) left plain apart from the name of the recipient and the date of the award. The medal hangs from a gold top ribbon suspender bar.

The medal is awarded in three divisions dependent upon the circumstances of the act or duty for which it is given. In each case the only difference is in the colour of the ribbon—white, red or green in descending order of importance. Second or subsequent awards are indicated by a clasp worn on the ribbon in the appropriate colour according to the division of the second award.

The Basque Police medal was the first to be awarded by any of the autonomous forces which were formed although the precedent set was later followed. Although an autonomous community was established in Catalania at the same time as in the Basque country, there was no provision made for the award of a medal to members of the *Mossos d'Esquadra*, the Autonomous Catalan Police, until 1995 when the Medal of Police Merit was introduced. The name of the new force is very old, dating from the days when Catalania was independent. The former force, in fact, was a part of the model adopted, along with the French Gendarmerie Nationale, when the Guardia Civile was established in 1844.

MEDALLA AL MERIT POLICIAL DEL CUERPO DE MOSSOS D'ESCUADRA

Instituted: 13 June 1995.

Ribbon: Plain red or blue according to the division of the award.

Metal: Gold, silver and bronze.

Description: (Obverse) a circular medal with the arms of the Corps in the centre (an oval consisting of vertical stripes of red and yellow) and the words GENERALITAT DE CATALUNYA around the upper circumference and AL MERIT POLICIAL (for police merit) at the bottom; (reverse) the words POLICIA (upper) and MOSSOS D'ESQUADRA (lower) around the circumference with the central field left plain for the recipients name. A ring suspender and buckled top ribbon bar are used.

The award of the medal follows the Spanish tradition of being issued in a number of divisions, two in this case (red or blue), dependent on the reason for the award. The gold medal is awarded only in the red division (the highest) but the silver and bronze medals are available in both, a total of five awards in all.

The gold medal is awarded to an officer who dies in the course of his or her duty or who suffers from a serious and permanent injury or disability provided that there was no evidence of negligence, through inexperience or otherwise, and the reputation of the Corps does not suffer. Where the award is made posthumously, it is given to the surviving spouse or next-of-kin.

The higher division (red) of the silver medal is also awarded where a serious injury is sustained in the course of duty but it does not need to result in a permanent disability to qualify. The blue division of the silver medal is restricted to officers who perform an act of courage at great risk to their lives or which displays particular merit bringing credit to the Corps.

The bronze medal can be awarded to individuals or groups in three circumstances. The red division is given to officers who sustain a wound or injury in the course of their duty with no qualifying remarks relating to the severity of degree of permanence. The blue division of the bronze medal is awarded to recognise an act of bravery where there was a degree of risk or danger and also to recognise particularly meritorious service which brings credit to the Corps.

Since the establishment of the first three autonomous regions, others have followed with their own police forces coming shortly afterwards. Several of these have introduced their own individual awards for their officers. Zaragozas issue three awards and Granada has available the *Medalla al Mèrito del Cuerpo de la Policìa Municipal* (Medal of Merit of the Municipal Police) awarded in gold, silver and bronze with a ribbon of red and green.

Apart from these new locally awarded medals, national awards are made to officers from the two national forces—the Policìa Nationale and the Guardia Civil, the equivalent of the Gendarmerie Nationale in France or Carabinieri in Italy, who have a nationwide responsibility irrespective of the existence of any autonomous forces. The Guardia Civil is a part of the Spanish Armed Forces and officers are eligible for a series of military awards although they are not usually awarded during peacetime. In 1976, in recognition of the fact that members of the Corps face dangers daily in the normal course of their duty unlike other members of the Armed Forces, a series of decorations were introduced—the *Order of Merit of the Corps of Civil Guards*. The order has four classes with the award made being appropriate to the service performed. The broad purpose of the Order is to reward acts of gallantry or outstanding service to the Corps or Spain.

CRUZ DE ORO DE LA ORDEN DEL MÈRITO DEL CUERPO DE LA GUARDIA CIVIL

Instituted: 29 May 1976.

Ribbon: Three equal bands of green, red and green with two laurel leaves in gold.

Metal: Gold.

Size: 25 mm.

Description: *(Obverse)* a cross pattée with the arms in emerald green enamel edged with gold and a central medallion in red enamel surrounded by a wreath of laurel in gold and a central motif of the emblem of the Guardia Civil (a crossed sword and bundle of staves around an axe—the fasces, the Roman symbol of authority) surmounted by an inscription in black which reads AL MERITO (for merit). The area between the arms of the cross consists of seven golden rays; *(reverse)* identical to the obverse but with the central medallion containing the old symbol of the Guardia—the intertwined letters GC surmounted by a royal crown.

The Gold Cross is the highest class and awarded to officers who are killed or seriously and permanently injured in the line of their duty where they have displayed conspicuous courage. It is also available to officers who display exceptional courage at the risk of their lives in the service of the Corps or the country. The award is given sparingly.

The second class of award—la Cruz de Plata (silver cross)—has an identical design but made of silver with the only enamel being on the central medallion (both sides) and in white. The ribbon consists of three equal bands of green, white and green with the two laurel leaves being of silver. The criteria for its award are also somewhat less demanding than those for the premier award. The medals are not intended to be worn with a ribbon and the colours are those of the gold (or silver) edged ribbon bar which is worn in undress uniform. The Silver Cross is awarded for acts of courage or exceptional and meritorious service to the Corps or Spain where the standard does not quite reach that necessary for the award of the Gold Cross.

The two lesser awards of the Order are very similar to the other but with the seven rays between the arms of the cross omitted and the central medallion larger in relation to the size of the cross. Both are also meant for wear with a ribbon of the same colour as the two higher awards hanging from a buckled top ribbon bar. The higher of the two—*la Cruz con distintivo rojo* (Cross of the Red Division)—is of gold and awarded where an officer performs an act of courage with a risk to his or her life or where death or injury is suffered in the course of duty in the face of danger to the officer's life.

La Cruz con distintivo blanco (Cross of the White Division) is the lowest of the four awards available but still demands a high degree of exceptional and meritorious service to the Corps or the country. The Cross differs from the Silver Cross with the absence of the seven rays between the arms of the cross pattée and the larger size of the central medallion.

The award of the Golden Cross and Cross of the Red Division, both of which are given to officers who are killed in the line of duty or who suffer serious and permanent injury, carries with it an increase in the pension paid to the officers, 20 % in the first instance and 15% in the second.

The Guardia Civil was formed in 1844 to provide a national public security force to combat the lawlessness of inland Spain and the activities of bandits since the War of Independence. It served dual masters in the early days, the Ministry of the Interior for operational activities and the Ministry of Defence for all other matters including discipline, equipment, personnel and pay. The initial force had an establishment of 3,250 officers and its area of responsibility was gradually enlarged to include the whole of Spain in the early years of the 20th century. It now boasts a strength of more than 70,000. Attempts to change the dual responsibility were made at intervals but without success until it became wholly answerable to the Ministry of the Interior only shortly before the outbreak of the Spanish Civil War. The Guardia was given responsibility for outbreaks of public disorder from the outset and this has been added to regularly since including the policing of Spanish roads through its Traffic Group, formed in 1959. It plays a leading rôle in combating terrorism, particularly that of the Basque separatist movement (ETA) and has also assisted in peacekeeping operations under the United Nations.

Working alongside the Guardia are the municipal police forces found in most towns and cities of any size and the Policìa Nationale which has a responsibility for most of rural Spain where autonomous forces have not yet been established. The national medal available to the majority of police officers in Spain (*Police Medal of Merit*) was established during Franco's time when all ambitions of independence or autonomy were surpressed. The design of the medal was changed once but it remains current today.

MEDALLA DEL MÈRITO POLICIAL

Instituted: 18 June 1943.

Ribbon: Light green with three stripes at each edge in the national colours, red, yellow and red.

Metal: Gold, silver and bronze.

Size: 40 mm.

Description: (Obverse) a circular medal with a reclining male figure at the base and the guardian angel above symbolizing sacrifice in the name of service. The words AL MÈRITO POLICIAL (for police merit) are inscribed between the two; (reverse) a sword (facing downwards) entwined with laurel leaves representing justice and the words SERVICIO (service) and SACRIFICIO (sacrifice) at the lower circumference. An ornate ring suspender is used with a buckled top ribbon bar in the same metal as the medal.

The medal is awarded to recognise outstanding police service and includes especially meritorious work in the scientific and technical fields which contribute to the overall aim of the police service in Spain. The class of award made is dependent upon the standard of service performed or the importance of an act or acts deserving official recognition. Any second or subsequent award is indicated by a bar worn on the ribbon, the bar being of the same metal as the later award(s). Particularly meritorious service in any of the three classes also brought with it an entitlement to an annual pension of 2,600 pesetas (gold), 1,850 (silver) and 1,180 (bronze). On 15 May 1945 an amendment to the regulations was made with the introduction of a broad central white band on the ribbon of awards made where a pension was granted. In 1964 further amendments were made which resulted in the bronze medal being discontinued and two crosses being introduced to replace it—*Police Cross of Merit*, red or white divisions.

CRUZ AL MÈRITO POLICIAL CON DISTINTIVO ROJO O BLANCO

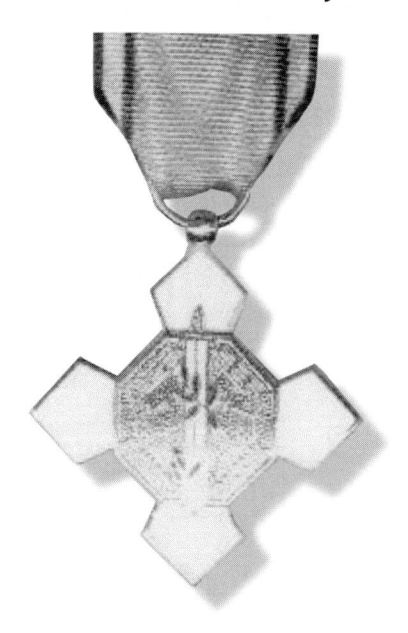

Instituted: 29 April 1964..

Ribbon: The same as the Medalla del Mèrito.

Metal: Gold and red or white enamel.

Size: 45 mm.

Description: (Obverse) a central octagonal medallion in gold depicting a sword (pointing downwards) entwined with leaves of laurel in white enamel with the arms of the cross in the shape of a pentagon at the cardinal points. The arms are of white or red enamel dependent upon the division of the award. The words AL MÈRITO POLICIAL are inscribed to the left and right of the sword; (reverse) left plain. A plain ring suspender is used

The introduction of the two crosses, bringing to four the number of awards available to police officers, was accompanied by a major revision of the criteria for the award of each. The general set of conditions laid down in 1943 was replaced by a far more specific list of what was necessary to be eligible for each of the four medals. The Medals of Merit in gold and silver are given to officers (or their next-of-kin) who were killed or seriously and permanently wounded or injured in the course of their duty, who perform an act of courage in the face of danger to their lives or who render some especially meritorious or distinguished service which enhances the reputation of the force or the police service in general. The level of the award is decided upon by the circumstances of the act.

The Cruz con distintivo rojo (Cross of the Red Division), with the arms enamelled in red, is awarded to any officer who is injured in the course of duty, has performed an act of courage in the face of danger to his or her life in circumstances which enhance the prestige of the force or the police service in general, who takes part in three or more actions where weapons are involved but no injury is sustained and, lastly, in recognition of a particularly meritorious or distinguished act of service where there was personal risk or danger.

Each of these awards can be accompanied by an increase in the officer's pension in similar fashion to the original awards but the fixed sum previously available was amended to a percentage to take account the loss of value of the earlier sums—20% (gold), 15% (silver) and 10% (Cross of the Red Division).

The final award, the Cruz con distintivo blanco (the Cross of the White Division), does not carry an entitlement to an increase in pension and is awarded where the service displays loyalty or professionalism not involving danger or injury but is of a standard sufficient, to merit official recognition. It can be given for particularly meritorious work in the scientific and technology fields which enhance the ability of the force or the police service in general to combat crime.

The range of local medals awarded to police officers in Spain is likely to increase, many autonomous governments already award their own medals for services to the region and this could well include police officers although the situation isn't easy to fathom at present. Devolution of government in Spain is more advanced than most European countries and the existence of autonomous police forces has no true comparison elsewhere within the European Community, I suspect that further local police medals will appear across the country before very long.

SRI LANKA

Sri Lanka has been inhabited since at least the 6th century BC when the very first Sinhalese people arrived from north India and displaced the previous inhabitants, the Veddah. It was first settled by Europeans in 1505 with the arrival of the Portuguese who displayed the worst aspects of European imperialism with a régime of greed, intolerance and cruelty. By the middle of the 17th century the Portuguese had been displaced by the Dutch who were themselves overthrown by the British in 1796. The British ruled the island from Madras until it was established as a Crown Colony in 1802. The first rumblings if discontent and stirrings towards independence began between the two 20th century world wars and it was finally granted following its larger neighbour to the north by a few months as the British Empire was unravelled. In 1948 Ceylon became an independent member of the British Commonwealth.

The present name—Sri Lanka—was not adopted until 1972 when the island became a republic and is based on the old Sinhalese name of Lanka with the addition of the prefix Sri meaning auspicious or resplendent in the native language. The precise translation of the Sinhalese character into our Roman alphabet is still subject to debate and the interpretation of Shri is now thought be much closer to the correct sound

Sri Lanka is not a large island, roughly the same size as Ireland, but with a population of more than 17 million, giving it one of the highest population densities in Asia. The predominant religion is Buddhism although the Tamil people in the north of the island represent a sizeable Hindu minority of about 18% of the total population—almost one million. Sri Lanka has the distinction of being the first country in the world to elect a female prime minister in 1960—Mrs Sirimavo Bandaranaike, the widow of the former leader who was assassinated by a Buddhist monk the previous year.

Not long after the arrival of the British in the early 19th century the first policing in a style we would recognise in the west was formed to suppress bandit activities. In 1844 the various forces that had sprung up in the towns, cities and provinces were amalgamated into a single body with their duties and responsibilities clearly defined by 1865. The first medal to be introduced to reward police officers appeared in 1925, awarded on completion of 15 years service.

CEYLON POLICE
LONG SERVICE AND GOOD CONDUCT MEDAL

Instituted: 1925.

Ribbon: Sand coloured with a red central band, all of equal width. A stripe of dark blue runs down the centre of the sand-coloured bands.

Metal: Silver.

Size: 36 mm.

Description: (Obverse) the uncrowned coinage profile of King George V; (reverse) an Indian elephant facing left in the centre, surmounted by a crown with the legend CEYLON POLICE along the bottom and FOR LONG SERVICE AND GOOD CONDUCT around the upper circumference. A ring suspender was employed.

In 1934 the medal was superseded by the Colonial Police Medal which stayed current until independence was granted in 1948 although a second medal, very similar to the first, was introduced at the request of the new Ceylonese government together with two others intended to reward gallantry and meritorious service, effectively mirroring the three different colonial police medals previously available.

CEYLON POLICE SERVICE LONG SERVICE MEDAL

Instituted: 1950.

Ribbon: Dark blue edged with stripes of khaki, white and pale blue.

Metal: Cupro-nickel.

Size: 36 mm.

Description: (Obverse) the effigy of King George VI or Queen Elizabeth II; (reverse) very similar to the 1925 version with an Indian elephant facing left in the centre but without the crown. The legend CEYLON POLICE SERVICE was inscribed around the upper circumference and FOR LONG SERVICE AND GOOD CONDUCT around the lower. A plain straight suspender bar was employed.

The necessary period of service for the long service and good conduct medal was extended to 18 years and two bars were introduced for award after 25 and 30 years total service. The medals issued in recognition of acts of gallantry or to reward meritorious service used the same design on the obverse, were of the same size but were cast in silver, hung from distinct ribbons and had different reverses.

CEYLON POLICE MEDAL FOR MERIT

Ribbon: Khaki with three stripes of silver, light blue and dark blue towards the edges.

Description: (Obverse) the effigy of King George VI or Queen Elizabeth II; (reverse) the badge of the Ceylon Police with the words CEYLON POLICE SERVICE above and FOR MERIT below. A plain straight suspender was used.

The medal awarded for gallantry differed only in the substitution of the words FOR GALLANTRY and the addition of a thin red line on the white bands of the ribbon. In 1972 when Ceylon became a republic and adopted its present name, all three medals were discontinued. At the time of independence in 1948 there were no official commemorative medals issued but this was rectified in 1955 for regular and reserve police officers who were serving on 4 February 1948.

CEYLON POLICE INDEPENDENCE MEDAL

Instituted: 1955.

Ribbon: A broad red central stripe flanked by a white line (1.5 mm), a fawn stripe (5.5 mm) and dark blue edges (4 mm).

Metal: Silver.

Size: 36 mm.

Description: (Obverse) the badge of the Ceylon Police within a circle containing the name of the Force with a circumscription which read THE CEYLON POLICE INDEPENDENCE MEDAL; (reverse) the Lion of Kandy within a circle surmounted by a crown all surrounded by the words ELIZABETH II QUEEN OF CEYLON & HER OTHER REALMS & TERRITORIES, HEAD OF THE COMMONWEALTH.

Information about the medals available to police officers since the establishment of republic status is hard to obtain through official sources. If the example of the large neighbour to the north is typical there will be a range of medals produced including awards for service against the rebel Tamil Tigers in the troubled north of the island but little detail has been forthcoming.

SWAZILAND

The Kingdom of Swaziland is a tiny country with an area of only 17,393 square kilometres and a population of 800,000 entirely surrounded by the Republic of South Africa on three sides and Mozambique on the other. It is an hereditary monarchy currently ruled by King Mswati III. A British protectorate since 1903, it became in independent kingdom under the father (King Sobhuza II) of the present monarch in September 1968 and introduced a range of three medals in 1970 for award to officers of the Royal Swaziland Police to acknowledge distinguished or meritorious service and long service and good conduct.

KING'S POLICE MEDAL FOR DISTINGUISHED SERVICE

Ribbon: *Dark blue with narrow red stripes in the centre and at each edge.*

Metal: *Silver.*

Description: *(Obverse) the King's head (Sobhuza II); (reverse) the Coat of Arms of Swaziland with the name of the medal around the circumference.*

The coat of arms has a shield at the centre with a motif of a native shield and spears and a crest of a flowering plant. The two supporters are indicative of the country's wildlife—an tusked elephant to the right and a male lion on the left.

The criteria for the award of the medal demand a display of exceptional resourcefulness and devotion to duty marked by outstanding and distinguished service. It was primarily a reward for the most senior officers of the Force—the Commissioner and his deputy were the first two recipients. Slightly less demanding criteria were applied to the next medal in the series which was awarded, in the main, to officers of the rank of assistant superintendent and above who had displayed exceptional ability and merit. The design of the Royal Swaziland Police Medal for Meritorious Service was the same as for the King's Police Medal with the only difference being the name of the award given on the reverse around the coat of arms. The ribbon was also of the same basic colour but with the stripes being in white, not red. It was made of cupro-nickel. The first two awards, to superintendents, were made in July 1972.

The third medal—Royal Swaziland Police Long Service Medal—also carried the King's head on the obverse but the reverse used the badge of the Force rather than the national coat of arms with the name around the circumference. It was made of cupro-nickel and hung from a dark blue ribbon with a thin white line at each edge. It was awarded to officers below the rank of assistant superintendent at the completion of 18 years exemplary service which was to be continuous with bars available after 25 years and each additional period of five years thereafter provided that the recipients conduct remained of the required standard.

With the death of King Sobhuza II in 1982 the medals were redesigned to include the effigy of the reigning monarch.

UGANDA

The Republic of Uganda is not a large country by African standards with an area of only 236,000 square kilometres and is has never experienced the large influx of European's settlers that led to early calls for independence from the local people in so many places. It is a land-locked country although Lake Victoria forms its south-east border and the River Nile runs through its heart making Uganda one of best-watered and fertile of central African states. Contact with Europeans was limited until the mid 19th century with Britain being the first colonial power to realise the potential of the fertile land there. In 1894 it was declared a British protectorate although a policy of indirect rule was adopted and the local kingdoms were given a high degree of autonomy.

Independence from Britain came in 1962 under the leadership of Dr Milton Obote who served as president through very troubled times until he was deposed by Idi Amin in 1971, a tyrant who led Uganda into a very dark and violent period which only truly ended in the 1990s when a more stable government was formed. Although Amin was the country's leader only until 1979 he presided over massacres of the people of horrific proportions. It is estimated that almost 300,000 Ugandans were murdered at the hands of the security forces with Amin's tacit approval. In the UK his régime is arguably best remembered for the forcible expulsion of the country's Asian population. Even after Amin had gone, Uganda endured a further decade of war and bloodshed and, for a time, was arguably the most dangerous country in Africa.

The first properly organised police force was established by the British in 1905 following the model of other protectorates and colonies and officers were, for a time, entitled to medals from the colonial series for acts of gallantry, distinguished service and long service and good conduct. With independence came a number of local medals including some exclusively for police officers.

POLICE DISTINGUISHED SERVICE MEDAL

Ribbon: Half green, half yellow with narrow stripes of red, white and black in the centre.

Description: (Obverse) a circular gold-coloured medal bearing the badge of the Uganda Police; (reverse) two crossed truncheons superimposed on a wreath with the words DISTINGUISHED SERVICE around the lower circumference. A ring suspender is used.

The badge of the Uganda Police consists of an oval wreath with the name of the Force in a banner at the base, all enclosing a representation of a Crowned Crane, a beautiful, colourful bird common over most of central and southern Africa but especially plentiful in Uganda. It is commonly domesticated and welcomed as a useful bird in and around gardens for its fondness for insects and reptiles which it scares out of the undergrowth by stamping its feet as it walks. It is a tall (almost one metre) slim bird, predominantly grey with a white breast and brown tail and a very conspicuous topknot of stiff golden feathers—its most outstanding feature.

POLICE MEDAL FOR GALLANTRY

Ribbon: Fifteen stripes each 2 mm wide. A white central stripe is flanked by light blue and groups of red, yellow and black repeated twice.

Description: (Obverse) a circular medal with a representation of a naked man armed with a spear fighting a lion and the word GALLANTRY below; (reverse) the badge of the Uganda Police.

POLICE JUBILEE MEDAL

Ribbon: White with a blue stripe at each edge and a blue central band dissected by two white lines.

Description: (Obverse) a circular medal with the UGANDA Police badge and the words 1905 POLICE JUBILEE 1955 around the upper circumference; (reverse) the map of Uganda superimposed by a motif of two crossed truncheons and a wreath with the words UGANDA POLICE at the lower edge of the circumference. A ring suspender was used.

SPECIAL CONSTABULARY SERVICE MEDAL

Ribbon: White with a blue stripe (5 mm) and a blue line (1.5 mm) towards each edge.

Description: (Obverse) a circular bronze medal with the bust of Idi Amin in uniform reaching to the lower rim and the words SPECIAL CONSTABULARY SERVICE around the upper circumference; (reverse) the police badge.

UNITED NATIONS

The United Nations was formally established on 24 October 1945 when the Charter drawn up by a grouping of delegates from 50 countries shortly after the end of the Second World War was ratified. Since the first test of its resolve in the Korean War it has been involved in 54 peacekeeping operations with 118 countries providing more than 750,000 military and police personnel. The majority of operations involved the military only but it became increasingly common in the last decade of the 20th century for officers from the civil police to take an active rôle although the first such involvement came in Cyprus in March 1964. After the Korean War the UN issued a specially struck medal for all personnel who took part followed by a second in November 1956 for troops from the eight countries sent to the Middle East to supervise the withdrawal of British, French and Israeli troops from Egypt after the Suez crisis. In 1966 the Secretary-General decided that a single medal would be issued for each qualifying operation with the only difference being the colouring of the ribbon used. The Regulations included a provision for the award of the medal to civilian police officers if they met the qualifying criteria. Several countries—Australia, Fiji and Ireland included—award their own medal to police officers who serve overseas in such situations in addition to any awarded by the UN and the recipient officers are entitled to wear both.

THE UNITED NATIONS MEDAL

Instituted: December 1951.

Metal: Bronze.

Size: 35 mm.

Description: (Obverse) The wreathed globe emblem of the United Nations with the letters UN above; (reverse) plain.

UN Peacekeeping Force in Cyprus (UNFICYP)

The first issue went to officers from the five countries who were a part of the ongoing peacekeeping mission in Cyprus, established in 1964 but given a renewed mandate after the Turkish invasion of 1974. The ribbon has three bands of UN blue, white and UN blue separated by lines of dark blue to represent the Mediterranean Sea. The qualifying period is three months service. Police officers from Australia, Austria, Denmark, New Zealand and Sweden have been involved.

UN Angola Verification Mission (UNAVEM)

This mission was established in January 1989 for a period of 31 months to oversee and verify the withdrawal of Cuban troops from Angola. The continuing troubles in the country after the Cubans had left caused the mandate to be renewed twice and enlarged to monitor the performance and activities of the Angola Police. The mission remains with the qualifying period for the award of the medal being 90 days. Civilian police officers from a number of countries from all corners of the world have been involved. The medal ribbon is yellow with a broad central band in UN blue flanked by lines of red, white and black.

UN Transition Assistance Group (UNTAG)

In April 1989 a UN mission was established in Namibia to ensure that the transition to independence was gained by free and fair elections supervised by UN personnel including civilian police officers from 24 countries. The mission was closed in May 1990. The ribbon is yellow with a broad band at each edge in UN blue. In the centre are five equal lines black, yellow, red. green and royal blue to represent the five continents who sent troops or police personnel. The qualifying period was 90 days.

UN Observer Mission in El Salvador (ONUSAL)

First established in May 1991 to monitor agreements between the El Salavador Government and FMLN insurgents this mission was expanded in the following January to verify the cease-fire between the two factions and the establishment of a new national police force. The qualifying period was 90 days and police officers from Austria, Spain, Mexico, Norway, France, Uruguay and the USA were provided as observers after the mission was extended. The medal was authorised in January 1992 and the ribbon consisted of five bars of dark blue, white, UN blue, white and dark blue, all of equal width. The dark blue and white were representative of the flag of El Salvador.

UN Transistional Authority in Cambodia (UNTAC)

UNTAC was established in February 1992 (replacing an existing mission) with a wide mandate which included the maintenance of law and order, the supervision of fair elections, monitoring of human rights and the rebuilding of the Cambodian infrastructure. The mission closed on 15 November 1993 and was replaced by a smaller unit with no police involvement. Thirty-two different countries sent troops or civilian police officers to Cambodia. The medal ribbon had green edges (to depict the colour of the paddy fields typical of the countryside) and a broad central stripe in UN blue flanked by dark blue lines. In the centre of the light blue band were three further lines of red, white and red, the red being indicative of the flags of the warring factions.

UN Operation in Mozambique (ONUMOZ)

In October 1992 the mission in Mozambique was established with a wide-ranging mandate to return the country to some semblance of normality following a period of conflict. The work was completed successfully and the mission closed in January 1995. Some 38 countries provided troops and civilian police observers to help in this huge task. The ribbon had a broad central band in UN blue with narrower band of white and green (to represent the tropical climate of Mozambique) on either side. The qualifying period of service was 90 days.

UN Assistance Mission for Rwanda (UNAMIR)

After the three missions established in 1992, the following year was less demanding on the countries involved although the ongoing situation in the three others placed a strain on the resources of many. UNAMIR was established in October 1993 but did not close for 30 months, in March 1996. More than 20 countries provided personnel including police observers to assist in the establishment and training of the new national police force. The colouring of the ribbon was intended to be symbolic of the region. The central band was of UN blue and flanks by narrow lines of white. Outside the white lines on both sides were three bands, all of equal width, in black (to represent the volcanic lava and mountain gorillas of the area), green (the colour of the lush vegetation of Rwanda) and red (symbolic of the soil of Africa). In keeping with the criteria established at other missions for the award of UN medals, the qualifying period of service was 90 days.

UN Preventative Deployment Force (UNPREDEP)

The break-up of Yugoslavia and the subsequent wars between the individual states of the former republic led to the establishment of a number of UN missions, several of which involved the use of civilian police officers to oversee a wide range of tasks. The first mission in which police officers became involved was established in March 1995 to replace an earlier mission in the Former Yugoslav Republic of Macedonia. Their mandate was to observe and report on any threat in the border areas which would compromise the stability of the country or threaten its territory. The mission is ongoing. The medal for a period of 90 days service was authorised in May 1996 and has been awarded to troops, military observers and civilian police officers the 29 countries involved. The medal ribbon has a broad central band in red with four narrow yellow lines separated from the ribbons UN blue edges by a white line.

UN Mission in Bosnia Herzegovina/ International Police Task Force (UNMIBH/IPTF)

The primary task of this mission was to monitor, observe and inspect law enforcement activities, train and advise personnel and pave the way for free and fair elections. The medal was authorised in August 1966 with its ribbon having five bands of equal width—the central band in white to symbolise peace, flanked to bands of UN blue and with a green band at the outer left edge (representative of the forests) and red to the right (symbolising sunrise over the mountains). Military personnel and civilian police officers from 41 countries are involved in the operation.

UN Transitional Administration for Eastern Slavonia, Baranja and Western Sirmium (UNTAES)

This mission was established in January 1996 to monitor the safe return of refugees and displaced persons to their homes and to restore peace and stability to this region of Croatia following the conflicts which resulted from the break-up of Yugoslavia. The medal was established in March 1996 with the customary qualifying period of 90 days. The ribbon is of United Nations light blue with a broad central band in red flanked by white lines. The blue outer bands carry a band of green (left) and yellow (right).

UN Interim Administration Mission in Kosovo (UNMIK)

In June 1999 a mission involving the presence of civilian police officers was established in Kosovo with the UN medal being authorised in September. The grave humanitarian situation in Kosovo prompted the formation of a force of military and police personnel from 51 countries to aid the return of displaced persons and refugees and to prevent an escalation of the conflict. The medal ribbon is UN blue with a dark blue central band flanked by white stripes.

UN Police Support Group Medal (UNPSG)

The importance of police officers as distinct from the military in peacekeeping operation has long been recognised by the UN and, in some circumstances, their use is the only true, practical option available. In January 1998 the UN decided to establish a group of 180 civil police officers to act as monitors in the Danube Region of Croatia to supervise the actions of the local police with particular importance being given to the return of displaced persons and refugees. Their duties were to include monitoring police operations, accompanying local officers on patrol, investigating human rights abuses and an overall supervisory and guiding rôle. In recognition of the work of the officers a special medal was introduced which remains the only medal awarded by the UN to police officers only.

The colouring of the ribbon has a significance to the region and the nature of the operation. The white of the background represents peace and a new beginning with the pale blue central stripe included to represent the UN and the River Danube which gives the region its fertility. The two narrow stripes of yellow and dark grey and indicative of the sunflowers which grow in profusion in the area and stone and mortar, both used in the rebuilding of the region and also the nation.

UN Transitional Administration in East Timor (UNTAET)

East Timor has been on the international agenda since 1960 when it was placed on the UN list of non-self governing territories. In 1974, the territory, administered by Portugal, was engulfed in a civil war as the Portuguese sought to establish a provisional government as a part of its withdrawal from its overseas territories at the end of the authoritarian government of Prime Minister Salazar. Portugal could not control the situation and withdrew leaving Indonesia to intervene and annex East Timor as a province. The UN never accepted the Indonesian claim to the territory was little was achieved until an agreement was signed in May 1999 between Portugal and Indonesia to hold a referendum of the East Timor people for them to decide if they wished to remain as a part of Indonesia or pursue independence. By a margin of three to one they chose independence on 30 August 1999. This led to a period of violence, looting and arson by pro-Indonesian groups resulting in the deaths of many East Timorese and the displacement of hundreds of thousands.

Intense diplomatic activity by the UN resulted in the agreement of the Indonesian government to help from the international community and the establishment of a UN mission (UNAMET) to restore order. A multi-national force of 17 nations headed by Australia undertook a huge relief effort and, slowly, peace, order and security were restored. As the situation calmed, the Indonesian army, police and civil authorities left the territory and a new mission (UNTAET) established in October 1999 to oversee the establishment of a new administration, the repatriation of displaced East Timorese, the first steps towards self-government and the maintenance of law, order and security. The force of almost 9,000 military personnel was supported by more than 1,300 police officers from a number of countries. At August 2000 military and civilian police personnel from 48 countries as diverse as the USA, Sweden, Cape Verde, Jordan and Bosnia-Herzegovina had assisted in the operation. Fatalities have occurred, including one police officer.

The award of the UN medal was authorised to all personnel, including police officers, on completion of 90 days service although this condition was waived by the UN for members of the Australian Federal Police (AFP) who had served from the outset although many did not meet the qualifying period. The changes were made to recognise the service of the officers in the most dangerous period and in the most inhospitable of conditions. Australian police officers have taken part in a number of UN peacekeeping operations although the deployment to East Timor was, by some margin, the most extensive with more than 250 taking part. The first deployment took place in Cyprus in 1964 with 40 officers followed by lesser detachments being sent to Thailand (1989), Cambodia (1992), Somalia (1993), Mozambique (1994), Haiti (1994) and Bougainville (1997).

Since its formation in 1975 overseas duty has fallen to members of the Australian Federal Police although small groups of officers from two state forces (Queensland and Victoria) were amongst the group of 30 Australians sent to Haiti. The deployment to East Timor was the largest and most dangerous when violence erupted following the referendum on the territorys future, a situation which led, ultimately, to the special recognition afforded to the AFP officers by the UN.

The lead rôle played by Australia in the operation to re-establish law and order in East Timor—the most significant deployment of Australian troops since WWII—led to the introduction of a special Australian medal for all those who served for at least 30 days.

INTERNATIONAL FORCE EAST TIMOR MEDAL

Instituted: 25 March 2000.

Ribbon: White with a red central stripe flanked by green and blue lines at the edges.

Metal: Cupro-nickel

Description: (Obverse) a dove bearing an olive branch superimposed on a map of East Timor with the words INTERNATIONAL FORCE EAST TIMOR around the circumference and a sprig of olive at the base. The straight suspender is attached by a seven-point star representing the Australian Commonwealth.

Although the introduction of an Australian campaign medal is not unique, the unusual step of offering it to other governments who contributed troops has been taken, the first time this has happened with an Australian award in recognition of the lead rôle played by Australia.

UNITED STATES OF AMERICA

The policing structure of the United States is very different from the United Kingdom and other European countries partly due to its vast size but also reflecting the political differences and the degree of autonomy granted to individual states, counties, cities and towns. There are in excess of 17,500 separate police forces ranging from those in small towns with four officers and one car responsible for a population of a few thousand (Hampstead, Maryland) to the huge organisation in New York City with 38,000 sworn officers and a population not far short of eight million. Differences in state and city laws exist but the overall range of policing duties and powers is the same irrespective of the size of the force. The award of medals to officers is very much a local affair, many forces, irrespective of their size, offering a range of methods of recognising bravery and meritorious work.

The range of awards available across the United States, in police departments large and small, is wide and typified by ornate design, the use of colour and enamels and the spread of reasons for their award some of which have no equivalent in the UK, Europe or Commonwealth countries although Australian police forces have introduced similar awards in some states in recent years. In a limited space its only possible to look at a sample of the hundreds, possibly thousands, of medals available to police officers in the US but it does show the range that exists across this vast country.

The most obvious omission of the American system of rewards for police officers has always been the lack of a national award. On 29 June 2000, President Clinton took the first steps towards rectifying this by signing an executive order establishing the Presidential Medal of Valor for Public Safety Officers, an award intended to reward these officers for acts of extraordinary valour above and beyond the call of duty in the course of their work. The medal will be available to any law enforcement officer and includes police, correctional, probation or parole officers and firefighters employed by the US Government, any state in the US, any officially recognised elected body in any state or any federally recognised tribal organisation. It can be awarded posthumously and the dangers faced by the groups of people defined are such that such awards are unlikely to be rare. Up to ten officers can be nominated each year and the presentations will be made on 15 May each year which has been designated as Peace Officer's Memorial Day and the week in which it falls as Police Week.

The design of the medal had not been decided when the executive order was signed and published with designs required to be submitted to the Attorney General for the President's approval by no later than 1 December 2000. The establishment of the medal was one of the final acts of President Clinton's eight years in the White House although the process stalled after he left office. The events of 11 September 2001 have caused the subject of suitable national awards for police officers, fire officers and other emergency services to be re-assessed.

NEW YORK CITY POLICE DEPARTMENT

The Police Department of New York City, the largest in the United States, recognises the dangers faced by its officers and their courage in dangerous situations by the award of its own range of medals. The highest award is the Medal of Honor which recognises courage of the highest order in circumstances of extreme personal danger to the officers life performed above and beyond the call of duty where the officer has full knowledge of the risks involved.

MEDAL OF HONOR

Ribbon: Green with twelve white stars to represent the original constables of the city's first organised police force in 1700.

Description: (Obverse) a gold eight-point star with a central circle showing the Seal of the City of New York; (reverse) inscribed with the name of the recipient and the date of the award. The medal hangs from a ring suspender with a gold top ribbon bar bearing the word VALOR.

Medals awarded in New York City are presented at a special Medal Day Ceremony held in October every year and the current design of the Medal of Honor was first awarded there in 1973. The award of medals to police officers in New York has occurred since the early 19th century but was not put on a regular basis until early April 1888 with the introduction of a bronze medal used to recognise any act of courage in a life or death situation. It was the only medal then awarded by the Department.

In 1912 the Medal of Honor (still cast in bronze) was introduced with the criteria for its award strengthened to reflect its intended position as the highest possible honour in the Department. It has been cast in gold since 1997. The medal is awarded sparingly to maintain its esteem and can be—and very often is—awarded posthumously as were three of the four Medals of Honor awarded in 1999. A second award of the Medal of Honor is signified by a gold oak leaf placed centrally on the breast bar.

COMBAT CROSS

Ribbon: Green silk.

Description: (Obverse) a gold Maltese cross with a central medallion bearing the Seal of New York City and the circumscription FOR VALOR - POLICE. The arms of the cross are of green enamel with black edges; (reverse) inscribed with the words NEW YORK CITY POLICE, the name of the recipient and the date of the award. It hangs from a ring suspender and gold top ribbon bar inscribed with the word VALOR.

The ribbon for wear in undress uniform is in green enamelled gold rather than a silk ribbon as in the UK. The use of enamelled metal breast bars is a feature of awards made by many United States police departments. A second award of the Combat Cross is indicated by the wearing of a gold palm leaf on the medal ribbon and breast bar. The Cross is the Department's second highest award, introduced in 1934 and first awarded on 19 July the same year to six officers for conspicuous gallantry in the course of their duty. The criteria for the award of the Cross limit it to officers who successfully perform an act of extraordinary bravery whilst engaged in personal combat with an armed person where the life of the officer is in extreme danger. Since its introduction it has been awarded more than 200 times.

At the medal ceremony held on 8 September 1994, eighteen officers were awarded the Combat Cross arising from thirteen incidents. A sample of one citation clearly illustrates the level of courage displayed. On 3 July 1992 Officer Michael O'Keefe was working with his partners in plain clothes when he saw what he thought was a man concealing a handgun. As he approached the man ran off into a nearby building pursued by Officer O'Keefe who caught him in the lobby and attempted to overpower him. The suspect punched and kicked Officer O'Keefe but could not get free and pulled the gun he was suspected of hiding from his coat and placed it in the officer's face. Officer O'Keefe managed to push it to one side and reached for his revolver. The man put his gun to the officer's face again but was shot and killed by Michael O'Keefe before he could pull the trigger.

MEDAL FOR VALOR

Ribbon: Blue.

Description: (Obverse) a gold central medallion with a representation of the statue at the New York Police Memorial which stands in the foyer of the Department's headquarters. It depicts a young boy standing next to a police officer and was sculpted in 1939. The medallion has a circumscription which reads FOR VALOR - POLICE DEPARTMENT - CITY OF NEW YORK and sits on a blue enamel disc with a gold wreath of laurel around the edge apart from the very top where there is a gold suspender ring; (reverse) inscribed with the name of the recipient. A gold top ribbon bar is inscribed with the word VALOR.

Assessing the level of courage displayed by anyone being considered for an award is far from easy if the act is to be properly recognised but the prestige of the highest awards maintained and not given so freely as to undermine their value. In any given set of circumstances the risk of death faced by the recipient is an important factor (not only in the United States) and as this risk decreases so does the level of award given. The Medal for Valor (the third highest award in New York City) recognises the actions of officers who display great courage but who are not in armed combat or facing an immediate threat of death although there is great potential danger to their lives.

PURPLE SHIELD

Ribbon: Crimson with a thin white stripe towards each edge.

Description: (Obverse) a gold shield shaped medal finished in purple enamel but with gold edges remaining, containing a gold bust of Theodore Roosevelt above the words FIDELIS AD MORTEM (faithful unto death) — the motto of the Department.

This is the most recent award introduced into the Department and is the equivalent of the Purple Heart available to members of the United States Military Forces. It was created in 1995 and is awarded to any officer who has died, suffered serious physical injury, permanent disfigurement or permanent or protracted impairment of health in the course of his or her duty. It was introduced following representations from the officers themselves.

Officers in New York are entitled to wear breast bars to indicate the grant of a number of other awards for a number of instances of bravery, grave personal danger, intelligent performance of duty, an extraordinary commitment to integrity or contribution to the improvement of life in the community with particular reference to the more disadvantaged areas of the city. Medals are not presented for any of the forms of award or citation which usually take the form of a certificate but breast bars are issued for wear when in uniform. Five of the awards use the same breast bar with the difference signified by the colour of a star added to the basic bar. A number of stars of different colours indicating the receipt of several awards can be worn on the same bar with the position laid down in the Department's procedural orders.

The basic breast bar is of gold and has a white central band with a dark blue band to the right and another in green to the left, thin stripes of orange separate the bands and are at each edge. An Honorable Mention, awarded for an act of bravery performed at imminent and personal danger to life, is indicated by a silver star.

Single stars are always placed on the central white band. An Exceptional Merit Award uses a light green star, a Commendation one of bronze and a Commendation—Community Service a light blue star. Further awards of the same type of commendation are indicated by additional stars worn in each of the three bands of the bar until a fourth award is earned and a second breast bar can be worn. Where different stars are worn on the same bar, the highest is worn centrally, the next on the green band and the third in the blue area.

The same basic bar used without the stars is given to officers granted the Meritorious Police Duty Award for acts of valuable service over an extended period or which demonstrate special qualities of faithfulness or perseverance. In the course of their career, officers could be receive this award many times and there is provision for a gold coloured numeral to be placed in the central white band to show the total number of awards received. There is no limit to the number of awards an officer could receive.

The NYPD, like many US police departments, also awards a Unit Citation where the performance of a group of officers acting together with a common purpose over a sustained period is considered to be worthy of official recognition. The Unit Citation breast bar—plain blue—is worn on the right breast in contrast to all other medals and awards and has in the centre the year of the award in gold. An officer is entitled to wear one bar only, irrespective of the number he or she has received.

In addition to the awards issued by the Department, police officers in New York City are eligible for no fewer than 48 other medals given by a host of societies, associations, clubs and individuals in the city to recognise acts of courage.

These medals are awarded at the annual medal day ceremony at the same time as the departmental awards are made. One officer is chosen to receive the medal each year and different medals are often awarded to different officers involved in the same action. The earliest of these awards dates from 1900 and the latest was made available in 1994.

Honor Legion Medal (1900).
Isaac Bell Medal for Valor (1900).
Brooklyn Citizens Medal for Valor (1906).
Doctor Ernest Fahnestock Medal for Valor (1932).
St George Association Medal for Valor (1937).
Patrolmen's Benevolent Association Medal (1940).
Police Anchor Club Medal of Valor (1941).
Detectives Endowment Association Medal for Valor (1942).
Columbia Association Medal for Valor (1945).
Shomrin Society Medal (1947).
Police Square Club Medal for Valor (1948).
Sergeant's Benevolent Association Medal for Valor (1948).
Lieutenant's Benevolent Association Medal for Valor (1950).
Holy Name Society, Manhatten, Bronx and Staten Island Medal for Valor (1950).
NYC Police Post No 460 American Legion Medal for Valor (1950).
Guardians Association Medal for Valor (1951).
Patrick J O'Connor Emerald Society Medal for Valor (1956).
Pulaski Association Medal for Valor (1960).
Steuben Association Medal for Valor (1965).
Hispanic Society Medal for Valor (1968).
International Police Association Medal for Valor (1972).
Captain's Endowment Association Medal for Valor (1973).
Retired Detective Association Medal for Valor (1973).
Traffic Squad Benevolent Association Medal for Valor (1975).
Police Reserve Association Medal for Valor (1977).
NY Finest Foundation Medal for Valor (1977).
NYC Police Foundation Medal for Valor (1981).
New York Yankees Captain's Medal for Valor (1981).
St Pauls Society Medal for Valor (1983).
Policewoman's Endowment Association Medal for Valor (1983).
US Senator Alfonse M D'Amato Medal for Valor (1984).
Regina Coeli Society Medal for Valor (1984).
Fire Department Honor Legion Medal for Valor (1984).
Police Commissioner William J Devine Medal for Valor (1984).
Major General Robert E Condon—
    Reserve Officers Association of the United States Medal for Valor (1984).
Patrolman Bernard F O'Reilly Memorial Medal for Valor (1985).
Retired Lieutenants Associated Medal for Valor (1985).
Centurian Foundation Memorial Award (1987).
Viking Association Medal of Valor (1988).
Police Self Support Group Medal for Valor (1990).
Survivors of the Shield Medal for Valor (1992).
NYC Westchester and Putnam Shield Medal for Valor (1992).
New York 10-13 Association Medal for Valor (1992).
Captain's Endowment Association Medal of Merit (1993).
Lieutenant's Benevolent Association Medal of Merit (1993).
Sergeant's Benevolent Association Medal of Merit (1993).
Detective's Endowment Association Medal of Merit (1993).
Asian-Jade Society Medal for Valor (1994).

On 13 April 1993 two police officers were on plain clothes duty when they saw a man fire several shots from a semi-automatic weapon on a crowded street corner. They pursued the suspect on foot who turned and fired at the officers twice. The chase entered a darkened school yard with the suspect turning twice more to fire four more shots at the officers. Both officers returned the fire and the suspects was arrested a short distance from the school. Officer Derrick Nash was awarded the Police Cross for his actions and Sergeant Kevin Gannon the Patrick J O'Connor Emerald Society Medal for Valor.

One incident on 21 April 1990 resulted in three of the special awards being made to the officers involved. At about 12.40 am the officers heard what sounded like shots being fired in the vicinity of a nearby building. As they approached they saw a man leaving the building. As soon as he saw the officers he fired several shots at them from a .45 semi-automatic pistol.

The three officers took cover, returned the fire and succeeded in hitting him. He was arrested and taken to hospital for treatment. Officer Eric Freese was awarded the St Pauls Society Medal for Valor, Officer William Best the Captain's Endowment Society Medal for Valor and Officer Kareen Noel-Hawthorne the Retired Detective's Association Medal for Valor.

Multiple presentations of the special medals arising from a single incident were not unusual. At the 1994 medal ceremony, ten awards were made to a group of officers who were involved in the arrest of two armed men robbing a bakery at gunpoint. In the pursuit after they were disturbed several shots were fired but both men were arrested and no-one was injured. Of the 65 awards made in 1994, all but four (the medals for merit) involved the use of firearms—an indication of the dangers of policing New York City.

CITY OF NEW YORK POLICE DEPARTMENT WORLD WAR ONE SERVICE MEDAL

At the end of the First World War the contribution made by those who took part was recognised in most countries by the award of a medal or medals of some description for their service to celebrate victory. Most countries made national awards but a large number of states, cities, towns, counties and organisations in the USA introduced their own local medal in addition to the federal issue. The total number of medals issued is not known accurately although there were more than 350 different designs introduced awarded by more than 1,300 different bodies. In some states there were no issues at all (Arizona, Arkansas, Mississippi and Nevada included) although in most there were some awards made ranging from one in Delaware, Florida, Louisiana, Montana and South Dakota to the highest number—at least 240—in New York State. In addition to the states, cities, towns and counties, medals were awarded by a variety of diverse organisations including trade associations, churches, universities and commercial bodies. The only police department in the US known to have awarded a medal to those of its members who served overseas was the City of New York Police Department.

Instituted: 1918.

Ribbon: There is some uncertainty about the colouring of the ribbon. Some references are made to three bands of red, white and blue (all of equal width), others to the colours being dark blue, white and pale blue edged with gold, the colours of the Police Department.

Metal: Bronze.

Description: (Obverse) a cross patée superimposed on a wreath of laurel with the upper and lower arms inscribed with the words WORLD and WAR and the dates 1917 and 1918 on the horizontal arms. There is a central medallion which has a shield at its centre showing three fleur-de-lys with a branch of laurel on either side all within an outer band bearing the words POLICE DEPARTMENT (upper) and CITY OF NEW YORK (lower); (reverse) the central medallion has the image of a charging soldier with the words FRANCE on the upper arm of the cross and COURAGE, HONOR and LOYALTY on the three others. A simple ring suspender is used attached to the upper arm of the cross.

Although the design of many local medals was common to a number of places, this particular design of medal is thought to be unique to the Police Department. It was awarded to all members of the Department who served in France after the entry of the USA into the War in 1917. Recipients were also awarded the Victory Medal issued by the federal government and another by the State of New York.

UNITED STATES VICTORY MEDAL

Instituted: 1919.

Ribbon: A double rainbow design with the red at the centre.

Metal: Bronze.

Size: 36 mm.

Description: (Obverse) the figure of winged Victory facing forward with a sword in her right hand and a shield in the left; (reverse) the American shield with a fasces superimposed and the names of the 14 allied nations on either side—FRANCE, ITALY, SERBIA, JAPAN, MONTENEGRO, RUSSIA and GREECE (left) with GREAT BRITAIN BELGIUM, BRAZIL, PORTUGAL, RUMANIA and CHINA (right). At the upper circumference is the inscription THE GREAT WAR FOR CIVILIZATION with six stars at the base.

Unlike the Victory Medal awarded in the other allied countries, the US award came with clasps for each of the major actions in which the recipient took part. For those who served overseas from the US but who were not entitled to a battle clasp, a series of five others were introduced bearing the name of the country in which they were based—England, France, Italy, Siberia or Russia. Entitlement for duty in Europe ceased on Armistice Day (11 November 1918) but duty beyond that date in European Russia or Siberia with the American Expeditionary Force up to 1 April 1920 also qualified.

NEW YORK STATE WORLD WAR ONE SERVICE MEDAL

Ribbon: Blue with a white band towards each edge.

Metal: Bronze.

Size: 33 mm.

Description: (Obverse) a figure of a soldier (facing right) with his rifle in his right hand and his left hand raised before the figure of an Victory both grasping an laurel branch against a background of a battlefield scene. The inscription WORLD WAR lies at the upper circumference either side of the laurel branch; (reverse) a wreath of laurel (left) and oak leaves (right) with three banners on each side and the coat of arms of New York State in the upper part of the central field between the tips of the wreath. An inscription FOR - SERVICE - 1917-1918 - PRESENTED BY THE - STATE - OF - NEW YORK. A simple ring suspender is used. Each medal is numbered.

CHICAGO (ILLINOIS) POLICE DEPARTMENT

The Chicago Police Department in Illinois has 13,500 sworn officers and more than 3,000 civilian staff to police a city of almost three million—it is one of the largest police departments in the country. The Department has no fewer than six medals and ten other methods of commending its officers for acts of courage, meritorious service or lifesaving and to recognise outstanding examples of police work in a demanding environment.

POLICE MEDAL

Ribbon: Gold with a wide blue central stripe.

Description: (Obverse) a round silver medal with the badge of the Chicago Police Department in the centre right, above a spray of oak leaves and a female figure holding a laurel wreath in her outstretched right hand and a flag in her left. There is a raised outer band covering the upper half of the medal bearing the inscription POLICE MEDAL. A ring suspender is used.

This award is presented each year by the Superintendent of Police to any sworn member of the Department who has previously received any one of the four other awards for bravery available but who, in the Superintendents opinion, deserves further recognition by virtue of the outstanding nature of their performance.

The ribbon for wear in undress uniform comes with a gold coloured scrolled metal surround and has a small blue five-pointed star in the centre—a recurring feature of the Department's awards to sworn officers. The Police Medal is the Department's highest award.

United States of America

SUPERINTENDENT'S AWARD OF VALOR

Ribbon: Red with a white central stripe, all of equal width.

Description: (Obverse) an irregularly shaped bronze medal with the emblem of the Chicago Police Department (the five-point star) and the words CHICAGO POLICE in a shield at the centre of a square in th lower half of the piece. At the bottom is the word VALOR. Above the square is an eagle with out stretched wings superimposed on a wreath of leaves with a plain central field to which is attached a ring suspender.

This award is available to any sworn member of the Department and is awarded to recognise an act of outstanding bravery demonstrating characteristics of selflessness, personal courage and devotion to duty. It is the Department's second highest award for bravery. The medal can be awarded posthumously and they are very often given for acts of courage involving the use of firearms against officers.

Officer James Camp was murdered on duty on 9 March 1999 whilst working with his partner—Kenneth King—as a part of the Gang Tactical Team concentrating on gang and narcotic suppression. They made a check on a vehicle with two occupants, a male driver and female passenger, which had stopped close to their position. They noticed that there were no keys in the ignition although the engine was running and ordered both occupants to leave the car. As soon as he had left the car, the driver attacked Officer Camp and managed to take his revolver from him in the struggle and fire it once, hitting him in the head and killing him instantly. Other officers witnessed the shooting and returned fire, wounding the murderer and arresting him.

The car had been reported stolen from Indiana a few days before. James Camp was posthumously awarded the Superintendent's Award of Valor for his courage.

Police officers in most US departments are expected to carry their firearms with them at all times, on or off duty, and most would not dream of venturing out unarmed under any circumstances—their caution is well-founded. On 10 August 1999 Officer Phillip Rider was off-duty and in civilian clothing when he noticed a large crowd gathered outside a liquor store, he was told that an armed robbery was taking place and that shots had been fired. At 10.20 pm four armed men had entered the store and shot two assistants, killing one, in addition to beating another with the butt of a gun. Two offenders left the store and waited in their car across the street whilst the others emptied the till. Officer Rider had no idea that the two were in the car as he approached the store with his weapon drawn. As he reached the door he was shot in the left shoulder by one of those in the car and had others shots aimed at him from close range by one who had now left the store with the cash. Under fire from two directions the officer managed to hit both occupants of the car, one three times and the other once. He then entered the store and succeeded in calling for assistance for himself and the wounded store staff. Two men were arrested, one gave himself up two weeks later but the fourth was not caught. For his great courage Officer Rider was awarded the Superintendent's Award of Valor.

These examples are typical of the level of courage required for the award of this second highest medal in the Chicago Police Department—to receive the supreme departmental honour for courage, the degree of bravery which must be displayed is of the very highest order.

HUNDRED CLUB OF COOK COUNTY MEDAL OF VALOR

Ribbon: *Halved in light blue and red.*

Description: *(Obverse) an oval gold medal with a wreath of oak leaves and the words THE HUNDRED CLUB MEDAL OF VALOR in the central field. It hangs from a ring suspender.*

Although this medal is not awarded by the Department, recipients are entitled to wear it alongside their other awards. It ranks third in the order of precedence. It is awarded to any sworn member of the Department who has displayed outstanding courage in the performance of his duties. The Hundred Club of Cook County (a part of the Chicago Police Department area of jurisdiction) is a group of local worthies and business people who wish to recognise the work of and dangers faced by their police officers. The blue star does not appear on the ribbon of this medal.

United States of America

SUPERINTENDENT'S AWARD OF MERIT

Ribbon: Blue with a white central stripe, all of equal width.

Description: (Obverse) an irregular shape bronze medal consisting of the Department emblem of a five-pointed star and the words CHICAGO (above) and POLICE (below) in a shield. The word MERIT is carried on a band above the shield with an eagle with outstretched wings at the top attached to the ring suspender. The lower half of the shield has a branch of laurel leaves on either side.

This is an unusual award by British standards with no real counterpart in any branch of the Police Service or Armed Forces. Sworn staff and civilian members of the Department are both eligible for this medal which is granted for an outstanding achievement resulting in improved administration or operation, substantial savings in costs or staffing levels where the recipient has gone beyond the normal contribution to effective policing. It can also be awarded for outstanding police work in cases of unusual public interest where the actions have brought credit to the Department. Civilian members of staff are not awarded a medal, having a certificate and lapel badge instead—a feature of the lesser awards given to sworn and unsworn staff.

BLUE STAR AWARD

Ribbon: Light blue with a broad white central stripe.

Description: (Obverse) a silver medal of irregular design. At the centre is a circle containing the five-pointed star familiar in many Chicago PD medals with the words CHICAGO POLICE above and BLUE STAR AWARD in a semicircular bar below. The circle stands at the centre of another five-point star with the area between each point filled in giving an overall pentagonal shape.

This is the Department's version of the military Purple Heart and given to anyone who has been seriously, critically or fatally injured in the performance of his police duty where the injury resulted from an attack, personal combat or whilst performing an act of bravery.

There is an unusual proviso which can result in its award although there was no actual injury suffered—where the use of body armour protected the officer from injury which would otherwise have occurred.

page 345

BLUE SHIELD AWARD

Ribbon: Light blue with a narrow white central stripe and a thin white edge.

Description: (Obverse) a silver medal of irregular shape. At the base is an elliptical bar bearing the words CHICAGO POLICE BLUE SHIELD AWARD in two lines. On the right above the bar a figure stands looking left towards a ship in full sail. Between the two is a shield with the Seal of the City of Chicago.

This award is the equivalent of the former medal but applicable where the injury arises accidentally and includes road traffic accidents, injuries of a non-violent nature and even heart attacks which occur in the direct performance of police duty.

In addition to any medals officers from the Department may have won, they may also wear ribbons signifying the award of a number of commendations. This has no direct equivalent in the UK although the mention in despatches oak leaf and emblems awarded to indicate that someone has received a Queen's Commendation offer some comparison. In Chicago the ribbons are worn with the gold coloured metal surround by sworn officers although the central blue star seen on medal ribbons is often absent. Civilian staff members are awarded lapel badges in cases where the award is applicable to them also. There are ten awards available:

Special Commendation—a yellow ribbon with a narrow central blue line and two thin blue lines on either side with blue edges. The award is made to any officer, civilian or member of the public who has made a significant impact on public safety or crime prevention.

Arnold Mireles Special Partnership Award—a pale blue ribbon with a central white band. On either side of the central band are a narrow blue and red stripe. This award is also available to members of the public in addition to sworn officers and civilian support staff for efforts which lead to an improvement in the quality of life in the community by identifying and solving problems.

Lifesaving Award—a plain green ribbon with the blue central star. It is only available to members of the Department, sworn and civilian, who successfully saved a human life in circumstances which involved exceptional courage or performance.

Police Officer of the Month Award—a plain orange ribbon with a central blue star. This can be awarded to an individual officer or each member of a team whose performance in a month showed exceptional professional skill to the degree that it merited special recognition.

Department Commendation—a plain purple ribbon, worn without the star. Available to sworn and unsworn members of the Department for any outstanding act or achievement bringing great credit to the Department involving a performance above and beyond the call of duty.

Unit Meritorious Performance Award—a plain rust-coloured ribbon, worn with a blue star. This award is available to all members of staff who display exceptional professional skill in the course of a co-ordinated campaign.

Special Service Award—a blue ribbon with a narrow white band towards each edge. Awarded to any member of the Department whose efforts contribute towards an event which has had a significant impact on the direction and operation of the Department.

Problem Solving Award—a pale blue ribbon with a red broad central stripe, red edges and a thin dark blue stripe towards each edge. An unusual award made to any member of the Department who shows exemplary efforts to identify, analyse and respond to causes, conditions and problems leading to crime and disorder.

Recognition Ribbon Award—a red ribbon with a thin blue central stripe bordered with white. At each edge are two further thin stripes of white and blue. Available to sworn officers only and worn to acknowledge that they have received an award for the performance of police duty from a civic group or other law enforcement agency.

Honorable Mention Ribbon Award—a red ribbon with a central white band bordered by a black stripe on both sides. The basic ribbon is awarded after an officer has received more than 50 mentions for exceptional performance or any act which is considered to be worthy of note. Receipt of 90 or more mentions entitles an officer to wear a bronze oak leaf on the ribbon and a silver oak leaf when 150 or more have been received.

1996 Democratic National Convention Award—the ribbon resembles a part of the Stars and Stripes. It is in two halves with the left half blue with a number of white stars and the right half white with three red vertical stripes. A very unusual award which nonetheless entitles officers to wear a medal ribbon on their chests. There are no British counterparts and would seem to be uniquely American. The certificate which accompanied the award showed it to be a Special Service Award but the political importance of the event and the presence of President Clinton was thought worthy of a special award. It was granted in recognition of the devotion to duty and professionalism of officers on duty ensuring a safe and secure convention.

DALLAS (TEXAS) POLICE DEPARTMENT

To most British people the city of Dallas is synonymous with two things—the TV series of the same name and the assassination of President John Kennedy in 1963. Although this was a defining moment for the city as well as the American people in general, Dallas is a thriving, prosperous city, the seventh largest in the US with a population of about two million. It was founded in 1841 by John Neely Bryan and grew quickly although the population in 1850 was still only 450. The Dallas Police Department grew from equally humble beginnings to a force now 2,845 strong supported by 727 unsworn members of staff. Dallas can be a dangerous place though, since the death of the first police officer in 1892—C O Brewer—68 other officers have been killed in the city up to April 1997. The years of 1972 and 1988 were the worst for police deaths with five officers losing their lives in the line of duty in both. The Department awards a range of medals and bars to its officers in recognition of acts of courage, meritorious service and devotion to duty.

MEDAL OF HONOR

Ribbon: *Gold—although the enamel ribbon bar for wear in undress uniform is yellow with two red stripes towards the edges.*

Description: *(Obverse) a cross flory in gold with a blue central medallion bearing the words DALLAS POLICE around a disc at the centre. The words HONOR (left) and VALOR (right) appear on two arms of the cross. A plain ring suspender is used.*

This is the highest award in the Department given to officers who voluntarily distinguish themselves by gallantry or extraordinary heroism in excess of the normal demands of duty of such a nature that they were fully aware of the imminent threat to their personal safety or danger to their lives. The actions must be above and beyond the call of duty and this precludes the award of the medal for any act, however courageous, which was performed in accordance with written or verbal orders. This rather unusual criterion makes the award of the medal very scarce and is a feature of two of the three highest departmental awards.

The medal which ranks second to the Medal of Honor is awarded only to officers who lose their lives in the course of their duty in honourable circumstances. It may be awarded in addition to any other medal arising out of the same set of circumstances which led to the loss of life.

THE POLICE CROSS

Ribbon: Dark blue.

Description: (Obverse) a round medal, cast in silver, depicting a Latin cross with lined arms superimposed on a wreath of laurel. At the centre is a medallion bearing the five-point star symbol of the Department on a blue enamel background with DALLAS POLICE inscribed on an outer ring. A plain ring suspender is used with a broad silver top ribbon bar.

Next in line is the last of the three medals awarded by the Department although there is a range of bars available for a host of achievements all of which are worn on the uniform on the left breast after any medal ribbons. The Medal of Valor demands a lesser degree of courage than the Medal of Honor but the criteria are still strictly applied and it is awarded sparingly.

MEDAL OF VALOR

Ribbon: Dark blue with the enamel bar also have two thin stripes of white towards each edge.

Description: (Obverse) a round silver medal with a wreath of laurel around the circumference and the Department badge in silver and blue enamel at the top above the words MEDAL OF VALOR. A plain ring suspender is used.

Any officer who receives this award must have displayed exceptional bravery at imminent risk of serious bodily injury whilst demonstrating exceptional courage by performing a voluntary course of action in an extremely dangerous situation. The Departmental orders detailing the criteria for the award of the medal add a rider to the effect that the use of the term voluntary course of action disqualifies all acts of courage, no matter how great, performed in the course of carrying out verbal or written orders—very similar to the proviso applicable to the award of the Medal of Honor.

A recent recipient of the Medal of Valor was Officer John Midyette, honoured for the courage he displayed on 31 May 1998 after his partner was shot whilst they investigated a suspected drug offence. The officer's partner was lying wounded in the line of fire and unable to move. Officer Midyette pushed open the door of the apartment where the gunman was hiding and returned fire with complete disregard for his own safety—he succeeded in arresting the three suspects found inside. His partner, Officer Edward Menchaca, made a full recovery from his wounds. John Midyette was awarded the Medal of Valor for his courage in very dangerous circumstances.

The range of bars available is large and follows a strict order of precedence starting with the *Meritorious Conduct Bar* awarded for an heroic deed and exceptionally meritorious conduct involving courage, risk and danger to an officers personal safety. The bar is half blue, half white enamel with a red central stripe on a base of gilded nickel.

Next in line is the *Police Commendation Bar* which is made available under any one of three provisions. First, in recognition of an outstanding performance involving great risk to personal safety, or second, the successful and professional completion of difficult police projects, programmes or situations or, lastly, to an officer who has received three or more acknowledgements of his or her ability in the form of Certificates of Merit or Civic Achievement—part of a range of lesser commendations both of which carry an entitlement to wear a bar. The Police Commendation bar is of red enamel with two dark blue stripes towards each edge.

The act of lifesaving is rewarded in Dallas in common with many US police departments and the conditions include circumstances where someones life is saved although they might later die of their injuries provided that the officers action prolong the victims life by six hours. The bar for the Life Saving Award is half white and half red enamel with a dark blue central stripe.

Amongst the range of bars available are two awarded for reasons which are totally alien to European police forces—the *Safe Driver Award* and the *Perfect Attendance Award*. To qualify for the first, an officer must complete at least five years free of involvement in a preventable accident with each five year period being rewarded. The bars are white with two dark blue stripes towards the edges and a gold shield placed in the centre bearing the total number of accident free years—5, 10, 15 and so on—in white enamel. The Perfect Attendance Award is also given in five year increments. To receive a five year award the officer must have worked for five consecutive years without taking sick leave and for the ten year award, ten consecutive years. If an officer should fall sick, all previous entitlement is cancelled and a new period starts on the day he or she returns to work. The bar is the same as the Safe Driver Award but with the substitution of two yellow stripes for dark blue.

In all there are three medals and at least fourteen bars available to officers from the Dallas Police Department, all with detailed and demanding criteria which are adhered to strictly by the Meritorious Conduct Board. There is one final procedure followed in Dallas and other US police departments that has no equivalent in the UK—an official period of mourning for a fallen officer. Should an officer be killed in the line of duty, all officers wear a black band across the centre of their shield of office for a period of seven days as a mark of their respect for their colleague.

In Dallas the shield of office carries a black band during a period of mourning for a fellow officer.

LOS ANGELES (CALIFORNIA) POLICE DEPARTMENT

On the west coast of the US the largest city by some distance is Los Angeles, a sprawling area which includes Hollywood and Beverley Hills with all that the immense wealth on display there means and the downtown districts of Compton and Watts at the very opposite end of the social scale where poverty is rife and life is cheap—areas described in one popular guide book as a zoo. The work of the officers of the LAPD is as difficult as anywhere in the US, often more so, and they are rewarded with a range of medals of very similar patterns to other police departments in the US in their name and criteria necessary for their award.

POLICE MEDAL

Ribbon: Half red and half white.

Description: (obverse) a gold-coloured cross with rounded ends and a central medallion bearing the seal of the Police Department in white on blue enamel, surrounded by a wreath of laurel. A small ring suspender is used.

The seal of the LAPD was designed by a serving officer and adopted in 1971 and incorporates ten symbolic elements. The centrepiece has three stylised figures representing the modern family unit and intended to signify the duty of the police to serve the community. The figures are faceless to reinforce the duty of an officer to serve impartially without regard to race, colour or creed. The figures are superimposed on the scales of justice and the American flag and stand on the badge of office worn by LAPD officers meant to symbolise the patrol officer, the mainstay of policing. Below the shield are four olive branches for peace and domestic tranquillity. The name of the Department is written in full around the upper circumference and the motto—TO PROTECT AND SERVE—around the bottom. The whole of the central motif is superimposed on rays of the sun meant to represent faith, hope and perseverance. The whole of the seal forms the central medallion of the Police Medal.

The acts for which officers awarded the Police Medal are very similar to those for the Medal of Valor with very little to choose between the two.

In May 1982, an officer was sent with his partner to the scene of a shooting at a bar. As they approached, two men left the bar, one with a gun in his hand. He raised it and pointed it at one of the officers using the second man, a hostage, as a shield. The officer managed to separate the two and wrestle the firearm from the suspect. He was awarded the Police Medal for his bravery and only denied the highest honour because he had a partner with him and reacted on reflex to the motion of a gun being pointed at him—a fine distinction.

In January 1983 three officers were sent to a four-storey hotel where a man was standing on the roof ready to jump. Two of the officer took hold of the man whilst the third held onto the belts of his colleagues and the man jumped. They succeeded in holding onto him and pulling him back to safety despite the risk of them all being pulled over the side. The two officers holding the man were awarded the Police Medal but the third was given the Police Star—a lower award—because he was not thought to have faced the same degree of danger or risk of being pulled over—an even finer distinction.

United States of America

MEDAL OF VALOR

Ribbon: Half blue and half white - a neck ribbon.

Description: (Obverse) a circular silver medal with an irregular outline. At the top centre is a representation of Los Angeles city hall with a chevron below bearing the words FOR VALOR above a small shield showing the city coat of arms. Two branches of laurel are on either side of the city hall. There is a band around the upper two-thirds of the circumference in blue enamel bearing the legend LOS ANGELES POLICE DEPARTMENT AWARD. A ring suspender is used.

In addition to the medal and ribbon bar presented, recipients are also given a small silver lapel badge in the same design as the medal which they are entitled to wear on their uniform. The medal is the Departments highest award for bravery and only considered in the most extreme circumstances although it is not solely given where the officers life is threatened by the use of firearms which can often be the case in a number of US police departments. An act of great courage, whatever, the circumstances, can result in the award of the Medal of Valor although incidents involving firearms figure prominently in the history of its award. A selection of citations illustrates the range of actions which have been rewarded with a Medal of Valor.

On 20 September 1980 Officer H Lane and his partner were chasing a suspect on foot after a car chase when the suspect turned and shot the partner three times hitting him once on his belt buckle and twice in the chest. Officer Lane had already fired all six rounds from his revolver when he saw his partner hit but immediately tackled the suspect in hand-to-hand combat and succeeded in overpowering him although he knew full well that he was armed and very prepared to use his firearm. For his courage he was awarded the Medal of Valor in 1982. Luckily Officer Lane's partner was wearing his bullet-proof vest and survived the shooting.

Slightly over a year later, two officers were called to the scene of a house fire where two children were thought to be inside.

Both officers went into the building which was well ablaze without hesitation several times and succeeded in finding and saving the lives of both children despite the heat and effects of smoke. The Los Angeles Fire Department gave evidence to the Commendations Board of the intense heat and dangers from the smoke. Officers P Verna and J Lafko were both awarded the Medal of Valor.

The Medal of Valor can be awarded posthumously as happened in 1984 when Officer S Taira was killed at the scene of a crash involving a helicopter from the Department. The pilot and observer were both dazed in the crash and there was great danger from a spill of aviation fuel and the rotor blades which were still spinning. Nine officers attended the scene and succeeded in rescuing both occupants but Officer Taira was hit by the rotor blades and killed. Seven of the officers, including the deceased were awarded the Medal of Valor.

The criteria for the award of the most prestigious medal are applied very strictly and each recommendation is scrutinised in some detail. The reasons why an application are downgraded are recorded in a guide issued in the LAPD used to illustrate why a certain medal might be awarded to one officer and a higher or lower award made to another in circumstances which appear, on superficial examination, to be almost identical. The second highest award in Los Angeles is very often given where one small factor prevents the recipient from receiving the top honour.

POLICE STAR

Ribbon: White with a thin red stripe at one edge and a thin blue stripe at the other.

Description: (Obverse) a plain, unadorned five-point star superimposed on a disc of light blue enamel with a gold edge. A ring suspender is used.

The Police Star is the last of the three medals available for personal heroism to officers from the LAPD and is awarded for acts of courage beyond the normal demands of duty but which are not deemed sufficient for the Police Medal. In addition to heroism, it has been awarded for the use of exceptional tactics or judgement in particularly stressful situations including the saving of life.

Acts of particularly distinguished police service which do not involve acts of bravery are rewarded by three service medals and two unit citation medals where the police work was carried out by groups of officers rather than individuals.

POLICE DISTINGUISHED SERVICE MEDAL

Ribbon: Three equal vertical stripes of red, yellow and black.

Description: (Obverse) the crest of the LAPD in white on blue enamel as a central medallion surrounded by a ten-point star.

To receive this medal the recipient must display exceptional service in an assignment of critical importance to law enforcement or one with great responsibility. An important factor is work in the employees own time to the benefit of the Department. It can be awarded to any employee, not solely sworn officers. The reasons for its award range from one to an officer who served for 16 years as an expert on the gang culture prevalent in the city which resulted in a reduction in gang-motivated crime to the head of a multi-agency task force established to solve a series of 45 homosexual murders committed over a period of eight years starting in 1972.

Awards of the medal have been made in circumstances which have no direct equivalent in the UK. In 1983, two officers received the medal for continuing to work although they had been diagnosed as suffering from terminal diseases. One officer suffering with incurable cancer worked right up to his death and inspired his colleagues with his courage. A second officer, diagnosed with leukaemia and who later contracted pneumonia, continued to work to within days of his death.

United States of America

POLICE MERITORIOUS SERVICE MEDAL

Ribbon: Red with a white broad central band and yellow edges.

Description: (Obverse) a circular silver medal with the representation of the family unit taken from the departmental crest at the centre surrounded by a wreath of laurel and the words MERITORIOUS SERVICE MEDAL along the base.

The criteria for this medal are the same as for the higher award but less stringent and take account of the fact that the employee performed most of the service off duty. It has been given for a suggestion made to the benefit of the Department in circumstances where a monetary reward might have been considered appropriate similar to the force suggestion panels in UK forces where ideas of benefit to the service are rewarded with money. Examples include an officer who organised and established a programme where clothing was collected and distributed to the needy and another who suggested and set up a tourist safety programme which ran successfully during the 1984 Olympic Games held in the city.

The two final awards made in Los Angeles are for units rather than individuals. The highest honour was introduced in 1974 specifically to honour members of the Department's Special Weapons and Tactics Team (SWAT) for their part in the confrontation with the Symbionese Liberation Army. It has been extended to cover acts of outstanding courage by any team or unit in extremely hazardous situations and there must be evidence of bravery during the incident. It is awarded by the Police Commission not the Chief of Police.

POLICE COMMISSION UNIT CITATION

Ribbon: Dark blue with a red central band, all of equal width.

Description: (Obverse) a circular gold coloured medal with the Great Seal of the City of Los Angeles in coloured enamel surrounded by a grey band forming the central medallion. Branches of laurel are on both sides of the circumference of the medal body.

The shield at the centre of the city seal has four elements to represent the different periods of the citys history. In the lower right quarter are a castle and lion taken from the arms of Spain to symbolise Los Angeles under Spanish rule from 1542 until 1821. The lower left shows an eagle holding a serpent, taken from the arms of Mexico to represent Mexican rule between 1822 and 1846. The upper right quarter has the bear of the Californian Republic established in 1846 and the top left, the stars and stripes of the current US flag to indicate that Los Angeles is an American city.

The citation has been awarded sparingly since 1972, one of the most recent being in 1992 following the riots that occurred across the city. Prior to the outbreak of violence, members of the Metropolitan Division which has responsibility for the most dangerous parts of the city had trained to be able to provide protection for police and fire officers in just such an eventuality. During the riots members of the Fire Department had come under fire whilst attending a blaze in the city centre and were protected by the police squad who engaged in a 90 minute fire fight. There were no injuries to officers from either department. The unit was awarded a citation in February the following year.

The final award is made by the Chief of Police to members of any unit or team for outstanding service displaying total team effort. Members do not need to have been a part of the team for the whole time for which the citation is awarded provided that they have spent of significant majority of that time with the unit or must have performed a significant specific commendable act during that time.

POLICE MERITORIOUS UNIT CITATION

Ribbon: Red with a central band of white, blue and white.

Description: (Obverse) a gold coloured circular medal with a representation of Los Angeles city hall in silver above a banner containing the words LOS ANGELES POLICE and a two small branches of laurel in green enamel. A small ring suspender is used.

Citations have been given for a wide range of reasons and include one to a task force set up to investigate a series of 50 violent crimes of murder, robbery, rape and assaults involving 20 suspects. The officers of the unit were commended for their investigative techniques, planning, tenacity and devotion to duty as they cleared up the majority of offences and brought all the suspects to trial. The Pornography Section of the Vice Division spent eight months investigating a ring involved in child and animal pornography which was thought to be responsible for 80 per cent of the national distribution of such material. They successfully broke the ring and sent many offenders to prison. They were awarded a citation for their skills in dealing with this particularly distasteful crime.

Los Angeles lies on one of the world's most seismically active zones and it is a matter of time only before a major earthquake hits the area with potential to cause a loss of life and level of damage that is frightening. Earthquakes are a regular occurrence in California and there have been three very destructive events in the past 25 years, the last being one of the worst natural disasters ever to hit the US in terms of financial loss, comparable with Hurricane Andrew in 1992 and the destruction caused to the east coast. The earthquake hit Northridge in the San Fernando Valley (32 km NW of Los Angeles) at 4.31 am on Monday 17 January 1994 and left 57 people dead, 1,500 seriously injured, 12,500 buildings moderately to severely damaged and tens of thousands without electricity, gas or water. Damage to the roads system was such that the area was effectively paralysed for weeks. Had the earthquake struck a few hours later the death toll would have been counted in the thousands in such a densely populated area. The performance of officers from the LAPD in the aftermath of the shock was such that a special medal ribbon was issued to recognise their services.

The ribbon was issued alone, there was no medal, and it is not worn in everyday uniform. The ribbon is of light blue with a dark blue broad central band and yellow edges. In the centre lies a silver representation of Los Angeles city hall and a circle carrying the figures 94.

The award of this commemorative ribbon is not unique in Los Angeles although very few incidents have merited their issue. The riots of 1992 following the acquittal of the police officers for the assault on Rodney King which left 54 dead and more than 2,000 injured was, however, another such incident where official recognition of the work of LAPD officers was thought necessary. The ribbon awarded was half dark blue, half light blue with a silver motif bearing the date—92—pinned in the centre.

Not all special issue medal ribbons commemorate disasters such as riots and earthquakes, particularly momentous events in the citys history have been remembered by such ribbons. The 1984 summer Olympics held in the city resulted in the issue of a ribbon for the large numbers of officers involved in making the event the success it was. The ribbon was of red, white and blue, all of equal width, with a gold motif (the five Olympic rings with the date —84—above) placed over the central white band. Similar recognition was made of the visit of Pope John Paul II in 1987 with the ribbon being in the papal colours—half yellow, half white—with a gold-coloured emblem of crossed papal keys above the date—87.

There is one other medal available which deserves a mention although it has only been awarded once in 1990. The Liberty Award is named after a Los Angeles police dog called Liberty who was killed in the line of duty in 1989 on a search for an armed suspect. It is available to any dog killed or seriously injured whilst engaged on police duties. The medal was presented to the dog's handler and is displayed at the K-9 Unit headquarters.

CITY OF CHICO (CALIFORNIA) POLICE DEPARTMENT

The practice of awarding medals to officers is not confined to the larger police departments in the United States, some forces of modest size issue a range of rewards to their officers to acknowledge acts of bravery and long or meritorious service. The Police Department of the City of Chico in California serves a city with a population of less than 55,000 with a strength of fewer than 75 sworn officers. In the UK this would be no more than an small sub-division in a rural force of modest size.

In the US it is a self-contained department and boasts its own collection of medals to reward its staff for acts of courage, lifesaving and distinguished service. The medals are available to all members of staff, sworn and unsworn, and includes reserve officers and volunteers. The highest award is given to anyone who distinguish themselves conspicuously by heroic action above and beyond the call of duty.

POLICE CROSS MEDAL

Ribbon: Purple with a white central stripe, all of equal width.

Description: (Obverse) a central medallion bearing the Great Seal of California with the words CHICO (above) and POLICE (below) around the outside, all superimposed on a Maltese cross with only the outer part of the arms visible. The top arm is almost totally obscured by a gold banner bearing the words POLICE CROSS in blue. The ribbon is attached across the width of the upper arm of the cross.

One of the latest awards of the Police Cross Medal was made in 1998 to two officers—Detectives Robert Merrifield and Tom McKinnon—for the bravery they displayed on 20 April attempting to arrest a man wanted for a parole violation in the city. The wanted man had armed himself with a knife and stabbed both officers as they tried to arrest him. Detective Merrifield received several wounds to his upper arm and Tom McKinnon was wounded in the leg. The officers would have been justified under United States law in shooting their assailant but they succeeded in taking him into custody without resorting to the use of their weapons. Both officers made a full recovery from their wounds and were awarded the Police Cross Medal for their courage.

Three years earlier (1995) another officer—Rod O'Hern—was wounded whilst taking a juvenile into custody for shoplifting, this time by a friend of the suspect who shot officer O'Hern in the face with a revolver loaded with snake shot. Although badly wounded he managed to call for assistance and provide a description of his assailant who was arrested a short while later. Rod O'Hern made a full recovery and was awarded the Police Cross Medal the following year.

The threat of violence is ever-present in the United States and a constant hazard for police officers in even the smallest towns and cities. Even if not in immediate danger themselves, officers can be faced with the consequences of the widespread ownership and use of firearms. In 1994 Officer Scott Franssen of the Chico Police Department put his first-aid skills to good use when he was called to attend the scene of a domestic dispute and found a woman who had been shot several times bleeding profusely from her wounds. He succeeded in controlling the bleeding until medical help arrived. His actions saved the woman's life and he was awarded the Lifesaving Medal for his actions.

LIFESAVING MEDAL

Ribbon: White.

Description: (Obverse) a central medallion bearing the Great Seal of California with the words CHICO (above) and POLICE (below) around the outside. This is superimposed on a six-point starburst with a banner above the central medallion bearing the words LIFE SAVING. A ring suspender is used attached to the medal by a device taking the form of an oil lamp.

The award of the medal need not involve an act of bravery, the saving of a human life in the course of an officer's duty is sufficient. Lifesaving medals are a feature of a number of police departments in the US and awarded to officers in circumstances where, in the United Kingdom, organisations such as the Royal Humane Society or Society for the Protection of Life from Fire would recognise their actions rather than their own police force or a national award would be made if the act showed the necessary degree of courage.

For meritorious or distinguished service not involving acts of bravery but deserving of official recognition, a third medal is awarded. The degree of merit necessary before the award will be considered need not be unique but it must be distinctive and the Commendation Review Board in the city will expect that several of a list of factors will be applicable:

(a) performance beyond the normal work assignment,
(b) an outstanding attendance record,
(c) contributions which result in improved efficiency, increased effectiveness, substantial cost savings, improved personal safety or an enhanced public image.
(d) superior work or high productivity of quality work,
(e) taking extra initiative,
(f) performance of community service work, on or off duty, that reflects favourably on the Department,
(g) personal development of expertise above and beyond the required duty,
(h) personal or professional accomplishment which brings credit to the Department as a whole as well as the individual employee,
(i) conducting follow-up investigations which result in an outstanding arrest or solution to a major crime.

MEDAL OF MERIT

Ribbon: Three equal bands of red, white and blue.

Description: (Obverse) a silver medal with the same central medallion as the previous medals but with a wider gold coloured outer band bearing the words MEDAL OF MERIT above and CHICO POLICE below all surrounded by a wreath of laurel tied at the base with a bow. A large ring suspender is attached to the medal by a device in the form of an oil lamp.

The Medal of Merit can be given for service over a number of years in recognition of quality of work, dedication and initiative in much the same way as the chief constable of a British force might award a commendation. In common with a number of US police departments, Chico City nominates an officer of the year and employee of the year. The recipients of both honours are awarded the Medal of Merit in addition to the special certificate of commendation.

Subsequent awards of any medal issued in Chico City are indicated by the award of a bronze star to be worn on the medal ribbon. Up to four bronze stars can be worn but, if the recipient is honoured for a fifth time, a silver star is awarded to replace all those of bronze. The ribbon for wear in undress uniform carries a gold numeral in the centre indicating the total number of awards made to the officer of that particular medal.

The Department's permanent staff is augmented by a corps of Reserve Police Officers who are all volunteers. There is a form of long service medal available to these any volunteer who performs 3,000 hours of service and who:

(a) is a current Reserve Officer of good standing,
(b) demonstrates a positive attitude,
(c) demonstrates a high degree of dependability, and
(d) whose work demonstrates an understanding of the Department's mission statement.

The Police Reserve Service Award is of the same design as the Medal of Merit but with the title in the band above the great seal changed to read RESERVE SERVICE. The ribbon is blue with a white central band, all of equal width.

Although Chico City is a modest town keen to retain its small town atmosphere, it suffers from problems more typical of larger American cities albeit on a much smaller scale. There are problems with gangs and the associated use of firearms. In 1998 three incidents involving gang members serve to illustrate the extent of the problem. In the first example, a local teenager was walking along a city street when he was shot in the head in what was thought to be a gang-related incident.

The boy survived and the gunman was arrested. Two particular gangs, the Norteno and Sureno, are especially active and sworn enemies. In a second incident the same year a group from the Norteno gang invaded a party being held by a member of the Surenos. Fighting broke out which led, almost inevitably, to gunfire and three people, including an innocent bystander, were shot. All the gunmen were identified and arrested. Not long afterwards, in what was possibly a revenge attack, a group of Norteno gang members were in a junior school car park when a car containing two rival gang members drove by and began to shoot into the crowd. Luckily, only one person was shot but survived.

In such circumstances and with the threat of violence and gunfire never far below the surface, police officers in the small city of Chico earn their awards.

The Great Seal of the State of California which forms the centrepiece of all medals issued in Chico City is a good example of the heraldry of the United States and illustrates clearly how it differs from the more formalised and restrictive rules applicable to the grant of coats of arms in Britain. The symbols used reflect the history, geography, wildlife and industry of California and are reproduced in a more contemporary fashion than would be permitted in Britain.

California is a relative newcomer to the United States, becoming a part of the Union in September 1850, many years after the Declaration of Independence and before the start of the Civil War. The Great Seal was designed and adopted a year earlier and anticipated entry into the Union is indicated by the use of 31 white stars near the upper edge to represent the number of states including California. The Seal is round and depicts the figure of Minerva, the Roman Goddess of Wisdom, seated in the foreground overlooking the Sacramento River with five ships, some in full sail, and a backdrop of the Sierra Nevada. At her feet are a grizzly bear and a cluster of grapes to represent the wildlife and agricultural richness with a gold miner working behind her on the shore of the river. The Greek word—"Eureka" (I have found it)—is at the top of the scene. The words—"The Great Seal of the State of California"—are inscribed around the circumference in an outer gold band.

All states have a great seal and many on the east coast show the influence of British rule although most were redesigned after 1776 as a sign of the new country's independence. The further west the state the less the impact of colonial days and British rule. The Great Seal of New Jersey is more traditional in design than that of California and uses a shield, supports and crest reminiscent of British achievements of arms although it was adopted in 1777, after the Declaration of Independence, and uses symbols designed to emphasise the newly won freedoms of the country.

The central shield of the New Jersey Great Seal depicts three ploughs to recognise the State's agricultural tradition and the helmet above is placed facing forward to denote sovereignty and make it clear that the newly-formed country was the sovereign, not the King of England. A horse's head, facing left sits above the helmet. The two supporters are both female—Liberty on the left holding a staff topped with the liberty cap and Ceres, the Roman Goddess of Plenty on the right, with a cornucopia of food in her left hand. Although the position of the elements follows the traditional British pattern, the choice of Liberty and a Roman Goddess as supporters were intended as a snub to the King, a gesture reinforced by the use of the forward-facing helmet—a position traditionally reserved for royalty.

Montana is in the far west of the USA and did not join the Union until 1889 as the 41st state although the Great Seal originated in 1865. It is far removed from the formalised design of New Jersey, more akin to the Seal of California but without any classical references or figures—it is a picture with features of the landscape of Montana and reminders of its mineral wealth. It shows the Great Falls of the Missouri River with a backdrop of mountains from which the State took its name and the rising sun. In the left foreground is a forest, a grove of smaller trees and a selection of mining implements on the river bank.

The state motto—*"oro y plata"* (gold and silver)—is shown in a banner at the bottom of the Seal.

In addition to the seals, all states in America have a range of official emblems from the obvious—motto, bird, animal, tree, fish and flag—through the more unusua—song, mineral, insect, fossil and dance—to the very obscure—troubador (Connecticut), soil (Oklahoma and California), percussive musical instrument (Oklahoma) and furbearer (Oklahoma again). Each has been officially adopted as representative of the traditions, patriotism and pride felt in the state and some very odd examples can be found.

MANCHESTER (CONNECTICUT) POLICE DEPARTMENT

The use of a state, city or town seal on medals is as widespread in the United States as it was in the UK when the smaller independent British forces also issued their own medals although the designs in the United States follow the principles seen in most state seals of using more contemporary elements than is usual in the UK where the traditions of heraldry go back centuries and where the range of permitted designs is strictly controlled.

The town of Manchester in Connecticut has an independent police department with 120 sworn officers and 38 members of its civilian support staff to police a population of less than 80,000. The Department (founded in 1896) issues no fewer than six different medals to all members of its staff and uses the Town Seal as its centrepiece on each. The Seal has a simple design with one main feature—the mulberry tree—the food plant of the silkworm, the basis of the towns major industry. It shows a stylised tree of six branches and mulberry leaves all giving an overall mulberry leaf shape. The date that the town was established—1823–is at the bottom formed by a silken thread.

The medals are awarded by the Police Department to its officers and members of the support staff to reward acts of courage, meritorious service and lifesaving.

All ribbons for medals awarded in Manchester are worn in the shape of a triangle with the apex at the bottom attached to a small ring suspender and all except one are of a single plain colour.

MEDAL OF HONOR

Ribbon: White

Description: (Obverse) the Town Seal in gold at the centre of an eight-point star with rayed arms. The inscription MEDAL OF HONOR is carried in gold on a blue banner beneath the centrepiece.

The medal is awarded to any person for an act of bravery above and beyond the call of duty whilst engaged in combat with someone known to be armed and dangerous. For other acts of courage where the officer is not in combat but nonetheless facing a dangerous situation there is a second medal with slightly less demanding criteria although the level of bravery necessary before its award would be considered remains very high.

MEDAL FOR VALOR

Ribbon: Red.

Description: (Obverse) a round gold coloured medal with the Town Seal in the lower half beneath a plain straight central bar. The back ground to the seal is rayed towards the circumference. There is a blue enamel banner below the seal bearing the words MEDAL OF VALOR in gold lettering. Above the plain bar is an eagle with outstretched wings.

MEDAL FOR DISTINGUISHED SERVICE

Ribbon: Dark green.

Description: Obverse) the medal also uses the Town Seal as its centrepiece with an outer band having a blue banner in its lower half bearing the words DISTINGUISHED SERVICE in gold lettering. Around this band lies a wreath of laurel tied at the base with a bow.

This medal is used to reward service beyond the ordinary course of duty in a wide range of circumstances where the officer displays alertness, perseverance or timely judgement in the performance of a difficult task which results in the protection of life, the recovery of stolen property, the prevention or solving of a major crime or arrest of an armed or dangerous person.

United States of America

LIFESAVING MEDAL

Ribbon: Pale yellow.

Description: (Obverse) an irregular shaped medal with the Town Seal in the lower half and the word LIFESAVING in gold lettering in a blue banner below. Above the rounded lower half sits a rectangle bearing a stylised motif to which is attached the small ring suspender. It is awarded to anyone who saves the life of another.

DEPARTMENT CITATION FOR MERITORIOUS SERVICE

Ribbon: Purple.

Description: (Obverse) another irregularly shaped medal using the Town Seal as the centrepiece of its rounded lower half. Above the seal sits an eagle with outstretched wings.

The use of medals to denote a citation has no comparison in UK police forces where a commendation from a chief constable usually takes the form of a certificate, never a medal, and is most usually made to individuals rather than units or squads. The award of a medal with the right to wear a ribbon, however, is a recurring feature of a large number of US police departments. The criteria for the award in the Manchester Police Department are wide and include the successful performance of an extremely complex and difficult investigation, the demonstration of exceptional skill and ingenuity in the arrest of a wanted person, the provision of outstanding service to the public or a display of continuous excellence over an extended period of time.

In addition to the Departmental Citation, the Chief of Police can award his own citation for acts or achievements which do not warrant the award of a higher medal but which are still thought worthy of official recognition. It also carries with it the right to wear the medal ribbon.

CHIEF'S CITATION

Ribbon: Five stripes of blue, white, red, white, blue—all of equal width.

Description: (Obverse) a central medallion bearing the Town Seal finished in blue superimposed on an eight-point star with the points coloured—top and bottom in blue, the two sides in white and the four intermediates in red with the webs between coloured gold. There is a gold banner below the town seal which bears the words CHIEF'S CITATION in blue enamel.

page 361

MASSACHUSETTS STATE POLICE

The policing structure of the United States can be complex with the jurisdictions of a number of separate departments overlapping even without taking into account the many federal agencies which include the FBI, Bureau of Alcohol, Firearms and Tobacco, US Border Patrol, US Marshals Service and others. Boston, the capital city of Massachusetts, boasts the oldest full-time professional police department in the country, founded in 1838 and is responsible for policing almost 600,000 people from a state population of almost six million. More than 340 other departments exist in the rest of the State ranging from Springfield PD caring for more than 150,000 in a large city to the Massachusetts Institute of Technology PD with jurisdiction only on the campus to care for 12,000 students and staff. Also at the lower end of the scale, the town of Grafton has less than 13,000 inhabitants but its own police department with a total strength of only 18 officers including the Chief of Police, the Lieutenant and three sergeants.

Although most urban areas of any size have their own police department there are large rural areas with small towns and villages where the policing responsibility rests with the state authorities. A similar situation exists in all states in the US and each has its own state police department to provide the necessary cover outside the towns and cities. The state troopers are also a familiar sight patrolling interstate roads although there is very often a totally separate highway patrol department for this purpose. Although not a large state by American standards the Commonwealth of Massachusetts has extensive rural areas inland from the area around Boston where the troopers of the Massachusetts State Police have the primary policing responsibility. They also patrol the main interstate roads running across the state.

The Department has its own range of four awards for its troopers, two to recognise acts of courage, one to acknowledge outstanding achievement and one for saving life. The highest award is the Medal of Honor given to all sworn personnel who perform acts of extraordinary heroism above and beyond the call of duty.

MEDAL OF HONOR

Ribbon: *Dark blue with a gold central stripe..*

Metal: *Gold.*

Description: *(Obverse) a central medallion of an eagle with outstretched wings against a circular background with the word HONOR in gold on a blue enamel banner below. Around the outside is a circle bearing the words MASSACHUSETTS (top) and STATE POLICE (bottom) separated by a set of five stars on either side of the band, all superimposed on a twelve-point star with only the points visible.*

Acts of courage which merit recognition but which fall below the high standards required for the Medal of Honor are rewarded by the Medal of Valor—a silver medal given for specific acts of bravery or for outstanding courage exhibited by troopers in the course of their duty. The design of the medal is almost identical to the Medal of Honor apart from the metal used and the substitution of the word VALOR in the banner below the eagle. The ribbon has five stripes of white, red, blue, red and white, all of equal width.

The Medal of Merit, the third award available, is given in recognition of acts of outstanding achievement, far exceeding the normal demands of the Department, which greatly contribute to its operation. The bronze medal hangs from a ribbon of halved blue and white. The design follows the same design as the two higher awards, differing only in the metal used and the word in the banner which reads MERIT.

The Medal of Honor is available only to officers of the State Police but the two others can be awarded to members of any other police department in Massachusetts. The final award, the Medal of Lifesaving, is awarded for significant action in the saving of a life. All four medals of the Massachusetts State Police are worn around the neck.

LIFESAVING MEDAL

Ribbon: Halved red and white.

Metal: Bronze and enamels.

Description: (Obverse) A Maltese cross in blue enamel with a star in the upper arm and a second cross with narrower arms in red enamel between the arms of the first. Both crosses overlie a wreath which is only partially visible. Over the lower arms of both crosses is a banner bearing the words LIFE SAVING which extends over the upper arms in the form of a wreath (in white enamel). At the centre is the Great Seal of the Commonwealth of Massachusetts within an outer band bearing the inscription MASSACHUSETTS STATE POLICE. A simple ring suspender is used.

THE GEORGE L HANNA AWARDS—MASSACHUSETTS

In many states medals are awarded by the state authorities to police officers from any department irrespective of any locally available honours system if the circumstances are such that the Governor feels the need to recognise the officers action at a much higher level. Massachusetts is such a state although the State Police, City of Boston and a number of other smaller forces have their own system of awards available for their officers. The state awards are the most prestigious of all awards and only given in the most extreme circumstances to recognise courage of the very highest order.

The George L Hanna awards for bravery are given state-wide and is the highest available to any police officer in any department in the Commonwealth of Massachusetts on the recommendation of any chief of police who considers that a member of his department should be considered. George Hanna was a trooper with the Massachusetts State Police who was killed in the line of duty on 26 February 1983 in circumstances which shocked the state authorities even in a country far more used to violent death than the UK. Trooper Hanna joined the State Police on 15 October 1974 and had stopped a suspicious vehicle with five occupants on the evening of Saturday 26 February. As he removed them from the car for questioning he was shot six times by one of the male occupants, dying later that evening. The three male occupants of the car were later arrested and convicted of first degree murder and sentenced to life imprisonment. George Hanna left a widow and three young children.

The shock felt in Massachusetts at the cold blooded brutality of the murder prompted the Governor to introduce a system of awards in George Hanna's memory to recognise the bravery of police officers who put their lives at risk in the service of their community. Since 1983 the awards have become a symbol of prestige in the Commonwealth as a whole not solely amongst those directly involved with law enforcement. The award is available at three levels.

The Medal of Honor is awarded to a sworn member of any police department who performs a specific act of bravery or act of extraordinary courage above and beyond the call of duty with no regard for their personal safety. In the 15 years up to the ceremony held in October 1999, 32 police officers have been awarded the medal although there were none given at that particular ceremony in recognition of the fact that no incident rose to the level of sacrifice demonstrated by George Hanna. The medals are awarded sparingly to reflect Trooper Hanna's courage in 1983. Officers awarded the medal wear an enamelled ribbon bar on their tunic which is of dark blue with a broad central white band bearing the word HONOR in gold lettering.

The Medal of Valor is given to recognise the actions of officers who have performed acts of extraordinary heroism above and beyond the call of duty. It had been awarded on 71 occasions since 1983 and the ceremony in 1999 saw the bravery of eight officers from three different police departments recognised. The use of firearms and knives figured prominently in six of the citations with the officers facing a very immediate threat to their lives. On 23 May 1998 Officer James Griffin of the Boston Police Department was in pursuit of a known drugs dealer who drove his car at him and pointed a handgun (later found to be fully loaded) at him. Officer Griffin shot and killed the dealer and found large amounts of cash and drugs in his car. In the same city, five months later on 19 October, Officer Raymond D'Oyley struggled with and disarmed a knife-wielding man who had previously slashed his ex-wife's throat and stabbed her boyfriend in a domestic incident.

Not all awards were made for incidents involving weapons however, on Christmas Eve 1998

Detective Robert Rogers, again from Boston PD, came across a car accident on the expressway on his way home from duty. He stopped to help and was trying to move an injured occupant to safety when he was struck by a car himself causing severe leg injuries. He continued to help the injured passengers of the first car despite his own wounds.

Both the Medal of Honor and Medal of Valor are of the same design as the Lifesaving Medal awarded by the Massachusetts State Police but with the arms of the crosses enamelled in different colours and the inscription below the central medallion amended to give the name of the award. It is a fine multi-coloured enamelled silver award which hangs from a ribbon of red, white and blue vertical stripes. The central medallion has the words COMM OF MASSACHUSETTS in silver on blue around the Great Seal of the State. The ribbon colouring also differs, dark blue for the Medal of Honor and red, white and blue stripes, all of equal width, for the Medal of Valor.

The third level of award—Award for Merit—does not have a medal and consists of a plaque mounted on wood. These awards are given for meritorious acts of bravery, courage and performance beyond the call of duty. At the ceremony held in October 2000, 29 officers from three different departments received the Award of Merit, many for assistance given to another officer who was subsequently awarded the Hanna Medal of Valor.

VIRGINIA BEACH (VIRGINIA) POLICE DEPARTMENT

Although the range of medals available in the United States is wide and varied, there are similarities in design between different departments and also those within an individual force. The Virginia Beach Police Department awards five different medals to its officers with four being of basically the same design although the colouring of the enamel, the legend bearing the name of the medal and, of course, the ribbon colour changes. The Medal of Valor is, in fact, identical to the George L Hanna Medal of Valor apart from the seal shown on the central medallion and the colouring of the ribbon. State Medals for Valor are also awarded in California and Arizona, both of the same basic design but with the appropriate great seal in the centre and the colouring of the ribbon.

Virginia Beach PD is a typical medium sized department with more than 750 officers responsible for a static population of almost 450,000 which is more than doubled by holidaymakers for much of the year. It is not a particularly dangerous city compared with many in the US although the levels of recorded crime are high by British standards. In 1998 there were 12 homicides, 75 forcible rapes, 2,500 burglaries and 450 robberies—figures which would cause uproar in a British force of similar size with questions in parliament and calls for the head of the chief constable.

The most prestigious award available is the Medal of Valor which requires that the recipients perform an act of courage of the highest order at great risk to their lives in circumstances which are above and beyond the call of duty.

MEDAL OF VALOR

Ribbon: *Plain medium blue.*

Description: *A Maltese Cross enamelled in dark blue with a second, smaller cross, enamelled in light blue, between the arms and the spaces between all the arms coloured silver and of a rayed design. The upper arm of the larger cross carries a small silver five-point star. Superimposed on the crosses in the centre is the Seal of Virginia Beach within a white band bearing the nam—VIRGINIA BEACH, VIRGINIA. Outside this band is a second one, open at the top, with the upper half in the form of a laurel wreath in white and the lower part in mauve bearing the name of the medal in silver—MEDAL of VALOR. It hangs from a simple ring suspender.*

Virginia Beach PD follows the pattern of many US police departments with the medal ribbon taking the form of an enamelled brooch, blue in the case of the Medal of Valor, with a silver border and a silver star placed centrally. The medal should be worn around the neck. It is awarded in recognition of a single act of gallantry and an accumulation of minor acts of heroism would not qualify an officer for the medal. These lesser acts of courage are rewarded by the grant of a second medal, also intended to be worn around the neck, which is very similar in design to the Medal of Valor. The Silver Cross differs only in the colouring of the enamels on the arms of the two crosses (light blue and red), the name on the lower half of the outer band (Silver Cross) and the ribbon which is plain red. It is awarded to any regular or auxiliary member of the Department who distinguishes himself by extraordinary heroism which does not merit the award of the Medal of Valor. The criteria remain demanding, however, and require the presence of great danger or personal risk.

In addition to the two medals for gallantry, the Department has available the Medal of Merit intended to reward officers who distinguish themselves by performing duties above those normally expected and which make a significant contribution to the achievement of the goals of law enforcement. These duties can be performed in a single act or by a sustained effort. The Department also issues a Special Commendation Award which takes the form of a certificate and any officer who receives five such awards is automatically considered for the Medal of Merit.

The medal itself again differs from the two previous awards only in the change of colours and the name inscribed on the lower half of the outer central band. The arms of the two crosses are purple and red and the ribbon is plain white. This medal is intended for wear on the breast.

The fourth of the similar medals is the Department's version of the military Purple Heart and awarded to any officer who is killed or wounded on duty or off duty but attempting to enforce the law. The individual must have required hospital treatment and the award is automatic if the wound was caused by a deadly or dangerous weapon. In any other circumstances the final decision will be made by the Department's Awards Committee.

The Blue Star hangs from a light blue ribbon with a broad central white stripe with the arms of the larger cross being light blue and the smaller one of crimson. The ribbon brooch is half blue and half white without the centrally placed star seen on the three other medals.

In common with a large number of US police departments and particularly relevant in a busy holiday resort on the Atlantic Coast, Virginia Beach awards a special medal to its officers who save lives. The criteria are quite complex with a number of basic elements which must be present before an award is considered:

(1) the performance of a physical act or first aid technique in the preservation of human life,
(2) the victim must have been in imminent danger of succumbing to an injury or illness unless some action is taken,
(3) the victim must have had active injuries or physical illness that are life-threatening, or
(4) the victim was incapable of retreating from an actual life-threatening situation and had to be moved to safety by the officer, and
(5) the officer had participated voluntarily in the life saving attempt.

If the officer manages to satisfy the Department's Awards Committee and Chief of Police, he or she will be awarded the Life Saving Medal.

LIFE SAVING MEDAL

Ribbon: Plain bright green.

Description: A six pointed star with the point bearing a rayed design. The Seal of the City of Virginia Beach is positioned at the centre of the star with a semicircular band superimposed over the lower three arms bearing the words LIFE SAVING in silver on mauve enamel.

The same basic design of medal used in Virginia Beach (apart from the Life Saving Medal) has also been adopted for the whole range of awards made in Salt Lake City, Utah where there are eight different medals available to police officers and members of the general public with the only differences being in the colouring of the enamels used, the ribbons and the name inscribed on the lower border of the central medallion.

KING'S COUNTY (CALIFORNIA) SHERIFF'S OFFICE

Working alongside the individual police departments, highway patrol officers and state troopers in all states are the sheriffs and deputy sheriffs with the differences between them being blurred and not easily understandable to those unfamiliar with the system. They are predominantly a feature of rural areas and often have a responsibility for running the local jails, prisoner escorts and court duties in addition to standard law enforcement. Sheriffs offices are usually older than many police departments and more evident the further west one travels. The County of King's in California appointed its first sheriff in 1893 and there have been eleven others since. The present office has all the trappings of a modern law enforcement agency—dogs, a SWAT team, scientific support and, common in the US, a team specially devoted to the suppression of gang related crime. The sheriffs area of responsibility covers 1,396 square miles with four main cities and a total population of almost 83,000.

The Detentions Division of the Department is responsible for two jails holding a maximum of 257 inmates, male and female, sentenced and pre-sentence with a staff of about 70. There is also a maximum security facility at the main jail. Each deputy sheriff is assigned his or her own vehicle which they use to travel to and from their station and which is always left in their driveways when off duty. The apparent wastefulness of such a system is offset by the high visibility in the County and the ease and speed of response by the deputies to any emergency.

The Department has its own medals available to reward deputies from the two divisions—operations and detention—for acts of courage and also if they are injured in the course of their duty. The highest award is given to acknowledge any conspicuous bravery above and beyond the call of duty.

United States of America

MEDAL OF VALOR

Ribbon: Green. The bar worn in everyday uniform is of green enamel with the word VALOR in gold.

Description: (Obverse) a gold medal with a central medallion carrying the Great Seal of California in coloured enamel surrounded by an outer band bearing the words KINGS CO SHERIFF'S DEPT in green enamel. This is superimposed on a star and Greek cross (edged in green enamel) with the words MEDAL OF in scrolls (above) and VALOR (below) the central medallion—all superimposed on a wreath of oak leaves.

Since its introduction eleven officers have been awarded the medal plus one award made in March 1995 to police dog Nero who was killed in the course of his duty in circumstances which were thought worthy of the highest honour the Department could bestow.

Any employees who distinguish themselves by any actions above and beyond the call of duty but which is not thought worthy of the Department's highest honour are rewarded with the Silver Star. It is a recent award, instituted only in 1997 and only one has been given to date. The criteria include acts that are brave and unselfish or where skills have been used to save a life.

SILVER STAR

Ribbon: Red. The bar for wear in undress uniform carries a small silver star at the centre.

Description: (Obverse) a central medallion in the form of the deputy sheriff's badge superimposed on six-point rayed star. There are two banners above and below the star bearing the words SILVER (upper) and STAR (lower) in green enamel. The suspender is in the form of a bird with outstretched wings. The deputy sheriff's badge at the centre consists of a six-point star with ball finials and a central medallion bearing the Great Seal of California in enamel with an outer band carrying the words DEPUTY SHERIFF (above) and COUNTY OF KINGS (below).

The third of the awards made in King's County is based on the national Purple Heart Medal and awarded to any deputies who sustain serious wounds or other serious bodily injury in the course of their duty as the result of an attack by another. The criteria for its award are that the injury was severe and required medical treatment beyond the application of simple first aid, the wound was caused by a weapon (gun, knife etc) and that a crime report had been made.

PURPLE HEART

Ribbon: Purple.

Description: (Obverse) a replica of the national military medal of the same name but with the portrait of George Washington in the centre replaced by a gold six-point sheriff's star similar to that used on the King's County Silver Star.

All three medals awarded in King's County can be awarded posthumously, a feature of a great many individual police departments and law enforcement agencies and a consequence of the dangerous nature of police work in the US.

TEXAS RANGERS

Arguably one of the most well-known of American policing agencies is, in reality, very small in terms of staffing levels although its area of responsibility is vast, large than most European countries, with an area of more than 673,400 square kilometres, a distance from border to border east to west not far short of 1,440 kilometres and from north to south of almost 1,280—Texas. All cities and most towns have their own police departments supported by the state police and highway patrol who all work with a force of no more than one hundred officers responsible for the vast area—the Texas Rangers—who have a mystique about them that rivals that of the Royal Canadian Mounted Police.

The Texas Rangers were formed in 1823 when the state was under Mexican control and consisted of ten men, all volunteers, who were given authority by the Mexican government to keep an eye on the movements of renegade Indians. The group was enlarged in 1835 and its area of responsibility extended to include protection of the settlers in Texas from outlaws and bandits. When the Republic of Texas was declared in 1836 with the break from Mexico the Rangers became involved in border disputes and conflicts with the Mexicans until Texas became a member of the United States in 1845. The State seceded from the Union during the American Civil War but was re-admitted at the end of the war.

In 1935 the Rangers were reorganised into the body that exists today under the control of the Texas Department of Public Safety with the same authority as any other law enforcement officer in the State but with jurisdiction across all parts of Texas. The number of Rangers is just over 100, a tiny number for such a huge area and a population of over 19 million but they perform a useful function in the policing of Texas and maintain their reputation with ease. The modern Ranger does not wear a uniform although he is always recognisable by his western hat. The Texas Rangers have one medal available to recognise acts of great courage at the risk of their lives although it has been awarded on five occasions only since its introduction, once posthumously and once as a second award to the same officer.

MEDAL OF VALOR

Ribbon: A red broad central stripe flanked by bands of white and blue.

Description: (Obverse) a five-point star with a central medallion containing a second five-point star with the word TEXAS spelt in the area between the points surrounded by an outer band inscribed with DEPARTMENT OF PUBLIC SAFETY in the upper half. In the lower half is a scrolled banner bearing the words COURTESY SERVICE PROTECTION. The whole is superimposed on a wreath of oak (left) and laurel leaves (right) above a banner bearing the word VALOR and two stars.

The double award was made to Ranger Sergeant John Aycock, the first in January 1987 and the second almost exactly eight years later in January 1995. On the first occasion he was involved with a fellow officer (Ranger Sergeant Stanley Guffey) during the rescue of a kidnapped 2-year old child being held to ransom by a man already on parole from prison who was also wanted for forgery and who was subsequently found to have committed one murder. The two officers hid in a car at the ransom exchange point although they were seen and Sergeant Guffey was shot and killed by the kidnapper although Sergeant Aycock himself killed the suspect. The child was freed without harm. Both officers were awarded the Texas Ranger Medal of Valor for their courage, Guffey unfortunately posthumously.

Sergeant Aycock's second award arose from another incident involving a young child, this time aged 14 months, who was being held at gunpoint. The offender had fired shots from a 12-bore shotgun and threatened to kill the child's mother before trying to escape in a stolen car. The car was disabled and a stand-off followed with Sergeant Aycock assuming the rôle of hostage negotiator. Over the next four hours he succeeded in persuading the suspect to hand over the child and surrender with no need to resort to force and brought the incident to a peaceful and successful end. He was rewarded for his skill, courage and judgement by the award of a second Medal of Valor.

CITY OF LAWTON (OKLAHOMA) POLICE DEPARTMENT

In some US police departments medals are given in addition to the usual range of rewards for heroic action where the officer concerned lost his or her life in the course of their duty. The award varies from department to department but the demanding and dangerous nature of police work in the US, even in small towns and cities far away from the areas normally associated with criminal violence, has meant that a range of such awards has been introduced.

The city of Lawton is a typical mid-western American city which sits in the south-west corner of Oklahoma, 160 kilometres from the state capital some 48 kilometres from the border with Texas. It has a population of approximately 90,000 and a police department of 152 sworn officers supported by 24 civilian members of staff who have been particularly successful in recent years in combating crimes from homicide and other crimes of violence to burglary and thefts from cars. From 1995 to 1999 the Department has managed to reduce burglaries from 1,689 to 1,062, auto thefts from 424 to 196 and assaults from 492 to 277—substantial reductions in all areas. The total of serious crimes in the same period has been reduced from 7,101 to 4,798, figures which should allow the officers some pride in their achievements. The work can, however, be dangerous and the Department has a range of award available for its officers who display conspicuous gallantry or meritorious service or who are killed or injured in the line of duty.

Police Medal of Honor—awarded to officers who distinguish themselves by gallant or extraordinary heroism above and beyond the call of duty where the officer was fully aware of the threat to his or her personal safety. The award of the medal is signified by a ribbon bar of orange with a red stripe towards the edges.

Police Cross—given to the next-of-kin of any officer who is killed in the line of duty under honourable circumstances. It is awarded in addition to any other award which may be given for the officers actions.

Police Medal for Valor—ranked next to the Police Cross it is a bravery award given to officers who display exceptional courage at an imminent risk to their life in an extremely dangerous situation. There is an unusual proviso in the conditions of the award which demands that the action should be entirely voluntary and which disqualifies officers from any entitlement to the medal if they were following verbal or written orders no matter how great the level of courage shown. The ribbon bar is dark blue with a white stripe towards each edge.

Meritorious Conduct Bar—in common with a number of awards made in the US this carries with it no entitlement to a medal but is indicated by a ribbon bar worn on the uniform in similar fashion to those signifying the award of a medal. It is awarded to officers for outstanding performance in circumstances which involve a great risk to their personal safety or for particularly meritorious service in the achievement of difficult projects or situations. The car is red with a dark blue stripe towards each edge.

Life Saving Bar—another common bar awarded in a number of US police departments and given to officers who save a human life. The bar is half red and half white separated by a dark blue stripe.

Police Shield—given to an officer who is seriously injured in the course of his or her duty which is usually awarded where the officer was assaulted but which is also available if the injury is sustained as a result of any police duty. In certain circumstances it has been awarded following road traffic accidents and falls on ice but only where it has been proven that the officer took all possible safety precautions and had no control over the circumstances. The bar is of pale green with a gold departmental police shield in the centre.

Certificate of Merit—the bar is available to all members of the Department, including the civilian support staff for any outstanding performance under unusual, complicated or hazardous circumstances It is possible the equivalent of a chief constables commendation in the UK but carries with it the right to wear a ribbon bar which is a red with a dark blue stripe towards each edge.

Lawson City Police Department also awards three other ribbon bars which have no equivalent in any force in the UK but which occur regularly in the US. There are no medals awarded.

Supervisor of the Year—awarded to officers of the rank of lieutenant or above who have contributed to the Department in an exemplary manner and whose actions exemplify leadership excellence. The ribbon bar is white with dark blue edges, the two separated by white stripes.

Officer of the Year—available to officers below the rank of lieutenant who have at least one years service who have performed in an outstanding and exemplary manner in the preceding year. The ribbon bar is red with dark blue edges the two colours separated by dark blue stripes.

Civilian Employee of the Year—awarded under similar criteria to the Officer of the Year Bar but available to members of the civilian support staff. The bar is half dark blue and half white separated by a red stripe.

United States of America

CITY OF ST MARY'S (GEORGIA) POLICE DEPARTMENT

The number of different awards available to officers from some very small police departments in the US and the range of ribbons they can wear can be bewildering, particularly in comparison with the situation in the UK. Even by American standards, the fact that officers from a police department with a strength of 33 sworn officers in a city with a residential population of only 15,000 are eligible for twelve different awards for bravery or service and a further five for marksmanship with a handgun is difficult for police officers from the UK to understand.

In addition to the 33 sworn officers of the Department, there are five administrative support officers, 20 members of the volunteer corps and four members of the sworn reserve but it remains a small department on the Atlantic coast of Georgia responsible for an area of 34 square kilometres and an unlikely place to be home to a total of 18 different medals and awards available for award to its police officers. The range of awards available is similar to many US police departments although there are some which are unusual. The ribbon colours are given after the award name.

Medal of Honor (dark blue with a central white band)—awarded for an outstanding act of courage in the line of duty with imminent danger to life where the officer was fully aware of the risks.

Lifesaving Medal (half red and half white)—given for an act performed with a disregard for personal safety or by prompt and alert action which results in the saving of a life.

Wounded in Combat Medal (yellow with green bands in the centre and at each edge)—awarded if an officer is severely wounded in the line of duty by an armed adversary.

Judge Brian Lynn Memorial Gallantry Star for Excellent Arrest (blue with a broad central red band flanked by white stripes and with white edges)—given for an act of great courage in the arrest of a person who is a major threat to the community or the officer.

Combat Cross (green with yellow edges)—awarded to recognise an act of courage in combat with an armed criminal with an imminent personal danger to the officers life.

Grand Cordon Departmental Citation (red with a white band towards each edge)—a unit award given to each member where the unit receives some form of official recognition for an action.

Meritorious Service Award (half green, half red separated by a white stripe)—given in recognition of a highly unusual act in adverse circumstances with a degree of danger to the officer or where death or injury to a third party is prevented.

Exceptional Duty Medal (red)—used to recognise an accomplishment which brings public acclaim to the officer concerned, the Department or the police service in general as a result of training, devotion to duty or service to the public.

Honorable Service Medal (blue)—awarded to acknowledge action of an unusual nature which shows special initiative.

Samaritan Officer of the Year (half blue, half white)—awarded for an act of humanity as a friend to someone in need during a time of crisis, accident or danger.

Advanced Academic Achievement Award (half dark blue, half orange)—an unusual award by UK standards given to recognise a years academic credit above the level of that required by law for a police officer in Georgia.

Good Conduct Award (green with a broad central band in yellow and two yellow stripes towards each edge)—available to acknowledge a years service without a written reprimand for any matter to officers who follow the tenets of friendly, fair, firm and faithful police duty.

Distinguished Volunteer Service Award (half black, half white)—given to volunteer members of the Department in recognition of 100 hours service in a year. Second and subsequent awards of any of the Department's medals are indicated by an oak leaf cluster with a gold star being worn for five or more awards of the same medal.

The remaining five medal bars which can be worn by members of the St Mary's Police Department are all presented on the basis of the results obtained on handgun marksmanship courses which each officer must undergo regularly during their police service. The basic ribbon of the Marksmanship Awards is green with one, two three or four yellow stripes according to the standard achieved. An officer who achieves 80 to 84% is entitled to the ribbon with a single stripe—a marksman. Scores of 85 to 89% (sharpshooter), 90 to 94 % (expert) and 95 to 100% (master) are indicated by extra yellow stripes. The achievement of three consecutive 100% scores carries with it the award of a gold star on the master ribbon and the title of Distinguished Master.

OWOSSO (MICHIGAN) POLICE DEPARTMENT

Smaller still than St Mary's with an area of responsibility of only ten square kilometres and 17,000 residents is the town of Owosso in Michigan. The Owosso Police Department has 22 sworn officers, ten reserve officers and three clerical staff to respond to 14,000 calls for service each year including traffic stops. For a small town the crime rate is alarming—in 1999 there were 300 assaults, 60 sexual offences, 214 burglaries, 605 thefts, 72 cases of fraud, four kidnappings and five robberies, figures which would cause an inspector in a town of similar size in the UK to suffer many sleepless nights. This small independent police department has no fewer than eight different medals available to its officers with the Medal of Honor being the most prestigious and awarded to recognise outstanding acts of courage in the line of duty accompanied by an imminent threat to the officers life in the full knowledge of the risks involved.

MEDAL OF HONOR

Ribbon: Green. The ribbon bar worn in everyday uniform is of dark blue enamel with gold borders and twelve gold stars positioned in two groups of six.

Metal: Gold and green enamel.

Description: (Obverse) a circular medal with a slightly lobed circumference and a central cross in green enamel bearing an eagle (in gold) with outstretched wings perched on a rock.

The first Medal of Honor was awarded in 1996 to Patrolman Roger Squiers (later sergeant) for his bravery in rescuing a woman from a blazing house in June of that year. He had been called to the scene with no idea what to expect and found a house engulfed in flames with the occupant still inside. He entered the house with a total disregard for his own safety, found the unconcious lady and succeeded in taking her to safety. The house was totally destroyed by the fire. Patrolman Squiers was later awarded the Medal of Honor by his Chief of Police and the County Dispatcher (Linda Mallory of the Shiawassee County Sheriff's Department) who controlled and co-ordinated the incident was awarded the Owosso PD Exceptional Duty Medal for her coolness and prompt action

The Combat Cross, the second highest award, is made to officers who perform an individual act of courage in combat with an armed person where there is an imminent threat to their life.

United States of America

COMBAT CROSS

Ribbon: Green with yellow edges.

Metal: Gold and enamels.

Description: (Obverse) a Maltese cross with the arms in white enamel and a central medallion in green enamel bearing the eagle with outstretched wings seen on the Medal of Honor (again in gold). The space between the arms of the cross is partially filled in (in blue enamel) to give the appearance of a circle behind the cross. There is an upper ribbon bar in green enamel bearing the name of the medal in gold lettering.

If an officer receives a wound in the course of his or her duty inflicted intentionally by an armed person and suffers an puncture wound, laceration, fracture, concussion or other serious injury, the award of the Purple Heart would follow as a matter of course, there is no requirement for any specific act of courage, suffering the wound is sufficient.

PURPLE HEART

Ribbon: Maroon with white edges and two white lines towards the centre.

Metal: Gold and purple enamel.

Description: (Obverse) in the shape of a shield with a purple enamel centre of the same shape and a small cross in the middle.

The remaining medals available are awarded to acknowledge a serious injury sustained on duty but not inflicted by an assailant (Legion of Honour), for saving life in the course of duty with a disregard for personal safety (Life Saving Medal) and a range of three awards for exceptional, honourable or meritorious service, given according to the level of professionalism, initiative and devotion to duty involved.

Owosso was founded in 1840 and named after a local Chippewa Indian chief—Wasso. The first police officer appeared in 1859 when the two districts of the town each appointed a single constable. By 1897 the town had grown to five districts with a constable in each with their duties covering such matters as ball playing in the street and shopkeepers forgetting to pull down a blind to cover his window display on a Sunday. As the car was introduced into the town a speed limit of 12 mph was imposed and took up a great deal of the officers time to prevent horses from panicking and becoming runaways—all very different from policing the town in the 21st century.

FARMINGTON (MAINE) POLICE DEPARTMENT

The award of ribbons only to recognise meritorious conduct, life saving or other outstanding achievements is not unusual in the US but the higher awards given for acts of courage are most usually in the form of traditional medals although the designs and names vary greatly from department to department. In a few departments, usually the small rural bodies that exist in large parts of the country, a ribbon bar alone is used in all circumstances. Farmington PD is a very small department in Maine with a total strength of 14 full time officers only including the chief of police and a lieutenant. The Department awards a series of eight different ribbon bars to its officers and one to civilians. The bars are all basically gold and use enamels in a range of colours.

Combat Cross (green with yellow edges)—awarded for an individual act of heroism in combat with an armed person with an imminent threat to the officer's life.

Gallantry Star (dark blue with a red central band flanked by yellow line and with red edges)—the second highest award given for an act of distinguished bravery in the arrest of someone who represented a major threat to the officer or the community.

Wounded in Combat (green with yellow stripes at the edges and two yellow stripes towards the centre, all equally spaced)—awarded for a wound received in the line of duty intentionally inflicted by an adversary which resulted in lacerations, a severe puncture wound, fractures or concussion being suffered by the officer.

Life Saving (half red, half white)—given to acknowledge any act carried out in the line of duty which results in the saving of a human life where the officer acted with a disregard for his or her personal safety or where particularly prompt and alert action was necessary.

Police Officer of the Year (red)—a typically American award with no equivalent in the UK or European countries, given to the officer who stands out from colleagues in the performance of his or her job and who makes a particularly marked contribution to the aims and objectives of the Department (instituted on 1 January 1996).

Commendation (dark blue)—awarded to recognise a highly creditable act performed in the line of duty which shows initiative and professional accomplishment (instituted on 1 January 1994).

Good Conduct Bar (yellow with green edges and two green stripes towards the centre, all equally spaced)—awarded for a continuous two year period without an official reprimand or adverse report (instituted on 1 January 1995).

Educational Achievement Bar (a central white band flanked by yellow lines with a dark blue band on the left and one of green on the right with yellow edges)—a most unusual award by European standards although it is not unique to Farmington. Awarded for attaining 65 credits towards a degree at an acknowledged institute. An associate's degree is marked by the award of the bar only, a bachelors degree by the addition of a gold acorn and a master's degree by an oak leaf. The bar is awarded irrespective of whether the officer gained the degree as a police officer or before.

Civilian Service Bar (bands of green, white and green, all of equal width)—available to civilian members of the community who help in the arrest of a criminal or provide prompt help to someone in danger with a risk to their safety.

With the exception of the Educational Achievement Bar, any second or subsequent award of any of the bars is indicated by a gold star worn on the original ribbon bar. Officers who are honoured receive a bar to wear on their uniform above the shield of office and another mounted on a plaque.

BOYNTON BEACH (FLORIDA) POLICE DEPARTMENT

A range of reasons for the award of a ribbon bar exists in the US, many with no direct equivalent outside the country certainly not in the UK, Europe of Commonwealth countries. Acts of courage, particularly distinguished service, lifesaving or suffering wounds in the course of duty are all recognised in a great many police departments, large and small. Other, more obscure, awards are more restricted. The Educational Achievement Bar awarded in Farmington has its equivalent in Boynton Beach with similar criteria and an identical bar adorned with one, two or three stars to indicate the level of degree held by the recipient. The Florida department, however, goes further in the range of bars available and grants them to officers who meet established standards of fitness, have achieved certain levels of command or who have been on active service in the US Armed Forces.

Fitness Ribbon (light blue with stripes of red, white and dark blue towards the edges)—awarded only to officers who attain certain levels of physical fitness above the norm for the Department.

Command Ribbon (light blue with narrow stripes of dark blue (four) and white (three) in groups in the centre and at each edge)—awarded only to senior staff officers to recognise achieving command of a bureau or division in the Department for a minimum period of one year.

Veteran's Service Ribbon (Light blue with stripes of red, white and dark blue in the centre and a group of green, yellow, red and dark blue lines at each edge)—awarded to every officer who served on active duty in the Korean War, Vietnam, the Granada conflict or the Gulf War.

Boynton Beach PD is not a large department with 135 staff of all ranks, including civilian support staff responsible for a population of approximately 50,000 in an area of less than 41 square kilometres. The Department has no fewer than sixteen different medals and ribbon bars available to reward its officers for a wide range of exceptional acts and achievements. The bars are all made of gold and coloured enamels with the different colours in each case separated by a thin gold line.

The policing structure of Lawton, Manchester, St Mary's, Owosso and Boynton Beach PDs is very typical of most parts of the US outside the larger cities, such forces form the backbone of the service for many Americans. The hazards officers from these forces face in comparison to their colleagues in Los Angeles, New York and Chicago may be less but the work is demanding, frustrating and potentially very dangerous exemplified by the variety of awards available to them. Although most policing in the USA is a local matter there are a number of federal agencies used to investigate crimes which fall beyond the remit of state, city or county departments for a number of reasons. The most well-known of these agencies—in the US and across the world is the FBI.

FEDERAL BUREAU OF INVESTIGATION

The FBI was formed in 1908 with a mere 34 agents at a time when there was little perceived need for a federal investigative body and a degree of resistance from state authorities and the general public. In the early days there were few federal crimes and their jurisdiction was confined to banking, bankruptcy, naturalisation and land fraud matters. As the use of the car expanded in the early years of the 20th century the problem of interstate crime grew with offenders being able to escape justice by crossing state lines. In 1910 an important piece of legislation was enacted—the Mann Act—which prohibited the transport of a woman across a state line for immoral purposes. It was used as a weapon by the FBI agents to investigate criminals who crossed state lines but who had committed no federal offences. After the Great War a further tool was handed to agents with the passage of the National Motor Vehicle Theft Act. The greatest expansion of the Bureau's powers occurred during prohibition when their work against the gangsters brought the agents firmly into public focus with their reputation increased.

The range of federal offences increased steadily in the latter half of the last century and the responsibility of the FBI grew to include matters of national security, terrorism, gambling, organised crime, white-collar crime, anti-drugs investigations and civil rights matters. At the turn of the millennium the Bureau had several thousand agents with a wide range of duties and responsibilities across the whole country. The work of the agents is dangerous and many have died or suffered injury in the course of their duty. The Bureau has, for many years, recognised the dangers involved and has available a range of five medals to acknowledge the work of the agents in special circumstances. In addition to FBI agents, the medals are all available to members of other law enforcement bodies in the US if they are working with the FBI or acting under its direction.

MEDAL OF VALOR

Ribbon: A central white band flanked by bands of red, green and blue, all seven of equal width. Worn as a neck ribbon.

Metal: Gold.

Description: (Obverse) a circular medal surmounted by a five-point star with a trefoil at the end of each arm and a central medallion bearing the seal of the FBI. The words FOR VALOR are inscribed in a banner at the base of the background disc between the two lower arms of the star. A small ring suspender replaces the trefoil of the upper arm.

The Medal of Valor is awarded in recognition of the most exceptional acts of courage where there is a very real threat to the personal safety and life of the recipient which was faced voluntarily. The FBI seal placed in the central medallion has several elements each with a special significance. At the very centre is a shield with five vertical stripes of red (three) and white (two) surmounted by the scales of justice. Red is intended to signify courage, valour, and strength with the white indicative of truth, cleanliness, light and peace.

The Bureau motto—FIDELITY, BRAVERY, INTEGRITY—is written in a banner below the shield with a laurel branch on either side of the shield. There are 46 leaves in the laurel branches to represent the number of states in the Union when the FBI was formed in 1908. Surrounding the central motif are 13 stars (the original states) in an endless circle to signify unity of purpose. The Bureau name is contained in an outer band.

SHIELD OF BRAVERY

Ribbon: The same as the previous award but worn on the breast.

Metal: Gold.

Description: (Obverse) a shield of the same shape as the centrepiece of the FBI seal with the five vertical stripes, scales of justice, laurel branches and an eagle above a scroll bearing the words FOR BRAVERY.

This award is made to recognise acts of courage which fall short of the demanding criteria applicable to the Medal of Valor. The award of the Medal of Bravery still demands voluntary risks in hazardous circumstances and includes undercover duties where the danger is ever-present.

MEDAL FOR MERITORIOUS ACHIEVEMENT

Ribbon: A neck ribbon in the same colours as the two previous awards.

Metal: Gold.

Description: (Obverse) a circular medal bearing the Great Seal of the USA with the words FEDERAL BUREAU OF INVESTIGATION around the upper two-thirds of the circumference and MERIT at the bottom. The disc has a protruding design of irregular shape at the two sides and top and bottom which is taken from the outer edge of the FBI seal and intended to signify the severe challenges faced by the FBI and the organisation's ruggedness.

Any act of courage performed in the line of duty which does not involve a risk of danger to the life or personal safety of the recipient but which is still thought worthy of official recognition is rewarded with the Medal for Meritorious Achievement. The criteria include direct and decisive acts where a life in danger is saved or protected.

Police Medals of the World

The threat of death or serious injury is ever-present in law enforcement work in many parts of the US and the nature of the work of the FBI is such that agents and those assisting them are placed in great danger throughout their careers. The Bureau has two methods of affording official recognition to those who do suffer serious injury or who pay the ultimate price.

MEMORIAL STAR

Ribbon: A neck ribbon in white with a central dark blue band, all of equal width.

Metal: Gold and dark blue enamel.

Description: (Obverse) a device in the form of a five-armed Maltese cross with the points of a five-point star between the arms and a central medallion bearing a five-point star in blue enamel placed centrally. On either side of the central star are the two leaves of laurel taken from the FBI seal with the initials—FBI—above in gold outlined in blue enamel.

The Memorial Star is presented to the next-of-kin of any agent or person working with them who is killed in the line of duty as a direct result of criminal activity. If the person concerned is seriously wounded in similar circumstances but survives they are rewarded with the FBI Star, identical in appearance to the posthumous award and with the same ribbon but intended to be worn on the breast.

In the early years of professional policing in the United States, a method of rewarding acts of bravery by officers did not exist, very similar to the UK where it was not until 1909 that the first national recognition of the dangers of police work was instituted in the form of the King's Police Medal for Gallantry.

In the US, no national award has ever been introduced and many towns and cities were obliged to recognise acts of courage performed by local officers in an individual fashion. A more formal arrangements now exists in many states, towns and cities but, in the early years of the 20th century, such rewards were very individual and quite often unique.

CITY OF ELIZABETH (NEW JERSEY) MEDAL FOR BRAVERY

The City of Elizabeth adjoins Newark, the largest city in the State, on the western shore of Newark Bay facing Staten Island (a part of New York State). It is a densely populated city—more than 110,000 in an area of just under 31 square kilometres. The history of the city's founding is rather confused and involved a prolonged dispute over the ownership of the land which had been sold by the native inhabitants of Staten Island to a group of traders for 20 fathoms of trading cloth, two coats, two guns, two kettles, ten bars of lead, 20 handfuls of powder and 400 fathoms of white wampum. Initial settlement of Elizabeth (originally known as Elizabethtown) began in 1665 and it was made the capital of the Province of New Jersey in 1668. The question of who owned the land was subject to much litigation but never settled. City status was granted in March 1855 by which time the population had grown to almost 9,000.

The first city seal was taken from the reverse of half-dollar coin showing the American eagle but changed early in the 20th century to the present design that appears on the central medallion of the Medal for Bravery. The seal shows a wooded landscape with four houses representing the first settlers behind the bay with a sailing ship at anchor and another smaller craft approaching. Superimposed on the scene is the coat of arms of the Sir George Carteret, a co-owner of the origin settlement and relative of the first governor of the Province of New Jersey. The coat of arms consists of a shield with four diamonds and a hand placed in the top left corner with a banner above the shield bearing the family motto—LOYAL—DEVOIR. The date of the city's founding—1665—lies at the base of the circular scene. An outer band bears the words SEAL OF THE (upper) CITY OF ELIZABETH (lower).

Ribbon: *Medium blue.*

Metal: *Gold.*

Size: *82.5 mm.*

Description: *(Obverse) a circular medal with a wreath of laurel forming the outer edge tied at the base by a bow. A central medallion bears the Seal of the City of Elizabeth; (reverse) plain but inscribed with details of the reason for the award—PRESENTED - TO - DETECTIVE (three lines)—name of recipient in a scroll—FOR BRAVERY FEB 8th 1922 - BY BOARD OF - POLICE COMMISSIONERS MAY 10th 1922. A simple three ring suspender is used. The medal hangs from a gold top suspender bar inscribed with the words FOR BRAVERY in two lines.*

Four medals are known to have been awarded on a single occasion on 10 May 1922 to reward four police officers from Elizabeth for their courage in arresting four men who had murdered a police officer in New York, robbed a man of $2,700 in Newark, New Jersey and shot two officers in Elizabeth. It is not known if any other medals had been awarded previously or have been authorised since.

On the morning of Wednesday, 8 February 1922 at about 10 am officers on patrol in Elizabeth were alerted to an armed robbery which had occurred in Newark thirty minutes earlier and given the descriptions of four men who had been seen acting suspiciously shortly before the attack had occurred. They were believed to be heading towards Elizabeth in a dark blue car. The blue car was not seen but four men riding in a yellow taxicab aroused the suspicions of Sergeant Brennan in Elizabeth and the vehicle was eventually stopped by the sergeant and two other officers.

Naturally the four men denied any knowledge of the robbery but Sergeant Brennan decided to take them to the police station for questioning. The two other officers—Hildebrand and Cochran—climbed into the taxi to escort them to the police station. Although the suspects had been searched, no weapons were found. As they neared the end of the short journey, one of the suspects reached down to the floor of the taxi and took hold of a gun he had dropped when first stopped. The two police officers were unable to disarm him in the confined space of the taxi and the suspect shot and seriously wounded Officer Cochran and caused a flesh wound to Officer Hildebrand. Other officers rushed to the scene and the suspects were overpowered and subdued. Detective Michael Manning, who was one of the first officers to reach the taxi after the two patrolmen had been shot, personally dragged two suspects from the cab and subdued them although one had been waving a revolver around and was prepared to use it.

A few phone calls made at the police station to their colleagues in Newark, soon confirmed that they had the right men who were also alleged to have killed a police officer in New York the previous August. When searched more thoroughly, one of the suspects was found to have a blood-stained piece of rubber filled with lead which had been used in the robbery at Newark which led to their arrest. All four men were charged with atrocious assault and battery with intent to kill the two patrolmen with the allegations of robbery in Newark and murder in New York awaiting them once the Elizabeth offences had been dealt with.

Sergeant Frank Brennan, Patrolmen Louis Hildebrand and John Cochran and Detective Michael Manning were all awarded a specially commissioned gold medal to recognise their bravery. The medals were presented at a special ceremony held on 10 May 1922 with a joint review and parade attended by 120 police officers and representatives of the Fire Department. The four officers were called from the police contingent to be presented with their awards by Mayor Mravlag.

VANUATU

The Republic of Vanuatu was formerly known as the New Hebrides and administered jointly by Great Britain and France from 1906 until independence from both was achieved on 30 July 1980. The islands which make up the Republic lie 800 kilometres west of Fiji and are strung out over 1,300 km of the Pacific Ocean. The total land area of the 82 islands is more than 12,000 square miles although only twelve are of any significant size.

In 1989 a new system of honours was introduced made up of the Order of Vanuatu (available in two classes) and a series of five medals to reward citizens and government officials, including the disciplined forces, for acts of bravery, distinguished or meritorious service and long service and good conduct. Police officers were amongst those eligible for medals from the series. All five medals were of similar design with the only differences being the colouring of the ribbon and the wording carried on the reverse. After the Order of Vanuatu, the award for gallantry ranks highest in the order of precedence.

GALLANTRY MEDAL

Instituted: 1989.

Ribbon: Red with a green stripe (4 mm) at each edge.

Metal: Rhodium plated cupro-nickel.

Size: 40.5 mm.

Description: (Obverse) a depiction of the sun rising over a mountain range within a wreath made up of a pair leaves of the hamele fern representing peace; (reverse) a further pair of leaves around the lower circumference and the word VANUATU around the top. In the central field were the words FOR GALLANTRY in two lines. A ring suspender was used attached to the top of the disc.

The wording in the central field of the reverse reflected the title of the medal, the next in the order of precedence—the Distinguished Service Medal—was inscribed with FOR DISTINGUISHED SERVICE in three lines and hung from a ribbon having five stripes of black, green and red (all 8 mm) in the centre with edges of yellow (4 mm). The Meritorious Service Medal carried the words FOR MERITORIOUS SERVICE (three lines) with the ribbon having a green central band (8 mm) flanked by stripes of red, yellow and black, all 4 mm wide and the Long Service and Good Conduct Medal with FOR LONG SERVICE AND GOOD CONDUCT in four lines and was suspended from a ribbon with 16 equal alternating stripes of green and red.

The final medal of the series is called the Vanuatu Service Medal and is a form of campaign medal for award to any member of the security forces who partakes in any operation abroad or at home in defence of the Republic.

VATICAN CITY

The most visible and familiar aspect of the policing and security arrangements for the Holy See are in the form of members of the Swiss Guard seen guarding the entrance to the Vatican and the Basilica of St Peter, the worlds largest church. The Vatican is the world's smallest independent state and consists of the Vatican City in Rome, three churches within the Italian capital which have been granted extraterritorial status and the Pope's summer residence at Castel Gandolfo, 40 kilometres south of Rome. It has been independent from Italy and Rome only since 1929 when Pope Puis XI and Mussolini agreed the terms of the Lateran Treaty formally establishing the Vatican City State with the Pope as head of the government.

Policing arrangements in the Vatican City are the responsibility of two separate bodies, the Swiss Guard (*Guardia Svizzera Pontifica*) and the Vatican City Police (*Corpo di Vigilanza dello Stato della Citta del Vaticano*). The policing of St Peters Square, however, is the responsibility of the Italian police. The Swiss Guard is the oldest of the two bodies, dating from the 15th century when a permanent force of 200 Swiss Catholics was first formed to act as a personal bodyguard for Pope Julius II. Today they are still recruited from Swiss nationals who must be under 25, unmarried, of legitimate birth, taller than five feet eight inches, of good character and free from any bodily disfigurement. Until quite recently they were only recruited from the German speaking cantons of Switzerland although this requirement has now been relaxed. Their duties include the special and continuous protection of the Pope and all the territories of the Vatican City State, acting as his escort during his travels abroad and performing honour guard duties at ceremonial occasions. On these ceremonial occasions and guard duty they still wear their uniforms of yellow and dark blue stripes trimmed with red, the colours of the Medici family and often described as being designed by Michelangelo although the basis for this belief in flimsy. The Swiss Guards are most visible when on sentry duty armed with their pikes and swords but they are members of a modern, fully armed force which performs a very real policing function for the Holy See.

The other current body—the Corpo di Vigilanza—performs a policing function in the Vatican more in keeping with the modern understanding of the term and was formed only in 1970 when Pope Paul VI disbanded three existing bodies which dated from the 18th and 19th centuries. The oldest of these forces—the Noble Guard (*Guardia Nobile*)—was a mounted unit created in 1744 from existing bodies and was made up of people from noble families. It performed little more than a ceremonial papal escort from the early 19th century. A second force—the Palatine Guard of Honour (*Guardia Palatina d'Honore*)—was formed in 1850 and grew to a strength of 750 ten years later. It was a true military force and took part in many actions outside the Vatican walls until it was reduced in strength after Rome was occupied by Italian troops in 1870. Until it was disbanded 100 years later its rôle was gradually diluted in similar fashion to the Noble Guard to one that was mostly ceremonial.

Working alongside the Swiss Guard and with a responsibility for the true policing of the Vatican City and its territories was the Papal Gendarmerie (*Gendarmeria Pontifica*) formed in the 19th century with recruitment criteria as stringent as the Swiss Guard. Members could only be Italian, taller than five feet nine inches, with an unblemished record of service in the Italian army and references of good character from both the religious and secular authorities. It ceased to exist with the two other bodies on the re-organisation of 1970 and the founding of the Corpo di Vigilanza.

The Vatican City awards a wide range of decorations and honours to people of all nationalities and faiths for services to the Pope personally, the Papacy, Roman Catholicism or the Vatican City State and this can include members of both policing bodies as a reward for acts of courage, meritorious or distinguished service and long service with good conduct. The structure of the Vatican awards system is complex and subject to changes as different popes introduce special temporary honours and amend the regulations of the long established and permanent orders of knighthood and honours to take account of changing times. In addition to the orders of knighthood there are two permanent minor decorations in the form of medals which have been awarded to police officers from any of the police forces in the Holy See, past and present.

The first of these two awards was originally introduced in 1888 as a temporary honour to mark the 50th anniversary of the entry into the priesthood of the pope then reigning—Leo XIII—although it was subsequently made a permanent feature of the Vatican honours system (1898) and given as a reward for meritorious or distinguished services to the Roman Catholic Church and the Holy See. In the latter years of the papacy of Paul VI (1963 to 1978) the medal was subjected to a major re-design following the wishes of the Pontiff who favoured modern art forms.

CRUZ PRO ECCLESIA ET PONTIFICE (ORIGINAL DESIGN)

Instituted: 17 July 1888.

Ribbon: Red with stripes of gold flanked by white lines towards each edge.

Metal: Gold, silver and bronze.

Description: (Obverse) a cross flory embossed with a representation of a comet and fleur-de-lys between the arms. A central medallion bears the head of Pope Leo XIII facing left with the words LEO XIII PM ANN X (Leo XIII, Pope for 10 years) in an outer band; (reverse) the central medallion shows the Papal regalia and the outer band bears the words PRO ECCLESIA ET PONTIFICE (for Church and Pontiff). The four arms of the cross bear the words PRID CAL IAN 1888 (the day before January 1888).

CRUZ PRO ECCLESIA ET PONTIFICE (CURRENT DESIGN)

Ribbon: Half white, half yellow, the papal colours.

Metal: Gold and gilt.

Description: (Obverse) a Greek cross with very broad pointed arms giving an almost octagonal appearance. In the centre are the images of the apostles—Peter and Paul—with the name of the medal to the left and right. On the upper arm of the cross are the papal emblems and a small shield bearing the arms of the reigning pope with his name on the lower arm below the figures. An inverted triangular suspender is used. The arms and name change with a new pope.

page 383

The second of the two medals is awarded to a wide cross-section of society for a range of reasons including meritorious or distinguished service, long service with good conduct and acts of courage by members of the police forces of the Vatican (past and present). The Benemerenti (literally good service) Medal was first awarded by Pius VI (1775 to 1799) and intended to reward military merit with others introduced by subsequent pontiffs for a number of reasons. In 1970 when the Palatine Guard of Honour was disbanded Paul VI introduced a special commemorative medal for members of the Guard as a reward for loyalty and faithful service. A medal intended to be permanent was not introduced until 1891 although it has remained in existence since. The design was changed with the election of each subsequent pope and it underwent a major re-design in similar fashion to the previous honour in the latter years of the papacy of Paul VI.

BENEMERENTI (ORIGINAL DESIGN)

Instituted: 1891.

Ribbon: Yellow with white edges, worn in triangular style with the apex downwards.

Metal: Silver and bronze.

Description: (Obverse) circular with the bust of the reigning pontiff in the centre with his name (left) and the words PONTIFEX MAX (right) all within a circle of laurel; (reverse) the word BENEMERENTI within the circle of laurel. The medal was suspended by two rings from the papal emblems to which were attached the ribbon. The papal emblems consist of the crossed keys of St Peter, the gatekeeper of Heaven, one in silver, one in gold surmounted by the papal tiara with its three crowns.

BENEMERENTI (CURRENT DESIGN)

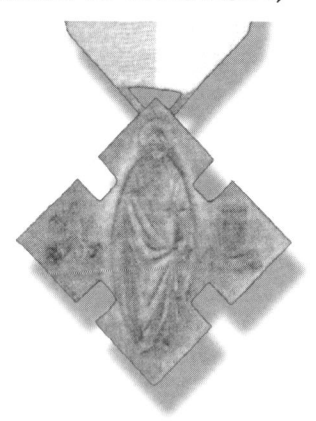

Ribbon: Half white, half yellow.

Metal: Gilt.

Description: (Obverse) has the appearance of a square with a small notch cut halfway along each side with an inverted triangular suspender attached to the top point. In the centre and extending into the upper and lower arms is a representation of Christ with the papal emblems on the left arm and the coat of arms of the reigning pontiff on the right; (reverse) the word BENEMERENTI.

The two orders of knighthood to which the most senior officers of the various police forces of the Vatican have most usually been admitted were both founded by Pope Gregory XVI (1831 to 1846). The highest of the two awards—the Order of Saint Gregory the Great—was originally instituted to reward Austrian troops and citizens for their faithful service to the Holy See during the turbulent times of the 1830s although the order was retained and the criteria for entry amended by Pope Pius X in 1905. The Order has two divisions—civil and military—with four classes in each. The two divisions are indicated in the Medal of the Order by a different method of suspension—a wreath for the civil division and a trophy of arms for the military.

ORDO SANCTUS GREGORIUS MAGNUS

Instituted: 1 September 1831.

Ribbon: Red with a yellow band at each edge.

Metal: Gold and enamel.

Description: (Obverse) a Maltese cross in red enamel with gold ball finials and a central medallion bearing the head of Pope St Gregory I (the Great) facing left and a dove both in gold on blue enamel with the words S GREGORIUS MAGNUS in an outer band; (reverse) the central medallion bears the words PRO DEO ET PRINCIPE (for God and Prince) and the outer band GREGORIUS XVI PM ANNO 1 (Gregory XVI Pope for one year).

Any civil or military services which are thought worthy of recognition but do not merit admission to the higher order are rewarded with another order also introduced by Gregory XVI and again amended in 1905 by Pius X. The Order of Saint Sylvester has three classes but no difference in the design for civil or military awards.

ORDO SANCTUS SILVESTRI PAPAE

Instituted: 31 October 1841.

Ribbon: Black with a red band placed centrally and at each edge.

Metal: Gold and enamel.

Description: (Obverse) a Maltese cross in white enamel with short rays between the arms and a central medallion bearing the image of Pope St Sylvester I in gold on blue enamel and the words SANCTUS SILVESTRI PM in the outer band; (reverse) the Papal emblems in the centre of the medallion and the dates 1841 and 1905 on the band.

The two orders were placed under the patronage of two popes who had a profound effect on the development of the influence, power and spread of the Catholic Church. Saint Sylvester (314 to 335) converted and baptized Constantine, the first Roman emperor to become a Christian, which saw the beginnings of the Christian Roman Empire. Saint Gregory was a renowned theologian and is considered to be one of the great teachers and reformers of the church.

ZAMBIA

In 1963 the Federation of Rhodesia and Nyasaland was dissolved and the three countries went their separate ways—two achieving independence the following year with the third (Southern Rhodesia) becoming embroiled in a dispute with Britain over majority rule which led ultimately to Ian Smith's unilateral declaration of independence and many years of bloodshed. Northern Rhodesia became the Republic of Zambia under President Kenneth Kaunda who was to stay in power for 26 years until he was persuaded to hold multi-party elections and was defeated. When independence was achieved the entitlement of the country's citizens to honours and medals from Britain ceased and a new system introduced in 1965 which included a number of medals available to police officers. The most senior award was available only to the highest ranking officers as a reward for distinguished service.

POLICE MEDAL FOR DISTINGUISHED SERVICE

Instituted: 1965.

Ribbon: Silver with a green central band, all of equal width and separated by lines of black.

Metal: Silver.

Size: 36 mm.

Description: (Obverse) the head of President Kaunda with the words PRESIDENT OF THE REPUBLIC OF ZAMBIA around the circumference; (reverse) a wreath of laurel with a police truncheon vertically across the centre surrounded by the inscription THE ZAMBIA POLICE MEDAL FOR DISTINGUISHED SERVICE.

A second award was introduced and made available to officers of any rank for valuable service marked by resourcefulness, devotion to duty, exceptional ability, merit or exemplary service although these three latter requirement were to be accompanied by long service. The design of the medal was similar to the higher award with the only differences being the substitution of its name—The Zambia Police Medal for Meritorious Service—around the circumference of the reverse and in the colouring of the ribbon—green with a black central band, all of equal width but separated by narrow silver lines.

A new long service award was also introduced to replace the Colonial Police Long Service Medal to which officers were previously entitled and made available to those up to and including the rank of chief inspector who completed at least 18 years continuous satisfactory service on or after 24 October 1964—independence day. Previous service with the Northern Rhodesia Police was counted.

POLICE MEDAL
FOR LONG SERVICE AND GOOD CONDUCT

Instituted: 1965.

Ribbon: Black with a green central band, all of equal width and separated by lines of silver.

Metal: Copper.

Description: (Obverse) an oval medal with the Coat of Arms of Zambia; (reverse) plain apart from the inscription FOR LONG SERVICE AND GOOD CONDUCT.

The ability to count service before independence was also applied to members of the Zambia Police Reserve formed after independence to replace the Northern Rhodesia Police Reserve. The Zambia Police Reserve Medal was awarded for 15 years continuous voluntary service and very similar in design to the medal awarded to regular officers although it was circular and cast in silver rather than copper. The obverse was the same but the wording on the reverse amended to read FOR VOLUNTEER SERVICE. The ribbon was also in three equal bands of black, green and black but with narrow lines of silver bisecting each band.

The national arms of Zambia consist of a central shield with a number of vertical wavy bars representing the Victoria Falls surmounted by a crossed hoe and pick (agriculture and mining) and an eagle which symbolises the freedom of Zambia and the country's ability to rise above its problems. The supporters are a man and a woman (in national dress). At the feet of the supporters are a small mine shaft head and zebra either side of a maize cob which, taken together, are intended to symbolise agriculture, minerals and game.

Acts of great bravery performed by police officers were rewarded with a medal available to any resident of Zambia including members of the Defence Force and recipients are entitled to the use of the post-nominal letters PGM. The medal is the country's highest award for courage other than one reserved for the Defence Force whilst on active service. It is awarded sparingly to reflect the high standards of courage required before its award would be considered.

PRESIDENT'S MEDAL FOR GALLANTRY

Instituted: 1965.

Ribbon: Green with a miniature eagle in copper placed centrally.

Metal: Silver.

Description: (Obverse) the President's head; (reverse) plain apart from the inscription FOR GALLANTRY.

After Kenneth Kaunda left power the new government amended the design of the country's range of honours and awards to remove any personal images and put in place a series of medals with features of national relevance and importance that would not be subjected to alteration with any future change of government or head of state.

ZIMBABWE

With the establishment of an independent Zimbabwe in 1980, the issue of the series of medals introduced by Ian Smith's regime in the Republic of Rhodesia ceased. In similar fashion to almost every newly independent country in Africa the new government of Zimbabwe introduced a medal to celebrate the achievement of independence for distribution to a great many people, including police officers from the UK who had been sent to supervise the conduct of the elections.

ZIMBABWE INDEPENDENCE MEDAL

Instituted: 1980.

Ribbon: Seven stripes of equal width with black in the centre and red, yellow and green on either side.

Metal: Silver and bronze.

Size: 38 mm.

Description: (Obverse) a scene from the settlement of Great Zimbabwe consisting of the Conical Tower above a crossed agricultural hoe and AK 47 assault rifle with the words ZIMBABWE INDEPENDENCE around the lower circumference and the date—18TH APRIL 1980—at the top; (reverse) a phoenix rising from the flames to symbolise the birth of the country from conflict.

The symbolism of the medal's features are reproduced on the country's coat of arms and reflect Zimbabwe heritage, history and legend. The dominant features—the Zimbabwe Bird and the Conical Tower—are both taken from the stone ruins at Great Zimbabwe, the remains of an African Iron Age city which was once home to somewhere between 10,000 and 20,000 Bantu people from the 12th to the 16th century. Its importance cannot be under-estimated and it was not until the early 20th century that archaeologists agreed that the ruins were not a relic of Greek, Phoenician or Egyptian rule but from a true African culture that thrived there until it was abandoned for reasons which will never be fully understood. When they were first seen by European explorers the ruins were thought to be the site of King Solomon's mines and attracted a great deal of interest although this waned and the area was left to archaeologists in the early to mid-1900s.

The Zimbabwe Bird which appears on the current coat of arms and the old arms of Rhodesia was first discovered amongst the ruins as a number of figurines carved from soapstone although their purpose is unknown. The stylised bird perched on a wall is believed to represent the Bataleur Eagle, a large, powerful and strikingly marked bird of prey which is usually seen soaring and sailing at great speed and which has the reputation of being one of the most agile and playfully acrobatic of the large eagles.

The ruins cover an area of more than 21 square kilometres and are a complete city but the most intriguing monument is the Conical Tower, a stone building, almost 10 metres high and 5 metres in diameter which doesn't seem to have served any practical purpose. Suggestions for its use have ranged from a symbolic grain bin to a phallic symbol. Its use in the coat of arms of Zimbabwe and on the Independence Medal represents the nation's historical heritage. The agricultural hoe and AK 47 assault rifle favoured by governments, armies, rebels and terrorists world-wide, are representative of the transition from war to peace. The name—Zimbabwe—is taken from the language of the Bantu people and means stone houses—such is the importance of Great Zimbabwe. The symbolism displayed on the Independence Medal was continued on a number of honours and awards subsequently introduced by the new government.

Zimbabwe

As the new regime became established a full range of awards was introduced to recognise and reward acts of courage, meritorious service and long service with good conduct for all branches of the disciplined services and those in public service, including police officers.

POLICE LONG AND EXEMPLARY SERVICE MEDAL

Ribbon: Black with three gold lines towards each edge.

Metal: Silver.

Description: (Obverse) the Zimbabwe Bird set against a rayed background within an outer raised band bearing the inscription LONG AND EXEMPLARY SERVICE; (reverse) the Coat of Arms of Zimbabwe. The recipient's name is engraved on the rim.

The medal was not an exclusively police award with the same design being used for any of the uniformed services, the difference being indicated by the colours of the ribbon and the design of the large suspender bar—for police officers it was embossed with the scales of justice. The medal was awarded on completion of 15 years service with bars available after an additional ten years and each subsequent five years thereafter.

SERVICE MEDAL

Ribbon: A multi-coloured ribbon with nine stripes—dark blue and old gold at each edge, a green central stripe flanked by silver and with a red stripe to the left and one of light blue to the right.

Metal: Bronze.

Description: (Obverse) in the shape of a decagon with the Roman numeral X within a wreath of laurel and the words ZIMBABWE (above) and FOR SERVICE (below) around the circumference; (reverse) a wreath of lilies with the number, rank and name of the recipient in the central field. The broad straight suspender bar carried a motif of several chevrons.

The Service Medal was awarded for ten years service on or after 18 April 1981 to regular or full-time members of the regular, auxiliary, reserve and territorial uniformed forces, including police officers.

The concept of the different branches of the uniformed services being identified by the use of differently coloured ribbons or alternative designs on the suspender bar of a medal was continued for the third medal in the series issued in 1982—the Efficiency Medal. For police officers the scales of justice were used, for the Territorial Army two oak leaves with acorns, for the Prison Service a key and for the Air Force a bataleur eagle with wings outstretched—believed to be the basis of the Zimbabwe Bird. The medal itself was silver, oval in shape with the coat of arms of Zimbabwe on the obverse surrounded by the words FOR EFFICIENT SERVICE and the reverse left plain apart from the number, rank and name of the recipient. If a second or subsequent award was made, this was indicated by the issue of a bar which followed the design of the suspender bar.

The range of awards introduced in 1981 to reward acts of courage were awarded to members of the uniformed services and civilians alike with three medals available according to the level of courage displayed by the recipient. The highest award—Gold Cross of Zimbabwe—is awarded very sparingly in only the most exceptional of circumstances. The silver and bronze awards are given where the standard of courage displayed does not merit a higher award.

BRONZE CROSS OF ZIMBABWE

Instituted: 1981.

Ribbon: Purple.

Metal: Bronze.

Description: (Obverse) a Greek cross with the arms in purple enamel. Superimposed on the cross is a four-point star with the points extending along the arms of the cross and a central medallion bearing the Zimbabwe bird within an outer band inscribed FOR BRAVERY (lower) and two branches of laurel (upper); (reverse) plain apart from the coat of arms of Zimbabwe on the lower arm of the cross.

At the lowest level of reward for acts of bravery, commendable action or devotion to duty for all branches of the uniformed services came a series of commendation medals. The principle of using a similar design for all services with the differences being only in the colouring of the ribbon and the design on the suspender bar was repeated.

POLICE COMMENDATION MEDAL

Instituted: 1981.

Ribbon: Fifteen stripes of equal width in dark blue (eight) and yellow (seven).

Metal: Bronze.

Description: (Obverse) a circular medal bearing only a lion's head facing forward. The suspender bar bears the scales of justice to indicate that it is a police award.